The Politics of
Global Governance

FIFTH EDITION

The Politics of
Global
Governance

International Organizations in an Interdependent World

edited by
Brian Frederking
Paul F. Diehl

LYNNE
RIENNER
PUBLISHERS

BOULDER
LONDON

Published in the United States of America in 2015 by
Lynne Rienner Publishers, Inc.
1800 30th Street, Boulder, Colorado 80301
www.rienner.com

and in the United Kingdom by
Lynne Rienner Publishers, Inc.
Gray's Inn House, 127 Clerkenwell Road, London EC1 5DB

Library of Congress Cataloging-in-Publication Data
The politics of global governance : international organizations in an
interdependent world / editors, Brian Frederking and Paul F. Diehl.
— Fifth edition.
     pages   cm
   Includes index.
   ISBN 978-1-62637-232-0 (alk. paper)
1. International agencies. 2. Non-governmental organizations.
I. Frederking, Brian. II. Diehl, Paul F. (Paul Francis)
   JZ5566.P65 2015
   341.2—dc23

                                          2015000924

British Cataloguing in Publication Data
A Cataloguing in Publication record for this book
is available from the British Library.

Printed and bound in the United States of America

The paper used in this publication meets the requirements
of the American National Standard for Permanence of
Paper for Printed Library Materials Z39.48-1992.

5   4

Contents

Part 6 International Organizations and the Future

1

Introduction

Brian Frederking and Paul F. Diehl

Global governance and the international organizations that form its backbone are worth studying because the most important issues in world politics today—poverty, terrorism, weapons proliferation, disease, regional conflict, economic stability, climate change, and many others—cannot be solved without multilateral cooperation. World politics is characterized by "security interdependence": no one state, not even the most powerful state, can manage these problems alone. Today's world requires both states and nonstate actors to coordinate action, often through international organizations, to address these issues. Security interdependence, in short, requires global governance, and international organizations are a central component of global governance. This volume addresses the role of international organizations in contemporary global governance.

The chapters presented here provide a more nuanced view of global governance and international organizations than the two predominant views held among the general public. One is the realist notion that international organizations are relatively insignificant actors because they are unable to overcome the strong influences of conflict, national interests, and state sovereignty in world politics. The other is the idealist notion that international organizations are destined to solve common human problems. This book attempts to present a more balanced view, one that recognizes both the necessity of multilateral cooperation and the inherent limitations of international organizations. We hope to show that international organizations play an important role in world politics, but that their influence varies across issue areas.

In this introductory chapter we do not attempt to review the interrelated academic fields of global governance and international organizations comprehensively.[1] Instead we provide a brief summary of both

1

the history of international organizations and the academic study of those organizations from World War I to the contemporary world. We discuss the broad range of issues that constitute security interdependence in the post–Cold War world. We emphasize the inherent tensions between a world of sovereign nation-states and the creation of global governance structures that can enable states to address contemporary issues adequately. We conclude with an overview of the sections and individual chapters in this book.

The Development of International Organizations

Early writings about the potential for international organizations to deal with common human problems include Jeremy Bentham's proposal for a "common legislature" and Immanuel Kant's advocacy of a "league of peace."[2] The academic study of international organizations began with the creation of the League of Nations after World War I and was largely descriptive and legalistic. The League represented an attempt at international cooperation to prevent war. The breakdown of the League in the 1930s had many factors, including a lack of will by the major powers and the unwieldy requirements necessary for collective action. Although the League was unable to prevent World War II, it did provide a means of cooperation and consultation among states on a variety of issues beyond security matters.

World War II had a stimulating effect on the development of international organizations, and world leaders again sought to form another general international organization.[3] Much of the scholarship at the time was explicitly normative, calling for improvements to global institutions to promote world peace.[4] Perhaps surprisingly, the new United Nations had many similarities with the League.[5] The Security Council and the General Assembly of the United Nations had comparable predecessors in the League system. The UN was also predicated on the notion that continued cooperation among the victorious coalition in the previous war would ensure global stability.

With the emergence of the Cold War, it seemed quite possible that the United Nations might follow the path of the League. "Realist" scholars criticized earlier "idealists" and began to dominate the discipline of international relations. Realists emphasized the importance of state sovereignty, military power, and national interests in world politics and thus were less likely to expect states to delegate important powers to international organizations.[6] Realists argued that order could only be established by the enlightened use of diplomacy and force. The traditional route of alliances and the balance of power, not some potentially transformative international organizations, would maintain order.

Ultimately, the UN survived because it faced a radically different environment than the League. First, the Cold War bipolar alliance structure, while undoubtedly prohibiting superpower cooperation, also provided more stability than the rapid systemic upheavals that characterized the interwar period. Second, there was a greater recognition of a need for cooperation among states. The early stages of security interdependence occurred with the threat of global devastation from nuclear war or environmental disaster. Third, the UN acquired a symbolic importance and a legitimacy that the League of Nations lacked. States felt obligated to justify their actions before the UN even when they appeared contrary to UN Charter principles. The United States felt compelled to make its case to the UN at important times such as the Cuban Missile Crisis or prior to the invasion of Iraq because the UN could legitimize such actions.[7] Most important, a state does not consider withdrawing its membership from the UN even when UN actions appear contrary to a state's national interests. The loss of significant actors plagued the League during most of its existence.

The academic study of international organizations during the Cold War attempted to conceptualize what we now call global governance and tried to identify the role that international organizations played in that process. Scholars began to study how international organizations were part of larger patterns of world politics, particularly regarding conflict and peacekeeping.[8] A second approach was the neofunctionalist argument that the scope of international problems often overwhelmed the jurisdiction of both states and international organizations; this approach often advocated the emergence of political forms "beyond the nation state."[9] A third area included a wide variety of critical, neo-Marxist, and poststructuralist arguments about international organizations.[10]

A final area focused on international regimes, defined as "governing arrangements constructed by states to coordinate their expectations and organize aspects of international behavior in various issue-areas."[11] Regimes included principles, norms, rules, and decisionmaking procedures. Examples include the trade regime, the monetary regime, the oceans regime, and others. The concept of international regimes was the first systematic attempt to theorize "complex interdependence" and the existence of global governance without global government. It challenged the realist notion of a world dominated by nation-states, emphasizing that economic, energy, and environmental issues could not easily be understood by referring to states with a particular distribution of power.[12] It also emphasized the role of nongovernmental organizations in influencing the beliefs, norms, rules, and procedures of evolving regimes. Realists incorporated this approach with "hegemonic stability theory," arguing that any stability brought about by regimes is associated with a concentration or preponderance of power in one state. That "hegemon" achieved multilateral cooperation, according to this approach, through a combination of coercive threats and positive rewards.[13]

The end of the Cold War signaled a new era for the UN and international organizations in general as the superpower rivalry had established many of the barriers that had prevented UN action in the security area. The UN authorized the use of force against Iraq in the First Gulf War, the first such collective enforcement authorization since the Korean War. The UN also authorized far more peacekeeping operations in the decades after the Cold War than in the forty-five years that preceded it. Those peacekeeping operations took on a wider scope of functions, including humanitarian assistance, nation building, and election supervision. Other international organizations also increased in scope. The European Union took further steps toward complete economic integration, and other regional economic blocs such as the Asia Pacific Economic Cooperation and the North American Free Trade Agreement took shape.

The Cold War's demise thus brought about greater prospects for expanding the roles, functions, and powers of international organizations in global governance. Nevertheless, a series of events underscored the limitations of international organizations in the contemporary era. The greater number of peacekeeping operations did not necessarily translate into greater effectiveness in halting armed conflict or promoting conflict resolution. The UN was extremely slow to stop the fighting in Bosnia and the Democratic Republic of Congo, it could not produce a political settlement in Somalia, and it did not prevent the genocide in Rwanda. With the United States under the George W. Bush administration at best ambivalent about the UN, the organization played little or no role in the 2003 US invasion of Iraq, both during and afterward. Despite its successes, the European Union stumbled badly in its peace efforts toward Bosnia, and attempts at further integration and expanded membership have produced significant domestic and foreign controversies. The North Atlantic Treaty Organization has struggled with the redefinition of its role, as the new environment significantly altered its original purposes. While international organizations continue to play a greater role than they ever have, state sovereignty and lack of political will continue to inhibit the long-term prospects of those organizations for creating effective structures of global governance.

The academic field of international organizations has more explicitly theorized "global governance" in the post–Cold War era.[14] The dominant trends of this era—particularly increased economic globalization and an emerging global civil society—suggest that the state is no longer the only source of authority for global governance. The rules of world politics are now generated through the interaction of international governmental organizations, nongovernmental organizations, norms, regimes, international law, and even private-public governance structures. Increasingly, the functions of governance—defining standards of behavior, allocating resources, monitoring compliance with rules, adjudicating disputes, enforcement measures—occur at a global level to deal with common security concerns and transnational issues.[15]

The dominant theoretical approaches in international relations explain these changes and the contemporary role of international organizations in different ways. Liberalism argues that international organizations provide an arena in which states can interact, develop shared norms, and cooperate to solve common problems. International organizations also coordinate action by providing information, monitoring behavior, punishing defectors, and facilitating transparency at a reduced cost to states.[16] They are also indispensable actors in the provision of public goods (for example, clean air and water) and in protecting the "global commons" (for example, oceans and polar regions).[17] Liberals also continue to emphasize regime theory and apply that concept to an increasing number of issue areas.[18]

Realists continue to argue that international organizations have little power over states because states can always leave those organizations.[19] To the extent that international organizations are important, it is because they are used as tools by great powers to pursue their interests. Realists argue that deterrence systems, alliance mechanisms, and the overall balance of power are more effective at maintaining peace than international organizations. They caution against great powers such as the United States relying on such institutions to further their own interests.[20] While realists generally dismiss the importance of nongovernmental organizations, international law, and transnational corporations to explain world politics, some aspects of the realist tradition (for example, hegemonic stability theory and alliances) continue to inform the study of international organizations.

A great variety of approaches to international organizations exists beyond the classic debate between liberals and realists. Critical theorists and neo-Marxists continue to argue that global governance is dominated by the logic of industrial capitalism, which in turn generates opposition from environmental, feminist, and other social movements.[21] Other analysts emphasize rational design, organizational processes (including the study of social networks), organizational culture, and principal-agent interactions.[22] A more recent approach is social constructivism, which emphasizes the role of social structure—norms, identities, and beliefs— in world politics. Constructivists have analyzed the potential for international organizations to socialize policymakers and states to embrace certain norms, identities, and beliefs.[23]

Overview of the Book

The chapters in this volume address a wide variety of issues regarding international organizations and global governance. Part 1 offers an overview of international organizations. In Chapter 1, Thomas Volgy and his colleagues attempt to define and identify international organizations to determine the extent to which a "new world order" is being created after the end of the Cold War. Using a variety of measures and comparing their results to others, they conclude that states have been less willing and/or able to create new organizations to meet post–Cold War challenges. In Chapter 2, Kenneth Abbott and Duncan Snidal provide the classic argument about why states create international organizations rather than pursue other approaches, such as bilateral agreements. They argue that two characteristics of international organizations—centralization and independence—allow states to perform various functions more efficiently, including norm creation and the arbitration of disputes. Together, these two chapters illustrate the overall argument that world politics is often not organized in a way that enables states to address contemporary issues effectively.

Part 2 details the decisionmaking processes of international organizations. The range of activities and the processes that are often hidden from public view or receive little media attention are revealed in these selections. Specifically, the types and roles of nongovernmental organizations are reviewed; these actors are increasingly important in influencing global governance actions. In addition, this section considers proposals to change the most visible UN organ—the Security Council.

The first two parts of the book give the reader a broad view of the place of international organizations in the world system and the patterns of their activities. Armed with this understanding, the reader is directed to the actions of international organizations in three major issue areas: peace and security, economic, and social and humanitarian. In Parts 3 through 5, one can appreciate the number of organizations involved, the scope of activities undertaken, and the variation in effectiveness across organizations and issue areas. While the first two parts highlight common patterns in international organizations, the next three parts provide more detail and reveal the diversity of these bodies.

Part 3 explores the changing aspects of global governance in the peace and security area. This includes the shift from traditional peace-keeping to peacebuilding and the emerging norm of "responsibility to protect," which would greatly expand the legal and moral conditions for international intervention into troubled countries around the world. In addition, these chapters look at the efficacy of nonmilitary options designed to promote peace and security: economic sanctions and international legal proceedings in the form of the International Criminal Court.

Part 4 emphasizes economic issue areas, particularly the tensions that often exist between developed and developing countries. These chapters discuss the development of poverty reduction as a central norm within the Millennium Development Goals, the contradictory food security rules within the trade and human rights regimes, the role of the World Trade Organization in resolving disputes between the United States and China, the changing state practices to more assertively regulate cyberspace, how the BRIC countries are challenging the hegemonic role of the United States since the global financial crisis, and the perennial debates about whether the European Union can succeed in its economic experiment.

Part 5, on social and humanitarian activities, shows how both public and private organizations influence a variety of important concerns. These chapters discuss the role of global health networks to control disease outbreaks, the role of private industry in adopting Kyoto Protocol rules on carbon emissions, the challenges of accumulating accurate information to monitor human rights violations, and the difficulties of combating the trafficking of women in our globalized world.

Part 6 returns to the more general concerns addressed at the outset of the book: What roles can international organizations play in global governance? This final chapter addresses the kinds of reforms that might be possible in the UN system given its seemingly continuous focus on reform proposals and actual implementations that fall short.

Notes

1. Few reviews of the field of international organizations exist. Two early reviews are John Gerard Ruggie and Friederich Kratochwil, "International Organization: A State of the Art on the Art of the State," *International Organization* 40 (1986): 753–775; and J. Martin Rochester, "The Rise and Fall of International Organizations as a Field of Study," *International Organization* 40 (1986): 777–813. See also Lisa Martin and Beth Simmons, "Theories and Empirical Studies of International Institutions," *International Organization* 52 (1998): 729–757.

2. Jeremy Bentham, *Plan for a Universal and Perpetual Peace* (London: Grotius Society, 1927); Immanuel Kant, *Eternal Peace and Other International Essays* (Boston: World Peace Foundation, 1914).

3. J. David Singer and Michael Wallace, "International Government Organizations and the Preservation of Peace, 1816–1964," *International Organization* 24 (1970): 520–547.

4. David Mitrany, *A Working Peace System* (London: Royal Institute of International Affairs, 1943).

5. Leland Goodrich, "From League of Nations to United Nations," *International Organization* 1 (1947): 3–21.

6. E. H. Carr, *The Twenty Years' Crisis, 1919–1939* (London: Macmillan, 1939); John H. Herz, *Political Realism and Political Idealism* (Chicago: University of Chicago Press, 1951); Hans J. Morgenthau, *Politics Among Nations* (New York: Knopf, 1948).

7. Ernst Haas, "Collective Legitimation as a Political Function of the United Nations," *International Organization* 20 (1966): 360–379.

8. Inis L. Claude, *Swords into Plowshares* (New York: Random House, 1959); Ernst B. Haas, "Types of Collective Security: An Examination of Operational Concepts," *American Political Science Review* 49 (March 1955): 40–62; Karl W. Deutsch et al., *Political Community and the North Atlantic Area* (Princeton: Princeton University Press, 1957).

9. Ernst B. Haas, *Beyond the Nation State: Functionalism and International Organization* (Stanford: Stanford University Press, 1964).

10. Immanuel Wallerstein, "The Rise and Future Demise of the World Capitalist System: Concepts for Comparative Analysis," *Comparative Studies in Society and History* 16 (September 1974); Richard K. Ashley, "The Poverty of Neorealism," *International Organization* 38 (1984); Robert W. Cox, "Social Forces, States, and World Orders: Beyond International Relations Theory," in Robert O. Keohane, ed., *Neorealism and Its Critics* (New York: Columbia University Press, 1986).

11. Stephen D. Krasner, ed. *International Regimes* (Ithaca, NY: Cornell University Press, 1983), p. 2; Robert O. Keohane, "Theory of Hegemonic Stability and Changes in International Economic Regimes," in Ole Holsti et al., eds., *Change in the International System* (Boulder: Westview, 1980); Duncan Snidal, "The Limits of Hegemonic Stability Theory," *International Organization* 39 (1985).

12. Robert O. Keohane and Joseph S. Nye, *Power and Interdependence* (Boston: Little, Brown, 1977).

13. Robert O. Keohane, *After Hegemony: Cooperation and Discord in the World Political Economy* (Princeton: Princeton University Press, 1984), pp. 57–60; Robert Gilpin, *U.S. Power and the Multinational Corporation* (New York: Basic, 1975).

14. James N. Rosenau, *Along the Domestic-Foreign Frontier: Exploring Governance in a Turbulent World* (Cambridge: Cambridge University Press, 1997); Anne-Marie Slaughter, *A New World Order* (Princeton: Princeton University Press, 2004); Michael Barnett and Raymond Duvall, eds., *Power in Global Governance* (New York: Cambridge University Press, 2005); Thomas G. Weiss and Rorden Wilkinson, "Rethinking Global Governance? Complexity, Authority, Power, Change," *International Studies Quarterly* 58 (March 2014): 207–215.

15. Joseph S. Nye Jr. and John D. Donahue, *Governance in a Globalizing World* (Washington, DC: Brookings Institution Press, 2000).

16. Robert Keohane and Lisa Martin, "The Promise of Institutionalist Theory," *International Security* 20 (Summer 1995): 39–51.

17. Elinor Ostrum, *Governing the Commons: The Evolution of Institutions for Collective Action* (Cambridge: Cambridge University Press, 1990).

18. Volker Rittberger and Peter Mayer, eds., *Regime Theory and International Relations* (Oxford: Clarendon Press, 1993).

19. Lloyd Gruber, *Ruling the World: Power Politics and the Rise of Supranational Institutions* (Princeton: Princeton University Press, 2000).

20. John J. Mearsheimer, "The False Promise of International Institutions," *International Security* 19, no. 3 (1994–1995): 5–49.

21. Craig Murphy, "Global Governance: Poorly Done and Poorly Understood," *International Affairs* 75, no. 4 (2000): 789–803.

22. Margaret Keck and Kathryn Sikkink, *Activists Beyond Borders: Advocacy Networks in International Politics* (Ithaca: Cornell University Press, 1998); Darren Hawkins, David A. Lake, Daniel L. Nelson, and Michael J. Tierney, eds., *Delegation and Agency in International Organizations* (Cambridge: Cambridge University Press, 2006); Barbara Koremenos, Charles Lipson, and Duncan Snidal, *The Rational Design of International Institutions* (Cambridge: Cambridge University Press, 2004).

23. Michael Barnett and Martha Finnemore, *Rules for the World: International Organizations in World Politics* (Ithaca: Cornell University Press, 2004); Jeffrey Checkel, "International Institutions and Socialization in Europe," *International Organization* 59, no. 4 (2005): 801–826.

Part 1

Overview

2

Identifying Formal
Intergovernmental Organizations

*Thomas J. Volgy, Elizabeth Fausett,
Keith A. Grant, and Stuart Rodgers*

In this effort, we probe conceptual and empirical dimensions for identifying the existence of intergovernmental organizations (IGOs) in international affairs and create a new database of IGOs. We do so because we are interested in two major research questions that we believe are not usefully addressed by existing data on IGOs. First, we wish to ascertain the extent to which a formal, institutional dimension of a "new world order" is being created after the end of the Cold War. From a theoretical standpoint, we see the possibility of such new institutional creation partly as a function of the strength possessed by the lead global power in the international system (the USA) and partly as a function of the capacity of other powers and the extent of their dissatisfaction with the dominant state's leadership. We assume that creating IGOs with little bureaucratic organization and very limited autonomy is less useful in stabilizing a new world order than a network of organizations that are significantly organized and autonomous. Additionally, it may be far easier to construct organizations that have neither of these characteristics than ones that do. By including in our analysis IGOs that are easy to assemble but produce little autonomous capability or organization, we would distort responses to research queries regarding the importance of great-power strength in formal institutional construction.

Our second research concern is about patterns of joining and participation by states in these IGOs. We wish to uncover whether or not states participate in these organizations for reasons similar to, or different from, factors correlated with their participation during the Cold War. We

Reprinted from *Journal of Peace Research*, vol. 45, no. 6: 837–850. © 2008 by Sage Publications. Reprinted by permission of the publisher.

assume that joining organizations that lack bureaucratic organization and offer little capacity to execute the collective will of members requires much less from states in terms of the costs of joining such organizations. Therefore, analyzing patterns of participation by states in such organizations may distort our understanding of the conditions under which states may invest resources in joining IGOs, including possibly confusing membership in minimalist organizations with the willingness of state policymakers to potentially surrender some of their sovereignty as a trade-off for their participation in more autonomous organizations.

We assume, too, that joining organizations is based both on opportunity and willingness. Measures of organizational participation based on simple counts of number of organizations joined fail to take into account the numbers of organizations a state is qualified to join. Since a simple count may distort the opportunities states have to join, we develop a denominator which allows us to factor in this dimension of participation.

Clearly, alternative definitions of IGOs have substantial impacts on their empirical enumeration. As Jacobson, Reisinger & Mathers note (1986: 144), different "reasonable" definitions yield population estimates that vary by as much as 300%. Below, we discuss previous efforts to enumerate systematically the population of IGOs in international relations, identify our conceptually based definition of an IGO and compare it with previous efforts, provide a series of criteria with which to identify an IGO, illustrate some of the empirical results, and compare the database with the most recent systematic data on IGO population.

The literature in international relations offers three major efforts that provide overlapping empirical criteria and quantify systematically—and longitudinally—the number of IGOs in the international system. None of the three, however, focuses explicitly on the broader conceptual meaning of an IGO that is associated with our research concerns, and therefore these efforts create both coding rules and empirical enumerations that differ substantially from those we identify below.

The earliest effort is by Wallace & Singer (1970), who posited four empirical criteria for identifying the existence of an intergovernmental organization: a minimum membership of two states; regular plenary sessions; a permanent headquarters arrangement; and independence from other IGOs (Wallace & Singer, 1970: 245–248). A second effort (Jacobson, Reisinger & Mathers, 1986; Shanks, Jacobson & Kaplan, 1996) provides a similar set of empirical criteria: intergovernmental organizations are "associations established by governments or their representatives that are sufficiently institutionalized to require regular meetings, rules governing decision making, a permanent staff, and a headquarters"

(Shanks, Jacobson & Kaplan, 1996: 593). Further, these authors define and identify separately emanations as "second-order IGOs created through action of other IGOs" (Shanks, Jacobson & Kaplan, 1996: 594).

Finally, Pevehouse, Nordstrom & Warnke (2003, 2005) represent the most recent and most comprehensive effort to measure annually the number of IGOs in the international system. They define an IGO as an organization with the following attributes: "(1) is a formal entity; (2) has [three or more] [sovereign] states as members; and (3) possesses a permanent secretariat or other indication of institutionalization such as headquarters and/or permanent staff" (Pevehouse, Nordstrom & Warnke, 2005: 9–10).

Defining IGOs

Taken together, the empirical criteria noted above share critical characteristics related to the institutionalization of enduring multilateral relationships: routinized interactions by state members, explicit methods of decision making within organizations, enduring bureaucratic structures, and evidence of organizational independence from other IGOs. These approaches seek to distinguish between IGOs and other types of cooperative arrangements, such as ad hoc agreements, ongoing but uninstitutionalized meetings between states, sub-units of other IGOs, or institutions controlled not by member states but by other entities (e.g., IGOs or NGOs).

While these authors provide essentially empirical measures, the indicators hint at a broader conceptual view of an IGO. That broader conceptual view is our starting point. We define intergovernmental organizations as *entities created with sufficient organizational structure and autonomy to provide formal, ongoing, multilateral processes of decision making between states, along with the capacity to execute the collective will of their members (states)*. This definition highlights both the process of interactions within IGOs and the possibility of collective outcomes from them, even though collective outcomes are contested among realist conceptions of international politics.

Furthermore, formal, ongoing processes of interaction within an organization and collective action require ongoing administration and organization. We concur with Abbott & Snidal (Chapter 3 of this volume) that the two primary functions of formal organizations are a stable organizational structure and some amount of autonomy in a defined sphere. Stability of organizational structure (in terms of routine interactions by states along with an administrative apparatus to ensure both institutionalized interactions and stability of organization) and autonomy are also critical for institutional conceptions of power (Barnett & Duvall, 2005), for assessing both global governance and hegemony.

This conceptual approach suggests that IGOs evidence attributes that (1) institutionalize state decision making and oversight in governance, (2) provide sufficient bureaucratic organization to assure some stability of management, and (3) demonstrate autonomy in organizational operation and in the execution of the collective will of the membership. All the operational definitions above seem to address some of the conditions under which these criteria can be observed. However, each of these criteria represents a continuum and suggests a *threshold*, below which institutionalization may not be in evidence, and for our theoretical concerns, an entity is not classified as an IGO. For instance, it is a rare IGO (perhaps not even the European Union) that exhibits fully autonomous characteristics in the execution of the collective will of the organization. Requiring absolute autonomy in a decentralized international system would, at that end of the continuum, leave virtually no empirical cases of formal organizations. At the same time, an IGO that relies completely on its members to carry out voluntarily the collective decisions made by the organization, without a secretariat that at least monitors and reports on the actions of its members, would represent the other end of the autonomy continuum, and it would be more realistic to view a structure of this type as a "discussion forum" rather than a viable, formal IGO. Somewhere between these two extremes exists some threshold, above which an organization qualifies as an IGO.

Where is that threshold? We turn now to the task of identifying thresholds below which an IGO loses one or more of its three qualifying characteristics.

Membership, Decision Making, and Oversight

First, we concur that the threshold for membership is one that consists of an IGO that contains three or more member states, consistent with the multilateral idea associated with IGOs. While it is plausible that an organization containing two members can be of theoretical interest, it falls within the area of bilateral relationships, and virtually all of the literature in the area focuses on multilateral dynamics effecting cooperation between states.

Second, we require that the membership be composed overwhelmingly of states and governed by them without a veto by non-state members. We recognize that some forms of cooperative arrangements have integrated into their deliberations non-state actors, including other IGOs and NGOs, and we have conceptualized IGOs, first and foremost, as mechanisms of cooperation between states. We are reluctant to exclude institutions that may contain non-state actors, but we require that decision making and oversight must reside overwhelmingly among states.

Third, we require that state membership entail representation by individuals or groups acting on behalf of the state, as individuals who are either directly part of the central governmental machinery of a state, or are temporarily (albeit primarily) acting in that capacity. If the individuals who represent their states are not expected to represent the preferences of their policymakers, then the state membership threshold is not reached. This would be the case if an organization's membership is designated for states, but each state appoints a citizen who is acting as an expert rather than in the role of government representative.

Fourth, we require that collective decision making and oversight be routinized: there are clear procedures governing the timing of meetings and decision making, and members meet routinely to make decisions and to exercise oversight over organizational operations. Procedural requirements are typically set out in the charters/constitutions/treaties of organizations and are easy to uncover. There is, however, much variation in the frequency with which organizational plenums are held, and a threshold value establishing a minimum is somewhat arbitrary. Ideally, meetings would occur on an annual basis. Recent efforts seem to have relied on the UIA [Union of International Associations] definition of inactivity: the lack of reported meetings for four or more years. We reluctantly accept the four-year threshold for regular meetings, although most viable organizations appear to hold annual meetings of their members.

Bureaucratic Organization and Autonomy

While conceptually distinct criteria, in practice, the empirical correlates of collective decision making, bureaucratic organization, and autonomy within an IGO may be difficult to separate, especially with respect to the last two dimensions. Viable administration requires professional staffing on a permanent basis; we anticipate the same for the execution of collective decisions, even if such staffing is only for the coordination or reporting on efforts of member states. Furthermore, permanent professional staffing is not feasible without a permanent source of funding.

Autonomy requires that both staffing and funding be relatively immune from control by either a single member state or outside forces (e.g., another IGO). Staffing that is not controlled by members of the organization and may not report primarily to the organization (e.g., the Andean Parliament initially was staffed by Colombia's foreign ministry) does not meet the staffing autonomy threshold. Likewise, if the primary funding for administration is provided by another IGO or overwhelmingly by one state—as is the case with some organizations—then it fails to meet the autonomous resources threshold.

Thus, we require evidence of the following thresholds for an IGO to have sufficient bureaucratic organization and autonomy. First, an IGO must demonstrate the existence of a *permanent headquarters and non-symbolic, professional staffing, independent* of other IGOs and/or one single state. Typically, the issue of a permanent headquarters is relatively unambiguous. Such headquarters may move periodically but is usually required within the charter of an IGO and specified as its address. By non-symbolic staffing, we are referring to an actual group of people who administer the organization. There are a few organizations that indicate a staff of one or two, which we assume to be either symbolic of an administration, or of a minor, clerical function, and does not represent an administration needed for a complex organization. By professional staffing, we are referring to people who administer the organization as their livelihood and are paid to do so (some organizations report a staff of volunteers). By independence of staffing, we are referring to an administration that is paid by, reports only to, and holds as its permanent assignment, the IGO in question.

Finally, we require that a majority of the funding for the ongoing operations of the IGO be *non-symbolic, systematically available, and independent* of any one state or another IGO. Extensive budgetary data are difficult to obtain for many IGOs, especially on an annual basis. Therefore, we settle for a relatively low set of thresholds. By non-symbolic, we require that the available funding is minimally sufficient to support staffing beyond one or two individuals. Funding that is systematically available requires provisions in the charter/constitution of the organization for a routine, recurring method of funding. Finally, independence of funding requires that a majority of the organization's budget is independent of any one member or other IGO(s).

Thus, we identify 11 threshold values as operational criteria for designating an entity as a formal intergovernmental organization (FIGO). The most consistent pattern of differences between our empirical criteria and those of other efforts relates to the nature of staffing and funding within FIGOs.

Constructing the Database

We create the FIGO database for three points in time: 1975, 1989, and 2004. These years are of interest to us for ascertaining changes to the web of organizations in the post–Cold War environment (2004), changes that require comparison with the two time periods that represent some mid-point during the Cold War (1975) and one that is directly at the end of the Cold War (1989). The three time points represent relatively equidistant intervals and the 1989–2004 period offers a 15-year time span in the development of post-Cold War institutional formation; 2004 is the most current point for reliable information on FIGOs.

Our compilation of FIGOs, similar to other efforts, starts with the UIA *Yearbook of International Organizations*. We use the online version and supplement it with the hardbound yearbooks as needed. In addition, we check our compilation against both the Jacobson database, *International Governmental Organizations: Membership and Characteristics, 1981 and 1992* (ICPSR 6737), and the Pevehouse and Nordstrom update of the COW IGO database: *Correlates of War 2 International Governmental Organizations Data Set*, Version 2.1. We supplement these sources with additional sources when information is insufficient: reading the websites of IGOs;[1] corresponding with the headquarters and/or executive committees of IGOs; reading the treaties and/or charters of the organizations; querying *Europa World Plus* online edition; and searching news sources and scholarly materials (Buzan & Waever, 2004; Grant & Soderbaum, 2003; Katzenstein, 2005; Pempel, 2005; Solingen, 1998, 2005).

The FIGO database yields 265 IGOs that are alive in 2004. Several patterns are worth noting regarding our concerns about new institutional world order construction, great-power contestation, and state membership. First, the dominant mode for FIGOs is a combination of regional and sub-regional organizations (accounting for nearly half of all FIGOs), consistent with earlier findings (Shanks, Jacobson & Kaplan, 1996); global FIGOs constitute approximately 26% of the overall FIGO population. At the same time, there is considerable variation in the number of FIGOs within regions (Figure 2.1). Africa and Europe—the poorest and richest regions—contain the largest number of FIGOs. By contrast, Asia has very few regional organizations. This is a region where the USA has worked to substitute bilateral mechanisms of coordination and cooperation, in lieu of multilateral arrangements from which it may be excluded or which it may not be able to control (Rapkin, 2001; Goh,

Figure 2.1 FIGO Population, by Region, 2004

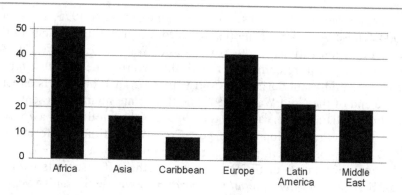

2004), and where there has been a culture of informal arrangements between state and non-state actors (Katzenstein, 2005).

Second, a decade and a half after the end of the Cold War, nearly two-thirds of all FIGOs are institutions that were created during the 1945–89 period. The number of FIGOs created during the 1970s alone accounts for approximately one-quarter of all FIGOs still alive in 2004, a number larger than all the FIGOs created since the end of the Cold War.

Third, classifying FIGOs by their primary original mandate indicates that approximately two-thirds of the organizations alive in 2004 have an economic mandate as their primary mission. Considerable variation exists, however, depending on when the organizations were created: 72% created prior to 1990 and surviving through 2004 have an economic mandate, compared with less than 50% of those created after the Cold War. Whether or not this is due to the higher survivability rate of economic FIGOs, or due to other factors, is not readily observable from the data.

Fourth, factoring in "opportunity" to join FIGOs should make a difference in assessing state membership. The average number of organizations joined by any one of the leading EU states (Germany, France, and the UK) is substantially higher than the membership rate of other major powers (Figure 2.2). This differential in membership is due, in part, to the opportunities for European states to join a large constellation of regional FIGOs; Japan and China are "penalized" by the virtual absence of a major network of regional FIGOs in Asia. At the same time, the differential between Japan and China indicates additional forces at work, beyond simple opportunity to join available FIGOs.

An additional example may indicate further the differences between a simple count of memberships versus a measure based on "opportunity"

Figure 2.2 FIGO Membership of Major Powers (as percentage of all FIGOs), 2004

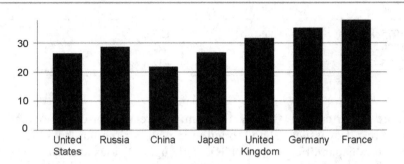

to join. Sudan actually has more memberships in FIGOs than does Australia. However, once we factor in the opportunity to join certain organizations, it appears that Sudan's joining rate is actually 15% below that of Australia, due in part to the much larger constellation of regional FIGOs in Africa compared with Oceania. Unsurprisingly, but masked by a simple frequency count, Australia's membership rate in global organizations (78%) significantly surpasses Sudan's membership rate (54%).

Comparing FIGO with COW IGO

In order to gauge the effects of our threshold criteria on the population of IGOs, we compare the FIGO population with the COW IGO series (Table 2.1). We do so for a number of reasons. Most important, the COW IGO effort is the current benchmark for IGOs, representing a careful process of data collection (meeting scientific standards for validity and reliability) and most current assessment (up through 2000) of the IGO population. A second reason is its wide utilization (see Volgy et al., 2006, for a sampling of literature) in quantitative analyses.

We compare the FIGO data with the COW IGO series in two ways: first, we update the number of COW IGOs formed between 2000 and 2004, in order to be able to make comparisons at the aggregate level between the two datasets for the years 1975, 1989, and 2004. Second, we compare state membership between the two datasets, using the existing COW IGO data and eliminating from FIGO the last four years uncovered in COW IGO.

The COW IGO database contains 340 IGOs classified as "live" for the year 2004. Of these, 105 organizations (30.9%) fail to meet one or

Table 2.1 **Comparison of Changes in Numbers of FIGOs and COW IGOs, 1975–2004 (as percentage change)**

Year	FIGO	COW IGO
1975–89	+26.4	+25.0
1989–2004	−2.9	+6.1
1975–2004	+23.6	+32.5

more of our criteria. Clearly, the dominant reason for exclusion occurs as a result of issues related to autonomy and/or the bureaucratic organization capabilities of these IGOs, although 29 cases also violate some provisions related to collective decision making and oversight by states.

Can we note significant differences as a result of these exclusions? Comparing the two sets of data yields substantial differences regarding both the population of IGOs and state membership in them. First, and at the macro level, the two populations are substantially different in size, in rates of growth over time, especially during the post–Cold War era. For example, the FIGO population in all time periods is substantially smaller (e.g., 28% smaller in 2004) than the COW IGO population. There are also significant differences between the two databases regarding rates of growth. While both populations show vigorous growth in the 1975–89 period, the net growth rate for FIGOs in the post–Cold War era is negative (reversing a long-term trend toward increased organizational development). The cumulative effect of these differences demonstrates a more modest net growth of FIGOs than COW IGO growth over a quarter of a century.

Second, the frequency of state memberships differs between the two databases: US membership in the FIGO web is roughly 20% smaller than in COW IGO; China's is approximately 18% smaller; for the three major states of the EU (combined)—the UK, Germany, and France—it is 13% smaller. As these differences suggest, the effects of differential IGO selection on membership frequency is not uniform across states, a point illustrated by considering that membership is nearly identical for Russia across the two sets of data and only minimally different for Japan. Apparently, a stricter definition of IGOs, requiring more states, may alter the enumeration of state membership in the web of intergovernmental organizations.

Do these differences matter? We believe they do, at both the macro and micro levels of analysis. With respect to the distinction between FIGOs, IGOs, and the Kantian peace, replicating Russett, Oneal &

Davis (1998), we find that generic IGO membership underestimates the importance of membership effects on conflict, with FIGOs demonstrating a stronger effect. The IGO variable yields a positive and significant effect when both measures are included in the same model (Volgy et al., 2006). The reversal in directionality of the IGO variable may be indicative of the aggregation of two distinct populations of organizations, with FIGOs reducing the likelihood of interstate dispute, while non-FIGOs possibly increase it. Future research will investigate further the dynamics underlying these relationships (Volgy et al., 2008).

At the macro level, a focus on IGOs substantially overestimates the ability of major powers to restructure the institutional dimension of the new world order (Volgy et al., 2008). Focusing on FIGOs and constellations of organizations created since 1989 indicates a substantial diminution in the capacity and/or willingness of global states to fashion new organizations to meet the challenges of the post–Cold War international system.

Conclusion

We conceptualized a FIGO as constituting three dimensions: (1) institutionalization of state decision making and oversight in governance, (2) bureaucratic organization allowing for stability of management, and (3) evidence of autonomy in organization and in the execution of collective decisions. Based on these dimensions, we identified 11 threshold criteria with which to mark an organization as being a FIGO. Comparing the resulting database with the COW IGO database, we found, as expected, significant differences in the size of the IGO population, changes in the growth of IGOs over time, and differences in state membership in the constellation of IGOs in international affairs.

It is important to note that data on all IGOs are both more "squishy" and "dynamic" than they appear on the surface. By "squishy," we mean that the disparate sources needed to trace their activities and membership make changes difficult to pinpoint. For example, while we are able to ascertain procedural requirements for organizational funding and can trace some amount of funding being spent, we are loath to estimate the exact size of FIGO budgets and the extent to which those budgets are resupplied annually. This is not a problem for many organizations, but it is probably so for a substantial number of them. A similar problem occurs with data on state membership, which is relatively accessible for organizations operating currently. But, when such membership changed over time, there are more formidable problems in pinpointing the exact year of the change. This issue is especially problematic for research based on annual observations of state membership in IGOs.

There is also the issue of "dynamism": organizations may acquire additional attributes (or lose some) over time, either lifting them across the minimum threshold to qualify as a FIGO, or drop them below the threshold. Detecting the precise time when such changes occur is difficult through self-reporting, especially in the case of lost attributes. Just as important, institutional design characteristics may change over time, and some of these structural changes may not be reported for several years. Again, research based on annual observations may be more susceptible to this problem.

Researchers working in this field may gain more valid observations through aggregating observations over periods larger than one year. This is the strategy we adopt by sampling three time frames—15 years apart—with the hope that we are able to minimize errors that we would likely generate utilizing annual observations.

Note

1. From this point forward, IGOs refer to the generic classification of intergovernmental organizations, while FIGOs refer to formal intergovernmental organizations.

References

Abbott, Kenneth & Duncan Snidal, 1998. "Why States Act Through Formal International Organizations," *Journal of Conflict Resolution* 52(1): 3–32.

Barnett, Michael & Raymond Duvall, 2005. "Power in International Politics," *International Organization* 59(1): 39–79.

Buzan, Barry & Ole Waever, 2004. *Regions and Powers: The Structures of International Security*. Cambridge: Cambridge University Press.

Goh, Evelyn, 2004. "The ASEAN Regional Forum in United States East Asian Strategy," *Pacific Review* 17(1): 47–69.

Grant, Andrew J. & Fredrik Soderbaum, 2003. *The New Regionalism in Africa*. Aldershot: Ashgate.

Jacobson, Harold K.; William R. Reisinger & Todd Mathers, 1986. "National Entanglements in International Governmental Organizations," *American Political Science Review* 80(1): 141–159.

Katzenstein, Peter J., 2005. *A World of Regions: Asia and Europe in the American Imperium*. Ithaca, NY: Cornell University Press.

Pempel, T. J., 2005. *Remapping East Asia: The Construction of a Region*. Ithaca, NY: Cornell University Press.

Pevehouse, Jon; Timothy Nordstrom & Kevin Warnke, 2003. "Intergovern-mental Organizations, 1815–2000: A New Correlates of War Data Set" (http://cow2.la.psu.edu/).

Pevehouse, Jon; Timothy Nordstrom & Kevin Warnke, 2005. "Intergovernmental Organizations," in Paul F. Diehl, ed., *The Politics of Global Governance.* Boulder, CO: Lynne Rienner (9–24).

Rapkin, David P., 2001. "The United States, Japan, and the Power to Block: The APEC and AMF Case," *Pacific Review* 14(3): 373–410.

Russett, Bruce; John R. Oneal & David R. Davis, 1998. "The Third Leg of the Kantian Tripod for Peace: International Organizations and Militarized Disputes, 1950–85," *International Organization* 52(3): 441–467.

Shanks, Cheryl; Harold K. Jacobson & Jeffrey H. Kaplan, 1996. "Inertia and Change in the Constellation of International Governmental Organizations, 1981–1992," *International Organization* 50(4): 593–627.

Solingen, Etel, 1998. *Regional Orders at Century's Dawn: Global and Domestic Influences on Grand Strategy.* Princeton, NJ: Princeton University Press.

Solingen, Etel, 2005. "East Asian Regional Institutions: Characteristics, Sources, Distinctiveness," in T. J. Pempel, ed., *Remapping East Asia: The Construction of a Region.* Ithaca, NY: Cornell University Press (31–53).

Union of International Associations (UIA), Various Years. *Yearbook of International Organizations.* New York: K. G. Saur (and online edition at https://www.diversitas.org/).

Volgy, Thomas J.; Elizabeth Fausett, Keith A. Grant & Stuart Rodgers, 2006. "Ergo FIGO: Identifying Formal Intergovernmental Organizations," Working Papers Series in International Politics: Department of Political Science, University of Arizona (October).

Volgy, Thomas J.; Zlatko Sabic, Petra Roter, Andrea Gerlak, Elizabeth Fausett, Keith A. Grant & Stuart Rodgers, 2009. *Searching for a New World Order.* Oxford: Blackwell.

Wallace, Michael & J. David Singer, 1970. "Intergovernmental Organizations in the Global System, 1816–1964: A Quantitative Description," *International Organization* 24(2): 239–257.

3

Why States Act Through Formal International Organizations

Kenneth W. Abbott and Duncan Snidal

- When the United States decided to reverse the Iraqi invasion of Kuwait, it did not act unilaterally (although it often does). It turned to the United Nations (UN) Security Council.
- When the Security Council sought to learn the extent of chemical, biological, and nuclear arms in Iraq, it did not rely on US forces. It dispatched inspectors from the International Atomic Energy Agency (IAEA).
- When the international community sought to maintain the suspension of combat in Bosnia, it did not rely only on national efforts. It sent in peacekeeping units under the aegis of the UN and North Atlantic Treaty Organization (NATO).
- When states liberalized trade in services and strengthened intellectual property protection in the Uruguay Round, they were not content to draft rules. They created the World Trade Organization (WTO) and a highly institutionalized dispute settlement mechanism.

Formal international organizations (IOs) are prominent (if not always successful) participants in many critical episodes in international politics. Examples in addition to those above include the following: Security Council sanctions on Libya, IAEA inspectors in North Korea, UN peacekeepers in the Middle East, and so forth. The UN secretary-general's 1992 Agenda for Peace sets out an even broader range of current and proposed UN functions in situations of international conflict: fact finding, early warning, and preventive deployment; mediation, adjudication,

Reprinted from *Journal of Conflict Resolution*, vol. 42, no. 1: 3–32. © 1998 by Sage Publications. Reprinted by permission of the publisher.

and other forms of dispute resolution; peacekeeping; sanctions and military force; impartial humanitarian assistance; and postconflict rebuilding. But IO influence is not confined to dramatic interventions like these. On an ongoing basis, formal organizations help manage many significant areas of interstate relations, from global health policy (the WHO) to European security (OSCE and NATO) to international monetary policy (IMF). What is more, participation in such organizations appears to reduce the likelihood of violent conflict among member states (Russett, Oneal, and Davis 1998).

IOs range from simple entities like the APEC secretariat, with an initial budget of $2 million, to formidable organizations like the European Union (EU)[1] and the World Bank, which has thousands of employees and multiple affiliates and lends billions of dollars each year. Specialized agencies like the ILO, ICAO, and FAO play key roles in technical issue areas. New organizations like UNEP, the EBRD, and the International Tribunal for the former Yugoslavia are regularly created. Older IOs like NATO and the Security Council are rethought and sometimes restructured to meet new circumstances.[2] As the examples illustrate, moreover, even the most powerful states often act through IOs. In short, "it is impossible to imagine contemporary international life" without formal organizations (Schermers and Blokker 1995: 3).

Why do states so frequently use IOs as vehicles of cooperation? What attributes account for their use, and how do these characteristics set formal organizations apart from alternative arrangements, such as decentralized cooperation, informal consultation, and treaty rules? Surprisingly, contemporary international scholarship has no clear theoretical answers to such questions and thus offers limited practical advice to policy makers.

We answer these questions by identifying the functional attributes of IOs across a range of issue areas. Although we are concerned with the concrete structure and operations of particular organizations, we also see IOs as complex phenomena that implicate several lines of international relations (IR) theory. From this vantage point, we identify two functional characteristics that lead states, in appropriate circumstances, to prefer IOs to alternate forms of institutionalization. These are centralization and independence.

IOs allow for the centralization of collective activities through a concrete and stable organizational structure and a supportive administrative apparatus. These increase the efficiency of collective activities and enhance the organization's ability to affect the understandings, environment, and interests of states. Independence means the ability to act with a degree of autonomy within defined spheres. It often entails the capacity to operate as a neutral in managing interstate disputes and conflicts. IO independence is highly constrained: member states, especially the powerful, can limit the autonomy of IOs, interfere with their operations, ignore their dictates, or restructure and dissolve them. But as in many private transactions, participation by even a partially autonomous, neutral actor can increase efficiency and affect the legitimacy of individual and collective actions. This provides even powerful states with incentives to grant IOs substantial independence.

The broad categories of centralization and independence encompass numerous specific functions. Most IOs perform more than one, though each has its own unique combination. We do not enumerate every such function or provide a comprehensive typology. Instead, we highlight several of the most important. We focus especially on the active functions of IOs—facilitating the negotiation and implementation of agreements, resolving disputes, managing conflicts, carrying out operational activities like technical assistance, elaborating norms, shaping international discourse, and the like—that IR theory has only sparingly addressed. Rational states will use or create a formal IO when the value of these functions outweighs the costs, notably the resulting limits on unilateral action.

Distinguishing formal IOs from alternative forms of organization is important from several perspectives. For IR scholars, who largely abandoned the study of formal IOs in the move from the legal-descriptive tradition to more theoretical approaches, developing such distinctions should "open up a large and important research agenda" with institutional form and structure as central dependent variables (Young 1994: 4; see also Koremenos et al. 1997). This will complement emerging work on international legalization, a closely related form of institutionalization (Burley and Mattli 1993; Abbott and Snidal 1997; Keohane, Moravcsik, and Slaughter 1997). Such research will also benefit practitioners of conflict management and regime design (Mitchell 1994). The policy implications of our analysis are significant as well. Many states, notably the United States, now resist the creation of IOs and hesitate to support those already in operation, citing the shortcomings of international bureaucracy, the costs of formal organization, and the irritations of IO autonomy. This is an ideal time for students of international governance to focus on the other side of the ledger.

The next section spells out our theoretical approach, drawing lessons from the ways in which different schools of theory have dealt with (or have failed to deal with) the questions posed above. It is followed by an analysis of the organizational attributes of centralization and independence and the functions they make possible—especially in contexts of cooperation and nonviolent conflict. The final section explores two composite functions that challenge conventional views of IO capabilities and demonstrate the complementarity of prevailing theories: developing, expressing, and carrying out community norms and aspirations and enforcing rules and commitments. We conclude with the example of the Security Council in the Gulf War, which draws together these themes in the context of violent conflict.

Putting IOs into Theory and Theory into IOs

Our primary approach is rationalist and institutionalist. We assume, for simplicity, that states are the principal actors in world politics and that they use IOs to create social orderings appropriate to their pursuit of shared goals: producing collective goods, collaborating in prisoner's dilemma settings, solving coordination problems, and the like. We start with the pursuit of efficiency and employ the logic of transaction costs, economics, and rational choice (Snidal 1996), using analogies with business firms and medieval trading institutions. Decentralized cooperation theory and, especially, regime theory provide a strong deductive basis for this analysis.

Regime theory (Krasner 1983; Keohane 1984) represents a major advance in understanding international cooperation. It is self-consciously theoretical and focuses directly on the institutional organization of international cooperation. But it has several shortcomings. Most important, regime scholars embrace an earlier turn in IR, which unnecessarily coupled a move to theory with a move away from consideration of IOs themselves. This resulted in "the steady disengagement of international organization scholars from the study of organizations, to the point that today one must question whether such a field even exists any longer except in name only" (Rochester 1986: 783–84). Indeed, regime theory deals with institutions at such a general level that it has little to say about the particular institutional arrangements that organize international politics. Our focus on the concrete operations of formal IOs not only brings them into regime theory but also provides a broader opportunity for IR theory to differentiate among institutional forms and recapture institutional details. We draw on the legal-descriptive literature to accomplish this.

Furthermore, regime theory has been rightly criticized for paying insufficient attention to issues of power and distribution in international politics. We draw on realist considerations to supplement our institutionalist approach in this regard. Finally, although regime theory has paid increasing attention to the role of ideas and norms in international politics (Goldstein and Keohane 1993), it has only begun to incorporate these important considerations. Here, we draw on constructivist theory for guidance. In sum, we enrich our primarily rationalist approach with important insights from several different traditions, which we see as complementary rather than competitive.

Decentralized cooperation theory takes as the problematic of international governance the existence of coordination and collaboration problems requiring collective action (Oye 1986; Stein 1983; Snidal 1985a). It assumes anarchy, often depicted in game models, and analyzes how states cooperate in that spare context through strategies of reciprocity and other forms of self-help. The dependent variable is typically cooperation in the abstract, and much of the research in this tradition has been directed to disproving the realist assertion that cooperation in anarchy is unlikely. There is no nuanced account of the forms of cooperation because the anarchy assumption makes IOs and other institutions largely irrelevant. However, the strong assumptions that underlie the theory, such as the need for high-quality information, suggest that cooperation is unlikely without an adequate institutional context although the theory is only beginning to analyze that context (Morrow 1994). For our purposes, however, it performs a useful service by emphasizing that institutional capacities other than centralized enforcement are crucial in mediating interstate relations.

Regime theory, in contrast, deals explicitly with institutional factors affecting cooperation, and regime scholars frequently mention IOs. But they downplay the distinctive institutional role(s) of IOs, perhaps in continued reaction against the earlier preoccupation with formal organizations. For example, Martin (1992) depicts the European Economic Community (EEC) and the Coordinating Committee for Export Controls (COCOM) as important but nevertheless quite rudimentary forums for intergovernmental bargaining; Weber (1994) emphasizes the broad political and symbolic goals of the EBRD. Neither discusses the organizations' primary operational roles. Keohane's (1984) *After Hegemony* also emphasizes intergovernmental bargaining, arguing that regimes help states reach specific agreements by reducing transaction costs, improving information, and raising the costs of violations. But this valuable analysis also excludes many significant operational activities of IOs.[3] In all these works, furthermore, regime scholars treat international institutions as passive. Regimes are seen, for example, as embodying norms and rules or clarifying expectations (Keohane 1984;

Yarbrough and Yarbrough 1992; Garrett and Weingast 1993), functions also performed by treaties and informal agreements. Regimes are also seen as forums in which states can interact more efficiently: like Keohane and Martin, Moravcsik's (1991) analysis of the Single European Act treats IOs as sites of, but not as agents in, cooperation. Indeed, the canonical definition of regime (Krasner 1983) encompasses only norms and collective choice procedures, making no provision for the active and independent IO functions—and the corresponding institutional forms that we emphasize below.

Legal scholarship continues to offer descriptive accounts of the history and institutional architecture of IOs, as well as doctrinal analysis of norms and texts, especially the normative output of organizations such as ILO treaties or General Agreement on Tariffs and Trade (GATT)/WTO panel decisions (Bowett 1982; Kirgis 1993). More important for present purposes, another strand of doctrinal theory addresses the constitutional law of IOs, including membership and voting rules, external relations, finance, and the authority of specific organs (Amerasinghe 1994; Sohn 1950, 1967; Dupuy 1988; Shihata 1991, 1995). The best of this work is comparative, examining how common problems of organization and operation are addressed in the constitutive documents and practices of various IOs (Schermers and Blokker 1995; Chayes and Chayes 1995). Unfortunately, "in the land of legal science, there is no strongly established tradition of developing theories on IOs" (Schermers and Blokker 1995: 8; see also Brownlie 1990: 679). Nevertheless, legal scholarship, like some earlier work in IR, notably Cox and Jacobson (1973), carefully differentiates among institutional forms and emphasizes institutional details, an important contribution that we use in our analysis.

Realist theory finds both legal and regime scholarship naive in treating IOs as serious political entities. Realists believe states would never cede to supranational institutions the strong enforcement capacities necessary to overcome international anarchy. Consequently, IOs and similar institutions are of little interest; they merely reflect national interests and power and do not constrain powerful states (Mearsheimer 1995; Strange 1983; for a more nuanced view, see Glaser 1995). We accept the realist point that states are jealous of their power and deeply concerned with the distributive consequences of their interactions. Yet, realists underestimate the utility of IOs, even to the powerful. The United States, at the peak of its hegemony, sponsored numerous IOs, including GATT, IMF, and NATO; these organizations have provided "continuing utility . . . as instruments . . . for regime and rule creation" (Karns and Mingst 1990: 29). Even the Soviet Union, the very model of a modern repressive hegemony, used the Council for Mutual Economic Assistance to organize economic relations within the eastern bloc. We argue that powerful states structure such organizations to further their own interests but must do so in a way that induces weaker states to participate. This interplay is embedded in IO structure and operations.

Finally, Kratochwil and Ruggie (1986) argue that only constructivist (interpretivist) theory focusing on norms, beliefs, knowledge, and understandings can satisfactorily explain formal organizations. We accept the insight that social constructions are fundamental elements of international politics (Wendt 1992, 1995; Barnett 1993) and agree that IOs are—in part—both reflections of and participants in ongoing social processes and prevailing ideas (Finnemore 1996; Kennedy 1987). But the role of IOs is best understood through a synthesis of rationalist (including realist) and constructivist approaches. States consciously use IOs both to reduce transaction costs in the narrow sense and, more broadly, to create information, ideas, norms, and expectations; to carry out and encourage specific activities; to legitimate or delegitimate particular ideas and practices; and to enhance their capacities and power. These functions constitute IOs as agents, which, in turn, influence the interests, intersubjective understandings, and environment of states (McNeely 1995). Potentially, these roles give IOs an influence well beyond their material power, which is trivial on conventional measures. Indeed, IO activities may lead to unintended consequences for member states, a fear often expressed by US politicians. Yet, IO autonomy remains highly constrained by state interests, especially those of the powerful, a fact often demonstrated by US politicians.

Although we adopt a predominantly rationalist theoretical approach, we are concerned with highlighting the importance of formal IOs as empirical phenomena rather than with maintaining a particular theoretical dogma. None of the individual approaches mentioned adequately explains why states use formal IOs; each holds key insights. In identifying formal IOs as an important category of institutionalization to be explained, therefore, we proceed in a more interpretive mode, drawing on different strands of argumentation to highlight ways in which formal IOs function to manage interstate cooperation and conflict.[4]

The Functions of IOs: Centralization and Independence

Two characteristics distinguish IOs from other international institutions: centralization (a concrete and stable organizational structure and an administrative apparatus managing collective activities) and independence (the authority to act with a degree of autonomy, and often with neutrality, in defined spheres).[5] The very existence of a centralized secretariat implies some operational autonomy, but this is often limited to administrative and technical matters and subject to close supervision by governments. In other situations sometimes involving the same organizations substantive autonomy and neutrality are essential. The range and potential importance of these activities lead us to treat independence as a separate category.

Centralization and independence enhance efficiency. An analogy to private business firms is instructive. The firm replaces contractual relations among suppliers, workers, and managers; it substitutes a centralized, hierarchical organization for the horizontal, negotiated relations of contract. In Coase's (1937) theory, firms are formed when the transaction costs of direct contracting are too high for efficient operation. Similarly, the move from decentralized cooperation to IOs occurs when the costs of direct state interaction outweigh the costs of international organization, including consequent constraints on unilateral action (Trachtman 1996).

Centralization and independence represent different forms of transaction cost economizing. Small businesses draw mainly on the centralization benefits of formal organization, interposing a legal entity with the ability to manage employees hierarchically and the capacity to contract, sue, and be sued. The owners still manage the business directly, though their interactions are more highly structured. Investors in larger firms additionally benefit by granting autonomy and supervisory authority to professional managers; in Berle and Means's (1968: 5) famous phrase, there is a "separation of ownership and control." The situation is similar in complex IOs, in which member states grant some authority to IO organs and personnel but supervise them through structures resembling the corporate shareholders meeting, board of directors, and executive committee. Introducing these new actors changes the relations among states and allows them to achieve goals unattainable in a decentralized setting.

Centralization and independence produce political effects beyond mere efficiency. In these respects, IOs resemble governments and private associations more than business firms. Independence, in particular, enables IOs to shape understandings, influence the terms of state interactions, elaborate norms, and mediate or resolve member states' disputes. The acts of independent IOs may be accorded special legitimacy, and they affect the legitimacy of members' actions. Even centralization, seemingly more mechanical, can alter states' perceptions and the context of their interactions.

Centralization

It is no great theoretical insight that an established organizational structure and centralized administrative support can render collective activities more efficient: even students of international governance are not
content to communicate by e-mail; they form the International Studies
Association and the International Law Association. This simple insight
goes far to explain the proliferation of IOs in this century in a period of
increasing issue complexity and a growing number of states. The
(inter)subjective effects of centralization are less apparent, though
equally important. We consider the benefits of centralization under two
headings—support for direct state interaction (the principal focus of
regime theory) and operational activities (the traditional focus of IO
studies). Here, we emphasize concrete activities in which governments
remain closely involved; the following section introduces broader functions also requiring IO autonomy.

Support for State Interactions

The organizational structure of IOs enhances even the passive virtues
recognized by regime theory. An established organization provides a
stable negotiating forum, enhancing iteration and reputational effects.
Such a stable forum also allows for a fast response to sudden developments. The Security Council, for example, is organized so that it can
function on short notice, with each member required to maintain continuous representation at UN headquarters. A permanent organization
also reinforces accepted norms: the most favored nation (MFN) principle instantiated in the WTO provides a sounder basis for state expectations than any informal arrangement.

In other ways too, centralization shapes the political context of state
interactions. IOs provide neutral, depoliticized, or specialized forums
more effectively than almost any informal or decentralized arrangement.
This enables a broader range of behavior: the superpowers could discuss
technical nuclear issues within the IAEA without the intrusion of high
politics, even at the height of the cold war. IOs also serve as partisan
forums for political coalitions: the United Nations Conference on Trade
and Development (UNCTAD) for developing countries, the Organization
for Economic Cooperation and Development (OECD) for industrialized
states. Finally, IOs strengthen issue linkages by situating them within
common organizational structures, as the WTO has done for goods, services, and intellectual property rights.

Formal organizations further embody the precise terms of state interaction. Representation and voting rules "constitutionalize" balances among states having different levels of power, interest, or knowledge. States with advanced nuclear technology and large supplies of nuclear raw material are guaranteed seats on the IAEA Board of Governors; states with major shipping and carrier interests have equal representation on the International Maritime Organization (IMO) Council. Such decision structures frequently guarantee disproportionate influence for powerful states. Yet, they may also constitutionalize protection for weaker states and hold the powerful accountable to fixed rules and procedures. For example, both the Security Council and the EU Council are structured so that the most powerful members can block affirmative actions but, even if united, cannot approve actions without support from smaller powers.

Such considerations often lead to elaborate organizational structures. The substantive work of many IOs takes place in specialized committees staffed by their secretariats. The OECD uses more than 200 committees and working groups; the IMO prepares treaties in substantive groupings like the maritime safety and marine environmental protection committees. Such committees are often formally open to all members, but specialization occurs naturally because of differences in interest, expertise, and resources. Delegation can also be encouraged institutionally: in the third UN law of the sea conference (UNCLOS III), the chairs of open-ended committees sometimes scheduled meetings in rooms capable of holding only 30 people![6]

Organizational structure influences the evolution of interstate cooperation as conditions change. For example, several environmental agreements were facilitated by appointing UNEP as secretariat and the World Bank as financial administrator, obviating the need for new institutions. These institutional links are often contested because of their distributional implications. The advanced countries fought to locate new intellectual property rules in the WTO (rather than in the World Intellectual Property Organization [WIPO]) so they could enforce their rights more effectively. In other cases, organizational structures create vested interests that impede change or politicize issues, as in the United Nations Education, Scientific, and Cultural Organization (UNESCO) during the 1970s. More generally, because IOs are designed for stability, they may not adapt smoothly to changing power conditions, as the continuing makeup of the Security Council attests. Yet, the gradual reduction of US voting power in the IMF, mandated by its declining share of capital contributions, illustrates how organizational structure can facilitate such adaptation.

Most IOs include a secretariat or similar administrative apparatus. In simple consultative organizations, the secretariat need only assist with the mechanics of decentralized interaction. The 1985 Vienna Ozone Convention assigned the following functions to its secretariat: "(a) To arrange for and service meetings . . . ; (b) To prepare and transmit reports based upon information received . . . ; (d) To prepare reports on its activities . . . ; (e) To ensure the necessary coordination with other relevant international bodies . . . ; (f) To perform such other functions as may be determined" ("Vienna Convention" 1985: 1532). The secretariat for the Convention on Long Range Transboundary Air Pollution (LRTAP) performed similar functions with only five professionals. Levy (1993: 84) notes that the staff had "little time to do anything else but keep the meetings running smoothly."

Even such modest activities can strengthen international cooperation. Here, we draw on the analogy to the medieval law merchant and the corresponding theoretical literature (Milgrom, North, and Weingast 1990; Calvert 1995; Morrow 1994). Informal consultations produced sufficient information on the identity of untrustworthy traders to support a substantial volume of trade. Yet, modest efforts by central administrators at commercial fairs to collect and relay additional information created a new equilibrium at a higher level of exchange.

Most IOs perform more extensive supportive functions. Law-making conferences like UNCLOS III or the Rio conference on the environment and development rely heavily on their secretariats. IO personnel coordinate and structure agendas, provide background research, and promote successful negotiations. They keep track of agreements on particular issues, trade-offs, and areas of disagreement, periodically producing texts that consolidate the current state of play. They also transmit private offers or assurances, improving the flow of information.

IO staffs support decentralized cooperation between major conferences. The large, expert OECD secretariat collects, produces, and publishes information relevant to national economic policy coordination. The WTO secretariat assists in numerous negotiations, from the settlement of disputes to sectoral talks under the services agreement. IO staffs also support the decentralized implementation of norms. UNEP, secretariat for the Basel convention on the transboundary movement of hazardous wastes, provides information states need to manage activities under the treaty; the ILO receives, summarizes, and circulates national reports on treaty implementation.

Experience under the international trade regime testifies to the importance of organizational structure and administrative support. The original GATT was a normative and consultative arrangement; almost all organizational features were removed at the insistence of the United States. Yet, member states soon needed more extensive organizational structure and support. As membership expanded and complex new issues appeared on the agenda, GATT began its metamorphosis into the WTO, a true IO.

Managing Substantive Operations

IOs do more than support intergovernmental negotiations; they manage a variety of operational activities. A prototypical operational organization is the World Bank, which finances massive development projects, borrows on world capital markets, reviews state investment proposals, provides technical assistance and training in many disciplines, generates extensive research and publications, and performs other substantive activities. Operational organizations normally have sizable budgets and bureaucracies, complex organizational structures, and substantial operational autonomy.[7]

Member states of an IO like the World Bank use the institution as an agent, taking advantage of its centralized organization and staff to carry out collective activities. The analogy of the large business corporation, with its dispersed owner-investors and professional managers, is apt. Compared with a decentralized approach based on ad hoc contracting, a formal organization provides efficiency gains that outweigh the accompanying costs in terms of money, human resources, and constraints on unilateral action. Especially when participating states differ in power, centralized operations will have significant distributional consequences.

IO operations also significantly influence the capabilities, understandings, and interests of states. This is most apparent with outputs such as information and rules. But it is also true of more material activities like technical assistance and joint production. Indeed, virtually all of the activities discussed below promote certain norms and practices among states, often in unanticipated ways.

Pooling

Many IOs are vehicles for pooling activities, assets, or risks. Some pooling can be accomplished on a decentralized basis, as in a business partnership, but a separate entity with a stable organizational structure and specialized staff can greatly reduce transaction costs while providing additional advantages.

Consider the World Bank again. As in other international financial institutions (IFIs), members pool financial resources through capital contributions and commitments. Pooling provides a solid cushion of capital that enables the World Bank to make credible financial commitments to borrowers, who rely on them for costly planning and investment decisions, and to world capital markets, in which the bank borrows at advantageous rates. In addition, this common effort promotes burden sharing in providing a collective good and may limit the competition for influence that characterizes some bilateral assistance. Similarly, by combining development loans in a common portfolio, bank members pool, and thereby reduce, their individual risk.

Pooling enables the World Bank to achieve economies of scale by carrying out a large volume of activities, establishing uniform procedures and building up a common body of data. These economies allow it to develop greater technical expertise on various aspects of country and project assessment than could most states and to innovate in emerging areas like "basic needs." Finally, the bank's broad jurisdiction creates a horizontal advantage akin to economies of scope: by dealing with virtually all needy countries, the bank can target global priorities while avoiding duplication and gaps in coverage.[8]

The largest states, especially the United States, could mobilize sufficient capital to accomplish their international financial objectives unilaterally.[9] They are unwilling to do so, however, for international and domestic political reasons and because of competing priorities. Indeed, the United States is actively working to strengthen the IFIs, in part because their broad membership and assessment structures encourage wide cost sharing.[10] In the meantime, although the G-7 countries bear most of the costs of the IFIs, they also retain the greatest share of voting power and influence on management. During the cold war, they successfully excluded the Soviet bloc and the People's Republic of China. Yet, the United States has been unable consistently to dictate IFI decisions on specific transactions.

Nonfinancial IOs provide similar advantages. The public health activities of WHO, like other UN-specialized agencies, are based on the pooling of national contributions and cost sharing (though the industrialized countries bear the bulk of the costs); economies of scale provide operational efficiencies. The WHO smallpox campaign illustrates the horizontal benefits of centralization: a single global campaign against a contagious disease is more effective than decentralized efforts because global scope avoids gaps in coverage. (The IAEA nuclear safeguards system offers a similar advantage.) In addition, the stable organizational structure of WHO and the reputation-staking effect of membership encourage participation. Free-rider problems remain, but the organization can alleviate them by using its own resources. WHO also provides effective technical assistance by pooling financial and technical resources and accumulating expertise; its global scope diffuses new technologies and allows rational prioritization of needs. By enhancing the development and transmission of ideas, technical activities of specialized organizations have significantly shaped the interests and identities of states. At the same time, they have helped less developed states acquire capacities essential to both national policy making and international activity.

An example of the limits of pooling illustrates these effects and the importance of realist and constructivist considerations. UNESCO's scientific arm was intended to promote the public goods aspects of scientific research by pooling international scientific facilities and creating a central clearinghouse. The organization was initially oriented toward the needs of scientists: executive board members did not represent governments. With the cold war, however, state interests asserted themselves. The board was reorganized to represent states, and UNESCO's orientation shifted to national science. Finnemore (1996) documents how UNESCO technical assistance subsequently promoted national science programs even in states where there was little need for them. Thus, UNESCO helped shape states' identities, interests, and capabilities in the area of science policy even though its initial global objectives were frustrated by interstate rivalries.

Joint Production

Alchian and Demsetz's (1972) theory of the firm suggests that a centralized organization is particularly important when workers, managers, and other "inputs" must work in teams, producing a joint output. In these situations, the hierarchical organization of the firm makes it easier for managers, themselves beholden to the owners ("residual claimants"), to monitor, reward, and discipline employees. IO personnel engage in similar teamwork and thus are typically organized hierarchically, with supervision by and on behalf of member states.

Beyond this, states themselves sometimes form multinational "teams" to engage in production activities. Experts from several European states cooperate in subatomic research through the European Organization for Nuclear Research (CERN), an IO that operates a nuclear laboratory; the Airbus project is a similar example. In addition to holding participants responsible, these organizations pool resources and risks, achieve economies of scale, avoid duplication and unproductive competition, and ensure that the outputs, including technological externalities, are shared. Projects like CERN and Airbus resemble business firms even more than the typical IO. Indeed, Airbus, originally created as a partnership under

French law, is being transformed into a private corporation to better coordinate the participants.

Perhaps the best example of interstate joint production is the NATO military alliance. Common war plans, specialization of military tasks, joint exercises, common equipment and interchangeable parts, and, of course, the conduct of battle are examples of teamwork par excellence. NATO's integrated command—operating hierarchically on behalf of member states as residual claimants—organizes, monitors, and disciplines participants in the joint activities of the alliance, probably the most successful in history.[11]

Norm Elaboration and Coordination

States arrange cooperative relationships through agreements. As Williamson (1985, 1996) and others have pointed out, bounded rationality and high transaction and information costs make it difficult for states—like the parties to any contract—to anticipate and provide for all possible contingencies. The longer and more complex the relationship, the more significant the contingencies; the greater the investment in specific assets, the greater the uncertainty and risk of opportunism. The domestic legal system helps alleviate these problems by supplying missing terms and decision rules, but the international institutional context is comparatively thin. "First, in international law, there is not a very complete body of law that can be applied to supply missing terms. . . . Second . . . there is generally no dispute resolution tribunal with mandatory jurisdiction. . . . The alternative, of course, is to write comprehensive contracts" (Trachtman 1996: 51–54).

There is another alternative: to create procedures for the elaboration of norms within an IO. Decentralized procedures do not address the problems of transaction costs and opportunism. Even with coordination issues in which equilibria can sometimes be reached without communication these problems can stymie cooperation when there are many actors, complex problems, and distributive conflicts. The stable organizational structure of IOs addresses both issues. Established procedures for elaborating rules, standards, and specifications enhance cooperation even when member states retain the power to reject or opt out—as they do even in IOs with relatively advanced legislative procedures, like the ILO. Nonbinding recommendations can become de facto coordination equilibria, relied on by states and other international actors. This gives IOs some power to affect international norms and state behavior and potentially much greater power with the backing of key states.

As always, powerful states exert disproportionate influence over norm elaboration and structure legislative processes to ensure their influence. Here, too, however, protection for weaker states may be the price of their participation, and the effectiveness of an established rule-making procedure requires that powerful states respect those arrangements. For example, powerful states often limit IO jurisdiction to technical areas with limited distributional impact; as a result, IO legislative procedures may go forward—up to a point, at least—less influenced by narrow national interests and differential power than direct intergovernmental bargaining.

Many IOs engage in norm elaboration, especially of a technical kind. The EU, most notably, has issued a huge number of directives, regulations, and other legislative acts—affecting everything from franchise agreements to telecommunication interconnectivity standards to tax policy—though many important issues have been addressed through interstate agreements and mutual recognition. The preparation of proposed legislation is housed exclusively in the commission to facilitate a depoliticized and expert approach.

Many other IOs carry out extensive legislative programs, frequently focusing on coordination rules. The ICAO promulgates international "rules of the air;" the International Telecommunications Union (ITU) coordinates national broadcasting standards; the Customs Cooperation Council implements common customs rules; and the Codex Alimentarius Commission harmonizes food standards. Although technical, these standards have important effects on (and within) states, as the concern over privileging Codex standards under the North American Free Trade Agreement (NAFTA) demonstrated. Although the associated IOs are quite weak, their influence is strengthened by the self-enforcing nature of coordination equilibria.

Independence

Although centralization often requires some operational autonomy, many valuable IO functions require more substantive independence. The participation of an IO as an independent, neutral actor can transform relations among states, enhancing the efficiency and legitimacy of collective and individual actions. These functions require a delicate balance among short- and long-term collective and distributional interests. Powerful states will not enter an organization they cannot influence, yet undermining the independence of an organization performing the functions discussed here will simultaneously reduce its effectiveness and their own ability to achieve valued ends.

Analogies from the business firm and the law merchant illustrate the point. Shareholders in a large corporation must monitor managers to limit agency costs. Yet, if major shareholders cause managers to favor their interests unduly, others may refuse to invest. If shareholders generally assert excessive control, moreover, they lose the advantages of professional management. The law merchant analogy is even sharper. Powerful princes granted monopoly privileges to independent guilds of foreign merchants, enabling them to embargo the princes themselves if they took advantage of the merchants (Grief, Milgrom, and Weingast 1994). By eliminating princes' incentives to cheat, these arrangements enabled them to make the binding commitments necessary to induce mutually beneficial trade. The princes could withdraw the guilds' privileges, of course, but were constrained from doing so by the resulting loss of trade.

Support for Direct State Interaction

Independent IOs promote intergovernmental cooperation in more proactive ways than those discussed earlier; they are *initiating* as well as supportive organizations. The governing body is often authorized to call together member states to consider current problems. IO personnel also influence negotiation agendas. On a high political plane, UNEP kept ozone protection alive when interstate negotiations deadlocked and built support for the Montreal Protocol. The UN secretary-general may put before the Security Council any matter that, in his opinion, threatens international peace and security. At the administrative level, the ILO governing body sets the General Conference agenda with assistance from the International Labour Office. At the technical level, IO and conference officials advance specific proposals and suggest linkages or trade-offs: the president of UNCLOS III was authorized to defer contentious votes to forge a consensus during deferment; the negotiating text advanced by GATT Director General Dunkel during the Uruguay Round catalyzed the faltering negotiations and helped bridge substantive differences.

IO officials are also prominent members of the epistemic communities that develop and transmit new ideas for international governance (Haas 1992). Drake and Nicolaidis (1992: 76) document the role of IOs in developing the concepts behind the liberalization of trade in services: a "comparatively small number of experts in the GNS [Group on Negotiation in Services] and on the GATT, UNCTAD and OECD staffs [were] the main source of the specific kinds of new ideas needed to carry the policy project to a conclusion." The UN Economic Commission on Latin America is well known as the source of many ideas regarding economic development that rallied the Group of 77. Such autonomous efforts can modify the political, normative, and intellectual context of interstate interactions. These factors are not purely exogenous, as in structural theories or constructivist approaches that locate them in general societal trends, but are tied to the agency and interests of IOs (Ness and Brechin 1988; Scott 1992).

Independence is equally important in implementation. The ILO committee of experts—a group of private individuals—comments on national reports. Some ILO organs use these comments to highlight noncompliance with ILO conventions and recommendations and to invite governments to submit additional information. Other IOs report on state compliance in addition to, or in lieu of, national reports. IO officials further monitor state conduct, in more or less intrusive ways, although enforcement remains decentralized. For example, the WTO regularly reviews the general effects of national trade policies.

Managing Substantive Operations

In the above examples, IOs facilitate interstate collaboration by pushing negotiations forward. This role could be played by, say, a dominant state, but suspicions of bias might impede cooperation; an independent IO may be more acceptable because it is neutral. For many substantive IO operations, however, it is the existence of a truly independent third party, not the absence of bias per se, that enables states to achieve their ends.

Laundering. Laundering has a negative connotation from its association with running ill-gotten gains through seemingly independent financial institutions until they come out clean, having lost their original character and taint. Without necessarily adopting that connotation, we use the term advisedly because the process at work in IOs is similar: activities that might be unacceptable in their original state-to-state form become acceptable when run through an independent, or seemingly independent, IO. The concept should be familiar to IR scholars who are reluctant to accept Central Intelligence Agency funds but eagerly accept National Science Foundation grants overseen by independent academic panels.

Appropriately enough, the World Bank, IMF, and other IFIs provide clear examples. States may prefer development assistance from an independent financial institution over direct aid from another state, especially a former colonial power or one seeking political influence. IFI restrictions on national autonomy (e.g., on project design or broader economic policies) may not carry the same domestic political implications of dependence and inferiority as would conditions imposed directly by, say, the United States or France. These considerations may make IFI conditions a superior means of promoting domestic reforms.

IFIs equally serve a laundering function for donor states seeking to avoid domestic and international controversies. The World Bank's charter requires, for example, that development loans be made without regard for the "political character" of the recipient; disregard of this factor is difficult within the United States, where financial assistance budgets require congressional approval. The United States called on the IMF to manage the 1980s debt crisis, keeping the issue less politicized and more technical. Similarly, the Soviet Union laundered subsidies to subordinate states in Eastern Europe through Council for Mutual Economic Assistance (CMEA) trading practices, muting domestic opposition to these political and economic arrangements both at home and in recipient states (Marreese 1986). IFIs also inhibit domestic special interests from distorting policy for other purposes, as in the case of tied aid.

Although the obligation to participate in IFIs may be strong, doing so helps donor states curtail aid recipients' expectations, thus preserving flexibility. Although international intermediaries diminish a donor state's leverage over recipient states, this factor is offset by decreases in other states' leverage and in competition for leverage among donors. Donor states as a group, of course, retain control over the IFIs. But it is the fund, not the United States or Germany, that imposes austerity on borrowers.

The autonomy needed for successful laundering gives IOs influence over the substance of their activities. For example, IFI staff have significant input into lending criteria and adjustment policies and, increasingly, into social, environmental, and other related policies. Robert McNamara was able to broaden development discourse beyond economic growth to include social factors and to reorient World Bank policy (Finnemore 1996; Sanford 1988). The point should not be overstated. McNamara's reforms were hardly radical, and Western countries were largely receptive. Subsequently, the Reagan administration pushed the World Bank partially back toward market policies. Thus, IO autonomy remains bounded by state interests and power, as reflected in institutional arrangements.

Such interventions can cause IOs to be perceived as politicized, responding to the interests of certain states or to issues beyond their regular purview. This occurred in the 1960s and 1970s, when the World Bank withheld loans from states that expropriated foreign property without compensation (Lipson 1985: 138–39); recently, the United States linked support for World Bank lending to human rights in cases, including China and Malawi (Kirgis 1993: 572–75). Whatever their justification, such measures reflect a partial failure we label dirty laundering. Powerful states face a tension between the immediate advantages of dirty laundering versus the long-run costs of jeopardizing IO independence.

Laundering is not limited to financial organizations. UN peacekeeping allows powerful states to support conflict reduction without being drawn into regional conflicts and discourages other powers from taking advantage of their inaction. This simultaneously reassures small countries that the conflict will not be enlarged. The IAEA performs two different laundering functions. First, recipients may prefer technical assistance from an independent agency rather than a particular nuclear state, even though nuclear states as a group dominate the agency. Direct assistance may create dependence, reduce policy flexibility, and be domestically controversial. IAEA technical assistance programs also distance provider states from recipient nuclear programs and inhibit the commercial rivalry among suppliers that otherwise facilitates proliferation. Second, states subject to nuclear safeguards may be more willing to admit independent international monitors into sensitive nuclear facilities than to permit entry by representatives of another state. Interestingly, when the United States transferred bilateral safeguard responsibilities to the IAEA in 1962, some recipients resisted the new arrangement, fearing that nationals of various states on the IAEA staff would conduct covert intelligence missions. This suggests, however, not that the logic of laundering is false but that it turns on the perceived independence of the organization.

Laundering thus has significant implications for the constitutive rules of IOs. Although member states retain ultimate control, organizations must be structured from their organs of governance down to their personnel policies—to create sufficient independence for laundering to succeed. A failing of the UN secretariat is that its personnel are viewed as retaining their national identities; by contrast, the "Eurocrat" is seen as having loyalties beyond his or her individual state.

Neutrality. Neutrality adds impartiality to independence. It enables IOs to mediate among states in contested interactions, including disputes and allocation decisions. UN neutrality underlies most of the functions discussed in the secretary-general's Agenda for Peace, from fact-finding and other forms of preventive diplomacy through dispute resolution and peacekeeping to postconflict consolidation of peace. Even more than laundering, neutrality demands that institutions be buffered from direct pressures of states.

IO as neutral information provider.   Regime theory recognizes the importance of information but does not emphasize differences in its quality. Information created or verified by an independent, neutral IO is more reliable than that provided by states because it is free of national biases. Consider the air pollution monitoring stations established in Europe under LRTAP. Data supplied by Sweden or Russia could be perceived as biased, but a neutral source of information was more credible and could support greater cooperation. The convention protecting Antarctic seals incorporated an existing institution, the Scientific Commission on Antarctic Research, as a neutral source and verifier of information on the status of seals and state activities. Based on this information, the parties attained a rather high degree of cooperation. Similar conventions without neutral sources of information, such as that concerning Antarctic marine living resources, have been less successful. Finally, the 1991 General Assembly declaration on fact finding strengthens the UN secretary-general's role as a neutral information source in politically charged situations; the General Assembly has similarly encouraged the secretary-general to develop early warning systems for international disputes and humanitarian crises.

International monitoring organizations, notably those operating under multilateral arms control treaties, provide outstanding examples of neutral information production. From the perspective of many participants, the neutrality of these organizations is their most important feature. Impartial information not only deters cheating by others but also helps states assure others of their own compliance (Abbott 1993). Although the literature on informal cooperation and the US-Soviet arms control experience suggest that states can perform these functions on their own (Glaser 1995), the widespread use of IOs testifies to the advantages of third-party neutrals.

IO as trustee.   In private commercial dealings, neutral parties often hold assets belonging to persons who cannot be trusted with possession until a transaction is completed. The "escrow agent," for example, protects assets until all elements of the transaction are ready for closing, while the trustee holds assets on behalf of owners who cannot take title immediately.

Such arrangements are not common in IR, but notable examples exist. The Security Council held Iraq responsible for losses caused by its invasion of Kuwait. It required Iraq to contribute a percentage of its oil export revenues to a UN compensation fund from which payments would be made. A compensation commission (whose governing council includes representatives of Security Council members) administers the fund as trustee for claimants. Subsequently, concerned about humanitarian needs in Iraq, the council authorized states to import limited amounts of Iraqi oil with payments to be made directly into a special escrow account for purchases of food and medicine. Similarly, an international oil pollution compensation fund is part of the IMO regime governing oil spills in territorial waters.

Building on the League of Nations mandate system, the UN charter established an international trusteeship system. Individual states were typically designated as trustees for various territories, with mixed results. But the charter did establish standards for trustees and a trusteeship council to monitor them. It even contemplated that the UN itself would perform the trustee function directly, an extraordinary example of the IO as a neutral party.

Traditional UN peacekeeping also illustrates the trustee function: UN forces patrol or even control territory to separate combatants, prevent conflict, and supervise negotiated cease-fires. UN neutrality also allows major powers to support peacekeeping without choosing sides among friendly states, as in Cyprus. Blue-helmet neutrality is crucial and guaranteed in multiple ways: operations are voluntary and require continuing consent of all parties, peacekeepers are from countries with no stake in the conflict and under UN command, operations are financed through general assessments, and troops are unarmed (observers) or lightly armed for self-defense to prevent uses of force inconsistent with neutrality. But these restrictions can limit the effectiveness of peacekeeping operations in some conflictual environments—as has been evident in Bosnia. To deal with these limitations, the secretary-general's Agenda for Peace proposes a preventive trustee function: UN-administered demilitarized zones, established in advance of actual conflict to separate contending parties and remove any pretext for attack.

Neutral activities must be keenly attuned to the realities of international power. U Thant's quick withdrawal of the United Nations Emergency Force (UNEF) at Egypt's request in 1967 was based on the legal principle requiring consent for UN operations but equally reflected the reality that two contributing countries had threatened to withdraw troops if Egyptian wishes were not respected. Nevertheless, like an escrow agent, peacekeeping is effective when it furthers state interests in limiting conflict.

The Acheson-Lilienthal (Baruch) Plan would have created an international agency to manage fissile material, contributed by the United States and the United Kingdom, the existing nuclear powers. This institutional arrangement (which was not, of course, adopted) resembled a trusteeship with the world community as beneficiary. It reflected the vital interests of donor states in preventing destabilizing proliferation, but the plan required a neutral trustee. The sponsors would not have been trusted to hold the material themselves.

Similarly, under the "common heritage" principle of UNCLOS 111, the convention declares that rights to seabed resources are "vested in mankind as a whole, on whose behalf the Authority shall act." The powers of the Seabed Authority were limited to accord better with market principles and US interests, but it retains its basic institutional structure, including important trustee characteristics that may evolve over time.

IO as allocator. A neutral party often allocates scarce resources among claimants to avoid paralyzing negotiating standoffs and lingering resentment: the parent, not the children, slices the birthday cake. IOs also serve this function.

The IAEA, for example, assists peaceful national nuclear programs. It necessarily evaluates proposed projects and allocates financial and personnel resources. Only a neutral body could be entrusted with such responsibility in a sensitive area. IFIs also allocate scarce resources according to project worthiness. The World Bank's charter tries to guarantee its neutrality by requiring that it ignore the political character of potential borrowers. The perception that the World Bank promotes pro-market policies on behalf of the Western powers and punishes governments that pursue other goals such as equity reduces its effectiveness. The World Bank defends its neutrality by presenting its policies as driven by technical analyses rather than value judgments. It has retained a sufficient aura of neutrality to be entrusted with allocating funds under the Global Environment Facility, the Ozone Trust Fund, and the climate change convention.

IO as arbiter. According to Morgenthau (1967: 272), "despite . . . deficiencies [in] . . . the legislative function [in international politics], a legal system might still be capable of holding in check the power aspirations of its subjects if there existed judicial agencies that could speak with authority whenever a dissension occurred with regard to the existence or the import of a legal rule." Few international institutions are truly designed to restrain state power, yet many help states resolve legal (and political) disputes. Neutrality is essential for such institutions, just as for a judge in the law merchant system (Milgrom, North, and Weingast 1990), the European Court, or a domestic court.

In *facilitative intervention,* an IO operates as "honest broker" to reduce transaction costs, improve information about preferences, transmit private offers, and overcome bargaining deadlocks. Chapter VI of the UN charter requires states to use traditional measures—including good offices, mediation, conciliation and fact finding—to resolve disputes that threaten international peace and security. The secretary-general frequently provides these services. The Human Rights Committee provides its good offices in interstate disputes and may appoint ad hoc conciliation commissions to propose possible settlements. Numerous international conventions, from the Antarctic to the NATO treaties, provide for similar measures if direct negotiations fail. Even the highly legalized WTO understanding on dispute settlement allows members to request mediation or conciliation by the director-general.

In *binding intervention*, international institutions issue legally binding decisions with the consent of all parties. The mere possibility of binding external intervention may bring recalcitrant states to the bargaining table and make negotiating positions more reasonable. The most common dispute resolution mechanism of this kind is arbitration. Participating states agree on arbitrators, procedures, and jurisdiction and agree to be bound by the arbitrators' decision. When agreement on these matters cannot be reached, other neutral IOs sometimes fill the gap—as when the Permanent Court of Arbitration selected the president of the US-Iran claims tribunal.

Arbitral tribunals resolve disputes on an ad hoc basis, as in the 1941 US-Canada *Trail Smelter* arbitration, a leading precedent in international environmental law, or in the secretary-general's "Rainbow Warrior" arbitration between France and New Zealand. They also handle classes of disputes such as the famous Alabama Claims arbitration following the Civil War, the special claims commission for allied property claims following World War II, and the Iran-US claims tribunal. The following comment on the Rainbow Warrior dispute applies to most of these cases: "This solution is not without critics in both countries. . . . However, . . . the settlement proved much more acceptable—precisely because of its unimpeachable source—than would have been the same, or any other, solution arrived at solely by the parties themselves. Neither government . . . could be accused by its internal critics of having yielded to the other" (Franck and Nolte 1993: 166).

Many international agreements, from bilateral commercial treaties to the law of the sea convention, rely on arbitration through ad hoc panels or more permanent institutions. The GATT-WTO dispute resolution process is similar to arbitration. In the interest of neutrality, the director-general maintains a roster of qualified panelists, suggests panelists to disputants, and names the panel if the parties cannot agree. NAFTA incorporates several arbitration procedures, including an innovative one whereby arbitrators review national antidumping and countervailing duty decisions to ensure that national law was followed. The International

Centre for the Settlement of Investment Disputes (ICSID), affiliated with the World Bank, provides neutral facilities for arbitrations between private investors and host governments.

The principal international judicial authority is the International Court of Justice (ICJ). Unlike domestic courts, it must be granted jurisdiction by parties to a dispute. Most cases have arisen under treaties that include submission to ICJ jurisdiction. The ICJ also issues advisory opinions to UN organs and specialized agencies. The court has issued a number of decisions of significance but has not been heavily used by states; GATT panels, for instance, have issued many more decisions than the ICJ. A relatively small number of states have accepted compulsory jurisdiction, and efforts to use the court during high-profile disputes led France and the United States to terminate their acceptance, although not without cost. The European Court of Justice and the European Court of Human Rights (which also requires acceptance of jurisdiction) have been more successful. Indeed, the former—whose judges are chosen "from persons whose independence is beyond doubt"— approaches the authority of the judicial institutions Morgenthau had in mind. Its judges have played a leading (independent) role in promoting European legal integration (Burley and Mattli 1993). Other international institutions, including the WTO appellate body, may also develop into successful judicial agencies.

IO as Community Representative and Enforcer

In this section, we consider broader and more controversial functions of formal IOs, some of which go beyond a simple state-centric approach. We examine how states structure and use formal organizations to create and implement community values and norms and to assist in the enforcement of international commitments. This discussion demonstrates further how the study of IOs forces different theoretical schools to engage one another. We discuss these two functions separately, then together in a brief examination of the role of the UN in the Gulf War—an example that also illustrates the significance of IOs in situations of violent conflict.

The IO as Community Representative

States establish IOs to act as a representative or embodiment of a community of states. This was a central aspiration in the postwar organizational boom and remains an important, if only partially fulfilled, aspect of IO operations today.

Community institutions take several forms. They may be inclusive bodies such as the General Assembly, the town square of international politics, created as a forum in which common issues can be addressed. Within such institutions, states work out and express their common interests and values. The process may be largely consensual, as when states consider some problem of common concern such as environmental change or the behavior of a rogue state, or it may entail one set of states pressuring another to accept new principles such as human rights, the oceans as a commons, or democracy. Other community institutions, such as the Security Council, are representative bodies. These incorporate the major actors (as realism would predict) as well as states representing other interests. These smaller bodies instantiate political bargains in their representation rules while providing a more efficient forum in which to deal with issues, especially those requiring operational responses. Finally, community institutions such as the ICJ are structured to promote independence and neutrality, their actions constrained by a charge to act in the common interest. All three types can advance community interests with special legitimacy.

The UN, established by the Allies when they had unchecked dominance, was undoubtedly intended to serve their own purposes. It was also based on a conception of shared interests and values that went well beyond laundering or even neutrality. The charter's broad goals presupposed a direct relation between national welfare, conditions around the globe, and the peaceful working of the international community as a whole. The principal goal was to maintain international peace and security, and UN organs were authorized to intervene not just mediate in interstate disputes that threatened peace. Other goals were to develop friendly relations among states based on the principles of equal rights and self-determination, to promote fundamental freedoms, and to promote cooperation on a wide range of global problems. Shared interests in many of these areas—human rights, democracy, and liberal economic relations—are still developing.

Perhaps the most important function of community organizations is to develop and express community norms and aspirations. Although the General Assembly lacks the Security Council's power of action, it can have substantial impact on international politics by expressing shared values on issues like human rights, apartheid, decolonization, and environmental protection in ways that legitimate or delegitimate state conduct. The Universal Declaration of Human Rights is a striking example. Although the declaration cannot be enforced, its explicit and sweeping formulation of standards has significantly affected state behavior. Its norms have been included in binding treaties, and the declaration itself has been incorporated into some national constitutions, thereby influencing the character and preferences of states and, thus, of the international system itself. Although smaller states have been disproportionately held to account on this issue, even large states like the former Soviet Union and reputed nuclear states like South Africa have been affected.

Similarly, although GATT (unlike the WTO) was intentionally created with as few attributes of an independent IO as possible, its contracting parties and council have formulated important policies for the trading community, including "differential and more favorable treatment" for developing countries. Although contested, this principle has been reflected in subsequent trade negotiations and the generalized system of preferences.

Courts as independent institutions also formulate and express community policy. By enunciating, elaborating, and applying rules publicly, they educate the community and strengthen underlying norms (Abbott 1992). A highly unusual IO, the UN tribunal dealing with war crimes in the former Yugoslavia, combines these public judicial roles with the closely related public role of prosecutor. But states have not fully embraced the community functions of courts. Even the ICJ is structured to minimize its community role: its jurisdiction rests on party consent, and its decisions have no formal status as precedents. Yet, ICJ decisions are regularly relied on, and the court has on important occasions acted as expositor of fundamental community values, as in the Iranian hostages case and, many would say, Nicaragua's suit against the United States. These decisions have important moral authority even when they cannot be enforced in the traditional sense. Similar functions are performed by the European and Inter American Commissions and Courts of Human Rights, and even by quasi-judicial bodies like the ILO governing body.

The most controversial example of community representation is the Security Council's "primary responsibility for the maintenance of international peace and security." The council is empowered to investigate any situation that might lead to international friction and recommend means of resolving the conflict, including terms of settlement. It is further empowered under Chapter VII to "take action" against any threat to peace. When using armed force, however, the council has proceeded much as with economic sanctions, calling on members to give effect to measures it has approved.

An IO with these powers could overcome free-rider problems hampering decentralized efforts to maintain peace. But the Security Council has the deeper rationale of representing the community. Because local disputes might spill over and disrupt the larger community, they affect the general welfare. Such disputes should not be dealt with exclusively by the parties themselves, or by third states intervening for their own private interests, but by collective bodies that consider the effects of the dispute and of external intervention on the general welfare. Chapter VIII of the charter even authorizes regional organizations like the Organization of American States (OAS) to deal with local disputes, although they only take "enforcement action" with council approval, lest such action itself threaten the peace of the larger community. Finally, situating private disputes in terms of community interests and institutions brings a heightened level of political and moral pressure to bear on disputants and potential intervenors.

The creation and development of IOs often represent deliberate decisions by states to change their mutually constituted environment and, thus, themselves. IOs can affect the interests and values of states in ways that cannot be fully anticipated. Yet, it is important to stress that these processes are initiated and shaped by states. Furthermore, IOs are constrained by institutional procedures—including financial contributions and leadership appointments—that are controlled by states and, ultimately, by the ability of (some) states to withdraw, albeit at some cost. These possibilities and limitations make IOs an important window into the relation between rationalist and constructivist analysis.

IOs as Managers of Enforcement

The role of IOs in ensuring compliance with international commitments can best be understood by integrating managerial and enforcement views of the process. Observing high levels of compliance with international agreements, even though strong enforcement provisions are rarely included or used, the managerial school concludes that IR has focused too heavily on coercive enforcement. In this view, noncompliance typically results not from deliberate cheating but from ambiguity in agreements, insufficient state capacity, or changing international and domestic circumstances (Chayes and Chayes 1995; see also Mitchell 1994; Young 1994). Resolution of such problems lies not in stronger enforcement but in better management of compliance. Downs, Rocke, and Barsoom (1996) counter that, without enforcement, states will cheat on agreements and that observed compliance levels largely reflect shallow agreements that require little change in state behavior.

An overly sharp distinction between managerial and enforcement functions is misleading. For many significant day-to-day activities—

especially ones involving coordination—incentives to defect are relatively small compared with the benefits of cooperation; here, the managerial approach is sufficient. In other cases, some enforcement may be necessary, at least potentially. IOs support both kinds of activities. More important, the strictly decentralized models that underpin the enforcement view do not apply strictly to the richer environment of international politics, especially when states are numerous and face significant informational problems. In these more complex settings, IOs can manage enforcement activities to make them more effective and to limit their adverse side effects.

Many IO functions identified earlier are valuable in implementing the managerial approach. Ambiguity can be resolved through dispute resolution and other third-party procedures, including fact finding, good offices, interpretation of international agreements, and mediation. State incapacity is addressed directly by financial and technical assistance. Emerging compliance problems due to changing circumstances can be managed by IO political and judicial organs with authority to interpret and adapt agreements and elaborate norms.

When enforcement is needed, IOs can facilitate decentralized action. They increase the prospect of continued interaction, often across issues, and generalize reputational effects of reneging across members of the organization. Some IOs directly monitor state behavior, producing credible neutral information necessary for effective enforcement. IOs further provide forums in which suspicious actions can be explained, lowering the risk that misperceptions will upset cooperation, and in which pressure can be brought on transgressor states. In these ways, international legal discussions about "mobilization of shame" can be understood not in the moral sense of creating guilt among states but in an instrumental sense of enhancing reputational and other incentives to abide by commitments.

IOs also have some direct avenues of enforcement. These include requirements of national reporting—wherein failure to report itself indicates improper behavior—and the issuance of findings by the IO itself. The ILO has issued such reports with respect to labor practices, even in the case of powerful states such as the Soviet Union and Britain. A less frequent sanction occurs through resolutions criticizing state behavior. Such practices pressure states to change their behavior both by impairing their international standing and by empowering private groups to pressure national governments, thus increasing "audience costs" (Fearon 1994). Currently, the G-7 states are working to empower the IMF to make findings on national economic policies and to issue public criticism with precisely these goals in mind.

A second means of direct enforcement is withholding IO benefits, as the IAEA suspended technical assistance after Israel bombed an Iraqi nuclear reactor. The IMF's "conditionality" requirements and the World Bank's requirements on development loans have expanded over the postwar period, and these agencies have frequently had strong effects on the policies of member states.

Finally, IOs play an important role as managers of enforcement, authorizing and giving meaning to retaliation, thus ensuring that enforcement activities are not excessively disruptive to the larger international community. This possibility is differentially developed. The GATT only once authorized retaliation, whereas WTO practice is still emerging; the Security Council, by contrast, has authorized economic sanctions on numerous occasions. Martin (1992: 245) finds IOs important in managing economic sanctions because they provide a framework for side payments among retaliating states and increase incentives to cooperate in sanctions so as not to jeopardize the "broad functional benefits these organizations provided."[12] Furthermore, such validation is akin to laundering: when an IO legitimates retaliation, states are not vigilantes but upholders of community norms, values, and institutions. The IO imprimatur clarifies retaliatory behavior so that it will be seen by the target state for what it is, not as noncooperation by the retaliating state, while reassuring third parties that the retaliating state is acting appropriately. (Again, influential states might seek IO approval to disguise their noncooperative acts as retaliation, a form of dirty laundering, but this practice is limited by its self-defeating character and IO independence.) IO approval frequently limits the severity and duration of state retaliation, as the WTO does by limiting the amount of retaliation and the economic sectors targeted. Indeed, the IO may negotiate a response with the retaliating state to maximize third-party support for the action. Such managerial activities counteract "echo effects" and are improvements over strictly decentralized enforcement.

Chapter VII: The Uses and Limits of Direct Enforcement

The Security Council's experience with Chapter VII illuminates the role of the community representative in constructing interests, the possibility of more forcible methods of direct enforcement, and, equally important, their limitations. As noted above, the original conception of Chapter VII involved independent action by the Security Council on behalf of the community of states, using military units provided "on its call" by member states and guided by a military staff committee. This was direct enforcement except that the units to be deployed, even the members of the committee, were to be provided by states. This distinguishes Chapter VII from, say, the independent ability of the IMF to cut off funds to a country that violates its financial commitments. Moreover, Chapter VII has never operated as originally intended. In the two principal episodes in which military force has been used—Korea and the Gulf War—the council instead authorized national military actions, led in both cases by the United States. How are these episodes to be understood?

In the more cynical view, both are examples of dirty laundering. By obtaining Security Council approval, the United States cast essentially unilateral action as more legitimate collective action. The same interpretation can be applied to various OAS enforcement actions against Castro's Cuba. Arguably, the organizations were not sufficiently independent of US influence to convert the measures taken into genuine community action. In the Gulf War, these measures were transparently national: the council simply called on other states to cooperate with the United States, which was already operating in the Gulf theater, and coalition forces were visibly dominated by the United States, whose troops even retained their own uniforms and commanders.

Yet, these episodes can also be seen in a more affirmative light. The institutional underpinnings essential to the original vision of Chapter VII had never been put in place: there were no agreements for the provision of national forces, no emergency units standing by, no military staff committee. Lacking appropriate institutional arrangements, the council carried out its community responsibilities in the only practicable way, by shifting from direct to indirect enforcement, lending its institutional authority to legitimate action by willing nations. Its membership structure and voting rules made the council sufficiently independent and representative to perform a genuine laundering function.[13] The United States, after all, assiduously courted council approval (partly by moving more cautiously) for reasons of both domestic and international politics. The imprimatur of the council was essential to other participants: Middle Eastern states, for example, needed it to justify cooperation with the coalition. In this episode, just as Claude (1966: 74) put it more than 30 years ago, "proclamations of approval or disapproval by organs of the United Nations, deficient as they typically are in . . . effective supportive power, are really important. . . . Statesmen, by so obviously attaching importance to them, have made them important."[14]

The affirmative view sees the council, especially during the Gulf War, as representing the community of states. This representative status, not simply the formal procedures of Chapter VII, led the United States and other states to seek council action: Security Council resolutions on Iraq carried unique political weight because they came from the established community institution with primary responsibility for international peace and security. Resolutions condemning the Iraqi invasion of Kuwait as unlawful, declaring void the incorporation of Kuwaiti territory into Iraq, denouncing human rights and environmental abuses by Iraqi forces, authorizing member states to cooperate with US forces, forcing the destruction of Iraqi weapons, and holding Iraq financially responsible for its actions are clear expressions of the shared moral and legal sense of organized international society. The IO was the locus for giving meaning to state action. The United States, even as the clearly dominant power in coercive activity, had good reasons to act not simply from might but from persuasion.

Thus, realist, constructivist, and rational-regime arguments come together in consideration of the role of IOs in the Gulf crisis. Although some might prefer to find a singular "winner" among the three explanations, we believe each explains a significant part of the episode and that any unidimensional explanation would be incomplete. In any event, IOs provide an important laboratory in which to observe the operation of these different aspects of international politics.

Conclusion

For several decades, states have taken IOs more seriously than have scholars. Whereas formal IOs have been seriously neglected in the theoretical study of international regimes, they have played a major role in many, if not most, instances of interstate collaboration. By taking advantage of the centralization and independence of IOs, states are able to achieve goals that they cannot accomplish on a decentralized basis. In some circumstances, the role of IOs extends even further to include the development of common norms and practices that help define, or refine, states themselves. At the same time, because issues of power and distribution are pervasive, states are wary of allowing IOs too much autonomy. Thus, we do not claim that IOs are supplanting the states system. We do claim that IOs provide an important supplement to decentralized cooperation that affects the nature and performance of the international system. Scholars must take IOs more seriously if they are to understand interstate relations.

Although we have presented the case for the importance of formal institutions in international cooperation, the shortcomings of many actual organizations go without saying. In addition, in emphasizing the possibilities for formal organizations, we should not ignore the difficulty and even impossibility of some of the tasks that are presented to them. Despite these severe limitations, the fact that IOs have not been abandoned by states is testimony to both their actual value and their perhaps greater potential. A better theoretical and empirical understanding of formal organizations should help improve their performance.

Notes

1. Although we discuss certain of its operations, we deliberately de-emphasize the EU because some would regard it as an exceptional case of institutionalization.

2. A discussion of IOs is an exercise in acronyms. The ones not identified in the text, in order, are the World Health Organization (WHO), Organization for Security and Cooperation in Europe (OSCE), International Monetary Fund (IMF), Asia-Pacific Economic Cooperation forum (APEC), International Labour Organization (ILO), International Civil Aviation Organization (ICAO), Food and Agriculture Organization (FAO), United Nations Environment Programme (UNEP), and European Bank for Reconstruction and Development (EBRD).

3. Keohane (1984) does discuss monitoring, but Glaser (1995) argues that regime theorists do not explain why monitoring must be done centrally.

4. On the use of rational choice as an interpretive device, see Ferejohn (1991), Johnson (1991), and Snidal (1985b).

5. Centralization and independence are matters of degree, not only among IOs but even between IOs and related institutions. For example, the Group of Seven is not a formal IO but merely a negotiating forum. Its organizational practices (e.g., a rotating chair) nevertheless provide some centralization benefits, and it partakes of some autonomy, as in legitimating members' actions.

6. Personal communication from Bernard Oxman, member of the US delegation, 21 May 1997.

7. We reserve for the following section discussion of those functions that turn directly on independence and neutrality.

8. Of course, as Kratochwil (1996) notes, large-scale centralized operations may not be necessary or desirable in all cases. The Maastricht Treaty's subsidiarity principle adopts this view, while authorizing supranational activity when the scale of the problem makes that appropriate.

9. The desire to benefit from pooling is nevertheless reflected in US Treasury Secretary Rubin's lament that the "United States cannot be the lender of last resort to the world" (quoted in Sanger 1995).

10. The G-7 countries also benefit from IFI independence, as discussed below.

11. The analogy is imperfect. NATO's organization differs from that of a firm. Nevertheless, team analysis suggests why a formal IO is valuable, whereas the standard public goods analogy reduces the problem simply to one of individual (under) provision. See Olson and Zeckhauser (1966).

12. Martin (1992: 245) also finds it important that the leading "sender" be willing to bear extra costs, suggesting a possible limitation to IO enforcement capacity in the absence of "leadership."

13. The current debate over the composition of the council reflects the idea that such an institution should be more representative of the community on behalf of which it acts.

14. See also Haas (1959) and, for a more skeptical view, see Slater (1969).

References

Abbott, Kenneth W. 1992. "GATT as a Public Institution: The Uruguay Round and Beyond." *Brooklyn Journal of International Law* 31:31–85.
———. 1993. "Trust but Verify: The Production of Information in Arms Control Treaties and Other International Agreements." *Cornell International Law Journal* 26:1–58.
Abbott, Kenneth W., and Duncan Snidal. 1997. "The Many Faces of International Legalization." Draft paper presented at the Conference on Domestic Politics and International Law, June, Napa Valley, CA.
Alchian, Armen, and Harold Demsetz. 1972. "Production, Information Costs and Economic Organization." *American Economic Review* 62:777–95.
Amerasinghe, C. F. 1994. *The Law of the International Civil Service.* 2d rev. ed. Oxford, UK: Clarendon.
Barnett, Michael. 1993. "Institutions, Roles and Disorder: The Case of the Arab States System." *International Studies Quarterly* 37:271–96.
Bowett, D. W. 1982. *The Law of International Institutions.* 4th ed. London: Stevens.
Berle, Adolf A., and Gardiner C. Means. 1968. *The Modern Corporation and Private Property.* Rev. ed. New York: Harcourt, Brace & World.
Brownlie, Ian. 1990. *Principles of Public International Law.* 4th ed. New York: Oxford University Press.
Burley, Anne-Marie, and Walter Mattli. 1993. "Europe Before the Court: A Political Theory of Legal Integration." *International Organization* 47:41–76.
Calvert, Randall L. 1995. "Rational Actors, Equilibrium and Social Institutions." In *Explaining Social Institutions*, edited by Jack Knight and Itai Sened, 57–94. Ann Arbor: University of Michigan Press.
Chayes, Abraham, and Antonia Handler Chayes. 1995. *The New Sovereignty: Compliance with International Regulatory Agreements.* Cambridge, MA: Harvard University Press.
Claude, Inis Jr. 1966. "Collective Legitimization as a Political Function of the United Nations." *International Organization* 20:367–79.
Coase, R. H. 1937. "The Nature of the Firm." *Economica* 4:386–405.
Cox, Robert W., and Harold K. Jacobson, eds. 1973. *The Anatomy of Influence.* New Haven, CT: Yale University Press.
Downs, George W., David M. Rocke, and Peter N. Barsoom. 1996. "Is the Good News About Compliance Good News About Cooperation?" *International Organization* 50:379–406.

Drake, William, and Kalypso Nicolaidis. 1992. "Ideas, Interests and Institutionalization." *International Organization* 46:37–100.

Dupuy, Rene Jean, ed. 1988. *A Handbook on International Organizations.* Hingham, MA: Kluwer Academic.

Fearon, James. 1994. "Domestic Political Audiences and the Escalation of International Disputes." *American Political Science Review* 88:577–92.

Ferejohn, John. 1991. "Rationality and Interpretation: Parliamentary Elections in Early Stuart England." In *The Economic Approach to Politics*, edited by Kristen R. Monroe, 279–305. New York: HarperCollins.

Finnemore, Martha. 1996. *National Interests in International Society.* Ithaca, NY: Cornell University Press.

Franck, Thomas M., and Georg Nolte. 1993. "The Good Offices Function of the UN Secretary-General." In *United Nations, Divided World: The UN's Role in International Relations*, 2d ed., edited by Adam Roberts and Benedict Kingsbury, 143–82. Oxford, UK: Clarendon.

Garrett, Geoffrey, and Barry Weingast. 1993. "Ideas, Interests and Institutions: Constructing the European Community's Internal Market." In *Ideas and Foreign Policy: Beliefs, Institutions and Political Change*, edited by Judith Goldstein and Robert O. Keohane, 173–206. Ithaca, NY: Cornell University Press.

Glaser, Charles. 1995. "Realists as Optimists: Cooperation as Self-Help." *International Security* 19:50–93.

Goldstein, Judith, and Robert O. Keohane, eds. 1993. *Ideas and Foreign Policy: Beliefs, Institutions and Political Change.* Ithaca, NY: Cornell University Press.

Grief, Avner, Paul Milgrom, and Barry R. Weingast. 1994. "Merchant Guilds." *Journal of Political Economy* 102:745–76.

Haas, Ernst. 1959. *Beyond the Nation-State.* Stanford, CA: Stanford University Press.

Haas, Peter M., ed. 1992. "Knowledge, Power and International Policy Coordination." *International Organization* 46 (Special issue): 1–390.

Johnson, James D. 1991. "Rational Choice as a Reconstructive Theory." In *The Economic Approach to Politics*, edited by Kristen R. Monroe, 113–42. New York: HarperCollins.

Karns, Margaret, and Karen Mingst, eds. 1990. *The United States and Multilateral Institutions.* Boston: Unwin Hyman.

Kennedy, David. 1987. "The Move to Institutions." *Cardozo Law Review* 8:841–988.

Keohane, Robert O. 1984. *After Hegemony.* Princeton, NJ: Princeton University Press.

Keohane, Robert O., Andrew Moravcsik, and Anne-Marie Slaughter. 1997. "A Theory of Legalization." Draft paper presented at the Conference on Domestic Politics and International Law, June, Napa Valley, CA.

Kirgis, Frederic L. Jr. 1993. *International Organizations in Their Legal Setting.* 2d ed. St. Paul, MN: West.

Koremenos, Barbara, Charles Lipson, Brian Portnoy, and Duncan Snidal. 1997. "Rational International Institutions." Paper presented at the American Political Science Association Meetings, 28–31 August, Washington, DC.

Krasner, Stephen D., ed. 1983. *International Regimes.* Ithaca, NY: Cornell University Press.

Kratochwil, Friedrich. 1996. International Organization(s): Globalization and the Disappearance of "Publics." Unpublished manuscript.

Kratochwil, Friedrich, and John Gerard Ruggie. 1986. "The State of the Art on the Art of the State." *International Organization* 40:753–75.

Levy, Mark A. 1993. "European Acid Rain: The Power of Tote-Board Diplomacy." In *Institutions for the Earth: Sources of Effective International Environmental Protection,* edited by Peter M. Haas, Robert O. Keohane, and Marc A. Levy, 75–132. Cambridge, MA: MIT Press.

Lipson, Charles. 1985. *Standing Guard: Protecting Foreign Capital in the Nineteenth and Twentieth Centuries.* Berkeley: University of California Press.

Marreese, Michael. 1986. "CMEA: Effective but Cumbersome Political Economy." *International Organization* 40:287–327.

Martin, Lisa L. 1992. *Coercive Cooperation.* Princeton, NJ: Princeton University Press.

McNeely, Connie L. 1995. *Constructing the Nation-State: International Organization and Prescriptive Action.* Westport, CT: Greenwood.

Mearsheimer, John. 1995. "The False Promise of International Institutions." *International Security* 19:5–49.

Milgrom, Paul R., Douglass C. North, and Barry R. Weingast. 1990. "The Role of Institutions in the Revival of Trade: The Law Merchant, Private Judges, and the Champagne Fairs." *Economics and Politics* 2 (1):1–23.

Mitchell, Ronald. 1994. "Regime Design Matters: Intentional Oil Pollution and Treaty Compliance." *International Organization* 48:425–58.

Moravcsik, Andrew. 1991. "Negotiating the Single European Act: National Interests and Conventional Statecraft in the European Community." *International Organization* 45:19–56.

Morgenthau, H. 1967. *Politics Among Nations.* 4th ed. New York: Knopf.

Morrow, James D. 1994. "The Forms of International Cooperation." *International Organization* 48:387–424.

Ness, Gary D., and Steven R. Brechin. 1988. "IOs as Organizations." *International Organization* 42:245–74.

Olson, Mancur, and Richard Zeckhauser. 1966. "An Economic Theory of Alliances." *Review of Economics and Statistics* 48:266–79.

Oye, Kenneth A., ed. 1986. *Cooperation Under Anarchy.* Princeton, NJ: Princeton University Press.

Rochester, J. Martin. 1986. "The Rise and Fall of International Organization as a Field of Study." *International Organization* 40:777–813.

Russett, Bruce, John R. Oneal, and David R. Davis. 1998. "The Third Leg of the Kantian Tripod for Peace: International Organizations and Militarized Disputes, 1950–85." *International Organization* 42.

Sanford, Jonathon. 1988. "The World Bank and Poverty: The Plight of the World's Impoverished Is Still a Major Concern of the International Agency." *American Journal of Economics and Sociology* 47:257–275.

Sanger, David E. 1995. "Big Powers Plan a World Economic Bailout Fund." *The New York Times,* 8 June, D 1.

Schermers, Henry, and Niels Blokker. 1995. *International Institutional Law: Unity Within Diversity.* 3d rev. ed. Cambridge, MA: Kluwer Law International.

Scott, W. Richard. 1992. *Organizations: Rational, Natural and Open Systems.* 3d ed. Englewood Cliffs, NJ: Prentice Hall.

Shihata, Ibrahim F. I., ed. 1991. *The World Bank in a Changing World.* Vol. 1. Norwell, MA: Kluwer Academic Publishers.

———. 1995. *The World Bank in a Changing World.* Vol. 2. Cambridge, MA: Kluwer Law International.

Slater, Jerome. 1969. "The Limits of Legitimation in International Organizations: The Organization of American States and the Dominican Crisis." *International Organization* 23:48–72.

Snidal, Duncan. 1985a. "Coordination Versus Prisoners' Dilemma: Implications for International Cooperation and Regimes." *American Political Science Review* 79:923–42.

———. 1985b. "The Game Theory of International Politics." *World Politics* 39:25–57.

———. 1996. "Political Economy and International Institutions." *International Review of Law and Economics* 16:121–37.

Sohn, Louis. 1950. *Cases and Other Materials on World Law.* Brooklyn, NY: Foundation.

———. 1967. *Cases on United Nations Law.* 2d rev. ed. Brooklyn, NY: Foundation.

Stein, Arthur. 1983. "Coordination and Collaboration: Regimes in an Anarchic World." In *International Regimes,* edited by Stephen D. Krasner, 115–40. Ithaca, NY: Cornell University Press.

Strange, Susan. 1983. "Cave! Hic Dragones: A Critique of Regime Analysis." In *International Regimes,* edited by Stephen D. Krasner, 337–54. Ithaca, NY: Cornell University Press.

Trachtman, Joel P. 1996. The Theory of the Firm and the Theory of International Economic Organization: Toward Comparative Institutional Analysis. Unpublished manuscript.

"Vienna Convention for the Protection of the Ozone Layer." 1985. *International Legal Materials* 26:1529–40.

Weber, Steven. 1994. "The European Bank for Reconstruction and Development." *International Organization* 48 (1):1–39.

Wendt, Alex. 1992. "Anarchy Is What States Make of It: The Social Construction of Power Politics." *International Organization* 46:391–425.

———. 1995. "Constructing International Politics." *International Security* 20:71–81.

Williamson, Oliver. 1985. *The Economic Institutions of Capitalism.* New York: Free Press.

———. 1996. *The Mechanisms of Governance.* Oxford, UK: Oxford University Press.

Yarbrough, Beth V., and Robert M. Yarbrough. 1992. *Cooperation and Governance in International Trade.* Princeton, NJ: Princeton University Press.

Young, Oran R. 1994. *International Governance.* Ithaca, NY: Cornell University Press.

Part 2

Decisionmaking

Paul F. Diehl and Brian Frederking

The common public perception of decisionmaking for global governance is a narrow one. Many see the decision process confined to formal, roll-call votes on symbolic resolutions by member states in large legislative sessions of international organizations; the various United Nations General Assembly resolutions are familiar examples that seem to confirm this perception. In this section, we hope to dispel this stereotype and give the reader a more sophisticated view of the activities and processes of global governance.

Although formal voting in international organizations is not the only aspect of decisionmaking, it is often an important component. Many international organizations adhere to the "one state–one vote" standard. This results in a situation whereby microstates such as Tuvalu have the same theoretical voting strength as the People's Republic of China. In other organizations, such as the International Monetary Fund and the World Bank, votes are weighted according to criteria such as economic wealth or level of budgetary contribution. At various times, the United States and other Western states have demanded a greater voice in the decisionmaking of the UN General Assembly based on the disproportionate amount of the organization's budget contributed by these states. However, the General Assembly bases its voting allocation on the concept of sovereign equality, the effect of which is that each state receives one vote.

Mirroring the Western demands for voting reform in the UN General Assembly has been the call from many states for changing the composition and voting rules of the UN Security Council. Germany, Japan, and other states have clamored for permanent seats on the Security Council based on their strong global economies and financial support of

UN activities. Third world countries have sought to expand the number of seats on the Security Council to give themselves a greater say in a body no longer stalemated by the Cold War. Various other proposals would weaken or share the veto power held by the five permanent members. A driving force behind all of these proposals is the importance of legitimacy and the perceived fairness of decisionmaking processes. In Chapter 4, Ian Hurd explores the debates regarding a proposed expansion of the UN Security Council and the widespread argument that the Council's legitimacy is undermined unless it reforms itself to account for recent changes in world politics. He concludes that all arguments for Security Council reform involve a trade-off between increasing the Council's legitimacy and other values such as efficiency, effectiveness, or power. Even with some desirable effects from Security Council reform, any alteration would require an amendment of the UN Charter (only once before has the United Nations altered the composition of the Security Council, increasing the membership to fifteen), something that must be approved by the five permanent members (whose veto could kill any amendments), exactly the states whose power would be diminished by certain kinds of changes.

Beyond states in international organizations are other important actors in global governance. Among these are nongovernmental organizations (NGOs) and groups that are linked together in "transnational advocacy networks." In Chapter 5, Margaret Keck and Kathryn Sikkink define such networks as including "those actors working internationally on an issue, who are bound together by shared values, a common discourse, and dense exchanges of information and services." These actors could be economic firms, scientific experts, or activist organizations (e.g., human rights or environmental NGOs) pursuing particular goals. The authors describe such actors in more detail and discuss how they emerge, what strategies they use, and under what conditions they are effective. In an era of globalization, such networks are increasingly influential in affecting decisions of international organizations as well as the policies of national governments.

4

Myths of Membership:
The Politics of Legitimation in
UN Security Council Reform

Ian Hurd

Among the competing proposals for reforming the UN Security Council, one theme is a near constant: that the Council's legitimacy is in peril unless the body can be reformed to account for recent changes in world politics. This consensus is driven by a number of developments: geopolitical changes (in the distribution of military and economic power), systemic changes after decolonization (which multiplied the number of UN members), and normative changes (in the value given to diversity, equity, and representation). . . . Most arguments in favor of Council expansion identify the gap between Council membership and international realities as a threat specifically to the *legitimacy* of the Council. The gap is an objective fact, but the link to legitimacy is what gives it its political salience and has made it a controversial matter in world politics. This article investigates this link. Conventional wisdom holds that the Council's outdated membership causes delegitimation but the causal mechanics behind this delegitimation are rarely explained.

The process by which institutions become legitimized or delegitimized is a hotly contested matter among organizational sociologists, and yet in the Council reform debates, the connection between legitimacy and membership has been treated as unproblematic, even self-evident. I set out below a number of potential causal mechanisms for delegitimation of the Council, which I derive from existing proposals for Council reform. Behind every proposal for Council reform is a different model for how legitimacy, effectiveness, and membership fit together. Compar-

Reprinted from *Global Governance*, vol. 14, no. 2: 199–217. © 2008 by Lynne Rienner Publishers. Reprinted by permission of the publisher. Edited for length.

ing these models is important to understanding the stalemate in Council reform and the utility of legitimation claims in world politics.

This article compares the various claims made in Council reform proposals regarding the effects of membership change on the legitimacy of the Council. Its goal is to isolate the discrete elements that make up these claims and assess their logical consistency. All Council reform claims contain hypotheses about the effects of membership change on Council effectiveness. The first section defends my claim that the conventional wisdom is that the current membership structure constitutes a *legitimacy* crisis for the Council. The second section extracts five distinct empirical hypotheses about the relationship between membership and legitimacy as put forward in defense of Council expansion. It typologizes these claims according to their underlying theory of legitimacy. These are all, in principle, testable, though the difficulties inherent in measuring legitimacy or its effects mean that perhaps in practice the most we can do is look for logical consistency. The third section addresses the question, Which among these claims are empirically plausible and logically sustainable? In conclusion, I speculate about the political interests that motivate these arguments and suggest implications about trade-offs, rhetorical entrapment, and legitimacy in international organizations.

. . . My goal in this article is not to find empirical evidence by which we might test theories of legitimation. Rather, I seek to compare the logic of the legitimacy claims themselves, taking advantage of the fact that they are cast in terms of generalizable principles. As such, I necessarily leave aside several interesting questions. For one, I do not examine the connection between the effectiveness of the Council and its legitimacy. That these two are mutually implicated is obvious but the link between membership and legitimacy is conceptually prior to, and separate from, the connection between legitimacy and effectiveness. For another, I do not focus on the privileges of permanent over nonpermanent membership, including the veto. The role of the veto for new members is important in the debate on enlargement, but it is generally kept out of the framing of the legitimation problems of the Council. No states link a defense of the veto for new members to arguments about legitimacy. For that reason, and because the High-Level Panel, among others, have largely set it aside as well, the veto does not play a large role in my analysis.[1] In focusing on the internal logic of the claim that changing the Council's membership will affect its legitimacy, I seek first to understand the causal mechanisms implicit in such a claim and then to chart the implications that arise from those mechanisms.

Legitimacy, Inequality, and Council Reform

. . . By far the most common malady identified at the Council is that the membership of the Council contains such inequalities that it threatens to delegitimize the body as a whole. The High-Level Panel said that "the effectiveness of the global collective security system . . . depends ultimately not only on the legality of decisions but on common perceptions of their legitimacy"[2] and that the anachronistic structure of membership rules "diminishes support for Security Council decisions."[3] . . . Kofi Annan has expressed "the view, long held by the majority, that a change in the Council's composition is needed to make it more broadly representative of the international community as a whole, as well as of the geopolitical realities of today, and thereby more legitimate in the eyes of the world."[4] The Open-Ended Working Group (OEWG) reported in 1995 a pervasive view among delegations that "an increase in the permanent membership would strengthen the United Nations and increase its legitimacy through bringing the organization closer to present-day global realities."[5] Changing the formal membership, it is said, is a necessary step to increasing, or to halting the loss of, the legitimacy of the Council and of its resolutions.

These claims treat the Council's legitimacy as a precious resource that is important to its effectiveness. Being seen as legitimate is important to the Council because, it is said, it increases the likelihood that states will respect the decisions it makes.[6] A more legitimate Council might be better at encouraging states to implement economic sanctions, or to contribute resources to peace missions, or to accept a Council-mandated solution to a dispute. Without coercive resources or financial power of its own, the Council must rely on its legitimacy to increase state compliance with its decisions.[7]

Legitimacy is rarely defined by those who use it to justify Council reform. As I use it here, it refers to the belief by states that the Council has the right to make authoritative decisions in its area of legal competence.[8] The "right" in question is a normative one, rather than a legal one, and so states that hold this belief will feel a normative obligation to respect the decisions of the Council. The belief rests within individual states but has its most significant effects when it is shared by many states. Four elements of the definition should be underscored: first, this is a *belief* of states, and so it is necessarily subjective and psychological—outsiders might disagree with one's belief, but the behavioral effects depend only on what the actor thinks, not on the assessments of others; second, the belief is held by *states*, and so I presume the corporate agency of the state; third, the belief is about the *right* of the body to make decisions, and this puts the Council in a position of authority over states, distinct from questions about its capacity to act or its effectiveness when it acts; and, finally, the legal structures of the Charter set a limit on the areas over which this right extends. The existence of this belief has consequences for how world politics proceeds. Disagreements on the consequences are examined below, but a conventional view is that a legitimate organization will find itself with higher levels of compliance, lower costs to enforcement, and higher levels of respect among its audience. All of these should add to its power.

The connection between legitimacy and Council reform is a chain of four linked steps. First, it is said that the inequalities inherent in the structure of Council membership are a drag on the legitimacy of the Council. The different powers given to permanent and nonpermanent members keep it from achieving the maximum potential level of legitimacy that might in principle be available to an international organization. Second, this lack of legitimacy is then said to reduce the effectiveness of the Council as a whole. This step in the argument relies on a theory of the power of international organizations (IOs) that identifies legitimacy as a crucial element of their corporate existence.[9] Third, the argument suggests that changing the Council's membership, or changing its membership rules, would remedy the legitimation deficit and so, by the fourth step, the Council's increased legitimacy will lead to a consequent increase in its effectiveness. Together, these stages constitute a thoroughly consequentialist defense of the importance of legitimacy for the Council: legitimacy is to be valued in the Council because it produces an outcome (greater Council power) that is thought to be desirable.

These are four distinct causal claims, with distinct independent and dependent variables. Steps 1 and 3 make up a mirror-image pair, as do Steps 2 and 4. The four can be summarized as follows:

Step 1: inequality → loss of legitimacy
Step 2: loss of legitimacy → loss of power or effectiveness
Step 3: change in structure → increase in legitimacy
Step 4: increase in legitimacy → increase in effectiveness

This causal chain as applied to the Security Council is derived from a more general model of legitimation in sociological theory but deviates from it in crucial respects. Step 1 is based on a central tenet of modern sociology—that inequality in a society reduces its stability. Disparities between groups in wealth, power, or status are thought to generate social discontent and thus instability, and the modern tradition from Marx to Weber to Habermas presents legitimacy as a countervailing force that can buttress the unequal social order. In this tradition, inequality is not itself seen as a threat to legitimacy but rather as a threat to the stability of the regime: as James Olson and Carolyn Hafer say, "When a group or system distributes inequalities unequally among its members, those members (or most of them) must view the inequalities as justified if the system is to survive."[10] Legitimacy is a device to mitigate the threat. Legitimation is one source of reasons for individuals to accept the existing inequalities of society as appropriate (or natural, or defensible).[11] It does not *eliminate* the inequalities; rather it *justifies* them and reduces their political salience. In this light, legitimacy is always a conservative force that acts to defend favored values against revolution.

The absence of legitimacy is therefore a dangerous condition for a social order based on inequalities, and Step 2 of the chain specifies the dangers. Without legitimacy, a society must rely on other tools to maintain order, notably coercion and inducement. This is particularly problematic for the Security Council, which cannot reliably use coercion to exert compliance with its decisions, and it has no resources to use as inducements. A Council without legitimacy would therefore have few tools with which to win states' support and so would quickly lose power, influence, and effectiveness in world politics.

The sociological story about legitimacy says that legitimation is a cure for the instability that arises from social inequality. The Council reform story suggests that the inequalities of the Council are damaging to its legitimacy and thus to its power, and so reducing the inequalities is a step toward maximizing the Council's effective authority (Step 3). The difference is that the latter believes that it is possible, or desirable, to reduce the inequalities in the society. Nevertheless, the key assumptions behind the two approaches are the same: that inequality is a threat to the effectiveness of the institution and that enhancing its legitimacy leads to an increase in its effectiveness (Step 4).

The practical dimension of the debate over the Council rests on Step 3. Competing theories of the link between Council structure and Council legitimacy produce very different proposals for Council reform. The policy debate is at present almost entirely over the question, What changes in the structure of the Council are most likely to lead to an increase in its legitimacy? The following sections address these arguments, first by specifying the competing answers to the question and then by assessing their empirical plausibility as accounts of legitimation. Resolving whether Step 3 is true or not is crucial to the institutional design of the Council and to the future of the UN more generally.

Council Structure and Legitimacy: Five Hypotheses

Ian Clark suggests that legitimacy is essential in resolving the question of who can rightfully be a member of the society. For him, one function of a consensus about legitimacy within society is that it provides a criterion for deciding "right membership."[12] In the debates on Council reform, however, the two concepts are usually put in the opposite order: manipulating the structure of the Council is believed to have effects on the level of legitimacy of the Council as perceived by the audience of nation-states. The views cited in the previous section all agree that the formal structure of the Council is an important factor in determining its legitimacy. In what ways might this be so?

The "empirical mechanics" by which changes in Council structure are hypothesized to affect Council legitimacy differ between different proposals. There are two main classes of claims for how this works, distinguished between the ideas that (1) *membership* produces legitimacy and (2) *deliberation* produces legitimacy. Variants of each are possible and they sometimes combine with each other, as we shall see, but a first cut into typologizing the claims must organize them according to whether they prioritize the legitimating effects of the practice of deliberation or of the formal structure of institutional membership. The two produce very different images of the work of the Council and therefore different policy prescriptions for improving it.

Membership

In 2005, the United States called for "a Security Council that looks like the world of 2005."[13] This could be operationalized in a number of ways, but the most logical is that the membership of the Council must be updated to reflect changes in the population of nation-states. The central element of these claims is a theory that the formal presence of certain states in the Council's membership will contribute to legitimizing the Council, and that conversely maintaining the present structure contributes to delegitimation. The goal of "equitable geographic distribution" is enshrined already in the selection of nonpermanent members, and it is not challenged by any state; but differences in how the clause is understood produce different versions of the "membership" argument on reform.[14]

Three variants of the membership argument are in common circulation, each premised on different assumptions about *which* states' presence or absence affects the Council's legitimacy. First, many argue that legitimation may come from the degree to which the Council faithfully *represents* the composition of the population of states in the General Assembly.[15] A Council that poorly reflects the population of states would be illegitimate. For instance, the chairs of the OEWG have stated "that the effectiveness, credibility and legitimacy of the work of the Security Council depend on its representative character."[16] The ambassador of Germany has said that "the legitimacy of the Security Council is based on its representativeness."[17] Bruce Russett hints at it when he says that "if the Security Council adds Germany and Japan as permanent members without also adding some major less-developed countries it risks losing legitimacy in the eyes of the great majority of UN member states."[18] These arguments are sometimes explicitly connected to a broader theory of democracy, but this is not logically necessary; whether an institution that is more representative is necessarily more democratic is a conceptually separate claim that should be evaluated on its own.

Second, legitimacy may come from having a Council that encompasses the *diversity* that exists in the General Assembly.[19] Distinct from representativeness, diversity might require over representing tiny minorities from the General Assembly in the interest of encompassing the full range of states and views into the Council. Reflecting diversity was one of the original motivations for the Council reform drive in the 1990s. . . . If the goal is to have inside the Council as full a sample as possible of the views in the General Assembly, then we would be justified in adding states based on how different they are from the current Council members. We would strive to maximize the differences among Council members, and this could result in a very different composition of the Council than might come about if one pursued the goal of representativeness. A number of countries in the Non-Aligned Movement (NAM) have argued that global diversity should be reflected in the composition of the Council. Cuba, for instance, has held that the diversity within a regional group should be taken into account when deciding how many seats the region should hold, implying that the purpose of a regional group is to project the region's diversity into the Council. Singapore has asked whether adding more large countries to the Council as permanent members is really progress, arguing instead that small states must be included in the interest of diversity. . . .

Both diversity and representativeness depend on a comparison with an appropriate referent population. Specifying this group is crucial and yet unavoidably political and controversial. The results will be different if we believe that the Council membership should faithfully represent the population of states in the General Assembly or the population of people in the world; striving to accommodate the diversity of world religions is different from accommodating the diversity of national economic capacities. These questions cannot be settled definitively outside the political process of negotiation. Most reform schemes based on membership agree that representativeness or diversity should be assessed compared to the regional distribution that exists in the General Assembly. This assumes that the relevant measure is *regional*, that states share their most important interests with others in their region rather than with those outside the region. Singapore, as cited above, suggests a different metric: small states have more in common with other small states than with large states, regardless of region.

Finally, legitimacy may be a product of having one's own country occupy a seat on the Council. Formal presence in a decisionmaking body may lead a state to support its decisions more than it would if it had not been present. If the change is a product of the *legitimating* effect of the presence, then we could sustain the argument that adding new members to the Council could increase its legitimacy in their eyes and thus add to its effectiveness. This argument, with its obviously self-serving implications, is rarely made publicly by diplomats, but its logic underpins the argument that only with a seat in the Council will a state's population continue to support paying its UN dues.

For all three variants of the membership argument, the crucial element is a conviction that the formal structure of Council membership is the key source of legitimation or delegitimation. It is the formal, legal presence of certain states, or of certain kinds of states, that affects the institution's legitimacy. This structural view is in sharp contrast with the procedural view of the "deliberative" argument, discussed next.

Deliberation

Many Council reform proposals interpose the concept of deliberation between the formal membership of the Council and the legitimacy of its outputs. Deliberation, in this view, is the source of legitimacy for organizations and opening up the Council's membership is a means to increasing its deliberative qualities. This view sees the Council as primarily a deliberative chamber rather than an interest-aggregating body. . . . The distinction between this approach and the membership approach above is clear when we trace the path for getting to legitimation: for the deliberative approach, participation in decisionmaking legitimizes outcomes; for the membership view, formal presence in the decisionmaking body legitimizes outcomes. If legitimacy is increased by deliberativeness, then changing the membership of the Council could lead to increased deliberation. Other strategies for increasing deliberation are contained in Cluster II issues in Council reform.

That deliberation might legitimize collective decisions is an important component of many theories of democracy. Amy Gutmann and Dennis Thompson argue that "deliberation contributes to the legitimacy of decisions made under scarcity . . . [because] the hard choices that democratic governments make in these circumstances should be more acceptable even to those who receive less than they deserve if everyone's claims have been considered on their merits."[20] James Fearon hypothesizes that "perhaps people feel that the decision process is fairer if they are allowed to have a discussion before voting, and this sense of procedural fairness then makes them more inclined to abide by or support the results."[21] This is confirmed by empirical surveys of Americans' attitudes toward legal and political institutions: Tom Tyler finds that "legitimacy is linked to judgments about the fairness of decision-making procedures. People are found to judge the legitimacy of institutions and authorities by focusing on the fairness of the procedures they utilize when making decisions. . . . [This] is demonstrated by their continued compliance with that decision over time, even in situations in which the incentives for complying . . . are weak or non-existent."[22] Deliberation is a key component of procedural fairness.

How does deliberation legitimize? Two mechanisms are possible: through change in the outcomes or through change in the deliberators. Diego Gambetta describes the former and John Dryzek the latter. Gambetta says that the "positive consequences of deliberation primarily concern the distribution of information" and its effect on the decision. He says, "If information and reasoning skills are, for whatever reason, unevenly distributed among deliberators, deliberation improves their allocation and the awareness of the relative merits of different means."[23] Fearon models deliberation as a strategy for lessening the problem of bounded rationality. To the extent that deliberation increases the amount of useful information available to decisionmakers, it should lead to better decisions.[24]

However, "better" decisions might not be the purpose of deliberation. Dryzek finds that "preferences can be transformed by deliberation" and sees the main value of deliberation to be the change it generates in participants themselves.[25] Independent of any effect it has on outcomes, deliberation might also have a "psychological effect," says Fearon, if "the opportunity to have one's say may make one more inclined to support the outcome of the discussion, even if one ends up opposing the collective choice."[26] If this is true, then deliberation might lead to higher rates of compliance regardless of whether it affects the substance of the decision.

Assessing the Five Hypotheses on Legitimacy and Council Reform

Taken together, the deliberative and membership arguments can be organized into five distinct hypotheses for how legitimacy is connected to Council membership. These are that a state will see the Council as more legitimate to the extent that:

> H1: the membership of the Council is representative of the General Assembly membership.
> H2: the membership of the Council is diverse.
> H3: the state is a member of the Council.
> H4: the state has an opportunity to participate in deliberations at the Council.
> H5: the level of deliberation at the Council is high.

The first three hypotheses are centered on membership, the last two on deliberation. Other hypotheses about legitimation are possible where the independent variable might be changes to working methods or changes in the Council's outputs, but these only indirectly justify a formal change in membership. Article 23 of the Charter ensures that regional diversity is included in membership selection, and these hypotheses provide possible explanations for why that criterion is valued by states.

Hypotheses 1 and 2 are closely related. They differ on the value that they aim to see institutionalized in Council membership, but they share the same structure and the same weaknesses. Both rest on three premises that, if all are true, would make it possible to construct an enlargement scheme that successfully uses representativeness or diversity as a means to legitimize the Council. I trace through the case in terms of "representation" here, and then show that the "diversity" case is essentially the same.

The proposition that the Council's representation of the General Assembly controls its legitimacy rests on three assumptions. First, states must really believe that representation is an important institutional norm. If states are simply posturing in their statements about the importance of representation, then the hypothesis will fail. Assuming they are genuine, we could conclude that states do indeed have an internalized attachment to the value of representation and the international system should, as a result, favor institutions that are believed to be representative. Second, states must agree on what constitutes an appropriate metric for representation. As discussed, disagreement over the metric will lead to substantive differences in assessing the legitimation effects of any particular change in membership. The history of the debates over enlargement seem to show that there is a good deal of disagreement over which dimension of representation is most important, with the result that we may well face a trade-off between increasing the legitimacy of the Council to one audience and reducing it for another. The existence of such a trade-off would mean that the potential legitimating power of representativity is small. Finally, the membership change must succeed in increasing representation along this metric. This depends on the particular countries chosen as new members. Not all enlargement schemes would increase representation, and some (such as adding Germany and Japan as permanent members) would create greater disparities of representation along many metrics.

The argument that legitimation is tied to diversity is analogous to that of representation, although the two values they put forward are different. H2 rests on versions of the same three assumptions as H1: that states really do value diversity in international organizations, that they possess a shared understanding of the appropriate metric for diversity, and that the specifics of the proposal do indeed increase diversity.

The degree of plausibility for both H1 and H2 turns out to be heavily dependent on a separate and prior question: Does the international community possess a reasonably consistent agreement on a metric for representation or for diversity? Only if this is true does it make sense to advance these values as a defense of enlargement. The debates over representation and over diversity would likely be more productive if they explicitly addressed the differences among states in their views of the correct metric.

There is less controversy in H3 because the issue of the metric does not arise. If H3 correctly describes the mechanics by which actors perceive legitimacy in institutions, its lesson for the Council is that its legitimacy will always remain limited to those few states that gain seats. Because it identifies legitimation as a product of having one's self-interest satisfied, this argument can justify the inclusion of individual states in the Council but cannot be generalized to all states. The legitimating effect does not extend beyond the particular state(s) added to formal membership. As a result, it is useful to the extent that we believe that the problem of delegitimation for the Council is limited to a few of the most important states but not beyond that. The United States, for instance, has said that its support for a Japanese permanent seat is a result of Japan's financial contribution to the UN. If the Japanese contribution is undermined by delegitimation that occurs due to not having a permanent seat, then adding it could be useful. Legitimacy in Japan's eyes could be served by adding it as a permanent member. But given that the maximum number of likely new members is around ten, the implication is that the legitimacy deficit of the Council cannot be improved for the rest of the world's states through membership changes. This would suggest that we could increase the legitimacy of the Council in the eyes of those ten countries but can do nothing, or only reduce it, for the rest of the UN population.

While membership is a scarce good, deliberation is in principle available to all. If we grant, for the sake of argument, that deliberation is the key to institutional legitimation, then we can inquire into how it might be manipulated for legitimation by expanding the Council. To assess both H4 and H5, we need to know the limits on Council deliberation at present.

The existing deliberative process at the Council includes some formal rights of participation for nonmembers. These represent an acknowledgment by the drafters of the Charter and of its rules of procedure, of the importance of deliberation to legitimizing outcomes. The Charter requires that the Council invite parties to a dispute to participate in its deliberations on the dispute (Article 32) and allows that the Council may invite any state whose interests it considers "specially affected" by the issue at hand (Article 31). In practice, the latter provision is used by nonmembers to request a seat in the deliberation. . . . It is almost automatic that a nonmember state can add its voice to the *formal* deliberations of the Council when it wants to. Because the deliberative model is mainly concerned with the breadth of information flowing into the process rather than the formal status of the speakers, this goes some distance toward satisfying a purely deliberative model of legitimation in that it opens the channel for states to express their views in the Council without distinction between members of the Council and nonmembers.

There are limits on this access, however, and they are illuminating because they point to unresolved issues in the deliberative model. For instance, only states that are "party to a dispute" have a *right* to participate (Article 32); other nonmembers are invited at the discretion of the Council. Even if these invitations are routinely granted, the formal control of access rests with the Council's members. Also, nonmembers are allowed "voice" only. That is, they may express views and participate in the substantive discussions, but they may not vote. Their contribution is restricted to the currencies of argument and information. These limits create distinctions in status and formal decisionmaking power among the participants in the deliberative process but do not affect their equality in the argumentative field. A purely deliberative model of legitimation should conclude that this does not matter, but one suspects that it does in practice. The opportunity to exercise voice through informal practices does not carry the same political status as does the chance to occupy a formal nonpermanent seat. The distinction needs to be accounted for by those who defend the deliberative approach in Council reform.

In this context, the only margin by which adding new formal members could increase the Council's deliberative quality is the same margin by which requests to participate (Article 31) are at present rejected by the Council. It is only the rejected states that stand to gain greater access to Council deliberation than they have at the moment. States that are accepted into the process under Article 31 already have the opportunity to contribute to the deliberation. Therefore, the potential increase in deliberation that could possibly come via adding new members must be quite small.

This conclusion may have to be amended based on changes in the Council's practice of informal consultations.[27] The issue depends on whether we see the many informal processes as extensions of Council deliberations or as circumvention of them. If Council members have greater access to these informal sessions than nonmembers have, then becoming a member might increase one's participation in the informal deliberative process outside of formal Council meetings. It is plausible that this might be true, though it probably depends on the state in question. Large states may already participate in informal consultations, even as nonmembers, and so giving them formal Council seats would not produce a net increase in deliberation. Small nonmember states are unlikely to be invited to informal sessions except in unusual circumstances—but even as formal members of the Council they might find themselves excluded from informal sessions too. The power of the informal process at present is precisely that it allows the dominant states on the Council to pick from among the members and nonmembers only those whose contribution to deliberation they feel is valuable to them. It allows the Council to ignore the distinction between member and nonmember and changes the patterns of deliberation. This has an ambiguous net effect on the quality and quantity of deliberation around the Council.

The fifth and final hypothesis is distinct from H4 in that it claims that it is the quality of deliberation in the organization that generates belief in its legitimacy by an actor, irrespective of whether that actor itself had the opportunity to contribute to the deliberation. Like H4, this argument is only as strong as the link between the deliberation that it sees as its goal and the expansion of formal membership that it suggests as its means. The identity of the deliberators is not important. What matters is that the Council be open to considering all morally relevant claims (and no irrelevant ones). Unless the limits of informal deliberation have already been reached, this argument looks hollow.

Assessing the Hypotheses

Does formal reform of membership contribute to legitimacy in any of the five hypotheses? The five are based on different empirical claims, but at least three general patterns emerge when one examines them as a group.

First, each claim ultimately rests on a trade-off, and each trade-off involves a political decision regarding one's priorities about the Council that cannot be resolved except by each state according to its own values and interests. Several of the hypotheses—H1, H2, and H3—set up a trade-off between increasing the Council's legitimacy for some states while necessarily reducing it for other states. We may not be able to predict which states will fall into each category, but we do know that the lack of consensus over metrics of representation and diversity means that privileging one interpretation over others will contribute to the delegitimation of an enlarged Council in the eyes of some states. This weakens H1 and H2. H3 can, at best, increase legitimacy in the eyes of the individual states that might be added to the Council while reducing it for those that are not. The deliberative models create a different kind of trade-off, one between increasing the range of voices and issues that can be raised in the Council (which is seen as the source of legitimation) and reducing the possibility of consensus in decisions. More interests on the table will necessarily mean that it will be harder to reach an agreement. Finally, all legitimation hypotheses involve a trade-off between increasing the Council's legitimacy and furthering other values, such as efficiency, effectiveness, or power. It is generally accepted that the size of the Council is negatively correlated to its effectiveness, and some countries raise this frequently as a cost of larger membership. A negative correlation here would mean that it was a fatal flaw for all legitimacy-through-enlargement arguments if, in fact, Council legitimacy was primarily a function of its substantive effectiveness rather than its membership.

Second, each hypothesis can be undermined by the possibility of "informal membership" in the Council. As the Council increases the opportunities for participation available to nonmembers, it steals the foundation from many of the reform arguments. The deliberative hypotheses, in particular, are weakened to the extent that Council rules of procedure, and Charter requirements, allow nonmembers of the Council to contribute to deliberation. The justification for adding new *formal* members is defeated if states' presence and participation can be solicited on a case-by-case basis. What remains is the potential legitimating power of the pure membership argument, where formal presence is thought by itself to have a legitimating effect (as in H1, H2, and H3). In the end, it is not clear that the formal structure of Council membership is the most important constraint on deliberation, or that adding new members would necessarily add to its deliberative quality.

Finally, the weakness of many of these arguments relative to empirical evidence makes it plausible to conclude that much of the "legitimacy talk" around which reform arguments are constructed is a false front, covering up the political interests of states. What aspirants to Council membership seem to be really seeking are the status and prestige that they believe go along with a seat. These real motives behind the rhetoric are not affected by the lack of evidence for the rhetorical claims. They are not without effect, however, given the nature of rhetorical power. Two new issues then come to the fore, each worthy of further research. First, the ubiquity with which reform arguments are defended by reference to the alleged "legitimacy deficit" of the Council suggests that the international community expects that proposals be couched in universal rather than particularistic values. Second, these generalizable claims may subject their speakers to the possibility of rhetorical entrapment, so that public statements about a principle of legitimation might be turned around by others in ways the speaker never intended but from which they can't escape.[28] International talk may be cheap, but it is never free.

Conclusion

My goal has been to assess the claim that adding members to the Security Council is a useful strategy to ensure the organization's legitimacy in the future. There are competing versions of this claim and I identified five distinct hypotheses about membership and legitimacy that are commonly presented in defense of changing the composition of the Council. Each is, in principle, testable by empirical methods, although in practice the evidence needed to confirm or falsify them is unobtainable. As a result, I presented assessments of the empirical and logical plausibility of each, drawn both from the past experience of the Council and from evidence on legitimation in other organizations. None of the five emerges with a strong defense. Each ultimately relies on prior assumptions that are themselves questionable—for instance, that states agree on a metric for measuring diversity or representation in the Council, or that states value the pure deliberative quality of the Council and not the status distinctions between members and nonmembers. Bardo Fassbender has suggested that "conflicting views of member states continue to block a solution" to Council reform.[29] The gaps in logic that undermine each of the five hypotheses may indicate that these "conflicting views" originate in incompatible notions about how legitimation works.

The hypotheses are not of a type that can be fully confirmed or disproved with evidence, but their evident weakness suggests that states may be largely insincere in their references to them. Assuming that what states really want is to gain a seat for themselves and to deny one to their rival, we should look at both *why* states find this to be an appealing goal and why talking in terms of legitimacy is seen as a useful strategy. While the hypotheses themselves may be weak, this article also shows the power that states see in using "legitimacy talk" to defend their interests. How this has come to be the case is itself an interesting question that combines the geopolitics of states competing over Council seats with the social construction of language resources.

Notes

1. Excellent analyses of the diplomatic history of the 1990s reform process are available in Mark W. Zacher, "The Conundrums of International Power Sharing: The Politics of Security Council Reform," in Richard M. Price and Mark W. Zacher, *The United Nations and Global Security* (New York: Palgrave Macmillan, 2004); Bardo Fassbender, *UN Security Council Reform and the Right of Veto: A Constitutional Perspective* (The Hague: Kluwer, 1998); Edward C. Luck, "Reforming the United Nations: Lessons from a History in Progress," AUNCS Occasional Paper No. 1, 2003.

2. United Nations, *A More Secure World: Our Shared Responsibility—Report of the Secretary-General's High-Level Panel on Threats, Challenges and Change*, A/59/565 (New York: United Nations, 2004), p. 57.

3. Ibid., p. 66.

4. Kofi Annan, "In Larger Freedom: Towards Development, Security and Human Rights for All," A/59/2005 (New York: United Nations, 2005).

5. United Nations, *Report of the GA Working Group on the Security Council for 1995*, A/AC.247/1 (New York: United Nations, 1995), www.globalpolicy.org /security/reform/secwg2.htm.

6. See Michael Barnett, "Bringing in the New World Order: Liberalism, Legitimacy, and the United Nations," *World Politics* 49, no. 4 (July 1997): 526–551.

7. Ian Hurd, *After Anarchy: Legitimacy and Power in the UN Security Council* (Princeton: Princeton University Press, 2007); Ian Hurd, "Legitimacy, Power, and the Symbolic Life of the UN Security Council," *Global Governance* 8, no. 1 (2002): 35–51.

8. This definition accords with Ian Hurd, "Legitimacy and Authority in International Politics," *International Organization* 53, no. 2 (1999): 379–408. See also Ian Hurd, "Theories and Tests of International Authority," in Bruce Cronin and Ian Hurd, eds., *The UN Security Council and the Politics of International Authority* (Abingdon and New York: Routledge, 2008). For competing definitions, see Allen Buchanan, *Justice, Legitimacy, and Self-Determination: Moral Foundations of International Law* (Oxford: Oxford University Press, 2003); and Erik Voeten, "The Political Origins of the UN Security Council's Ability to Legitimize the Use of Force," *International Organization* 59, no. 3 (2005): 527–557.

9. Michael Barnett and Martha Finnemore, *Rules for the World: International Organizations in Global Politics* (Ithaca: Cornell University Press, 2005); and Hurd, *After Anarchy*.

10. James M. Olson and Carolyn L. Hafer, "Tolerance of Personal Deprivation," in John T. Jost and Brenda Major, eds., *The Psychology of Legitimacy: Emerging Perspectives on Ideology, Justice, and Intergroup Relations* (Cambridge: Cambridge University Press, 2001), p. 157.

11. Tom Tyler, "A Psychological Perspective on the Legitimacy of Institutions and Authorities," in Jost and Major, *The Psychology of Legitimacy*.

12. Ian Clark, *Legitimacy in International Society* (Oxford: Oxford University Press, 2005), pp. 26–28.

13. US Department of State, 20 June 2005, www.state.gov/r/pa/scp/2005 /48332.htm (accessed 14 September 2005).

14. On nonpermanent members, see Article 23(1). Also see Ramesh Thakur, ed., *What Is Equitable Geographic Distribution in the 21st Century?* (Tokyo: United Nations University, 1999).

15. See, for instance, the Canadian position: "The membership of the Security Council should more clearly represent the international community of the 21st century," statement of the Ministry of Foreign Affairs, Canada, www.dfait -maeci.gc.ca/cip-pic/IPS/IPS-Diplomacy7-en.asp (accessed 13 September 2005).

16. United Nations, *Report of the GA Working Group on the Security Council for 1997*, A/51/47 (New York: United Nations, 1997), www.globalpolicy.org /security/reform/wk97-3.htm.

17. Ambassador Pleuger to General Assembly, 14 October 2003, archived at www.germany-un.org/archive/speeches/2003/sp_10_14_03.html.

18. Bruce Russett, "Ten Balances for Weighing UN Reform Proposals," in Bruce Russett, ed., *The Once and Future Security Council* (New York: St. Martin's Press, 1997), p. 20.

19. See Gordon, "Scenarios for Reforming the United Nations."

20. Amy Gutmann and Dennis Thompson, *Democracy and Disagreement: Why Moral Conflict Cannot Be Avoided in Politics, and What Should Be Done About It* (Cambridge: Harvard University Press, 1996), p. 41.

21. James D. Fearon, "Deliberation as Discussion," in Jon Elster, ed., *Deliberative Democracy* (Cambridge: Cambridge University Press, 1998), p. 57.

22. Tyler, "A Psychological Perspective," pp. 419–420.

23. Diego Gambetto, "'Claro!' An Essay on Discursive Machismo," in Elster, *Deliberative Democracy*, p. 22.

24. Fearon, "Deliberation as Discussion," p. 50.

25. John Dryzek, *Deliberative Democracy and Beyond: Liberals, Critics, Contestations* (Oxford: Oxford University Press, 2000), p. 1.

26. Fearon, "Deliberation as Discussion," p. 57.

27. Susan C. Hulton, "Council Working Methods and Procedure," in David M. Malone, ed., *The UN Security Council: From the Cold War to the 21st Century* (Boulder: Lynne Rienner, 2004); Luck, "Step One."

28. Thomas Risse, "'Let's Argue!' Communicative Action in World Politics," *International Organization* 54, no. 1 (2000): 1–40; Ian Hurd, "The Strategic Use of Liberal Internationalism: Libya and the UN Sanctions, 1992–2003," *International Organization* 59, no. 3 (2005): 495–526; Frank Schimmelfennig, *The EU, NATO, and the Integration of Europe: Rules and Rhetoric* (Cambridge: Cambridge University Press, 2003).

29. Bardo Fassbender, "Pressure for Security Council Reform," in Malone, *The UN Security Council*, p. 341.

5

Transnational Advocacy Networks in International and Regional Politics

Margaret E. Keck and Kathryn Sikkink

World politics . . . involves, alongside states, many non-state actors who interact with each other, with states, and with international organizations. This article considers how these interactions are structured in networks, which are increasingly visible in international politics. Some involve economic actors and firms. Some are networks of scientists and experts whose professional ties and ideas underpin their efforts to influence policy (Haas, 1992). Others are networks of activists, distinguishable largely by the centrality of principled ideas or values in motivating their formation. We call these *transnational advocacy networks.*

Advocacy networks are significant transnationally, regionally and domestically. They may be key contributors to a convergence of social and cultural norms able to support processes of regional and international integration. By building new links among actors in civil societies, states and international organizations, they multiply the opportunities for dialogue and exchange. In issue areas such as the environment and human rights, they also make international resources available to new actors in domestic political and social struggles. By thus blurring the boundaries between a state's relations with its own nationals and the recourse both citizens and states have to the international system, advocacy networks are helping to transform the practice of national sovereignty.

Scholars have been slow to recognize either the rationality or the significance of activist networks. Motivated by values rather than by material concerns or professional norms, they fall outside our accustomed categories. Yet more than other kinds of transnational networks,

Reprinted from *International Social Science Journal,* vol. 51, no. 149: 89–101. © 1999 by Wiley Publications. Reprinted by permission of the publisher. Edited for length.

advocacy networks often reach beyond policy change to advocate and instigate changes in the institutional and principled bases of international interactions. When they succeed, they are an important part of an explanation for changes in world politics. *A transnational advocacy network includes those actors working internationally on an issue, who are bound together by shared values, a common discourse, and dense exchanges of information and services.*[1] Such networks are most prevalent in issue areas characterized by high value content and informational uncertainty, although the value-content of an issue is both a prerequisite and a result of network activity. At the core of the relationship is information exchange. What is novel in these networks is the ability of non-traditional international actors to mobilize information strategically to help create new issues and categories, and to persuade, pressurize, and gain leverage over much more powerful organizations and governments. Activists in networks try not only to influence policy outcomes, but to transform the terms and nature of the debate. They are not always successful in their efforts, but they are increasingly important players in policy debates at the regional and international level.

Simultaneously principled and strategic actors, transnational advocacy networks "frame" issues to make them comprehensible to target audiences, to attract attention and encourage action, and to "fit" with favorable institutional venues. By framing, we mean "conscious strategic efforts by groups of people to fashion shared understandings of the world and of themselves that legitimate and motivate collective action" (McAdam et al., 1996, p. 6). Network actors bring new ideas, norms and discourses into policy debates, and serve as sources of information and testimony. Norms "describe collective expectations for the proper behaviour of actors with a given identity" (Katzenstein, 1996, p. 5; see also Klotz, 1995; Finnemore, 1996).

Shared norms often provide the foundation for more formal institutional processes of regional integration. In so far as networks promote norm convergence or harmonization at the regional and international levels, they are essential to the social and cultural aspects of integration. They also promote norm implementation, by pressuring target actors to adopt new policies, and by monitoring compliance with regional and international standards. As far as is possible, they seek to maximize their influence or leverage over the target of their actions. In doing this they contribute to changing the perceptions that both state and societal actors may have of their identities, interests and preferences, to transforming their discursive positions, and ultimately to changing procedures, policies and behaviour. We thus believe, with Finnemore, that

"States are embedded in dense networks of transnational and inter-national social relations that shape their perceptions of the world and their role in that world. States are socialized to want certain things by the international society in which they and the people in them live" (Finnemore, 1996, p. 2).

Networks are *communicative structures*. To influence discourse, procedures and policy, transnational advocacy networks may become part of larger policy communities that group actors from a variety of institutional and value positions. Transnational advocacy networks may also be understood as political spaces, in which differently situated actors negotiate—formally or informally—the social, cultural and polit-ical meanings of their joint enterprises. In both of these ways, transna-tional networks can be key vehicles for the cultural and social negotia-tions underpinning processes of regional integration.

We refer to transnational networks (rather than coalitions, move-ments, or civil society) to evoke the structured and structuring dimension in the actions of these complex agents. By importing the network concept from sociology and applying it transnationally, we bridge the increasingly artificial divide between international relations and comparative politics. Moreover, the term "network" is already used by the actors themselves; over the last two decades, individuals and organizations have consciously formed and named networks, developed and shared networking strategies and techniques, and assessed the advantages and limits of this kind of activity. Scholars have come late to the party.

Our theoretical apparatus draws upon sociological traditions that focus on complex interactions among actors, on the intersubjective con-struction of frames of meaning, and on the negotiation and malleability of identities and interests. These have been concerns of constructivists in international relations theory and of social movement theorists in com-parative politics, and we draw from both traditions. The networks we study participate simultaneously in domestic and international politics, drawing upon a variety of resources, *as if they were part of an inter-national society*. However, they use these resources strategically to affect a world of states and international organizations constructed by states. Both these dimensions are essential. Rationalists will recognize the lan-guage of incentives and constraints, strategies, institutions and rules, while constructivists and social constructionists will be more comfortable with our emphasis on norms, social relations and intersubjective under-standings. We are convinced that both matter; whilst recognizing that goals and interests are not exogenously given, we can think about the strategic activity of actors in an intersubjectively structured political universe. The key to doing so is remembering that the social and political contexts within which networks operate contain contested understandings as well as stable and shared ones. Network activists can operate strategically within the more stable universe of shared understandings at the same time as they try to reshape certain contested meanings.

Part of what is so elusive about networks is how they seem to embody elements of agent and structure simultaneously. Our approach must therefore be both structural and actor-centered. We address five main questions:

(1) What is a transnational advocacy network?
(2) Why and how do they emerge?
(3) How do they work?
(4) Under what conditions can they be effective—that is, when are they most likely to achieve their goals?
(5) What are the implications of network activities for the social and cultural processes of regional integration?

Although we had initially expected that transnational networks would function in quite different ways from domestic social movements, we found that many of the characteristic strategies, tactics and patterns of influence resembled those outlined in the literature on social movements. Organizations and individuals within advocacy networks are political entrepreneurs, mobilize resources like information and membership, and show a sophisticated awareness of the political opportunity structures within which they operate (Tarrow, 1994). Our emphasis on the role of values in networks is consistent with some arguments contained in the literature on "new social movements" (Dalton et al., 1990). Most importantly, however, over the last decade social movement theory has increasingly focused on the interaction between social-structural conditions and action, on the social context of mobilization, and on the transformation of meanings among activists and among mass publics that make people believe they can have an impact on an issue.

What Is a Transnational Advocacy Network?

Networks are forms of organization characterized by voluntary, reciprocal and horizontal patterns of communication and exchange. Organizational theorist Walter Powell calls them a third mode of economic organization, distinctly different from markets and hierarchy (the firm). "Networks are 'lighter on their feet' than hierarchy" and are "particularly apt for circumstances in which there is a need for efficient, reliable information . . . ," and "for the exchange of commodities whose value is not easily measured" (Powell, 1990, pp. 295–6, 303–4). His insights into economic networks are extraordinarily suggestive for an understanding of political networks. Policy networks also form around issues where information plays a key role, and around issues where the value of the "commodity" is not easily measured.

In spite of differences between the domestic and international realms, the network concept travels well because it stresses the fluid and open relations among committed and knowledgeable actors working in specialized issue areas. We call them advocacy networks because advocates plead the causes of others or defend a cause or proposition; they are stand-ins for persons or ideas. Advocacy captures what is unique about these transnational networks—they are organized to promote causes, principled ideas and norms, and often involve individuals advocating policy changes that cannot be easily linked to their "interests."

Some issue areas reproduce transnationally the webs of personal relationships that are crucial in the formation of domestic networks. Advocacy networks have been particularly important in value-laden debates over human rights, the environment, women, infant health, and indigenous peoples. These are all areas where through personal, professional and organizational contexts, large numbers of differently situated individuals became acquainted with each other over a considerable period, and developed similar world views. When the more visionary among them proposed strategies for political action around apparently intractable problems, the potential was transformed into an action network.

Major actors in advocacy networks may include the following:

(1) international and domestic NGOs, research and advocacy organizations;
(2) local social movements;
(3) foundations;
(4) the media;
(5) churches, trade unions, consumer organizations, intellectuals;
(6) parts of regional and international intergovernmental organizations;
(7) parts of the executive and/or parliamentary branches of governments.

Not all these will be present in each advocacy network. Initial research suggests, however, that international and domestic non-governmental organizations (NGOs) play a central role in most advocacy networks, usually initiating actions and pressuring more powerful actors to take positions. NGOs introduce new ideas, provide information, and lobby for policy changes.

Social scientists have barely addressed the political role of activist NGOs as *simultaneously* domestic and international actors. There is a literature on NGOs and networks in specific countries (Fruhling, 1991; Scherer-Warren, 1993). Much of the existing literature on NGOs comes from development studies, and either ignores interactions with states or spends little time on political analysis (see, for example, Korten, 1990). Examining their role in advocacy networks helps both to distinguish NGOs from, and to see their connections with, social movements, state agencies and international organizations.

Groups in a network share values and frequently exchange information and services. The flow of information among actors in the network reveals a dense web of connections among these groups, both formal and informal. The movement of funds and services is especially notable between foundations and NGOs, but some NGOs provide services such as training for other NGOs in the same, and sometimes other, advocacy networks. Personnel also circulate within and among networks.

Relationships *among* networks within and between issue areas are similar to those that scholars of social movements have found in the case of domestic activism. Individuals and foundation funding have moved back and forth among them. Environmentalists and women's groups have looked at the history of human rights campaigns for models of effective international institution-building. Because of these interactions, refugee resettlement and indigenous peoples' rights are increasingly central components of international environmental activity, and vice versa; mainstream human rights organizations have joined the campaign for women's rights. Some activists consider themselves part of an "NGO community." This convergence highlights important dimensions that these networks share: the centrality of values or principled ideas, the belief that individuals can make a difference, creative use of information, and the employment by non-governmental actors of sophisticated political strategies in targeting their campaigns. Besides sharing information, groups in networks create categories or frames within which to organize and *generate* information on which to base their campaigns. The ability to generate information quickly and accurately, and deploy it effectively, is their most valuable currency; it is also central to their identity. Core campaign organizers must ensure that individuals and organizations with access to necessary information are incorporated into the network; different ways of framing an issue may require quite different kinds of information. Thus, frame disputes can be a significant source of change within networks.

Why and How Transnational Advocacy Networks Have Emerged?

The kinds of group characteristics of advocacy networks are not new; some have existed since the nineteenth century campaign for the abolition of slavery. Nevertheless, their number, size, professionalism, and the density and complexity of their international linkages have grown dramatically in the last three decades, so that only recently can we speak of *transnational* advocacy networks (Keck and Sikkink, 1998).

International networking is costly. Geographical distance, nationalism, the multiplicity of languages and cultures, and the costs of fax, telephone, mail, or air travel make the proliferation of international networks a puzzle that needs explanation. Under what conditions are networks possible and likely, and what triggers their emergence?

Transnational advocacy networks appear most likely to emerge around those issues where:

(1) channels between domestic groups and their governments are hampered or severed where such channels are ineffective for resolving a conflict, setting into motion the "boomerang" pattern of influence characteristic of these networks;

(2) activists or "political entrepreneurs" believe that networking will further their missions and campaigns, and actively promote them;

(3) international conferences and other forms of international contacts create arenas for forming and strengthening networks.

The Boomerang Pattern

It is no accident that "rights" claims may be the prototypical language of advocacy networks. Governments are the primary "guarantors" of rights, but also among their primary violators. When a government violates or refuses to recognize rights, individuals and domestic groups often have no recourse within domestic political or judicial arenas. They may seek international connections to express their concerns and even to protect their lives.

Many transnational advocacy networks link activists in developed countries with others in or from less developed countries. These kinds of linkages are most commonly intended to affect the behaviour of *states*. When the links between state and domestic actors are severed, domestic NGOs may directly seek international allies to try to bring pressure on their states from outside. This is the "boomerang" pattern of influence characteristic of transnational networks where the target of their activity is to change a state's behaviour. This is most common in human rights campaigns. Similarly, indigenous rights campaigns, and environmental campaigns supporting the demands of local peoples for participation in development projects that would affect them, frequently involve this kind of triangulation. Where governments are unresponsive to groups whose claims may none the less resonate elsewhere, international contacts can "amplify" the demands of domestic groups, pry open space for new issues, and then echo these demands back into the domestic arena. Needless to say, in such cases the use of a boomerang strategy is politically sensitive, and is subject to charges of foreign interference in domestic affairs.

Linkages are important for both sides. For the less powerful Third World actors, networks provide access, leverage and information (and often money) they could not expect to have on their own. For northern groups, they make credible the assertion that they are struggling with, and not only "for," their southern partners. Not surprisingly, such relationships can produce considerable tensions. It is not uncommon to see reproduced internally the power relations that the networks are trying to overcome. Increasingly, network members are forced to address this problem.

Just as injustice and oppression may not produce movements or revolutions by themselves, claims around issues amenable to international action need not produce transnational networks. Activists are "people who care enough about some issue that they are prepared to incur significant costs and act to achieve their goals" (Oliver and Marwell, 1992, p. 252). They form networks when they believe it will further their organizational missions—by sharing information, attaining greater visibility, gaining access to different publics, multiplying channels of institutional access, and so forth.

Networks are normally formed around particular campaigns or claims. Networks breed networks; as networking becomes a repertoire of action that is diffused transnationally, each effort to network internationally is less difficult than the one before. Over time, in these issue areas, participation in transnational networks has become an essential component of the collective identities of the activists involved. The political entrepreneurs who become the core networkers for a new campaign have often gained experience in earlier ones.

Opportunities for network activities have increased over the last two decades, in part through the efforts of the pioneers among them. Network activists have been creative in finding new venues in which to pursue claims—a process we discuss in the next section. The proliferation of international organizations and conferences has provided foci for the contacts. Cheaper air travel and new electronic and communication technologies speed information flows and simplify personal contact among them.

Underlying the trends discussed here, however, is a broader cultural shift. The new networks depended on creating a new kind of global public (or civil society), which grew as a cultural legacy of the 1960s. The activism that swept Western Europe, the United States, and many parts of the Third World during that decade contributed to this shift, alongside the vastly increased opportunities for international contact.

Obviously, internationalism was not invented in the 1960s. Several long-standing ethical traditions have justified actions by individuals or groups outside the borders of their own state. Broadly speaking, we could designate these as religious beliefs, the solidarity traditions of labor and the left, and liberal internationalism. While many activists working in advocacy networks are from one of these traditions, they no longer tend to define themselves in terms of these traditions or the organizations that carried them. This is most true for activists on the left, for whom the decline of socialist organizations capped a growing disillusionment with much of the left's refusal to address seriously the concerns of women, the environment, and human rights violations in eastern bloc countries.

Advocacy networks in the north often function in a cultural milieu of internationalism that is generally optimistic about the promise and possibilities of international networking. For network members in developing countries, however, justifying external intervention or pressure in domestic affairs is a much trickier business, except when lives are at stake. Linkages with northern networks require high levels of trust, because arguments justifying intervention on ethical grounds often sound too much like the "civilizing" discourse of colonial powers, and can work against the goals they espouse by producing a nationalist backlash.

How Do Transnational Advocacy Networks Work?

Transnational networks seek influence in many of the same ways that other political groups or social movements do, but because they are not powerful in the traditional sense of the word, they must use the power of their information, ideas and strategies to alter the information and value context within which states make policies. Although much of what networks do might be considered persuasion, the term is insufficiently precise to be of much theoretical use. We have developed a more nuanced typology of the kinds of tactics that networks use. These include:

(a) *information politics,* or the ability to move politically usable information quickly and credibly to where it will have the most impact;
(b) *symbolic politics,* or the ability to call upon symbols, actions or stories that make sense of a situation or claim for an audience that is frequently far away (see also Brysk, 1994, 1995);
(c) *leverage politics,* or the ability to call upon powerful actors to affect a situation where weaker members of a network are unlikely to have influence; and
(d) *accountability politics,* or the effort to oblige more powerful actors to act on vaguer policies or principles they formally endorsed.

The construction of cognitive frames is an essential component of transnational networks' political strategies. David Snow has called this strategic activity *frame alignment*—"by rendering events or occurrences meaningful, frames function to organize experience and guide action, whether individual or collective" (Snow et al., 1986). *Frame resonance* concerns the relationship between an organization's interpretive work and its ability to influence broader public understandings. The latter involves both the frame's internal coherence and its fit with a broader political culture (Snow and Benford, 1988). . . . Snow and Benford (1992) and Tarrow (1992), in turn, have given frame resonance a historical dimension by joining it to Tarrow's notion of protest cycles. Struggles over meaning and the creation of new frames of meaning occur early in a protest cycle, but over time, "a given collective action frame becomes part of the political culture—which is to say, part of the reservoir of symbols from which future movement entrepreneurs can choose" (Tarrow, 1992, p. 197).

Network members actively seek ways to bring issues to the public agenda, both by framing them in innovative ways and by seeking hospitable venues. Sometimes they create issues by framing old problems in new ways; occasionally they help to transform other actors' understandings of their identities and their interests. Land-use rights in the Amazon, for example, took on an entirely different character and gained quite different allies when viewed in a deforestation frame than in either social justice or regional development frames.

Transnational networks normally involve a small number of activists in a given campaign or advocacy role. The kinds of pressure and agenda politics in which they engage rarely involve mass mobilization, except at key moments, although the peoples whose cause they espouse may engage in mass protest (for example, the expelled population in the Narmada Dam case). Boycott strategies are a partial exception. Instead, network activists engage in what Baumgartner and Jones (1991), borrowing from law, call *venue shopping:* "This strategy relies less on mass mobilisation and more on the dual strategy of the presentation of an image and the search for a more receptive political venue" (p. 1050). The recent coupling of indigenous rights and environmental struggles is a good example of a strategic venue shift by *indigenista* activists, who found the environmental arena more receptive to their claims than had been human rights venues.

Information Politics

Information binds network members together and is essential for network effectiveness. Many information exchanges are informal—through telephone calls, e-mail and fax communications, and the circulation of small newsletters, pamphlets and bulletins. They provide information that would not otherwise be available, from sources that might not otherwise be heard, and make it comprehensible and useful to activists and publics who may be geographically and/or socially distant.

Non-state actors gain influence by serving as alternative sources of information. Information flows in advocacy networks provide not only facts, but also *testimonies*—stories told by people whose lives have been affected. Moreover, they interpret facts and testimony; activist groups frame issues simply, in terms of right and wrong, because their purpose is to *persuade* people and stimulate them to take action.

How does this process of persuasion occur? An effective frame must show that a given state of affairs is neither natural nor accidental, identify the responsible party or parties, and propose credible solutions. This requires clear, powerful messages that appeal to shared principles, and which often have more impact on state policy than the advice of technical experts. An important part of the political struggle over information is whether an issue is defined primarily as technical, subject to consideration by "qualified" experts, or as something that concerns a much broader global constituency.

Even as we highlight the importance of testimony, however, we have to recognize the mediations involved. The process by which testimony is discovered and presented normally involves several layers of prior translation. Transnational actors may identify what kinds of testimony would be valuable, then ask an NGO in the area to seek out people who could tell those stories. They may filter through expatriates, through travelling scholars, through the media. There is frequently a huge gap between the story's telling and its retelling—in sociocultural context, in instrumental meaning, and even in language. Local people, in other words, sometimes lose control over their stories in a transnational campaign.

Non-governmental networks have helped to legitimize the use of testimonial information along with technical and statistical information. Linkage of the two is crucial: without the individual cases, activists cannot motivate people to seek to change policies. Increasingly, international campaigns by networks take this two-level approach to information. In the 1980s even Greenpeace, which initially had eschewed rigorous research in favor of splashy media events, began to pay more attention to getting the facts right. While testimony does not avoid the need to manage technical information, it helps to make the need for action more real for ordinary citizens.

A dense web of north-south exchange, aided by computer and fax communication, means that governments can no longer monopolize information flows as they could a mere half-decade ago. These technologies have had an enormous impact on moving information to and from Third World countries, where mail services are often both slow and precarious. We should note, however, that this gives special advantages to organizations that have access to such technologies.

The central role of information in all these issues helps to explain the drive to create networks. Information in these issue areas is both essential and dispersed. Non-governmental actors depend upon their access to information to help make them legitimate players. Contact with like-minded groups at home and abroad provides access to information necessary to their work, broadens their legitimacy, and helps to mobilize information around particular policy targets. Most NGOs cannot afford to maintain staff in a variety of countries. In exceptional cases, they send staff members on investigation missions, but this is not practical for keeping informed on routine developments. Forging links with local organizations allows groups to receive and monitor information from many countries at low cost. Local groups, in turn, depend on international contacts to get their information out, and to help to protect them in their work.

The media are essential partners in network information politics. To reach a broader audience, networks strive to attract press attention. Sympathetic journalists may become part of the network, but more often network activists cultivate a reputation for credibility with the press, and package their information in a timely and dramatic way to draw press attention.

Symbolic Politics

Activists frame issues by identifying and providing convincing explanations for powerful symbolic events, which in turn become catalysts for the growth of networks. Symbolic interpretation is part of the process of persuasion by which networks create awareness and expand the constituency. Awarding the Nobel Peace Prize to Rigoberta Menchu, during the International Year of Indigenous People, heightened public awareness of the situation of indigenous peoples in the Americas. The ability of the indigenous people's movement to use 1992, the 500th anniversary of the voyage of Columbus to the Americas, to raise a host of indigenous issues revealed the ability of networks to use symbolic events to reshape understandings (Brysk, 1994).

The coup in Chile played this kind of catalytic role for the human rights community. Often it is not one event, but the juxtaposition of disparate events that makes people change their minds and take action. For many people in the US, it was the juxtaposition of the coup in Chile, the war in Vietnam, Watergate, and civil rights that gave birth to the human rights movement. Likewise, the juxtaposition of the hot summer of 1988 in the US with dramatic footage of the Brazilian rainforest burning may have convinced many people that global warming and tropical deforestation were serious and linked issues. The assassination of Chico Mendes at the end of that year crystallized the belief that something was profoundly wrong in the Amazon.

Leverage Politics

Activists in advocacy networks are concerned with political effectiveness. Their definition of effectiveness often involves some policy change by "target actors" which might be governments, but might also be international financial institutions like the World Bank, or private actors like transnational corporations. In order to bring about policy change, networks need to both persuade and pressurize more powerful actors. To gain influence the networks seek *leverage*—a word that appears often in the discourse of advocacy organizations—over more powerful actors. By exerting leverage over more powerful institutions, weak groups gain influence far beyond their ability to influence state practices directly. Identifying points of leverage is a crucial strategic step in network campaigns. We discuss two kinds of leverage: material leverage and moral leverage.

Material leverage usually takes the form of some kind of issue-linkage, normally involving money or goods (but potentially also including votes in international organizations, prestigious offices, or other benefits). The human rights issue became negotiable because other governments or financial institutions connected human rights practices to the cut-off of military and economic aid, or to worsening bilateral diplomatic relations. Human rights groups obtained leverage by providing US and European policymakers with information that persuaded them to cut off military and economic aid. To make the issue negotiable, NGOs first had to raise its profile or salience, using information and symbolic politics. Then more powerful members of the network had to link cooperation to something else of value: money, trade or prestige. Similarly, in the environmentalists' multilateral bank campaign, linkage—of environmental protection with access to loans—was very powerful.

Moral leverage involves what some commentators have called the "mobilisation of shame," where the behaviour of target actors is held up to the bright light of international scrutiny. Where states place a high value on international prestige, this can be effective. In the baby-food campaign, network activists used moral leverage to convince states to vote in favor of the WHO/UNICEF Codes of Conduct. As a result, even the Netherlands and Switzerland, both major exporters of infant formula, voted in favor of the code.

Although NGO influence often depends on securing powerful allies, making those links still depends on their ability to mobilize the solidarity of their members, or of public opinion via the media. In democracies, the potential to influence votes gives large membership organizations an advantage in lobbying for policy change; environmental organizations, several of whose memberships number in the millions, are more likely to have this added clout than are human rights organizations.

Accountability Politics

Networks devote considerable energy to convincing governments and other actors to change their positions on issues. This is often dismissed as inconsequential change, since talk is cheap—governments change discursive positions hoping to divert network and public attention. Network activists, however, try to make such statements into opportunities for accountability politics. Once a government has publicly committed itself to a principle—for example, in favor of human rights or democracy— networks can use those positions, and their command of information, to expose the distance between discourse and practice. This is embarrassing to many governments, who may try to save face by closing the distance.

Under What Conditions Do Advocacy Networks Have Influence?

To assess the influence of advocacy networks we must look at goal achievement at several different levels. We identify the following types or stages of network influence:

(1) issue creation and attention/agenda setting;
(2) influence on discursive positions of states and regional and international organizations;
(3) influence on institutional procedures;
(4) influence on policy change in "target actors" which may be states, international or regional organizations, or private actors like the Nestlé corporation;
(5) influence on state behaviour.

Networks generate attention to new issues and help to set agendas when they provoke media attention, debates, hearings and meetings on issues that previously had not been a matter of public debate. Because values are the essence of advocacy networks, this stage of influence may require a modification of the "value context" in which policy debates take place. The theme years and decades of the United Nations, such as International Women's Decade and the Year of Indigenous People, were international events promoted by networks that heightened awareness of issues.

Networks influence discursive positions when they help to persuade states and international organizations to support international declarations or change stated domestic policy positions. The role that environmental networks played in shaping state positions and conference declarations at the 1992 Earth Summit in Rio de Janeiro is an example of this kind of impact. They may also pressurize states to make more binding commitments by signing conventions and codes of conduct.

At a more concrete level, the network has influence if it leads to changes in policies, not only of the target states, but also of other states and/or international institutions. These changes are easier to see, but their causes can be elusive. We can speak of network impact on policy change where human rights networks have pressured successfully for cut-offs of military aid to repressive regimes, where repressive practices diminish because of pressure, or even where human rights activity affects regime change or stability. We must take care to distinguish between policy change and change in behaviour; official policies may predict nothing about how actors behave in reality.

We speak of stages of impact, and not merely types of impact, because we believe that increased attention and changes in discursive positions make governments more vulnerable to the claims these networks raise. This is not always true, of course—discursive changes can also have a powerfully divisive effect on networks, splitting insiders from outsiders, reformers from radicals. Nonetheless, a government that claims to be protecting indigenous areas or ecological reserves is more vulnerable to charges that such areas are endangered than one that makes no such claim. Then, the effort is no longer to make governments change their position, but to hold them to their word. Meaningful policy and behavioural change is thus more likely when the first three types or stages of impact have occurred.

Both *issue characteristics* and *actor characteristics* are important parts of our explanation of how networks affect political outcomes and the conditions under which networks can be effective. Issue characteristics like salience and resonance within existing national or institutional agendas can tell us something about where networks are likely to be able to insert new ideas and discourse into policy debates. Success in influencing policy depends on the strength and density of the network, and its ability to achieve leverage.

As we look at the issues around which transnational advocacy networks have organized most effectively, we find two characteristic issues that appear most frequently: (1) those involving bodily harm to vulnerable individuals, especially when there is a short and clear causal chain (or story) about who bears responsibility; and (2) issues involving *legal* equality of opportunity. The first responds to a normative logic, and the second to a judicial and institutional one.

Issues involving physical harm to vulnerable or innocent individuals appear more likely to resonate transnationally. Of course, this alone does not ensure the success of the campaign, but is particularly compelling. Nor is it straightforward to determine what constitutes bodily harm, and who is vulnerable or innocent. Both issues of "harm" and "innocence" or vulnerability are highly interpretive and contested. Nevertheless, we argue that issues involving bodily harm to populations perceived as vulnerable or innocent are more likely to lead to effective transnational campaigns than other kinds of issues. This helps to explain why it has been easier to work on torture or disappearance than some other human rights issues, and why it has been easier to protest against torture of political prisoners than against torture of common criminals or to abolish capital punishment. It is also useful for understanding that those environmental campaigns that have had the greatest transnational effect have been those that stress the connection between protecting environments *and* the (often vulnerable) people who live in those environments. We also argue, following Deborah Stone (1989), that in order to campaign on an issue it must be converted into a "causal story"— establishing who bears responsibility or guilt. But in addition to the need for a causal story, we argue that the causal chain within that story needs to be sufficiently short and clear to make a convincing case about responsibility or guilt.

The second issue around which transnational campaigns appear to have greater effectiveness is that of greater legal equality of opportunity. Notice that we stress *legal* equality of *opportunity,* not of outcome. One of the most successful international campaigns was the anti-apartheid campaign. What made apartheid such a clear target was the legal denial of the most basic aspects of equality of opportunity.

Transnational Networks and Regional Integration

Many scholars now recognize that the state no longer has a monopoly over public affairs and are seeking ways to describe the sphere of international interactions under a variety of names: transnational relations, international civil society, and global civil society (Lipschutz, 1992; Peterson, 1992). In their views, states no longer look unitary from the outside. Increasingly dense interactions among individuals, groups, actors from states and regional and international institutions appear to involve much more than re-presenting interests on a world stage.

Recent empirical work in sociology has gone a long way towards demonstrating the extent of changes "above" and "below" the state. The world polity theory associated with John Meyer, John Boli, George Thomas and their colleagues, conceives of an international society in a radically different way. For these scholars, it is the area of diffusion of world culture—a process that itself constitutes the characteristics of states (Thomas et al., 1987; Boli and Thomas, in press). The vehicles for its diffusion become global intergovernmental and non-governmental organizations, but neither the sources of norms nor the processes through which global cultural norms evolve are adequately specified (Finnemore, 1996). Proponents of world polity theory present international organizations and NGOs as "enactors" of some basic cultural principles of the

world culture: universalism, individualism, rational voluntaristic authority, human purposes, and world citizenship. There is thus no meaningful
distinction between those espousing norms that reinforce existing institutional power relationships, and those that challenge them.

We argue that different transnational actors have profoundly divergent
purposes and goals. To understand how change occurs in the world polity
we have to unpack the different categories of transnational actors, and
understand the quite different logic and process in these different categories. The logic of transnational advocacy networks, which are often in
conflict with states over basic principles, is quite different from the logic
of other transnational actors who provide symbols or services or models
for states. In essence, world polity theorists eliminate the struggles over
power and meaning that for us are central to normative change.

Our research suggests that many transnational networks have been
sites of cultural and political negotiation rather than mere enactors of
dominant Western norms. Western human rights norms have indeed
been the defining framework for many networks, but how these norms
are articulated is transformed in the process of network activity. For
example, issues of indigenous rights and cultural survival have been at
the forefront of modern network activity, and yet they run counter to the
cultural model put forward by the world polity theorists.

In other words, as modern anthropologists realize, culture is not a
totalizing influence, but a field that is constantly changing. Certain discourses—like that of human rights—provide a language for negotiation.
Within this language certain moves are privileged over others; human
rights is a very disciplining discourse. But it is also a permissive discourse that allows different groups within the network to renegotiate
meanings. The success of the campaign for women's rights as human
rights reveals the possibilities within the discourse of human rights. We
believe that studying networks is extraordinarily valuable for tracking
and ultimately theorizing about the emergence of shared norms and cultural meanings underpinning processes of regional and international
integration.

Network theory can thus provide an explanation for transnational
change, a model that is not just one of "diffusion" of liberal institutions
and practices, but one through which the preferences and identities of
actors engaged in transnational society are sometimes mutually transformed through their interactions with each other. Because networks are
voluntary and horizontal, actors participate in them to the degree that they
perceive mutual learning, respect and benefits. Modern networks are not
conveyor belts of liberal ideals, but vehicles for communicative and political exchange, with the potential for mutual transformation of participants.

Note

1. We developed this definition based on a discussion in Mitchell (1973, p. 23).

References

Baumgartner, F.; Jones, B., 1991. "Agenda dynamics and policy subsystems," *Journal of Politics* 53, pp. 1044–74.

Boli, J.; Thomas, G., in press. *World Polity Formation since 1875: World Culture and International Non-Governmental Organizations*. Stanford.

Brysk, A., 1994. "Acting globally: Indian rights and international politics in Latin America." In D. Van Cott (ed.), *Indigenous Peoples and Democracy in Latin America*, New York: St Martin's/InterAmerican Dialogue, pp. 29–51.

Brysk, A., 1995. "Hearts and minds: bringing symbolic politics back in," *Polity* 27 (Summer), pp. 559–85.

Dalton, R., Kuechler, M.; Burklin, W., 1990. "The challenge of new movements." In R. Dalton, M. Kuechler (eds.), *Challenging the Political Order: New Social and Political Movements in Western Democracies*, Cambridge: Polity.

Finnemore, M., 1996. *National Interests in International Society*. Ithaca: Cornell.

Fruhling, H., 1991. *Derechos Humanos y Democracia: La contribución de las Organizaciones Nogubernamentales*. Santiago: IIDH.

Haas, P. (ed.), 1992. "Knowledge, power and international policy coordination." *International Organization*, vol. 6.

Katzenstein, P. (ed.), 1996. *The Culture of National Security: Norms and Identity in World Politics*. New York: Columbia.

Keck, M.; Sikkink, K., 1998. *Activists beyond Borders: Advocacy Networks in International Politics*. Ithaca: Cornell.

Klotz, A., 1995. *Norms in International Relations: The Struggle against Apartheid*. Ithaca: Cornell.

Korten, D., 1990. *Getting to the 21st Century: Voluntary Action and the Global Agenda*. Hartford, CT: Kumarian.

Lipschutz, R., 1992. "Reconstructing world politics: the emergence of global civil society," *Millennium* 21, pp. 389–420.

McAdam, D., McCarthy, J.; Zald, M. (eds.), 1996. *Comparative Perspectives on Social Movements: Political Opportunities, Mobilizing Structures, and Cultural Framings*. New York: Cambridge.

Mitchell, J., 1973. "Networks, norms, and institutions." In J. Boissevian, J. Mitchell (eds.), *Network Analysis*, The Hague: Mouton.

Oliver, P.; Marwell, G., 1992. "Mobilizing technologies for collective action." In A. Morris, C. Mueller (eds.), *Frontiers in Social Movement Theory*, New Haven, CT: Yale University Press.

Peterson, M. J., 1992. "Transnational activity, international society, and world politics," *Millennium* 21.

Powell, W., 1990. "Neither market nor hierarchy: network forms of organization," *Research in Organizational Behaviour* 12, pp. 295–336.

Scherer-Warren, I., 1993. *Redes de Movimentos Sociais*. São Paulo: Loyola.

Snow, D.; Benford, R., 1988. "Ideology, frame resonance, and participant mobilisation." In B. Klandermans, H. Kriesi, S. Tarrow (eds.), *From Struc-

ture to Action: Comparing Social Movement Research across Cultures, Greenwich, CT: JAI, pp. 197–217.

Snow, D.; Benford, R., 1992. "Master frames and cycles of protest." In A. Morris, C. Mueller (eds.), *Frontiers in Social Movement Theory*, New Haven, CT: Yale University Press, pp. 133–55.

Snow, D., et al., 1986. "Frame alignment processes, micromobilisation, and movement participation," *American Sociological Review* 51.

Stone, D., 1989. "Causal stories and the formation of policy agendas," *Political Science Quarterly* 104, pp. 281–300.

Tarrow, S., 1992. "Mentalities, political cultures, and collective action frames: constructing meanings through action." In A. Morris, C. Mueller (eds.), *Frontiers in Social Movement Theory*, New Haven, CT: Yale University Press.

Tarrow, S., 1994. *Power in Movement*. New York: Cambridge University Press.

Thomas, G.; Meyer, J.; Ramirez, F.; Boli, J. (eds.), 1987. *Institutional Structure: Constituting State, Society, and Individual*. Newbury Park, CA: Sage.

Part 3

Peace and Security Affairs

Paul F. Diehl and Brian Frederking

The realist view of international organizations has been most prevalent in the area of peace and security affairs. The incidence of war around the world over the past seventy years, especially civil wars in the past several decades, attests to the mostly failed efforts of international organizations to prevent the outbreak of war. With no international police force on the immediate horizon, there is little prospect for global governance mechanisms that can prevent large-scale violence. Furthermore, the collective security provisions in Chapter VII of the UN Charter have never been fully implemented (the Korean and Kuwaiti efforts were not truly international operations, conducted under international command with broadly representative groups of contributing states).

Historically, there are several reasons for the relative ineffectiveness of the United Nations and other regional organizations in preventing war. First, and most obviously, was the stalemate among the permanent members of the Security Council, with the split largely along ideological lines. Cold War tensions and the great power veto in the Security Council often prevented the United Nations from launching concerted actions when faced with threats to international peace and security. The superpower rivalry was also manifested in proxy conflicts around the world, making the ability of regional bodies to form consensus on actions difficult. Second, international organizations have been hampered by a lack of political will on the part of the members to take strong action, even when consensus exists. The financial and human costs associated with security operations are considered too high by many key states who believe they have few direct national interests affected by conflicts far from their home base. Finally, international organizations usually become involved in disputes only after one or more of the disputants has

105

threatened or actually used military force. At that stage, it becomes very difficult to resolve the dispute without further violence.

The end of the Cold War created the possibility for a greater role for international organizations in the realm of peace and security affairs. Greater consensus on the Security Council led to increased peacekeeping missions and the use of economic sanctions. There was increased attention to early warning systems and preventive diplomacy in order to detect nascent conflicts before they reach militarized stages. Even though the political environment enabled decisions to be more easily reached, the complexity of the conflicts on the ground prevented international organizations from achieving more success. The world continues to struggle with the new global environment and to search for the right mix of organizational structures, procedures, and strategies to deal with the various security challenges of the contemporary era, one increasingly characterized by complex emergencies that involve civil war, human rights abuses, and humanitarian crises. The chapters in Part 3 consider these issues and seek to shed some light on how the international community might adapt to a world without a superpower rivalry but one still threatened by international militarized conflict.

Early on, the United Nations adopted the peacekeeping strategy to deal with various conflicts around the world. Traditional peacekeeping operations are characterized by the deployment of a small number of neutral, lightly armed troops, with the consent of the host state, to act as an interposition or buffer force between protagonists, usually after a cease-fire, but prior to conflict resolution. By the beginning of the 1980s, however, international peacekeeping efforts were largely moribund, and it was thought that this strategy for dealing with international conflict might be abandoned. Yet the peacekeeping strategy was renewed with vigor starting in 1989, with more than twice as many UN peacekeeping operations being deployed in the decade following the Cold War period than in the almost forty-five years of the period itself. This trend has continued into the twenty-first century and by some estimates there are now just under 200 peace operations carried out by the United Nations, regional organizations, and multinational coalitions. Along with the expansion in the number of peacekeeping operations, however, there has been a shift away from the traditional model and an expansion in the type and scope of duties for peacekeeping operations, including humanitarian assistance, election monitoring, and other "peacebuilding" functions.

In Chapter 6, Alexandru Balas, Andrew Owsiak, and Paul Diehl explore the reasons for the increase in the number of operations as well as the shift from traditional peacekeeping to peacebuilding missions. Specifically, they focus on the "demand" for peacekeeping and the increase in civil wars in recent decades. Nevertheless, they conclude that it is not simply the increase in opportunity occasioned by more civil wars that accounts for more peace operations. Rather, an increase in peace settlements that include peacekeeping and a greater willingness to take action by the international community also help explain why the rate of intervention has increased since the end of the Cold War and why operations now take on additional tasks beyond monitoring cease-fires.

Going beyond peacekeeping, Christopher Joyner analyzes a more proactive strategy in Chapter 7: the "responsibility to protect" or R2P. This norm moves beyond the idea that states have the *right* to intervene in situations in which there are large-scale human rights abuses—they actually have an *obligation* to do so. This norm has generated criticism from some developing countries that it will be used to justify military intervention. The chapter examines the historical bases and specific elements associated with R2P. Joyner also lays out a series of practical and ethical guidelines on when and how R2P might be employed. R2P is not yet international law or widely practiced, but the motivations to protect civilians and prevent large humanitarian disasters have increased over time, and this norm could become established policy in the future.

Beyond the use of military force, there are alternative approaches that represent global governance attempts at addressing threats to international peace and security. Economic sanctions, which limit trade and impose other penalties, have long been used to alter the cost-benefit analysis for states pursuing a policy (e.g., invasion, human rights abuses) to which the international community or segments of it object. Yet such sanctions often have hurt the citizens of the targeted states and have not made their leaders alter the offending policies. Accordingly, there has been a shift in strategy toward "smart" sanctions that focus on leaders and individuals in the target country, imposing personal costs on them (e.g., freezing assets) in hopes of changing policy. Chapter 8 looks at the efficacy of such a strategy. Peter Wallensteen and Helena Grusell examine the cases of 450 individuals targeted by UN sanctions. This was a mixed bag in terms of effectiveness, but focusing on leaders and key traders can under some circumstances produce the desired effects.

Finally, when conflict cannot be prevented, the world retains an interest in bringing to justice those who commit war crimes that violate international law and shock the consciences of the world's people. The creation of the International Criminal Court (ICC), first operative in 2002, was a landmark event in addressing genocide, rape, and other war crimes. One of the ways in which a case can be referred to the ICC is through the United Nations Security Council; this is essential to prosecute crimes that occur on the territories of states that are not members of the ICC. Rosa Aloisi examines the relationship between the Security Council and the ICC in Chapter 9. She examines the politics of referral with respect to those cases that were sent to the ICC (e.g., Darfur, Sudan) and perhaps more importantly those that might have been but were not referred (Syria, at least as of early 2015). Her conclusion is not an optimistic one about the future viability of this method of ensuring that the ICC is able to deal with serious human rights abuses.

6

Demanding Peace: The Impact of Prevailing Conflict on the Shift from Peacekeeping to Peacebuilding

Alexandru Balas, Andrew P. Owsiak, and Paul F. Diehl

> So many of today's conflicts are within States rather than between States. The end of the Cold War removed constraints that had inhibited conflict in the former Soviet Union and elsewhere. As a result there has been a rash of wars within newly independent States, often of a religious or ethnic character and often involving unusual violence and cruelty.

—Boutros Boutros-Ghali, *Supplement to "An Agenda for Peace,"* 1995

During his tenure as Secretary-General of the United Nations, Boutros Boutros-Ghali authored a seminal document, *An Agenda for Peace*, which both captured the spirit of cooperation permeating the organization (and the international community) in the immediate aftermath of the Cold War and charted a novel course for United Nations' peace operations. Speaking about the new challenges faced by the organization at that time, Boutros-Ghali noted that the number of United Nations (UN) peace operations had increased dramatically in the Cold War's wake. Among the reasons for this increase, the Secretary-General asserted that the end of the Cold War unleashed a wave of intrastate conflicts. These new conflicts demanded more peace operations and required these operations to develop and include innovative—peacebuilding—tasks.[1]

This idea—that an explosion of intrastate conflicts after the collapse of the Soviet Union prompted increased UN intervention and drove the UN toward peacebuilding efforts—did not die in the years after the Cold War ended, nor did it rest only within the minds of policy-makers. Scholarly work conveys a similar sentiment.[2] Such a position is not without superficial merit; indeed, some basic data support it at first glance. The

---

Reprinted from *Peace and Change*, vol. 37: 195–226. © 2012 by Wiley Publishing. Reprinted by permission of the publisher.

sheer number of peace operations admittedly increased dramatically after 1989. Between 1945 and 1989, the UN Security Council authorized and deployed 18 peace operations. In contrast, during the period from 1990 to 2009 (the post–Cold War era), the UN authorized forty-five different operations. This translates into roughly a fivefold increase in UN operations across the two periods on an annualized basis. Furthermore, this trend is not restricted to the UN. Both regional organizations and multilateral groups of states exhibit a similar (and even stronger) tendency. The international community clearly opted to rely increasingly on peace operations after 1989 to address the conflicts that plagued states.

Increased deployments, however, are only half of the story. The mandates for many of the authorized operations simultaneously shifted from traditional peacekeeping toward multifaceted peacebuilding missions. These latter missions—which sought to create a lasting peace through reconciling conflicted parties and repairing the social fabric of war-torn societies—slowly supplanted the traditional interposition missions of the Cold War. The UN (and the international community at large) embraced the belief that well-constructed political and economic structures supported peace and prevented conflict relapses.[3] Thus, peace operations in the post–Cold War environment have been tasked with, *inter alia*, monitoring elections, providing humanitarian assistance to displaced persons, restoring law and order (for example, training local police forces or constructing an independent judiciary), rebuilding societal infrastructure, and reintegrating former belligerents into society.

What accounts for the increased number of peace operations after the Cold War and the shift within these missions from traditional peacekeeping strategies to those under the umbrella of peacebuilding? More specifically, do the trends in peace operations mirror trends involving international conflict? This work explores one widely advanced mechanism for the change in mandates and, by implication, the rise in the raw number of peace operations as well: an increase in the number and a change in the predominant type of conflict prevalent in the international system. Such a "demand side" explanation (as articulated by Boutros-Ghali above) argues that conflict drives the response of the international community—in this case, the authorization of peace operations. According to this argument, organizations simply respond to the challenges posed by the international environment. As the predominant conflict in the system changes from interstate to intrastate, the tasks shift accordingly from the traditional peacekeeping missions of the Cold War (well-suited for interstate conflict) to the peacebuilding missions of today (well-suited for intrastate conflict). If the pattern of conflict changes markedly after 1990 (that is, toward more intrastate conflict), then the expansion into peacebuilding merely reflects a response of the international community to the needs of the system, rather than a larger, sea change in international relations behavior.

The analysis below explores the validity of this demand side argument. Specifically, we ask whether or not conflict truly changed once the Cold War ended. Did conflict situations *demand* a different volume and type of international peace operations after, as opposed to during, the Cold War? Both scholars and practitioners have asserted this fact, but no systematic study of the argument exists. We therefore derive a number of testable hypotheses from the demand side argument, which we subsequently evaluate using multiple conflict datasets. In the end, we find some support for a demand side argument, but it is not as clear-cut as is often presented.

We do not observe a large enough shift in conflict patterns to account for the dramatic changes in operations that occurred. Nevertheless, we do uncover a substantial increase in the number of negotiated agreements that terminate conflicts in the post–Cold War era. These agreements often contain requests for peace operations, particularly to perform peacebuilding tasks. Thus, while the international community does *not* appear to be reacting to changes in overall conflict trends, they *are* responding to increased demand from the disputants themselves.

Such findings yield two specific policy prescriptions. First, practitioners should not stress overall conflict trends when forecasting the international community's potential need for peace operations. Although these trends should not be ignored entirely (after all, intervention requires conflict), the primary focus should be upon the agreements that resolve conflicts, because this is where the demand for peace operations (both in number and mandate) originates. Second, and related to the first point, practitioners concerned about the carrying capacity of organizations or wanting to alter the mandates of peace operations (that is, to narrow or widen their scope) can best achieve this goal by getting more actively involved in the negotiations that end conflicts. Both prescriptions contain seeds of optimism. Rather than being passively subject to overall conflict trends, international actors have clear opportunities to control their fate more actively.

Peacekeeping and Peacebuilding: Some Distinctions

The literature on peace operations contains terminology that often is not conceptually clear. This is particularly true with peacebuilding, which is used to describe different activities depending on the context.[4] We adopt the "maximalist" definition of peacebuilding,[5] which proposes that the goal of peacebuilding is to achieve "positive peace" by employing such activities as disarming warring parties, training indigenous security personnel, facilitating elections, strengthening institutions, providing humanitarian aid, repatriating refugees, and supporting the reconciliation process between parties to the former conflict.[6] Given the tasks associated with peacebuilding, it usually takes place in the aftermath of traditional peacekeeping and peacemaking. Parties must often agree to a cease-fire (a traditional peacekeeping goal) and sign a peace agreement (a peacemaking goal) before the comprehensive tasks associated with peacebuilding can begin. Although peacebuilding tasks can occur after either interstate or intrastate (or civil) wars, scholars have generally associated peacebuilding with the latter.[7]

In contrast, traditional peacekeeping forces are deployed to war-torn areas in order to achieve slightly different purposes.[8] Most notably, they seek to limit the violent conflict that occurs in a specific area. The primary mechanism for this is the deployment of troops as an interpositionary, or buffer, force that separates the combatants following a cease-fire. Traditional peacekeeping is also predicated, at least in part, on promoting an environment suitable for conflict resolution. Peacekeepers are thought to create the conditions conducive for the hostile parties to resolve their differences, and thus, most traditional operations are deployed after a cease-fire, but prior to the conclusion of a peace agreement.

Although there are numerous differences between traditional peacekeeping and peacebuilding (for example, the size of forces and integration with other actors), there are three key differences for our purposes. The first is that peacebuilding operations are primarily sent to intrastate conflicts, whereas traditional peacekeeping may be sent to any context. Second, traditional peacekeeping is usually deployed prior to a final peace settlement, whereas peacebuilding missions are typically designed for the post-settlement phase of conflict. Finally, the scope of the missions differ, with peacebuilding operations performing numerous and varied tasks beyond cease-fire monitoring or the creation and maintenance of a buffer zone.

The Demand Side Argument

As noted above, the use of peace operations changed substantially after the Cold War—both in terms of the frequency of their deployment and the mandates given to the missions that were authorized. What is the causal mechanism that produced this shift? Generally speaking, any possible mechanisms fall into two camps. First, the trend could be driven by "supply side" factors. Those deploying (or supplying) peace operations may suddenly change the rate at which they authorize operations, as well as the mandates they assign to the authorized operations. Scholars have not missed this explanation. Indeed, they frequently assert that peace operations changed (in part) because of the new, cooperative international environment ushered in by the Cold War's end.[9] For example, noting the difference in Cold War versus post–Cold War peace operations deployment rates, Gilligan and Stedman include the Cold War among various factors in their models that attempt to predict the speed with which the UN deploys operations.[10] They find that the systemic constraints of the Cold War (for example, the use of vetoes in the Security Council) greatly slowed UN peace operation deployments during that period. This suggests that the superpower competition (not conflict trends) drove UN intervention behavior.

Such a supply side approach most often focuses on the UN and argues that members of the Security Council and the international community writ large were more willing to intervene in conflicts throughout the world once United States–Soviet Union tensions eased. The narrative is an optimistic one, emphasizing a new spirit of cooperation in which vetoes in the Security Council decreased and the major world powers began to collaborate on issues involving international conflict.[11] As Diehl notes, however, this explanation seems better able to explain the increase in the number of missions, rather than the expansion of the scope of authorized duties.[12] That is, a greater willingness to intervene does not automatically indicate a growth in the scope and purpose of those interventions. Additional factors are needed to provide a holistic explanation. For this reason, scholars have turned to the demand side as well.

The "demand side" argument focuses on the locations to which peace operations are deployed. It is predicated on the assumption that the international community reacts to threats to international peace and security in a consistent fashion. As the situations requiring intervention change, so too must international responses. This might be compared to the behavior of police and fire departments, which respond to crimes and fires respectively but not often to those events outside of their expertise. Accordingly, traditional peacekeeping and peacebuilding are seen as actions commensurate with the kinds of conflicts faced at a given time. Because of the tasks and timing associated with traditional peacekeeping operations [see above], scholars expect these missions to deploy when interstate conflict prevails. In contrast, when intrastate conflict dominates, the international community should instead shift to peacebuilding missions.

To our knowledge, Jakobsen is the only one to examine (very briefly) the possibility that conflict trends influenced intervention patterns, although his work does not represent a systematic examination of this possibility. After reviewing some very basic conflict data within the period 1985–1993, he concludes that ethnic and civil conflicts could not possibly explain the increase in UN-authorized peace operations. He then quickly turns his attention to globalization, democracy and human rights, which he believes to be the real causal factors that drive UN behavior. From our perspective, Jakobsen's analysis is not sufficient to assess the merits of the demand side argument; it is not only restricted temporally (1985–1993) and spatially (UN operations), but also does not consider all conflict trends (for example, interstate conflict) or derive and evaluate the full implications of the demand side argument.

To move beyond Jakobsen's analysis, we therefore need to deduce the detailed hypotheses associated with a demand side argument. At a general level, if the rise of peacebuilding missions is attributable directly to changes in conflict types (or demand), then we should expect to see shifts between the Cold War and post–Cold War periods that highlight the differences between peacebuilding and traditional peace-keeping, with an emphasis on the need for the former. More specifically, incidents of civil war must increase after the Cold War with a corresponding decrease in interstate conflict in order to establish a *prima facie* case for the demand side explanation. Note that both conflict trends are required. If interstate conflict remained prevalent in the post–Cold War period, then any "shift" to peacebuilding would be somewhat muted; those deploying peace operations in such an environment would then seek a balance between peacebuilding and traditional peacekeeping. Furthermore, the changes in conflict should be *proportional* to the observed changes in intervention patterns; otherwise, there is little face validity to the argument that the international community responded to conflict trends. These considerations lead us to our first hypothesis:

Hypothesis 1: Peacebuilding operations increased after the Cold War because of a (proportional) increase in the prevalence of intrastate (or civil) conflicts (and a decrease in interstate [or state-state] conflicts).

Although the rate of conflict occurrences represents one aspect of demand, it is not the only one. Indeed, such a conceptualization implicitly assumes that every conflict is an appropriate context in which a peace operation might intervene. We recognize, however, that this assumption may be inaccurate. We therefore entertain a second possibility: that demand originates not from the conflicts themselves, but rather from the *disputants* involved in the conflicts.

Empirical evidence and scholarly work seems to support the possibility that negotiated agreements drove a shift toward peacebuilding. Beginning around 1989, a number of agreements emerged that both ended conflicts and requested a peace operation to assist with peacebuilding tasks. For example, in Central America, state leaders asked for the UN to perform two peacebuilding tasks. First, they requested that the UN monitor elections in the aftermath of the (linked) intrastate conflicts there, a proposal Secretary-General Perez de Cuellar reluctantly accepted. His reluctance stemmed from the fact that observing elections pushed the organization into the domestic politics of states—a place that the Secretary-General thought was both "uncharted" and "potentially treacherous" for the UN.[13] According to Karns, two contextual characteristics of the situation persuaded him to change his mind: the existence of an international agreement and a direct request from state leaders.[14] Given that the UN had previously supported the goals of the agreement that emerged, it was difficult for the organization then to deny the request for observers.

Second, the foreign ministers from five Central American nations asked the UN for an international military observer force. In addition to traditional peacekeeping tasks, leaders asked the force to perform peacebuilding functions, particularly the monitoring of elections and human rights violations, as well as the demobilization of sub-state groups that engaged in the conflict.[15] This request produced two missions: the United Nations Observer Group in Central America (ONUCAL) and the United Nations Observer Mission in El Salvador (ONUSAL). The former involved primarily traditional peacekeeping tasks, while the latter forayed more heavily into peacebuilding.[16]

Similar agreements in Namibia (1989), Angola (1991 and 1994), Cambodia (1991), Mozambique (1992), Macedonia (2001), Liberia (2003), and Indonesia (2005) also asked the UN to assume peacebuilding tasks.[17] In the case of Namibia, the UN was asked to ensure the occurrence of free and fair elections, the repeal of discriminatory laws, the release of political refugees, and the maintenance of law and order.[18] The organization's success in Namibia prompted its mission there to serve as a template for other peacebuilding missions.[19] The UN role in, *inter alia*, Cambodia expanded upon the tasks it performed in Namibia. More specifically, the

UN was asked to focus upon the Cambodian societal infrastructure and serve as a civilian administrator for the state (that is, conduct its foreign, defense, financial, and civil police affairs), in addition to monitoring elections, repatriating refugees, and maintaining law and order.[20] This was a tall order, but although reluctant, the UN did as it was asked.[21]

In addition to the tasks already noted, disputants also frequently request peace operations to assist with the disarmament, demobilization, and reintegration (DDR) of former belligerents. For example, the government of Indonesia and the Free Aceh Movement (GAM) signed a memorandum of understanding in 2005, in which the two parties asked the European Union and the Association of Southeast Asian Nations to deploy a peace operation that would help disarm, demobilize, and reintegrate GAM members, monitor human rights violations, and generally underwrite their agreement by investigating and reporting on potential violations of it.[22] Similarly, Macedonia and the National Liberation Army (NLA) asked the North Atlantic Treaty Organization to perform disarmament, demobilization, and reintegration functions with respect to NLA members in 2001.[23] Agreements that resulted from conflicts in Angola, Mozambique, and Liberia contain similar requests.

These cases suggest that the demand for peacebuilding arose not merely from the occurrence of conflicts, but from the *agreements* that ended them.[24] As parties negotiated an end to violent conflict, they requested that the UN underwrite their commitments, thereby making those commitments more credible.[25] From a theoretical perspective, this makes sense. As we noted during our discussion of the differences between the concepts of traditional peacekeeping and peacebuilding, the former often comes *before* a comprehensive settlement agreement, while the latter comes *after* those agreements. This implies that if the number of comprehensive agreements that settled outstanding conflicts rise, there should be a greater demand for peacebuilding, as opposed to peacekeeping. Such thinking leads to our second hypothesis:

> *Hypothesis 2:* Peacebuilding operations increased after the Cold War due to an increase in the number of negotiated agreements that settled conflicts (of any type) in the system.

To be sure, the content of the comprehensive agreements certainly matter as well, for it is within the agreements that disputants often request peacebuilding assistance. Yet we believe that if the number of such agreements rises after the Cold War ends, such evidence suggests a *prima facie* case for the demand side argument and opens the door to additional research.

Empirical Data and Analysis

To evaluate the first hypothesis presented above, we turn to data on inter-state and civil conflict drawn from several sources. The Correlates of War Project's (COW) Interstate and Intrastate War Data tracks state-state and civil wars with 1,000 or more battle deaths.[26] For this analysis, we have restricted the temporal domain of the COW war data to the period 1945–2009 (post–World War II), the end point representing the final year for which data are available. Because the COW data has a high severity threshold (that is, it captures conflicts with at least 1,000 fatalities), we also examined violent conflicts reported by the Uppsala Conflict Data Program (UCDP).[27] This latter collection records interstate and intrastate conflicts with greater than 25 fatalities during the period 1946–2008.[28]

By looking at both of these data collections, we are able to detect changes in the frequency of threats to international peace and security that might prompt the international community to authorize peacekeeping or peacebuilding operations. The different levels of severity reflected in the two datasets also permits us to control for the possibility that not only has there been a shift in the types of conflict, but also that post–Cold War conflicts became more (or less) severe. This is an important factor to consider, given that previous studies have shown that peace operations are more likely to be deployed in the most dangerous or hostile conflicts.[29] In other words, it is possible that there are not more conflicts in the post–Cold War period, but rather that the conflicts that do occur are more severe, thereby eliciting the authorization and deployment of a greater number of peace operations.[30] Examining less severe conflict allows us to check this possibility and ensures that any results are not an artifact of data measurement decisions.

To examine the second hypothesis, we employed data from the UCDP Conflict Termination Dataset.[31] This dataset collects information on how conflicts ended during the period 1946–2009. For our purposes, the most important data includes information on any agreements that might have helped end each conflict. Such agreements fall into three categories: cease-fire agreements, cease-fire agreements with conflict regulation, and peace agreements.

As noted earlier, peacekeeping and peacebuilding typically enter conflicts at different junctures. Traditional peacekeeping tends to enter conflict situations after the signing of a cease-fire agreement (but before a peace agreement), while peacebuilding operations generally intercede after a more comprehensive agreement. This suggests that the *type* of agreement should matter for whether a peacekeeping or peacebuilding operation emerges. We therefore create two categories of agreements to use in our analysis. The first indicates whether *only* a cease-fire was signed. The second notes whether either a peace agreement *or* a cease-fire with conflict regulation was signed. We aggregate these two categories together because in both cases parties are likely to request more than just cease-fire monitoring. Nevertheless, we note that retaining three separate categories does not alter our conclusions.

The numbers of interstate and intrastate conflicts initiated in each decade, as well as the number of negotiated agreements resulting from those conflicts, are reported in Table 6.1. Within each dataset and conflict type, the first column indicates the frequency with which conflicts were initiated (or agreements signed). Because comparison across and within the datasets requires standardization (primarily to deal with truncated decades, especially in the 1940s and 2000s), the second column under each conflict type annualizes the frequency counts found within the first column (that is, it takes the frequency and divides it by the number of years for which we have data in that decade). The resulting statistic indicates the *average* number of conflicts initiated per year during a specific period (decade or pre/post–Cold War). The key breakpoint for the purpose of evaluating the demand side explanation (outlined above) lies between the pre-1990 (Cold War) and post-1990 (post–Cold War) periods, where 1989 designates the end of the Cold War and 1990 signals the beginning of the post–Cold War era.

With respect to intrastate (civil) conflict, the results are consistent across different levels of severity (COW vs. UCDP datasets). Civil wars (COW data) were approximately 39% more frequent on an annual basis in the post–Cold War era (averaging 3.39 per year) as opposed to the earlier period (averaging 2.44 per year). Similarly, less severe intrastate conflict (UCDP data) was more common after 1990 than during the Cold War (averaging 3.16 incidents per year versus 2.86 per year respectively), although the magnitude of this increase (11%) was not as great as that for full-scale wars (39%, as noted above). There are numerous reasons for the increase in intrastate conflicts after 1989, including a greater number of independent states, an increase in ethnic tensions, and the like.[32] Nevertheless, the general pattern is consistent with the demand side argument. One cannot help but note, however, that there were significant numbers of civil wars and lesser internal conflicts during the Cold War era as well. Thus, the development of peacebuilding in the post–Cold War (and, inversely, its absence during the Cold War) cannot be attributed to a dearth of civil conflict opportunities before 1990, casting some doubt on the demand side's first hypothesis.

Also consistent with the demand side argument is the decline in the number of interstate conflicts. Nine interstate wars (COW data) occur between 1990 and 2007, compared to the 29 interstate wars during the

Table 6.1 Conflict Frequency, Cold War and Post–Cold War Periods

| | High-Severity Conflicts (COW, 1945–2007) | | | | All Conflicts (UCDP, 1946–2008) | | | | Negotiated Agreements (UCDP, 1946–2008) | | | |
| | Interstate Wars | | Intrastate Wars | | Interstate Conflict | | Intrastate Conflict | | Cease-fires Only | | More Comprehensive Agreements | |
Decade	Initiated	Per Year	Initiated	Per Year	Initiated	Per Year	Initiated	Per Year	Initiated	Per Year	Initiated	Per Year
1940s	2	0.40	10	2.00	6	1.50	23	4.60	0	0.00	3	0.60
1950s	6	0.60	11	1.10	4	0.40	15	1.50	0	0.00	7	0.70
1960s	7	0.70	24	2.40	6	0.60	34	3.40	3	0.30	9	0.90
1970s	9	0.90	35	3.50	7	0.70	32	3.20	4	0.40	13	1.30
1980s	5	0.50	30	3.00	7	0.70	22	2.20	2	0.20	6	0.60
Cold War Totals	29	0.64	110	2.44	30	0.68	126	2.86	9	0.20	38	0.84
1990s	7	0.70	41	4.10	4	0.40	48	4.80	7	0.70	37	3.70
2000s	2	0.25	20	2.50	2	0.22	12	1.33	4	0.40	20	2.00
Post–Cold War Totals	9	0.50	61	3.39	6	0.32	60	3.16	11	0.55	57	2.85

Cold War (annualized rates of 0.64 and 0.50 for the two respective periods). These data, however, require 1,000 fatalities, which may be a high threshold. Examining the UCDP data, which includes conflicts with a lower fatality threshold (of 25), supports the conclusion that fewer interstate conflicts occur in the post–Cold War era. Such figures indicate a decline from 30 Cold War interstate conflicts to 6 similar conflicts after the Cold War's end (annualized decrease from 0.68 to 0.32). In short, the yearly rate of initiation declines by roughly 22–53% for interstate conflict in the post–Cold War world compared to its predecessor period, and any militarized threats that do occur are less likely to produce fatalities.[33] These findings suggest that we might expect fewer traditional peace operations after 1989, as state-state conflicts have become less frequent and are often not severe.

Data on negotiated settlements yield conclusions that complement those derived from the conflict data (right-hand columns of Table 6.1). On average, there were 0.84 episodes per year in which a conflict ended with more than a cease-fire (n=38) prior to 1990. We do find a subsequent increase in the frequency of these agreements after 1990; in the post–Cold War era, the annualized number of agreements rises from 0.84 to 2.85 (n=57). This indicates a growth rate of 239% across the two periods. Cease-fires also increased in the post–Cold War era, although the growth rate was somewhat lower (175%).[34] As with civil wars, more comprehensive agreements are not merely a characteristic of the post–Cold War period. Yet they did increase substantially after the Cold War ended, suggesting that any demand side explanation may be driven not by the demands of conflict itself, but rather by the demands of the disputants involved in those conflicts. This lends support to the demand side's second hypothesis.

Patterns of interstate conflicts, intrastate conflicts, and negotiated agreements provide some limited support for the demand side argument. For the demand side argument to hold merit, however, changes in conflict patterns must also correspond with changes in intervention patterns. That is, increasing conflict in the world (generally) needs to yield a similar increase in intervention, while the prevalence of intrastate conflicts or an increase in the number of more comprehensive, negotiated agreements should make peacebuilding a necessary tool for any successful intervention. To address this proposed relationship, we cross-referenced the conflict data with those on peace operations drawn from the same time period. We present intervention data on both UN peace operations (Table 6.2) and peace operations undertaken by regional organizations (Table 6.3).

Table 6.2 provides summary information on the propensity for UN peace intervention over time and across different conflict contexts and

Table 6.2 Patterns of UN Intervention in Conflicts (peace operations only)

	Interstate Conflicts			Intrastate Conflicts			Totals		
	Conflicts	Interventions	Intervention Rate	Conflicts	Interventions	Intervention Rate	Conflicts	Interventions	Intervention Rate
High-Severity Conflicts									
Cold War	29	7	0.24	110	6	0.05	139	13	0.09
Post–Cold War	9	4	0.44	61	20	0.33	70	24	0.34
Total	38	11	0.29	171	26	0.15	209	37	0.18
Low-Severity Conflicts									
Cold War	30	6	0.20	126	7	0.06	156	13	0.08
Post–Cold War	6	3	0.50	60	20	0.33	66	23	0.35
Total	36	9	0.25	186	27	0.15	222	36	0.16

Table 6.3 Patterns of Regional Organization Interventions in Conflicts (peace operations only)

	Interstate Conflicts			Intrastate Conflicts			Totals		
	Conflicts	Interventions	Intervention Rate	Conflicts	Interventions	Intervention Rate	Conflicts	Interventions	Intervention Rate
High-Severity Conflicts									
Cold War	29	0	0.00	110	5	0.05	139	5	0.04
Post–Cold War	9	0	0.00	61	12	0.20	70	12	0.17
Total	38	0	0.00	169	17	0.10	209	17	0.08
Low-Severity Conflicts									
Cold War	30	2	0.07	126	5	0.04	156	7	0.04
Post–Cold War	6	0	0.00	60	12	0.20	66	12	0.18
Total	44	2	0.05	183	17	0.09	222	19	0.09

severity. A pure demand side explanation for the rise of peacebuilding would require that the overall rate of intervention remain roughly constant while the number of intrastate conflicts would rise (that is, the UN should deploy peace operations with equal frequency across the two periods, but because they face a new conflict context in which to intervene, they should shift to peacebuilding). As we noted above, the latter has some validity; intrastate conflicts do increase somewhat. Yet the rate of UN intervention does *not* remain constant across the two time periods, suggesting that the organization is doing more than merely responding to conflict trends. Among the most severe conflicts (captured by the COW data in the top rows of Table 6.2), the annualized rate of UN peace operations has soared approximately 278% after the Cold War ended across both civil and international wars (a jump from 0.09 to 0.34; top rows, far right column). These UN deployments after 1990 include both traditional peace missions in the aftermath of state-state wars such as the one between Ethiopia and Eritrea, as well as peacebuilding missions to intrastate conflicts such as the one in Kosovo.

Patterns for full-scale wars are mirrored by UN intervention in less severe conflicts (captured by the UCDP data in the lower rows of Table 6.2)—roughly a 338% increase in UN involvement between the two periods across all conflicts (an increase in annualized rates from 0.08 to 0.35). In the bottom half of Table 6.2, it is clear that the UN has sent peace missions (on average) more frequently to interstate conflicts after 1990 than before (annualized rates of 0.50 and 0.33 for interstate and civil conflicts respectively), although these conflicts occur considerably less often than in previous decades (see Table 6.1). More significantly, however, is the finding that *the rate* of intervention for civil conflict has been substantially greater since 1990 (annualized rates of 0.06 and 0.33 for the Cold War and post–Cold War periods respectively). Such an increase occurs even as the opportunities for intervention have increased as well. That is a significant feat, for the rate of intervention can only rise in the presence of more conflict if the organization takes on a *significant* number of new operations (otherwise, the rise in conflict would mute any increase in intervention behavior and the annualized rates would be similar across the two periods). The UN appears to have done just that.

Comparing the changes found in Tables 6.1 and 6.2 reveals the shortcomings of the demand side argument: the UN does not seem to be responding to changes in conflict trends alone. Interstate conflict falls in the post–Cold War period, but the average rate of UN intervention in these conflicts actually *rises*. And although intrastate conflict increases

11–38% between the Cold War and post–Cold War eras, the increase in UN intervention rates *vastly exceeds* that (approximately a 450% increase in intervention rates using annualized figures). The first hypothesis does not seem to receive strong empirical support.

Despite this finding, the demand side argument is not without some merit. The increase in intervention rates across the Cold War and post–Cold War periods (450%; see above) mirrors the increase in the number of comprehensive, negotiated agreements across these two periods (an increase of approximately 239%). Once again, this suggests that although the UN may not be responding to a significant increase in the number of conflicts throughout the world, they *are* more than likely responding to requests from disputants for UN assistance, which have increased since the Cold War ended. Coupled with the spirit of cooperation that permeated the organization after 1990, such a finding implies that there was more than just a *willingness* on the part of the UN to get involved in more conflicts, there was also an increased *opportunity* for the UN to do so.

Regional organizations display similar intervention patterns to those noted for the UN. Table 6.3 provides summary information on regional organizations' intervention in both interstate and intrastate conflict across varying levels of severity. As before, the evidence suggests that the demand side argument has some validity; regional organizations are not equally likely to send peace operations to interstate or intrastate conflicts in the Cold War and post–Cold War eras. Instead, the rates with which regional organizations deploy peace operations escalated dramatically after 1990. Within the most-severe conflicts (listed in the top half of Table 6.3), the annualized rate of regional organizations' intervention across all conflict types climbed by 325% after the Cold War ended (from 0.04 to 0.17). This behavior is mirrored by regional organizations' use of peace operations to intervene in less severe conflicts (listed in the lower half of Table 6.3). Compared to the Cold War period, regional organizations' annualized intervention rate in the post–Cold War period rose 350% (from 0.04 to 0.18). The UN's intervention patterns are therefore not unique. Instead, the patterns cumulatively signify a shift in how the global community views its responsibilities (and the appropriate method to use) for handling conflict throughout the world.

Three additional factors are worth mentioning about the data in Tables 6.2 and 6.3. First, the interventions listed in those tables appear low at first glance. This is because we focused on the *conflict* as the unit of analysis. In several instances, the international community sent multiple peace missions to the same conflict (for example, Haiti, Angola, and Kosovo). In cases such as these, the relevant organizations (UN vs.

regional) were only credited with intervening once within any given conflict (although both the UN and regional organizations were each given credit for intervention if they both intervened in the same conflict). This decision prevents us from overstating the intervention rates of the international community.

Second, critics might argue that the intervention rates for regional organizations are less meaningful, because peace operations lay within the UN's domain until the Cold War's end. Yet such an argument is not supported by the data. Regional organizations did send peace operations to conflicts during the Cold War. The interventions they undertook during that time were primarily within intrastate, rather than interstate, conflicts, suggesting that they reserved intervention in interstate conflicts for the UN. Although they may still follow this precedent in the post–Cold War world, it is clear that their overall intervention rate accelerated markedly beginning in 1990. We address some of the reasons for this shift below in more detail.

Finally, the international community has recently begun to cooperate more in peace operations, with multiple organizations sending missions to the same conflict. For example, Kosovo hosts complementary missions sent by the UN, the Organization for Security and Cooperation in Europe (OSCE), the European Union (EU) and the North Atlantic Treaty Organization (NATO). This requires greater inter-organizational cooperation, as multiple mandates must govern the various organizations' behavior. Yet even when the same organization sends multiple missions to a conflict (for example, the UN in Haiti), multiple mandates appear, only some of which might be labeled as peacebuilding. This secular trend toward greater involvement (and cooperation) in peace operations by the international community writ large calls for an explanation beyond merely a greater incidence of conflict events.

Although some portion of the new peacebuilding operations can certainly be attributable to the rise in intrastate conflicts, this is far from a monocausal explanation. Opportunities for peacebuilding activities clearly existed during the Cold War, but the international community chose to intervene with only traditional peacekeeping operations, if at all. Perhaps only the United Nations Operation in the Congo (1960–1964) approaches what might be labeled peacebuilding today.[35] To be sure, there is some evidence that civil conflicts have become more severe over time, with the rise of failed states and various negative externalities (for example, refugees, cross-border fighting). Yet we found no evidence that the severity of conflict has led to an increase in UN missions, much less accounting for the shift in strategies toward peacebuilding.

In addition, in the post–Cold War era, the international community has not responded to certain civil conflicts with peacebuilding missions, even when such operations might have been justified by the conditions on the ground (for example, Rwanda). Regional organization and multinational operations have also exploded in number since 1990, targeting many of the world's hotspots such as Liberia, Azerbaijan, and Burundi. Yet these have not generally involved a wide range of peacebuilding activities, albeit for a variety of reasons including limited resources of the sponsoring agency. In short, the evidence indicates that conflict context does not automatically drive peace operation deployment and that there is ample room for non-peacebuilding operations, even when host states might actually need such services. The conflict trends and characteristics in the post–Cold War era simply do not explain the disproportionate rise in the deployment of peace operations or the much greater use of peacebuilding activities.

The Demand Side Argument: Integration and Future Research

The merits of the demand side argument are mixed. Clearly, an increase in overall conflict has limits in accounting for the development of peacebuilding. Civil wars existed (in significant numbers) prior to 1990, and their increase in the post–Cold War era cannot account for the disproportionate increase in peace operations. Yet this is not to say that the demand side argument should be dismissed entirely. More comprehensive, negotiated agreements did end an increased number of conflicts in the post–Cold War era, suggesting that disputants may be directly driving intervention trends (as in the examples of Angola, Cambodia, Indonesia, Liberia, Macedonia, Mozambique, and Namibia demonstrated earlier). Thus, the demand side argument has some explanatory value. Taken collectively with a handful of interrelated arguments, we believe that a more complete explanation of the shift to peacebuilding can be constructed. This explanation, however, will require additional research.

[In order to] account for the rise of peacebuilding, one first has to explore a substantial shift in three related norms: sovereignty, democratization, and humanitarian intervention. During the Cold War, before a peacekeeping operation could be deployed, the state upon whose territory the peacekeepers would be deployed had to agree to the operation. In contrast, during the post–Cold War era, peace operations have been frequently deployed both to conflicts in which host state cooperation was complete and those in which it was absent (and at several points in between). Such changes reflect a transformation in international norms toward state sovereignty.[36] The traditional notion held that sovereignty was nearly absolute—what happened inside state borders being solely the domain of national governments. More recently, exceptions to state sovereignty have been carved out and the idea that the international community has a vested interest in and can play a role in internal matters has been increasingly accepted.[37] Whereas during the Cold War, the international community largely ignored internal conflicts and the superpowers armed competing sides, the last two decades have seen states intervene more frequently in internal conflicts. Yet we know that the pendulum has not swung completely in the other direction as most civil wars do not prompt intervention and sovereignty concerns are still part of intervention debates over Darfur and other conflicts.

Democratization has also clearly influenced intervention behavior, and a commitment to democratic principles strengthened in the wake of the Cold War. Although the number of democratic states in the international system has consistently been rising since 1946, the number of democratic states escalated dramatically from 1989–1995.[38] During that period, the number of democracies climbed from roughly 50 states to 80 states, at which point it eventually leveled off. Simultaneously, the international community and disputants turned their attention to building stable *democratic* states through intervention. For example, in *An Agenda for Peace*, Boutros-Ghali noted that social stability requires domestic institutions through which people can freely express their will.[39] In his view, "Democracy at all levels is essential to attain peace for a new era of prosperity and justice." Disputants apparently shared the Secretary-General's position, for when they signed agreements to end conflicts after 1989 that requested a peace operation, they often asked the operation to accept tasks associated with democratization, such as monitoring either elections (for example, in Angola, Liberia, Mozambique, Namibia) or the legislative changes associated with the emergence of a new, democratic entity (for example, in Indonesia). In short, as the norm of democratization strengthened after the Cold War, disputants asked for assistance to build democratic states and organizations offered to expand their mandates to include such peacebuilding tasks.

Finally, in line with a decline in the absolutist view of state sovereignty and a preference of greater democratization has been the rise of the norm of humanitarian intervention.[40] This norm establishes a right for the international community to intervene in the event of humanitarian disasters and widespread human rights violations; still, there is no legal obligation or "responsibility to protect" that would assure that the international community responds to every such situation.[41] Of course, in the case of failed states, no sovereign barriers to intervention exist, but there has not been an expectation of an affirmative response by the global community until recently. Accordingly, peace operations have been sent to areas without the full cooperation of the legally sovereign state (for example, KFOR in Kosovo) or where no functioning government existed (for example, UNOSOM I in Somalia). Both illustrate a shift in international norms that include a more expansive role for peace operations. Enhancing the norms for intervention, globalization allowed the media to bring human suffering across the globe to developed countries in great detail. This "CNN effect" generated domestic pressure on Western governments for greater intervention in war-torn states.[42]

The timing of the normative shifts regarding sovereignty, democratization, and humanitarian intervention coincide largely with the systemic break between the Cold War and post–Cold War periods.[43] For example, UN Secretary-General Boutros-Ghali released *An Agenda for Peace* in 1992 (updated in 1995), shortly after the Cold War ended.[44] In that document, Boutros-Ghali noted that the tides were shifting in favor of democracy and humanitarian intervention—the primary aims being to halt conflict and human rights abuses despite a lack of host state consent and rebuild stable democratic states in the aftermath of conflict. As he wrote in 1992, "Respect for fundamental sovereignty and integrity are crucial to any common international progress. The time of absolute and exclusive sovereignty, however, has passed."[45] Combined with norms of democratization and humanitarian intervention, the erosion of the norm of absolute sovereignty indicates that the shifts toward peacebuilding and more frequent interventions might require a partially normative explanation, which the demand side argument does not immediately anticipate.

Such thinking was not confined to the UN either. Instead, it permeated regional organizations at the same time as well. For example, the Secretary-General of the Organization of African Unity (OAU), Salim Ahmed Salim, expressed the same sentiment as Boutros-Ghali, albeit in more forceful language. He released a report to his organization in 1992, entitled *Resolving Conflicts in Africa: Proposals for Action*. Besides proposing a formal peacekeeping mechanism within the organization, the Secretary-General notes that although signatories to the OAU Charter of 1963 pledge respect for the sovereignty of all member states (and claim to respect non-intervention in the internal affairs of other members), "sovereignty can legally be transcended, by the 'intervention' of 'outside forces,' by their will to facilitate prevention and/or resolution, particularly on humanitarian grounds."[46] The timing of these documents makes it easy to attribute responsibility for the increased authorization of peace operations and their shift to peacebuilding to greater cooperation among the major powers. These events happened side-by-side. Yet organizational records indicate that something larger occurred; greater cooperation is only part of the story. The international community changed how it viewed its responsibilities, believing that sovereignty was no longer a barrier to intervention when humans experienced great suffering and that peace required democratization.

The discussion so far suggests that the rise of peacebuilding was largely altruistic. Nevertheless, the motives of those intervening, specifically the major powers behind UN interventions, deserve consideration. It is not merely that international norms permit intervention, but states in the international community also must be willing to commit to action. Some have suggested that economic or other motives have been at work in peace operations that seek to remake individual countries.[47] Related and perhaps with a more benign conclusion, scholars have suggested that the ideology of liberalism encouraged Western liberal democracies to use peace operations to intervene legitimately throughout the world to spread their norms.[48] A modified version of this ideological explanation proposes that individual and human rights became center-stage concepts in the international system after 1990.[49] In most peacebuilding operations, the host state is encouraged to adopt democratic institutions and processes, often borrowed from Western models. Economic reforms typically encourage market mechanisms to promote growth and rebuild economies. Human rights provisions in new constitutions and laws resemble those in Western legal traditions, emphasizing individual rights, rather than what may be indigenous political or legal traditions. In these ways, peacebuilding operations serve the interests of the leading states in the international system.

In some ways, the need for peacebuilding was also conditioned by the failure of previous Western aid policies. The use of International Monetary Fund conditionality by Western governments often formed the premise upon which financial and developmental aid were given to developing states, leading to an increased number of failed states and civil wars when economic targets negatively impacted the target nations.[50] This context required a different type of peace operation.

For all these reasons, we believe that future research should continue to explore the normative shifts that might underlie the change to peacebuilding. A normative explanation holds great promise for adding to our understanding of how peacekeeping has changed over time. That said, we also believe that scholars have minimized the potential role that the demand side argument plays in these normative shifts. Although the international community has changed the criteria for the interventions it is willing to undertake (a supply side story), it also seems that disputants might encourage this shift by requesting assistance more often (a demand side story). Further, it is also possible that normative shifts occur at the disputant level, rather than at the organizational or systemic level.[51] Far from eschewing the demand side explanation, we conclude that it should be more carefully considered in research that evaluates the normative tides that might have produced peacebuilding trends.

Conclusion

What accounts for a shift from traditional peacekeeping to a peacebuilding approach and the accompanying increase in the number of peace operations? The conventional explanation of great power cooperation after the end of the Cold War is best able to explain the increased frequency of intervention, but not a shift in strategy. In this paper, we explored a demand side perspective that argues that peace operations responded to a shift in the kind of conflicts facing the global community (specifically a change from predominantly interstate conflicts to internal ones), a general increase in conflicts of all varieties, and an increase in the number of more comprehensive, negotiated agreements that terminate conflicts. Generally, we find mixed support for the demand side argument.

There has been an alteration in the configuration of conflict since 1990, with both intrastate conflicts and disrupted states more frequent and interstate disputes declining somewhat. Nevertheless, changes in conflict patterns do not explain the disproportionate increase in the rate of intervention by the UN and regional organizations. The more substantial cause may lie within the increased prevalence of comprehensive, negotiated agreements that terminated conflicts. These agreements appeared far more frequently in the post–Cold War world. Combined with evidence from specific cases, this suggests that disputants may have requested peacebuilding activities with increasing frequency after the Cold War ended. Yet the story is not so simple. The rise of peacebuilding and the increase in peace operations generally are not merely functions of the *opportunities* available to the international community, but also its *willingness* to take action—and in a more expansive fashion. A complete understanding of the shift to peacebuilding requires that we consider the merits of the demand side story, specifically the role of disputants in requesting (and thereby encouraging) the proliferation of peacebuilding activities.

Our analysis suggests that explaining the trends in peace operations requires more than a simple reference to greater cooperation among major states. One must also account for conflict context, disputant requests, changing international norms, and major power interests. These factors each contribute toward the evolution and expansion in peace operations throughout the international system. They also lay the groundwork for such cooperation, indicating that cooperation may only last until conflicts, norms, or major power interests render the deployment of peace operations less desirable. Finally, they offer policy-makers hope. Beholden simply to the will of major powers (and their vetoes), overarching conflict trends, or larger normative changes, there is little the international community can practically do but react. If disputant requests (through peace agreements) help drive trends in peace operations, however, policy-makers have a way to influence the mandates undertaken by peace operations, as well as the contexts to which they are deployed. Getting involved in such negotiations offers leaders a much more active way to influence the peace operation trends that they sometimes lament.

Notes

1. Boutros Boutros-Ghali, *An Agenda for Peace* (New York: United Nations, 1992, S/24111); Boutros Boutros-Ghali, *Supplement to "An Agenda for Peace"* (New York: United Nations, 1995, S/1995/1).

2. For example, see Boutros Boutros-Ghali, *Unvanquished: A U.S.-U.N. Saga* (New York: Random House, 1999), 30–64; James H. Lebovic, "United for Peace: Democracies and United Nations Peace Operations after the Cold War," *Journal of Conflict Resolution* 48, No. 6 (December 2004): 910–36; Karen A. Mingst and Margaret P. Karns, *The United Nations in the Post–Cold War Era* (Boulder, CO: Westview Press, 2000), 74–116.

3. See, for example, Boutros Boutros-Ghali, *An Agenda for Peace* and *Supplement to "An Agenda for Peace,"* op. cit.

4. Michael Barnett, Hunjoon Kim, Madalene O'Donnell, and Laura Sitea, "Peacebuilding: What Is in a Name?" *Global Governance* 13, No. 1 (January 2007): 35–58.

5. Paul F. Diehl, "Paths to Peacebuilding: The Transformation of Peace Operations," in *Conflict Prevention and Peacebuilding in Post-War Societies*, eds. David Mason and James Meernik (London: Routledge, 2006): 107–29.

6. See Boutros-Boutros Ghali, *Agenda for Peace*, for the clearest and most cited use of the term.

7. Paul F. Diehl, *Peace Operations* (Cambridge: Polity Press, 2008), 10.

8. Diehl, *Peace Operations*, op. cit., 28–67.

9. This is effectively used as a baseline explanation from which Jakobsen further expands. See Peter Viggio Jakobsen, "The Transformation of United Nations Peace Operations in the 1990s: Adding Globalization to the Conventional 'End of the Cold War' Explanation," *Cooperation and Conflict* 37, No. 3 (September 2002): 267–82.

10. Michal Gilligan and Stephen Stedman, "Where Do the Peacekeepers Go?," *International Studies Review* 5, No. 4 (December 2003): 37–54.

11. David Malone and Karin Wermester, "Boom and Bust? The Changing Nature of UN Peacekeeping," *International Peacekeeping* 7, No. 4 (December 2000): 37–54; Steven Ratner, *The New UN Peacekeeping* (New York: St. Martin's Press, 1995), 1–24.

12. Diehl, "Paths to Peacebuilding," op. cit.

13. Javier Pérez de Cuéllar, *Pilgrimage for Peace: A Secretary-General's Memoir* (New York: St. Martin's Press, 1997), 412.

14. Margaret Karns, "Searching for the Roots of UN Post-Conflict Peacebuilding" (paper presented at the Annual Meeting of the International Studies Association, San Francisco, CA, March 26–9, 2008).

15. Karns, op. cit.

16. United Nations, "Department of Peacekeeping Operations: Past Operations," accessed January 4, 2011, http://www.un.org/en/peacekeeping/pastops .shtml.

17. See United Nations, *Agreements on a Comprehensive Political Settlement of the Cambodia Conflict, Paris, 23 October 1991* (New York: United Nations, 1991); Conciliation Resources, accessed September 9, 2011, http://www.c-r .org/our-work/accord/); North Atlantic Treaty Organization Update, "Skopje Requests NATO Assistance," accessed September 9, 2011, http://www.nato.int /docu/update/2001/0618/e0620a.htm; United States Institute of Peace, "Comprehensive Peace Agreement, Liberia," accessed September 9, 2011, http://www.usip .org/files/file/resources/collections/peace_agreements/liberia_08182003.pdf; Aceh Monitoring Mission, "Memorandum of Understanding," accessed September 9, 2011, http://www.aceh-mm.org/download/english/Helsinki%20MoU.pdf.

18. United Nations Security Council, "Resolution 435" (New York: United Nations).

19. Cedric Thornberry, *A Nation Is Born: The Inside Story of Namibia's Independence* (Windhoek: Gamsberg Macmillan Publishers, 2004), 375.

20. Karns, op. cit.

21. Pérez de Cuéllar, op. cit.

22. Aceh Monitoring Mission, op. cit.

23. North Atlantic Treaty Organization Update, op. cit.

24. See Karns, op. cit.

25. Disputant requests for third-party assistance with disarmament, demobilization, and reintegration may be critical for the success of civil war agreements. See Barbara Walter, "The Critical Barrier to Civil War Settlement," *International Organization* 51, No. 3 (Summer 1997): 335–64.

26. Meredith Reid Sarkees and Frank Wayman, *Resort to War: 1816–2007* (Washington, DC: CQ Press, 2010), 75–78. Data available at: http://correlates ofwar.org.

27. See Nils Petter Gleditsch, Peter Wallensteen, Mikael Eriksson, Margareta Sollenberg, and Håvard Strand, "Armed Conflict 1946–2001: A New Dataset," *Journal of Peace Research* 39, No. 5 (September 2002): 615–37; Lotta Harboom and Peter Wallensteen, "Armed Conflict 1989–2006," *Journal of Peace Research* 44, No. 5 (September 2007): 623–34. The analysis uses data version 04-2009, which is available at: http://www.prio.no/CSCW/Datasets /Armed-Conflict/UCDP-PRIO/Armed-Conflicts-Version-X-2009/.

28. To facilitate comparisons and prevent duplicate counting, we aggregated the Uppsala data to the conflict level; any series of event that contained the same start date and conflict identifier were considered to be part of the same conflict.

29. Gilligan and Stedman, op. cit.; Virginia Page Fortna, *Does Peacekeeping Work? Shaping Belligerents' Choices after Civil Wars* (Princeton: Princeton University Press, 2008), 18–46.

30. For a similar sentiment, see Boutros-Ghali, *Supplement to "Agenda for Peace,"* op. cit.

31. Joakim Kreutz, "How and When Armed Conflicts End: Introducing the UCDP Conflict Termination Dataset," *Journal of Peace Research* 47, No. 2 (March 2010): 243–50.

32. Mary Kaldor, *New and Old Wars: Organized Violence in a Global Era* (Cambridge: Polity Press, [1999] 2007), 69–89.

33. Ghosn, et al., op. cit.

34. Note that because the frequency of cease-fires is relatively low and the two periods under examination differ in length, a marginal increase (from 9 to 11) across the two periods can produce a large change in the annualized figures.

35. Alan James, "The Congo Controversies," *International Peacekeeping* 1, No. 1 (Spring 1994): 44–58.

36. Janice Thompson, "State Sovereignty in International Relations: Bridging the Gap Between Theory and Empirical Research," *International Studies Quarterly* 39, No. 2 (1995): 213–33; Francis Deng, "Frontiers of Sovereignty: A Framework of Protection, Assistance, and Development for the Internally Displaced," *Leiden Journal of International Law* 8, No. 2 (Autumn 1995): 249–66; Saskia Sassen, *Losing Control: Sovereignty in an Age of Globalization* (New York: Columbia University Press, 1996), 1–32; Sohail Hashmi, ed., *State Sovereignty: Change and Persistence in International Relations* (University Park, PA: Penn State Press, 1997), 1–14 (*inter alia*).

37. For example, Pérez de Cuéllar was much more hesitant to intervene in such conflicts than Boutros-Ghali. See Pérez de Cuéllar, op. cit.; Boutros-Ghali, *Unvanquished*, op. cit., 30–64.

38. See Bruce Russett and John Oneal, *Triangulating Peace* (New York: W.W. Norton, 2001), 81–124 (especially figure 3.1).

39. Boutros-Ghali, *An Agenda for Peace*, op. cit.

40. Thomas Weiss, *Humanitarian Intervention: Ideas in Action* (Cambridge: Polity Press, 2007), 88–118; Christopher Joyner, "The Responsibility to Protect: Humanitarian Concern and Lawfulness of Armed Intervention," *Virginia Journal of International Law* 47, No. 3 (Spring 2007): 693–724.

41. Alex Bellamy, *Responsibility to Protect* (Cambridge: Polity Press, 2009), 1–34.

42. Peter Viggio Jakobsen, "National Interest, Humanitarianism or CNN: What Triggers UN Peace Enforcement after the Cold War?," *Journal of Peace Research* 33 (1996): 205–15.

43. Karns, op. cit.

44. Boutros-Ghali, *An Agenda for Peace* and *Supplement to "An Agenda for Peace,"* op. cit.

45. Boutros-Ghali, *Supplement to "An Agenda for Peace,"* op. cit., para. 10.

46. African Union, *OAU Charter* (Addis Ababa: Organization of African Unity, 1963); Ahmed Salim Salim, *Resolving Conflicts in Africa: Proposals for Action* (OAU Press and Information Series, 1, 1992), 17.

47. Ronald Hatto, "Les Interventions Militaires Après la Guerre Froide: Humanitarisme ou Néocolonialisme?," *Romanian Political Science Review* 6, No. 1 (2006): 9–22; Lebovic, op. cit.

48. Roland Paris, *At War's End: Building Peace after Civil Conflict* (Cambridge: Cambridge University Press, 2004), 40–54.

49. Andrea Talentino, "One Step Forward, One Step Back? The Development of Peacebuilding as Concept and Strategy," *Journal of Conflict Studies* 24, No. 2 (Winter 2004): 33–60; Martha Finnemore, *The Purpose of Intervention: Changing Beliefs about the Use of Force* (Ithaca, NY: Cornell University Press, 2003), 52–84.

50. Jakobsen, "The Transformation of United Nations Peace Operations in the 1990s," op. cit.

51. Karns, op. cit.

7

"The Responsibility to Protect": Humanitarian Concern and the Lawfulness of Armed Intervention

Christopher C. Joyner

During the twentieth century, at least 170 million deaths resulted from internal state conflicts, mostly by tyrannical regimes killing their own citizens. . . . These statistics indicating innocent people killed by their own governments are of such a magnitude that it is difficult to relate to or appreciate their meaning. In fact, it remains an irony of psychology that all too often it is easier to evoke pathos over the plight of a single individual's death than over the fate of many millions of victims. . . .

The puzzle is how best to legally reconcile respect for the preeminent principle of state sovereignty with the critical human rights necessity of protecting municipal populations from their own governments. What is the solution to this legal incongruity? The answer lies in the concept of the "responsibility to protect." The key is to rethink the fundamental meaning of sovereignty, which should be conceived as the preeminent requirement for the government of a state to exercise responsibility for, not merely control over, its actions. In addition, this responsibility must be motivated by the supreme duty of a government to protect its population, without a legal license to kill massive numbers of that population.

This article examines the legality of armed intervention by putting into context the role of governmental responsibility as it relates to national sovereignty. [The first part] examines the concept of humanitarian intervention and the criticism of its use as a legal rationale for international interference into another state's internal affairs. [The second part] deals with the UN Charter framework and sets out the legal premises on

Reprinted from *Virginia Journal of International Law*, vol. 47: 693–725. © 2007 by University of Virginia School of Law. Reprinted by permission of the publisher. Edited for length.

which contemporary international intervention may be permissible. [The third part] treats sovereignty as a legal principle that explicitly requires a state to exercise responsibility as an ingredient necessary for its governance to be considered legitimate. To this end, [the fourth part] identifies certain criteria that ought to be weighed in the event an international intervention to halt genocide or ethnic cleansing is contemplated. Finally, a number of reflections are proffered on how the growth of human rights law has impacted the evolution of the "responsibility to protect" as a norm, as well as the prospects for mobilizing international political will for converting moral rhetoric into legal opportunity.

Humanitarian Intervention

An important debate arose in the international legal community over the permissibility of outside actors using armed force to halt humanitarian atrocities. Primarily beginning in the 1970s and culminating in the 1990s, the dilemma of states employing armed intervention to halt such massacres was critically proclaimed and discussed.[1] Known as humanitarian intervention, the concept involved an armed intervention into another state, without the agreement of that state, to address the threat or actual infliction of grave and large-scale violations of fundamental human rights. The main question centered on whether it was ever lawful for a state or group of states to take military action against a sovereign state in order to protect that state's citizens from their government.

As a polemical legal issue, humanitarian intervention became the subject of increasingly acrimonious academic debate during the 1990s.[2] During this period, several government-instigated human rights atrocities spotlighted the killing fields and the failure, apathy, or incompetence of the international community to respond. There was the debacle of the United States–led armed intervention into and withdrawal from Somalia in 1993;[3] the pitifully inadequate international response to the horrific genocide of 800,000 Tutsis in Rwanda in 1994; the shameful unwillingness of UN peacekeeping forces to prevent the murderous ethnic cleansing of 7,000 to 8,000 Muslim men and boys in Srebrenica in Bosnia in July 1995; the ethnic cleansing in Kosovo of Kosovar Albanians, which left 700,000 persons displaced and thousands killed. [A] reprehensible genocide perpetrated in Darfur [left] perhaps as many as 400,000 persons dead and 2.5 million displaced. None of these cases was well handled, and the sense of acute failure to do anything compounded frustration over the capability and responsibility of the United Nations, when set against the impenetrable nature and limits of state sovereignty. Other cases involving large-scale human rights violence further aggravated that concern: the desperate plight of the Kurds in northern Iraq, and murderous civil strife in Liberia, Haiti, Sierra Leone, and East Timor. To be sure, intractable tensions between the exigent need to intervene militarily in horrendous human rights situations versus unimpeachable state sovereignty in all circumstances, made the issue of humanitarian intervention legally, politically, morally, and ethically contentious. Humanitarian intervention was deemed by many to be an impermissible assault on state sovereignty. If that indeed is the case, how can the United Nations or the international community successfully halt pervasively violent abuses of human rights and massive carnage? For any real policy to proceed, common sense must prevail to square this contradiction.

The fact is, however, that these conceptual questions are not new, and they require answers to determine what actions states are permitted to take when confronted with real or perceived attacks on their territory or against their own nationals, as authorized by the principle of self-defense as set out in Article 51 of the UN Charter or through the authority of the Security Council "to maintain international peace and security" under provisions in Chapter VII. While enormously important in international law, these questions remain distinct from the issues posed by the debate over the lawful permissibility of humanitarian intervention. Whereas the former pertain to conflicts between states, the latter is concerned with the justification for external actors intervening militarily into intrastate conflicts, an issue on which the UN Charter is conspicuously silent.

Most governments and jurists are reluctant to endorse unilateral humanitarian military intervention under modern international law because of the potential that powerful states will abuse such a doctrine. The history of humanitarian military intervention is replete with examples of powerful states or coalitions invoking a humanitarian doctrine to conceal their own geopolitical interests. In very few cases, if any, has the right to intervene for humanitarian purposes been declared under circumstances that were actually humanitarian, rather than motivated or driven by self-interest and power-seeking. To be sure, the doctrine of forcible intervention in the name of international justice usually gave rise to serious abuses, and was reserved for the most powerful states.

The UN Charter Framework

Under the UN Charter framework, three principal goals are proclaimed: the preservation of peace, the protection of human rights, and the promotion of self-determination. The Charter system, however, creates a tension between these goals, with peace upheld as predominant among them. "Justice"—the pursuit of human rights, self-determination, and other goals such as economic development and the correction of past wrongs—was to be sought, but not at the expense of "peace." Given the experience of two world wars, the framers of the Charter believed that force was too dangerous to be seen as a legitimate means of altering the political or territorial status quo. Under the Charter, other mechanisms were established to allow states the means to seek justice peacefully.

The cornerstone of the Charter framework for recourse to force is Article 2, paragraph 4. This Article provides that "[a]ll Members [of the United Nations] shall refrain in their international relations from the threat or use of force against the territorial integrity or political independence of any state, or in any other manner inconsistent with the Purposes of the United Nations." Article 2(4), therefore, constitutes a basic proscription on the use and even the threat of force that in some manner violates the territorial integrity or political independence of states, or that in some other way transgresses the purposes of the United Nations. In the Charter, there are only two explicit exceptions to this prohibition that are still applicable: (1) force undertaken in self-defense and (2) force authorized by the Security Council. First, under Article 51 of the Charter, states maintain "an inherent right of individual" and "collective self-defense if an armed attack occurs . . . until the Security Council has taken measures necessary to maintain international peace and security." Hence, if one state commits an armed attack against another state, the aggrieved state may use force to repel the attack until such time as the Security Council acts. Moreover, the victim state may call upon other states to assist it in collective self-defense. Second, under Article 39, the Security Council is empowered to determine if there is a "threat to the peace, breach of the peace, or act of aggression." If the Council so determines, it is permitted under Article 42 to authorize the use of military force against the offending state. Under Chapter VIII of the Charter, regional organizations are allowed to deal with "matters relating to the maintenance of international peace and security," but those organizations cannot undertake an "enforcement action" absent authorization by the Security Council.

Under UN Charter law, for armed force to be a permissible remedy for a humanitarian crisis, the Security Council must first determine under Chapter VII provisions that massive violations of human rights are occurring, or are about to occur. Additionally, it must then conclude that such an event actually constitutes a threat to international peace, and finally, it must authorize an enforcement action to prevent or halt those violations. In the absence of such Security Council consent, resort by other governments to military means for compelling a state not to perpetrate, or even not to tolerate, human rights atrocities within its territory would constitute a breach of Article 2(4) of the Charter. Accordingly, that situation would be considered unlawful. In addition, as long as that humanitarian crisis did not spill over national borders and give rise to armed attacks against other states, recourse to Article 51 as a justification would not be available.

Human rights law aims to promote and protect the dignity and worth of the human person. The UN Charter in fact makes promotion of human rights a fundamental purpose of the United Nations, and asserts so in the Charter's preamble. Articles 55 and 56 of the Charter obligate each UN member to "take joint and separate action" to ensure the "universal respect for, and observance of, human rights and fundamental freedoms." Thus a conflict arises in the UN Charter between the core objectives of ensuring human rights and preserving state sovereignty when a regime deprives its citizens of fundamental human rights. Vital questions are raised for diplomats and policymakers: Do certain acts, even if they are the most heinous crimes imaginable, remain within the sovereign prerogatives and jurisdiction of that state? Do they pose any actual military threat to world peace? If not, is the United Nations still empowered to act? But, what if the Security Council should opt, for whatever reason, not to act? Must tens of thousands or even millions of people die from violence, starvation, and disease for the sake of sovereignty? International legal commentators are divided on such key issues underlying the concept of humanitarian intervention. The focal problem is the legal principle of state sovereignty and the explicit command within it concerning nonintervention.

Rethinking Sovereignty as Responsibility

Since the mid-seventeenth century, sovereignty, supported by the prerogatives of authority and control, has underpinned the Westphalian system of international relations. It is said that sovereignty endows a government with the lawful capability to make authoritative decisions concerning the people and use of resources within the territory of its state. The traditional view is that international law empowers a sovereign state to exercise exclusive, absolute jurisdiction within its territorial borders, and that other states and multilateral actors have the corresponding duty not to interfere in a state's internal affairs. Since the end of the Second World War, gaining membership in the United Nations became viewed as symbolic attainment of independent sovereign statehood and lawful acceptance into the community of states. Moreover, the United Nations was deemed to be a world organization dedicated to maintaining interstate peace and security, as it functioned largely to protect the territorial integrity, political independence, and national sovereignty of its member states.

Over the past six decades, however, the character of the international system and its conflicts has changed. Whereas originally only fifty-one polities were members of the United Nations, the process of decolonization has produced [more than 190] today. Moreover, since 1945, a spate of new actors have entered the international scene and gained status as subjects under international law. Nonstate actors have proliferated on the international scene. Intergovernmental organizations, non-governmental organizations, multinational corporations, and even the individual person have all acquired recognized status under international law.[4] Relatedly, certain subnational groups—terrorists, crime syndicates, and narco-traffickers, *inter alia*—operate transnationally in carrying out their unlawful activities. Perhaps more significantly, no longer do armed conflicts primarily occur between states. The vast majority of armed conflicts today are internal wars—uncivil wars—that leave mainly innocent civilians, not soldiers, as casualties and victims. Thus, as new realities and challenges emerged since the end of the Second World War, so too have new expectations for action and new standards of behavior arisen in national and international relations.

As a concept, the responsibility to protect evolved from mere aspirations voiced by Secretary-General Kofi Annan to the status of a norm in process of becoming a legal principle. At the United Nations General Assembly in 1999, and again as a pillar of UN reform in his Millennium address in 2000, Secretary-General Annan made compelling appeals to the international community to find international consensus for resolving the dilemma of humanitarian intervention. In his 2000 address before the Millennium Summit, he tersely and soberly presented the question to the critics of humanitarian intervention: "[I]f humanitarian intervention is, indeed, an unacceptable assault on sovereignty, how should we respond to a Rwanda, to a Srebrenica—to gross and systematic violations of human rights that offend every precept of our common humanity?"[5] This question summed up the essential dilemma confounding the lawful permissibility of humanitarian intervention. . . .

Conceiving sovereignty in terms of governmental responsibility fosters certain implications. First, it suggests that state officials are responsible for policies that ensure the protection of their citizens and the promotion of their welfare.[6] Secondly, it implies that governments are obligated to their own nationals and to the international community. Third, sovereignty as responsibility means that government officials are responsible for their own policy decisions and are accountable for their own actions.

The rationale for conceiving sovereignty in terms of responsibility is increasingly being justified by the escalating influence that human rights norms exert as they are accepted as genuine components of human security. In this regard, the equation of sovereignty as governmental responsibility is increasingly being codified in international human rights instruments and recognized in state practice. Since 1948, the adoption of several salient international human rights instruments have established legal benchmarks for state conduct and erected the global legal regime that mandates national and international protection for and promotion of individual human rights.

No less important is that, during the last two decades, a salient shift occurred in thinking about security as a national concept. The traditional view held that security pertained preeminently to states, their borders, and their ability to protect themselves from external aggression. Today, the conceptualization of security has broadened considerably beyond the physical defense of states to include the welfare of their populations—their citizens' physical safety, socio-economic well-being, and safeguarding their basic human rights and freedoms. At the same time, it has become recognized that the basic elements of human security—the safety of people against threats to life, liberty, health, personal well-being, and human dignity—can be imperiled not only by external aggression, but also by circumstances and forces within a state, including actions by its military and police forces. Here again, emphasis is placed not so much on what governments are permitted to do under the guise of sovereignty, as what they are not permitted to do in carrying out legal responsibilities to their own people.

During the past six decades, disparities have widened between the presumed lawful conduct of sovereign states as defined in the UN Charter and actual state behavior in international relations as justified under the pretext of sovereign rights. It seems evident that the United Nations' founders never intended for the Charter to justify government officials possessing unrestrained power to do whatever they wanted to their own citizens. Rather, the Charter and UN practice both indicate that sovereignty entails a dual responsibility: On the one hand, sovereignty implies the duty to respect the sovereignty of other states and to refrain from interfering in their internal affairs. On the other hand, sovereignty summons the concomitant duty of the government to respect the fundamental rights of all peoples within the state and take action to protect them. The point here is clear. By construing sovereignty as a principle of state responsibility, relations between states can proceed with less conflict and greater cooperation. At the same time, however, the basic rights of persons within states can be guaranteed under internationally agreed upon legal standards.

Use of "responsibility to protect," instead of the more proverbial "right to intervene," furnishes greater worth to the humanitarian issues in question. It adds a positive, more humane context to what is clearly a terrifying situation inside a state. The puzzle here is how best to legally reconcile respect for the preeminent principle of state sovereignty with the critical human rights necessity of protecting municipal populations from their own governments. What must be done to fix this legal incongruity? The answer lies in the concept of the "responsibility to protect." The key is to rethink the fundamental meaning of sovereignty. The notion of sovereignty should be conceived as the preeminent need for the government of a state to exercise responsibility, not merely control over its actions. In addition, this responsibility must be motivated by the supreme duty of a government to protect its population without any alleged legal license to kill massively selected members within it. The Charter of the United Nations establishes international obligations for states in their international relations. Among these duties are to refrain from the threat or use of force, to settle disputes peacefully, to promote human rights and self-determination, to respect the sovereign equality of states, to respect the territorial sovereignty and political independence of states, and to conform with general principles of international law. There are other advantages as to why the term "responsibility to protect" should be heralded as a normative principle for guiding international behavior. For one, the responsibility to protect invites consideration of the issues from the perspective of those who urgently need help, as opposed to governments that might undertake a military intervention. "The responsibility to protect" casts international attention where concern should fall: on the obligation to protect people from mass murder, women from systematic rape, and children from starvation. For another, the responsibility to protect underscores the crucial role for the government concerned to assert the paramount duty to protect its citizens. If that government is unable or unwilling to perform that protective role, or if it itself is the perpetrator of massive human rights crimes, then the responsibility devolves to the international community to act in its place. Finally, the responsibility to protect is multidimensional, as it entails not merely a responsibility to react, but also the responsibilities to prevent and to rebuild. The responsibility to prevent means taking action to curtail internal discontent and the roots of violence that put populations at risk. This requires use of the toolbox of measures available, including political means, diplomatic initiatives, legal processes, economic strategies, and, if necessary, military force. Indeed, the single most important feature of the responsibility to protect is prevention. To prevent harm from occurring is to exercise the responsibility to protect against harm.

The responsibility to rebuild connotes reconstructing civil order in a state in the aftermath of an intervention. Reconstruction involves facilitating the recovery of a society from violent upheaval and the reconciliation of its people into a civil society. This means full assistance with recovery, reconstruction, and reconciliation after the military intervention. There must be genuine commitment to build both a durable peace and a society under legitimate authority, governed by the rule of law.

As might be expected, the most critical aspect of the responsibility to protect, as well as the most difficult to implement conceptually and politically, is the requisite responsibility to react. This means responding to situations of compelling human need with appropriate measures, including armed force, if necessary. At its core, the responsibility to protect inculcates the responsibility to take action in response to extreme situations in which there is a compelling need for protecting against threats to innocent persons. When preventive efforts fail to check or constrain internal violence and the government is unable or unwilling to remedy the state of affairs, then measures of coercive intercession by other members of the international community may be necessary. Such coercive means might involve the use of political, economic, or judicial remedies, and in extraordinary and extreme situations, they could necessitate the use of armed force. But herein lies a critical obstacle that must be overcome, namely what precisely entails an "extreme" case? What threshold must be reached for violations of human rights to trigger action that amounts to legitimate military intervention? What conditions are applicable for determining whether intervention should occur? Perhaps thorniest of all, who makes these determinations? Who retains the ultimate authority to decide whether, when, where, and how intervention involving deadly force on a possibly massive scale should proceed? The answers to these critical questions rest in the identification of criteria that must be considered in weighing a decision to intervene. To that end, six threshold criteria are suggested under the principle of the responsibility to protect. These criteria can be weighed and factored into the calculus for deciding whether to intervene militarily into a state. They are just cause, legitimate intention, last resort, proportionality, reasonable prospects, and legitimate authority.

The Threshold of Just Cause

Resort to the use of armed force must be taken only when the cause is just and when circumstances reach extreme conditions. Extreme conditions fall into two categories of internal situations. The first occurs when a massive loss of life, real or potential, with or without genocidal intent, results from either deliberate government action or the inability of the government to exercise the responsibility to protect its own citizens. The second involves a situation in which massive or "large-scale" ethnic cleansing is being or might be perpetrated, regardless of whether it is carried out by mass murder, forced depopulation, extensive evictions, premeditated acts of terror, or premeditated strategies of using rape pervasively as an instrument of war. While the adjectives "massive" or "large-scale" are used as qualifiers for determining the need for a military intervention, neither concept can be precisely quantified. Nor should they have to be. If the responsibility to protect is to have any legal credibility or political integrity, military action must be legitimized in anticipation of the onslaught of pervasive killings or ethnic cleansing in a society. Genuine protection demands the here and now. The international community does not have to wait until genocidal atrocities commence before initiating forceful action to stop them from occurring in a state.

It must be understood, however, that certain situations involving human rights deprivations are excluded from the just cause threshold because they fall short of being genocide or ethnic cleansing. Accordingly, such cases that would not justify military action for protection purposes include those earmarked by political oppression or methodical racial discrimination, the overthrow of a democratically elected government, or the rescue by a government of its own nationals in a foreign state. These latter circumstances do not attain the threshold of just cause.

The Threshold of Rightful Intention

The primary purpose motivating a "responsibility to protect" action must be to stop or prevent human suffering. That is, if military intervention is undertaken, the preeminent motivation for that action must be the clear and present protection of endangered persons.[7] This stipulation might seem reasonable enough, but it is difficult to gauge with compelling precision. In any event, intervention taken to protect must be carried out so as to ensure respect for the general rule of law and not to pursue the realization of any government's individual advantage. In effect, under the responsibility to protect, governments act as trustees and defenders of the law of humanity when that law is violated in some state. Intervening governments must not use the law to prosecute their own self-interested ends under the guise of humanitarian concerns.

A legacy of past large-scale atrocities can furnish a legitimate prerequisite for exercising preemptively the responsibility to protect. If the government of a state has a history of killing, torturing, or creating conditions of intolerable suffering for large numbers of its own citizens, then intervention taken under the responsibility to protect may be a viable prospect in the future. The right to life is a fundamental human right that civilized governments are supposed to protect through due process, not take away *en masse* through genocidal acts.

The Threshold of Last Resort

Before using force to execute the responsibility to protect, governments are legally bound to pursue all reasonable peaceful means available to resolve the situation. These means might include diplomatic protests, appeals to the UN Security Council, and even economic sanctions. Even so, the time available for resort to these peaceful means remains contingent upon the situation in the delict state. If human rights conditions worsen, or the threats to the security of persons in that state escalate, the lawful justification—and need—for military intervention will rise correspondingly. The prerequisite requirement to undertake peaceful means of dispute settlement dissipates as human rights conditions deteriorate in the offending state. It makes no sense to say that the search for means to restore domestic peace in a state must go forward while thousands of innocent persons in that state are killed. In such circumstances, the procedural search for conflict resolution must give way to the responsibility to protect potential victims through preemptive armed intervention. To do otherwise could prompt the perpetrators to start killing, and might instigate the slaughter of innocents on a massive scale.

In any event, clear and compelling evidence must indicate that gross and egregious violations of human rights involving the deaths of hundreds or even thousands of innocent people are actually going to occur in the territory of a sovereign state. The threat of these atrocities, which would amount to genocide or crimes against humanity, is made real either with the complicity or support of the governmental authorities, or because those authorities are unable or unwilling to prevent them. The bottom line is this: The responsibility to react with military force can only be justified if the responsibility to prevent through means of peaceful dispute settlement has been attempted to a reasonable degree of effort.

The Threshold of Proportionate Means

The magnitude, duration, and power of the military intervention used for human rights protection must be limited to the minimum level necessary to halt impending human rights violations. The intervening state or states must plan and carry out the military action carefully so as not to inflict more harm, death, or injury than is sought to be prevented. Generally, the authority structure of the offending state should not be overthrown, nor should the domestic political process of that state be permanently altered. If, however, the government of an offending state is responsible for planning or committing massive human rights abuses, it does so at the risk of being removed by an intervening humanitarian force, but only if necessary to halt the loss of life. An action undertaken on grounds of responsibility to protect must also be limited in duration to the time that is necessary to stop the atrocities from taking place or to halt their execution. Upholding the right to protect innocent persons cannot be a rationale for military occupation of some state, nor is it acceptable as a justification for annexation or integration of territory by another state.

The armed force taken should be used exclusively for the limited purpose of preventing or halting the atrocities and restoring respect for human rights. Such humanitarian coercion must be stopped as soon as the purpose of the intervention is secured. The use of force, moreover, must be proportionate to the threat that it seeks to address.

The critical point remains that human rights have evolved such that the rights of all people merit protection under international law. International law should be directed at protecting the sovereignty inherent in people, not merely the legal polity known as the state. That is, sovereignty resides in the citizens of the state, not in the government as sovereign, particularly when that government by commission or omission fails to halt brutal depredations of human rights, or is actually engaged in perpetrating them against its own citizens.[8] The bottom line here is this: If force is used consistently with other principles in the UN Charter without being directed against the territorial integrity or political independence of another state, it may well be held as commendable rather than condemnable under the UN Charter.

The Threshold of Reasonable Prospects for Success

Resort to military invention can only be legitimized if it has a realistic chance of successfully stopping or preventing large-scale atrocities or suffering. Armed intervention cannot be justified if actual protection cannot be achieved, or if the action appears likely to produce adverse consequences or suffering greater than if there were no intervention at all. Here is an important point: A military action taken for human protection should not be justified if in the process it touches off a more deadly conflict.

This observation obviously poses an inherently troublesome question relating to the Great Powers on the Security Council. Given their relative superior military might, an armed intervention into their territories would likely spark a major conflict, with little chance for ultimate success. Here again, the issue of double standards arises, as interventions might not be possible in every case where genuine reason exists to do so.

The Threshold of Legitimate Authority

When authorization is needed for human protection purposes, the first stop must be the UN Security Council. The United Nations was created to be the primary instrument for determining legitimate action and, accordingly, the link between authority and state recourse to force. Under the UN Charter framework, it is the Security Council that first and foremost bears responsibility for dealing with issues concerning the maintenance of international peace and security, including violently brutal anarchic situations within states. But what if the Security Council is unwilling or unable to take coercive action to prevent or halt massacres or massive human rights atrocities in some country? Such UN inaction could originate from disagreement among permanent members on the council, or from one of them casting a veto, or simply from that body opting to adopt a resolution condemning the situation and admonishing the state in question to refrain from any massive atrocities, rather than taking any effective preventive action aimed at stopping human rights atrocities. The decisive question then becomes, should this impasse be the last stop for the international community in its efforts to avert large-scale human carnage?

The answer must be a resounding no. The United Nations undoubtedly remains a vital institution for constructing, securing, and applying international legal authority. It was founded to provide a foundation for world order and international stability. It was to serve as the structure within which governments could negotiate legal agreements to resolve problems of global import, while establishing norms for the appropriate behavior of states that might foster peace and security, as opposed to conflict or confrontation. Thus the United Nations was viewed as the forum for mediating great power rivalries, for overseeing political adjustments within the international community, for promulgating new legal norms, and for bestowing the imprimatur of international legitimacy. In that regard, the authority of the United Nations rests not on any power of armed force, but rather on its ability to confer legitimacy on interstate actions.

Other legitimate options are available under the emerging norm of the responsibility to protect. For one, the United Nations General Assembly could convene in an Emergency Special Session under the "Uniting for Peace" procedure that furnished the legitimizing authority for operations in Korea (1950), Egypt (1956), and the Congo (1960). It seems likely that if serious efforts had been made by major powers to use the Uniting for Peace Resolution to deal with the situations in Rwanda (1994) and Kosovo (1998), the General Assembly may well have authorized emergency protective action. For another, there is the option to take action with regional organizations under Chapter VIII of the UN Charter, subject to their seeking authorization from the Security Council. Again, this alternative also is susceptible to being frustrated by political paralysis in the Security Council.

It is clear that armed interventions by a state, or even ad hoc coalitions of states, that are undertaken without the umbrella of legitimacy furnished by Security Council or General Assembly authorization are viewed as highly suspect by the international community.

Reflections

The Rise of Human Rights

A cardinal principle of contemporary international law is state sovereignty. The condition of sovereignty identifies the state as a legitimate actor entitled to protection under international law. Possession of sovereignty imbues the government of a state with supremacy over its territory and independence in international relations. In principle, however, such independence is neither absolute nor unlimited.

In light of recent developments, there is clearly a fundamental tension between the concept of state sovereignty and the concern for human rights. If intervention is permitted by any and all states to protect human rights in some other state, then an invitation is issued for widespread abuse of military intervention and disruption of international stability. On the other hand, if a flat prohibition is placed on the use of any forcible intervention under any circumstances, including genocide, massacres, pervasive torture, or other human rights atrocities, then the principle of nonintervention takes on an immoral character. An international law founded to promote justice for all peoples is sacrificed on the altar of national sovereignty by the principle of nonintervention. . . .

[A] new understanding of the principle of nonintervention surfaces when a government obligates itself through international agreements to protect human rights conditions within its territory. The legal scope of these agreements effectively removes human rights from being a matter exclusively within the domestic jurisdiction of a state, and converts them to a matter of concern to the international community. Accordingly, the principle of nonintervention into the internal affairs of states cannot be used as a protective shield behind which human rights can be massively and systematically violated with impunity. . . .

When certain actions by a state's government offend the very conscience of civil society, then the legitimacy of that government must be called into question. A legitimate government undertakes legitimate acts for legitimate purposes. But a government that is unable to perform legitimate acts, or undertakes illegitimate action as premeditated policies, or fails to protect fundamental human rights to which all people are entitled under international law, can be said to lose some part of its legitimacy in the eyes of international law. Thus, it is not unreasonable to expect that remedial measures should be possible by other states, or the international community, to redress what are obviously gross, large-scale violations perpetrated by a government on its citizens. Intervention should be permissible by a state or group of states to redress the illegitimate situation of massive human suffering at the hands of some government.

If the "responsibility to protect" does emerge full-fledged as an accepted norm of international law, it will generate a revolution in consciousness in international relations. The essential leitmotif of the responsibility to protect maintains this: Each individual state has the responsibility to protect its populations from genocide, war crimes, ethnic cleansing, and crimes against humanity. The responsibility to protect starts before the carnage begins. If this responsibility is to be fulfilled, a government must strive to prevent such crimes from occurring through proper and necessary means. If a government fails in its duty to exercise this fundamental responsibility to protect its citizens, either through its inability to act or through malicious intentions, then that government forfeits any entitlement to sovereignty that might prohibit other states from intervening into its internal affairs to stop the bloodshed. The responsibility to protect demands the capacity and willingness of a government to do just that: protect the people in its state. If that government fails in this critical duty, the international community becomes empowered and is permitted to exercise protection by military intervention for humanitarian purposes.

The moral principle of the responsibility to protect applies to all governments and is unmistakable: Mass murder and other gross violations of human rights will not be tolerated within a government's borders. As the sovereign power, it is a government's responsibility to maintain internal law and order and to prevent or stop genocide and crimes against humanity from occurring. If a government cannot carry out this protection on its own, the international community will assist it. If, however, a government is the problem and it is unable or unwilling to act, then the international community, either through the United Nations or as individual states, must be prepared to take action by whatever means, including use of armed force, to halt the atrocities.

Mobilizing Political Will

There is a compelling need to mobilize action to rescue populations who are at risk of slaughter, ethnic cleansing, genocide, and starvation. The governments of sovereign states have the responsibility to protect their own people from harm, and if they are not able or willing to do so, the international community must exercise that responsibility. If a government fails to uphold its responsibility to protect its own people from harm, then coercive international action for human protection purposes, including use of armed force, might be warranted.

But there is need to reconcile the principle of shared responsibility with that of nonintervention. Intervention gains the greatest legitimacy if authorized by the UN Security Council and carried out as the collective responsibility of several states. All too often in the past, however, when confronted with situations of grave humanitarian concern, the Security Council failed to respond in a timely, authoritative manner. Moreover, even when the Security Council did act, there was no guarantee of an operational response or that action would be taken effectively.

The key question remains how to get the necessary political commitment to halt the atrocities. How can sufficient political will be mustered by governments to act when action is necessary to ensure human protection?

Essential for marshalling international collaboration is the need to assemble domestic support. How popular opinion in a state reacts to a government's decision to employ armed force abroad, along with the anticipated costs in human lives and financial resources, remain central considerations in international decision-making. In this regard, various contextual factors, such as military capability, geography, and the nature of political institutions come into play. Some states are more internationalist than others and will respond more readily to pleas for multilateral cooperation. Middle powers and small powers tend to be more interested in multilateralism than Great Powers.

Much also depends upon the quality of leadership among decision makers and organizations in states and how appeals for humanitarian action are made. Three types of appeal seem relevant here. First, there is the public appeal on moral grounds. Moral appeals argue that averting or halting human suffering and the catastrophic losses concomitant with mass slaughter, ethnic cleansing, and genocidal atrocities provides inspiring and legitimizing motives to take action. Common decency and compassion within domestic constituencies can move leaders to commit to participate in human protection actions. To get a moral motive to stick, however, entails having the ability to convey a situation's urgency and its exceedingly grave threat to human life. That is not always easy to do. Second, there is also a financial appeal, that is, earlier action is always cheaper than action later. Prevention is obviously the most preferred option, since it alleviates the need to respond through military action, humanitarian relief assistance, and post-conflict reconstruction of the society. A third compelling appeal is that of the national interests of states. Clearly, neighboring states could be profoundly affected by refugee outflows, and regional security will likely be destabilized by spillovers from the chaos and anarchy in an afflicted state.

International political will entails more than merely the aggregate of attitudes and policies of each state. There are also interactions of diplomats and governmental representatives in intergovernmental organizations. The Secretary-General must play a crucial role in mobilizing international support for an intervention, as well as in constructing multilateral coalitions that might take military action. Similarly, the media can have great impact on public opinion by reporting and showing real world suffering. The so-called "CNN effect" can be compelling and contagious, although it can be unbalanced in how it depicts various crises, as well as push decision-makers into taking action before serious operational planning and analysis of consequences are complete.

What else might be done? For one, the General Assembly should consider and adopt a draft declaration embodying the fundamental principles of the right to protect, highlighting that: sovereignty means responsibility; the international community of states has the responsibility to protect human life when governments are not able to do so; certain thresholds must be met before military force is used to protect human life; and certain "precautionary principles" must be observed when military intervention is undertaken for human protection purposes.

Another strategy might have the Security Council consider and adopt a set of guidelines that detail the chief principles or "rules of engagement" that must govern responses when military intervention is done to protect human life. Moreover, there should be an agreement among the five permanent members of the UN Security Council not to use their veto power in matters where their vital interests are not at stake. Such a veto would obstruct passage of resolutions authorizing the use of military force for the purposes of human protection; it would do little or nothing to serve the interests of the vetoing power. In fact, some permanent members might oppose UN intervention on general principles, or feel such intervention might jeopardize economic or political ties with the offending government. Reaching such an understanding would not be easy to do politically, but if accomplished, it would add tremendous symbolic weight to the credibility of the responsibility to protect within the international community. . . .

Notes

1. Philip C. Jessup, 1948, *A Modern Law of Nations*, Macmillan, pp. 172–74; Ian Brownlie, 1974, "Humanitarian Intervention," in John N. Moore (ed.), *Law and Civil War in the Modern World*, Johns Hopkins Press, pp. 217; Ian Brownlie, 1989, "The Principle of Non-Use of Force in Contemporary International Law," in W.E. Butler (ed.), *The Non-Use of Force in International Law*, Martinis Nijhoff Publishers, p. 17; Richard Lillich, 1980, "Forcible Self Help Under International Law," in Richard Lillich and John N. Moore (eds.), *Readings in International Law From the Naval War College Review*, pp. 133–38.

2. Fernando Teson, 1997, *Humanitarian Intervention: An Inquiry Into Law and Morality*, Martinis Nijhoff Publishers.

3. Sean D. Murphy, 1996, *Humanitarian Intervention: The United Nations in an Evolving World Order*, University of Pennsylvania Press, pp. 202–12; Oliver Ramsbotham and Tom Woodhouse, 1991, *Humanitarian Intervention in Contemporary Conflict: A Reconceptualization*, Polity Press, pp. 33–65; Daphne Richemond, 2003, "Normativity in International Law: The Case of Unilateral Humanitarian Intervention," *Yale Human Rights & Development Law Journal*, Vol. 45, pp. 48–49.

4. Christopher C. Joyner, 2005, *International Law in the 21st Century: Rules for Global Governance*, Rowman and Littlefield, pp. 24–28. Among transnational actors in 2006, there are at least 6,400 intergovernmental organizations, 44,000 international nongovernmental organizations, 500,000 multinational corporations and foreign affiliates, and 6.4 billion persons.

5. Kofi Annan, 2000, "'We the Peoples': The Role of the United Nations in the 21st Century," U.N. Sales E.00.1.16, available at http://www.un.org/millennium/sg/report/full.htm.

6. International Commission on Intervention and State Sovereignty, 2001, *The Responsibility to Protect: Report of the International Commission on Intervention and State Sovereignty*, available at http://www.iciss.ca/report-en.asp.

7. Michael J. Bazyler, 1987, "Reexamining the Doctrine of Humanitarian Intervention in Light of the Atrocities in Kampuchea and Ethiopia," *Stanford Journal of International Law*, pp. 601–602.

8. W. Michael Reisman, 1990, "Sovereignty and Human Rights in Contemporary International Law," *American Journal of International Law*, p. 869.

8

Targeting the Right Targets?
The UN Use of Individual Sanctions

Peter Wallensteen and Helena Grusell

The Rise of Smart Sanctions

Economic sanctions constitute one of the main tools for the United Nations to react to international crises. It is mentioned in the Charter under Chapter VII. Therefore it is important to analyze the operations of sanctions, most recently in the form of the targeting of particular individuals. In this article we build on a unique inventory of the close to 450 individuals who have been targeted by the UN, in the first decade of the twenty-first century, in nonterrorist cases of sanctions. We analyze the individuals with respect to their closeness to power and, thus, their ability to effect the changes the UN demands. Hence, this is a study of compliance to UN sanctions.

The UN Security Council is the prime organ with a responsibility for international peace and security. In theory, when the Council acts, there is general agreement among the major powers and there is considerable political will behind its actions—an application of global power. In practice, many decisions are compromises, which may affect the design and implementation of the Council's measures. In this article, we study one such policy option pursued by this collectivity: the sanctioning of individuals to achieve member state compliance with the Council's decisions.

In the late 1990s the Security Council started the practice of targeted sanctions, which meant dealing with particular commodities (e.g., diamonds, minerals, or oil), arms, aviation, and particular individuals when imposing sanctions. Previously, the focus had been on entire

Reprinted from *Global Governance*, vol. 18, no. 2: 207–230. © 2012 by Lynne Rienner Publishers. Reprinted by permission of the publisher. Edited for length.

countries. This approach ran into humanitarian trepidations, which were much discussed in the case of the sanctions on Iraq. The chief concern was the possible adverse impact that comprehensive sanctions could have on the most vulnerable segments of the populations.[1] The targeting of individuals took on a new dimension when confronting international terrorism. This was seen as action by small groups and, thus, diffusely targeted sanctions would not get the intended compliance. To target the actual or potential culprits seemed to be a valid form of action. If coupled to bans that prevent the target's sale of some commodities or purchase of some others (e.g., arms), this could be a more effective tool without negative consequences for bystanders or outsiders. Quickly, such UN sanctions were labeled "smart sanctions." The European Union, African Union, and individual countries have since embarked on a similar policy. Today, targeted sanctions against individuals, particular commodities, and arms embargoes are the only types of sanctions used by these international organizations and by governments. The Council has acted to preserve the legitimacy of the sanctions measure. An effect is that sanctions debates have focused less on the humanitarian impact and more on the human rights of the targeted individuals.[2] It is time to take stock of this development and go back to the original ideas: how smart are the smart sanctions?

The idea of targeting sanctions at individuals not only was an innovative way for making sanctions legitimate in the international system. It also was in line with a global development of giving accountability a stronger role in international affairs. It was morally appealing to demonstrate that decisionmakers were not personally exempt from the impact and reactions that their policies were causing. Thus, the idea of freezing financial assets for such individuals and preventing them from international travel was attractive. It was expected to lead to a change of policy and behavior in the direction desired by the senders (compliance). In this article, we consider whether these were realistic expectations or if there is a need for further reform of the sanctions instrument.

A debate on the human rights of the listed individuals has questioned the UN procedures and tarnished the image of the "smartness" of this type of sanctions. Clarity of the reasons for listing (and delisting) was seen as a matter of human rights of the listed individual and a question of the effectiveness of the sanctions tool. Without knowing the reasons for the sanction, it is difficult for the listed individual to change his or her behavior. Clarity also makes it easier to monitor the individuals' actions—to know when they in fact comply with the sanction and when they can be delisted. The reforms in the practices of the Security Council taken in Resolution 1904 of 17 December 2009 was a response to this, and it remains to be seen whether these measures are sufficient. For instance, the office of the ombudsperson was created to ensure the human rights of a listed individual. The officer is to receive requests for delisting, evaluate and consider them, and serve as a link between the individual, the state, and the UN.[3] These measures may have resulted in fewer names being listed because the reason for each listing has to be specified. This, furthermore, will make it easier to follow the individuals and their behavior because the monitoring teams now know what behavior to evaluate. These measures would serve to improve fairness and credibility of the UN procedures.[4] It remains, however, to be considered whether the measures also achieve desired compliance.

Thus, we evaluated whether the sanctions are aimed at individuals that can change government policy and, then, to what extent that takes place. We did this by first developing the theory of targeted sanctions and then conducting an empirical study of targeted individuals based on open sources. We protected the listed persons' identities in this work, unless such information was already in the public domain. We scrutinized reports of compliance and violations of the sanctions to evaluate the implementation of the actions. This empirical analysis, then, applies a typology of the closeness of the individuals to the powers that be in the targeted country. In other words, is the targeted individual really in a position to affect the policies pursued? Finally, we provide conclusions for sanctions research and sanctions policy.

The Theory of Targeting Individuals

The literature on sanctions draws on practical experience, but there is relevant research (e.g., in social psychology) that should also be part of the discourse. Going to the public policy debate, there are many different logical expectations of what individually targeted sanctions may accomplish. In the context of counterterrorism, it is assumed that the freezing of assets may prevent new terrorist attacks, as it deprives the individuals from nonstate organizations that survive without taxation possibilities or access to other important resources. However, if the purpose is to stop a civil war, change a regime, or change basic security policies of a country, the argument has to be different. In these cases, assets held by the individual are not essential for governments or the organization. The expectation is instead that the exposure to sanctions makes the individual an advocate for a change of policy. Targeting a particular individual is a way to get him or her to act in consonance with the sanctions initiator (the sender) and contribute to change in the ultimate target (the recalcitrant government or organization). We have organized the seven predicted effects or types of outcomes that we found under three main labels (see Table 8.1). The outcomes can be seen as steps on a ladder beginning with small incentives for improved behavior culminating in threats of or actual escalation. This will be the basis for our assessment of the present practice of targeting international sanctions.

Table 8.1 demonstrates that there are many and varied expectations when senders impose sanctions. To some extent, they may be formulated into a coherent targeting policy. If the sender (the UN in our case) is pursuing theories belonging to categories 1, 2, and 3 the idea is that sanctions will be removed once behavior has changed. This is an instrumental use of sanctions. In such a case, the sanctions may result in direct or indirect negotiations between the sender and the ultimate target (the government or the organization to which the targeted individual belongs).

Table 8.1 Types of Logically Expected Effects of Individually Targeted Sanctions

---

Initiate bargaining for compliance

1. The sanctions give individuals a personal stake in making their country or government comply with particular international demands.
2. The sanctions deter the individuals from deciding on or supporting policies that would make a particular situation more complicated (e.g., prevent escalation).
3. The sanctions make targeted individuals interested in negotiating a way out of a particular predicament, thus resulting, for instance, in peace talks and peace agreements.

Deprive resources from the target (shift balance of power)

4. The sanctions make it impossible for the actor to carry out activities, either immediately (not pursue war as there are no arms deliveries) or for the future (not be able to travel to set up a plot).
5. The sanctions are a punishment for past lack of compliance by the targeted individuals, or for the policies they were pursuing or supporting in place of other forms of accountability for their actions. For instance, not being able to consume luxury goods and send children to expensive schools abroad is expected to affect the private conditions of sanctioned individuals.

Threaten potential target (sanctions escalation)

6. Sanctions on some individuals signal to others still not listed, thus making them willing to comply (in line with points 1, 2, or 3) rather than becoming exposed to these measures.
7. Sanctions are a step on a ladder leading to other, more coercive actions against the government and the state, constituting larger threats to the survival of the incumbent regime.

Furthermore, to the sender there is also a fallback position. If there is no change, sanctions may still have type 4 and type 5 ambitions. They are a way of increasing pressure on the target. The same is true, explicitly or implicitly, for type 6 and 7 goals. If even more hardship is threatened or actually implemented, the target will comply. This could amount to a unified theory behind targeting individuals. The personal conditions in which the targets find themselves would give them particular incentives to change behavior and also influence others to do the same. However, as we show below, this is not necessarily the way these sanctions are applied.

Unfortunately, a review of literature from social psychology, criminology, and law complicates the picture.[5] There are many rational and emotional reasons for why decisionmakers still may not change policy. They may even turn the imposed measures into their advantage.[6] The literature lists a number of factors that speak against compliance. To these factors belongs the significance of the sender to the target (the less important, the less reason to change). Legitimacy is a measure of such a connection. Peter Verboon and Marius van Dijke argue that authorities enacting sanctions in a fair manner are considered more legitimate in communicating what is morally acceptable. Tom R. Tyler also argues that a sense of obligation increases effectiveness.[7]

The first three ways in which sanctions work draw on such psychological insights. The sanctions are seen as an appeal to common understanding and, thus, would result in negotiations. However, if this communality does not exist, there will be no compliance.

Douglas D. Heckathorn points to the (lack of) clarity of the purpose with the sanctions, which means that the target does not know what to respond to. Effectiveness is also reduced if considerable time has lapsed between the deplorable behavior, the sanctions decision, and imposition of sanctions. The severity of the measures for the individual and his or her family will affect the individual's motives and will to resist. There is also a degree of calculation of what compliance will mean and what can be achieved without complying. These are considerations that influence how an individual reacts when exposed to external pressure, and the same factors are likely to have an impact on the efficacy of the sanctions in achieving the outcome desired by the sender.[8] The second and third categories of sanctions impacts actually point to sanctions as coercive and punitive instruments rather than inducements for change. The sender tries deliberately to eliminate the target's resources for continued political existence.

By listing these conditions, we make clear that there is not likely to be a straightforward connection between imposing sanctions and recording compliance. The Security Council may, in fact, be unclear about its aims and not pursue the actions as eagerly as might be expected or necessary. On the targeted side, the individuals will have incentives to find ways in which to compensate themselves from the impact of the sanctions by circumventing the measures and building counter-alliances, domestically and internationally. The hardships that follow may even be turned into marks of honor, demonstrating solidarity, patriotism, and loyalty with the established course of action. Furthermore, the lower an individual is placed in the hierarchy of decisionmaking of the targeted country, the fewer opportunities there will be for an individual to actually influence the course of action that the sanctions aim at changing. The individual may not even be able to change the operations in which he or she participates (e.g., in a nuclear production facility) other than possibly delaying action or making errors that will be hard to notice on the outside and rather risk their employment. In other words, there are compelling reasons to hypothesize that the sanctions will lead to changes in behavior only under very specific conditions. Such conditions may relate only partly to the seven types of expected outcomes.

The scholarly literature is limited with respect to the impact of sanctions on particular individuals. A first work was Erica Cosgrove's 2005 interview study of two individuals listed for a travel ban under the Liberia sanctions in 2001.[9] She reports that one of the individuals felt this to be a stigmatization, but it did not influence his view of the conflict. The second individual, a cabinet minister at the time, did not see the sanctions as targeted on him specifically but on the government as a whole. Thus, the sanctions did not change his view either. Interestingly he studied the UN sanctions reports on violations, which revealed to him what President Charles Taylor was doing with the resources. This made him question whether the president could perform properly. The minister managed to escape abroad and then could resign. New information, in other words, may have a stronger impact on a person than a particular targeted measure. He chose this dramatic course of action because he felt he could not influence Taylor's policies. Still, the sanctions are likely to have affected these two individuals: they were aware of the measures and they seem to have tried to handle their dilemma on a personal level (e.g., by escaping) rather than in a political way.

Following Cosgrove, other authors have conducted interviews with targeted individuals, for instance, in Western Africa and Zimbabwe.[10] Sometimes these individuals have also gone public with their situation, such as Jewel Taylor, a former wife of Charles Taylor, who has described some of the effects in detail and has repeatedly stated that the sanctions imposed on her should be lifted.[11] However, the individual sanctions also have humanitarian exemptions so that the individual should not experience crippling personal effects. Too punitive measures might generate public sympathy.

A number of court cases have arisen from the listing of individuals based on the protection of the human rights of these individuals. These cases give little guidance, however, on the impact of sanctions on individuals, apart from testimony to their personal plight. Also, leaders have been brought to courts, for example, when accused of war crimes. The Special Court for Sierra Leone is presently trying the former president of Liberia, but the sanctions are not important in this connection.[12]

Given the paucity of ideas for the conditions under which individuals may comply, we embarked on an empirical investigation. At present the number of individuals listed is large, the names are openly available, and it is possible to pursue a systematic study. In this project, we reported on eight UN sanctions active in the ten-year period from 2000 to 2009. We traced the individuals listed for the eight cases in open sources in order to find observations on their compliance with the sanction measures (travel bans and frozen assets) and their change of political behavior in the direction demanded by the UN. In particular, we were interested in their ability to actually change the direction of a government's policy in the country (i.e., their closeness to the ultimate decision-making). As is obvious from the sanctions theory shown in Table 8.1, the targeted individuals are expected to be able to exert influence. However, as Cosgrove found, even cabinet ministers can have little power over the decisions that result in the imposition of sanctions.[13] We first review the eight cases.

Eight Cases of UN Sanctions

The dataset includes all cases and all persons listed for a travel ban or assets freeze by the UN under Chapter VII in the ten-year period from 1 January 2000 to 31 December 2009 with the exception of the cases that concerned terrorist actions. Thus, the dataset has information on eight countries. As of this writing, in only one case (Angola 2002) has the sanctions measure been fully lifted. The total number of persons listed (446) and the type of sanctions to which they are subject are shown in Table 8.2. (Many individuals from Liberia and Sierra Leone have now been removed by the UN, often without any specific reason given; in other cases, because of death.)

Table 8.2 UN Nonterrorist Sanctions

Country	Sanction		
	Individuals	Travel Ban	Assets Freeze
Angola (UNITA)	166	166	166
Côte d'Ivoire	3	3	3
Democratic Republic of Congo	20	20	20
Iran	39	39	39
Liberia	152	152	29
North Korea (DPRK)	5	5	5
Sierra Leone	57	57	57
Sudan	4	4	4
Total	446	446	323

Sources: Compiled by the authors from UN Security Council Sanction Committees' annual reports, reports of the panel of experts, and press releases, www.un.org/sc/committees /751/pdf/1844_cons_list_12Apr10.pdf.

Notes: Total number of individuals listed. Travel bans and assets freeze measures, 1 January 2000 to 31 December 2009. Countries in alphabetical order.

There is a threat of sanctions in connection with the investigation of the assassination of former Lebanese prime minister Rafic Hariri in 2005, but no individuals have been listed as of this writing. In December 2009, sanctions were also imposed on Eritrea, where one organization and eight individuals were listed in April 2010, too late to be included in this study.

The dataset includes events describing listed individuals' behavior of evasion or compliance in relation to the sanction measure. For instance, we recorded if an individual continued the sanctioned activity (evasion) or changed the sanctioned behavior in a positive way such as being engaged in a peace process or handing in weapons (compliance). Also we recorded public statements such as whether the listed person denied all reasons for the listing (evasion) or admitted that the listing did change his or her behavior (compliance). For each listed individual, we searched for information in open data sources and databases, such as Dow Jones Factiva and in annual reports of the various Security Council Sanctions Committees, reports from panels of experts, and press releases. We also collected reasons for listing and delisting. We found most of the information in the material from the Security Council. For some key persons on whom several events were reported in the first search round, we carried out a second search in the Factiva database to get deeper into the specific case. We also conducted interviews with some key persons in their respective home countries, notably Liberia and Côte d'Ivoire.[14]

We now present descriptive information from the dataset. Mostly the sanctions measures aim at preventing travel of the individuals. This has been more common than the freezing of assets held by the individuals (Table 8.2). All the targeted countries are classified as developing countries, which means that most of the population depends on agriculture and not on international connections. This means that the travel bans hit at typical elite resources. For most of the countries, the leaders are likely to benefit from exportable resources and therefore need to be able to travel to make trade agreements or personal economic arrangements. Thus, reduction in the ability to travel may have particularly severe repercussions that may induce compliance or negotiations with the sender.

The travel bans and asset freezes may have some merits as separate actions. Preventing travel means limiting interactions and thus reduces private information sharing (e.g., because phone lines may be monitored). On the whole, however, travel bans and asset freezes have been used simultaneously and probably with a supporting argument. The travel ban prevents a targeted person from physically entering the banks, financial institutions, or other locations holding his or her assets if they are outside the country. Not having access to these assets makes the person willing to comply, according to one of the expected effects presented in Table 8.1. Furthermore, without direct access to one's assets, travel is more difficult. Theoretically, the individual is boxed in and the sanction measures reinforce each other. Seeing no way out, compliance follows according to the logic of type 1. This logic can be questioned: in today's world of instant communication financial resources can be moved without travel, making it necessary to have an independent argument for travel bans. Also, the country of residence for this individual may not apply the sanctions, which, for instance, has been the case of Liberia. This means individuals may have access to local banks. Lately, nationally owned banks have also been listed under UN sanctions, notably in the cases of nuclear [proliferation] (Iran and North Korea).

This leads us to a first conclusion: given this financial mobility, it might now be necessary for the Security Council to explain the use of the travel ban. For example, it might be argued that it is the measure felt most strongly for the individual. He or she may be able to borrow money, but not easily disguise himself or herself. The travel ban may give the most personal discomfort of these measures.

This suggests that the travel ban has not been a measure to prevent listed persons from accessing funds. Rather, it has been a way of preventing them from continuing their luxury lifestyles. To travel to Europe, Asia, and the United States for children's schooling, for nonurgent medical treatments, and for luxury shopping has a value in itself. It is seen as evidence of social success and political legitimacy, particularly in an African context. This argument has support in social psychology. Social motivations have to do with earning approval and respect from significant persons with whom the target interacts.[15] By depriving (or at least complicating) this behavior, the travel ban accomplishes the type 5 effects that we describe in Table 8.1. It is not likely to be something that is revealed in interviews, and was not mentioned by any of our interviewees. More likely the targeted individuals mention hardships that generate human sympathy (e.g., medical concerns).

The travel ban imposed against Liberians under Security Council Resolution 1342 (2001) was originally recommended by the Panel of Experts on Sierra Leone. The recommendation was that the travel ban should be in effect until Liberia's support to the Revolutionary United Front and Liberia's violation of other UN sanctions ended conclusively.[16] Thus it was imposed in a bargaining mood, notably according to the types 1–3 ambitions in Table 8.1. However, only gradually were these sanctions removed and by mid-2010, forty-five individuals were still listed for travel ban and twenty-two for asset freeze.

The first listings were clearly done in a somewhat haphazard way. The theory of targeting was poorly developed at the time. This type of unpredictability is one of the critical concerns that have been raised. Many individuals did not know why they had been listed, what they could do about it, and how they could be delisted.[17] Needless to say, this does not reinforce a willingness to comply with the sanctions. On all these points, however, the sanctions have been gradually improved; in particular, the reforms of December 2009 have strengthened the transparency of this measure, even creating a position as an ombudsman for complaints. This clearly enhances the legitimacy of this measure.

The data in Table 8.2 actually present a downward trend over time in listing of individuals. The large numbers are from the early cases of targeted sanctions (Angola, Liberia, Sierra Leone), with more than fifty names listed for each of the cases. Later sanctions do not have lists anywhere near as close. This appears to reflect a change in the Council's approach. The extensive listing in the earlier cases implied considerable enthusiasm for this measure. Later, however, human rights concerns emerged, no doubt impacting on the entire listing procedure. Also, there were new arguments favoring lower numbers. In the case of Côte d'Ivoire, the group of experts reported in October 2006 that the sanctions had a calming effect and that the targeting of a few individuals with clear criteria was an effective tool for the UN. It also said it would be counterproductive to target more individuals, particularly if there was no effective monitoring system in place.[18] Monitoring of a few persons is obviously easier than dealing with a large number. The present practice of naming only a few individuals means there is an awareness of the complications of large lists, but it may also leave open the addition of new names, thus implying a threat of escalation according to impact types 6 and 7.

This leads, however, to a new question. How many should be targeted for the sanctions to achieve desired political change? The different expectations listed in Table 8.1 do not give clear guidance. The idea of gradually escalating sanctions, according to categories 6 and 7, would suggest sanctions should start with a few, thus generating fear among others. A gradual increasing of the number of individuals would thus be a signal to the target that the sanctions are tightening and getting more teeth. To avoid being targeted, the argument goes, the potentially targeted individuals would be willing to comply, thereby also getting their compatriots off the list.

In addition, one may argue in social psychological terms that, if an entire group is targeted (i.e., a large number of individuals), the effect is likely to be that they all unite in opposition against the sender. It may have the same effect as comprehensive sanctions: stimulating an attitude of "we are all in this together." A stronger differentiation by focusing on some well-identified individuals would then have—at least potentially—a greater chance of achieving political change.

However, in the interviews we conducted in Côte d'Ivoire in 2006, the sanctions against only three persons—seen as fairly peripheral in political power, although they had violated the UN resolution—threatened the credibility of the sanctions. The measure appeared not to be as dangerous as first believed, centrally placed informants said, also describing them as hitting "small fish."[19] The sanctions, which initially seemed tough and dangerous to leading persons, turned out to be targeted at others than those actually responsible for the policies pursued. Furthermore, as the idea of gradually enlarging the group—following the dynamics of types 6 and 7 in Table 8.1—did not gain support in the UN, the individual sanctions were no longer seen as threatening. The three remained the only ones listed up to the end of the period studied.[20] The targeted sanctions lost credibility in this case. As there were other measures in place parallel to the sanctions, international actions still had some clout (e.g., peacekeeping, arms embargo, mediation).[21] Ineffective actions affect the standing of an international organization, such as the UN and European Union, not just the credibility of the particular measure.

We cannot prove it with available information, but it is also likely that bigger fish will still learn something from the sanctions on citizens of the country. They are likely to take precautions, notably moving assets out of reach or hiding them in less identifiable forms (e.g., nominally turning over bank accounts or real estate to relatives, turning assets into other resources). Thus, rather than complying, leading targets may take the threat of sanctions seriously and act to undo the sanctions before they even have been brought into place. This means that the threat of gradually escalating the sanctions may backfire and, thus, make targeted sanctions less able to succeed. The dynamics of type 6 become less likely.

We pose this as a second conclusion: the Council may use targeting as a gradual process, where a few are listed first and, with a lack of compliance, new individuals are added to the list. However, it is possible that sanctions will work as an early warning signal, for instance, giving reasons and time for other actors to move or cover their assets. Thus, this policy may be most effective if initiated at the top, rather than lower in the hierarchy. Perhaps a strategy of targeting big fish would be more in line with both sanctions theory (as outlined in Table 8.1) and with reality. We look at this strategy more systematically in the following section.

Closeness to Power

The sanction theories suggest that sanctions on those that make the final decisions should be the most effective. Thus, we need to identify the relationship of the listed persons to such ultimate decisionmakers or whether the listed persons actually *are* such decisionmakers.

The targeted persons can be categorized with respect to their closeness to policymaking. This is a way to gauge if they have power and influence in the society. Those responsible could be expected to have different reaction patterns than those without much influence on the policies chosen. The theory of targeted sanctions assumes that leadership is a key issue. Attempting such a differentiation, we developed four target categories with respect to closeness to ultimate decisionmaking in the society.

- Leaders (L) are obviously those directly responsible for the actions that the international community is objecting to.
- Administrators (A) [make up] a separate group, indispensable for the execution of policy, but possibly less able to actually formulate or change such policies.

- A third group consists of the supporters (S) of the leadership, ranging from family members to party members and local decisionmakers. They are all needed for the leadership, but largely without much influence on what that leadership actually does.
- Finally, a more difficult group to relate to the policies [is] the traders (T), the agents that deal with the actual international transactions that the sanctions aim to reduce (e.g., individuals involved in commerce, transportation, banking, or smuggling). They are likely to be significant for the conduct of policy, but again probably have little direct impact on the formulation of such policies.

Thus we assume that the four groups are distinct and stand in different relationships to ultimate policymaking. The logical order of influence would go from leaders, to administrators and supporters, and finally to traders.

We applied these categories to the 446 names using publicly available information of the targeted individuals and were able to place 85 percent of them in one of the four categories. Some remain unidentified or have unclear relations to decisionmaking and were kept in a separate group (O, others). In all, there were 59 leaders, 209 administrators, 80 supporters, and 34 traders listed. For 64 individuals, there was little or no information available and they were kept in the fifth group.

This result shows that administrators constitute about one-half of all the targeted individuals. The logic behind this targeting pattern is not easy to understand. The original idea of sanctions was that it would deal with the (ultimately) responsible actors. Clearly, the responsible elite is a small group in any society. It is dependent on administrators to function, but at the same time administrators are likely to have less of a chance to change prevailing policies. They may be necessary, but not sufficient for a particular policy.

Table 8.3 suggests an important trend in the use of individual sanctions: in the Liberia case, the targeted leaders constituted a considerable part of all listed (thirty-eight in all, including the two mentioned in Cosgrove's work), whereas later sanctions, such as those on North Korea and Iran, have not listed any leaders at all.[22] In the latter cases, administrators and supporters constitute the overwhelming number as only two traders had been listed.

However, the case of Sudan goes against the trend. In this case, only individuals in the leadership category were targeted. Thus, the data may not reflect a consistent trend, but rather the lack of a coherent general sanctions policy: each case may be dealt [with] entirely in its own right.

Table 8.3 Individual Sanctions and Closeness to Power (number of individuals by category)

	Leaders	Administrators	Supporters	Traders	Others	Total
Angola (UNITA)	4	73	21	5	63	166
Côte d'Ivoire	1	0	2	0	0	3
Democratic Republic of Congo	10	3	0	7	0	20
Iran	0	22	15	2	0	39
Liberia	38	51	42	20	1	152
North Korea (DPRK)	0	5	0	0	0	5
Sierra Leone	2	55	0	0	0	57
Sudan	4	0	0	0	0	4
Total	59	209	80	34	64	446

This suggests that there is no clear theory about the selection of targets. For instance, to achieve types 6 and 7 reactions of Table 8.1, credibility in signaling and deterrence builds on consistency in behavior. If the potential target knows that he or she is likely to be targeted, as seen by previous action, this may have an impact. The case-by-case targeting of sanctions does not reinforce such a notion. Instead, the lack of a consistent targeting strategy may strengthen the targeted actor's belief that the sanctions are a punishment (i.e., belong to categories 4 and 5) rather than a bargaining tool (according to logics of categories 1, 2, and 3).

There is, no doubt, a case for targeting administrators in the situations of nuclear energy programs. They may be the technical staff that is necessary for running the operations. Thus, listing them may affect their willingness to carry out the orders of the regime. However, their personal hardship—if any—is not likely to sway the regimes. Most likely the nuclear programs are defined as "patriotic" undertakings and "worthy of personal sacrifice." We surmise that the administrators have little choice but to continue to carry out their orders. In fact, doing the opposite would get them into trouble. They would know this and, thus, they may work more diligently than before in order to demonstrate their loyalty. The only alternative may be to escape the country (as we mentioned above in the case of the cabinet minister from Liberia; although belonging to the group of leaders, he said he had little chance to influence policy). There are reports on such escapes in the Iran case, although not by persons who were on the target list. It suggests—from the UN point of view—that allowing technical staff to travel may be more effective than banning them from going abroad.

A third conclusion then is: it makes more sense to target only those responsible for making the strategic decisions, in line with the original idea of making leaders accountable for their actions. This is where realpolitik enters. Sanctioning top leaders has often proven difficult. In the case of Africa, leaders have obviously been considered for sanctions, but in the end no action has been taken. There has not been sufficient consensus or political will for such high-profile measures. Looking at the list of names in the studied cases, we find only ten top leaders. Two were listed in the case of Angola (Vice President Antonio Dembo and President Jonas Savimbi, both leaders of UNITA), six in the case of Liberia (among those were Vice President Moses Blah and President Charles Taylor), one in the case of Sierra Leone (Johnny Paul Koroma, who reportedly died under mysterious circumstances in 2003)[23] and one in the case of Sudan (the general commanding Sudanese forces in Darfur).

What we can see in this data is that, more recently, there has been a reluctance to target leaders in several highly authoritarian countries such as Iran and North Korea as well as in civil war–divided Côte d'Ivoire. Also, in Sudan the president himself is not on the list. This is remarkable in view of the fact that the targeting of lower echelons is likely to be less effective in generating dynamics toward compliance, as mentioned above, and that the arguments for sanctions focus on the top leaders. Indeed, the moral argument of accountability also points to this level as the central one for sanctions. In the case of Sudan, the International Criminal Court has actually been more willing to identify the ultimate decisionmaker. . . .

Still, we have to conclude that the targeted sanctions had a stronger focus on the top levels of decisionmakers in the early uses and lately have turned toward the lower levels. This means that the individual sanctions may now work more to test the loyalty of lower echelons to the present regime rather than undermining its policies. For people on this level, notably administrators in nuclear programs or heads of particular government agencies, being listed on sanctions lists is likely to be uncomfortable and also to induce them to demonstrate their adherence to established policies by pursuing them more effectively than before. The only rewards and protection they can get is to be more supportive with the established order than before. This form of targeting sanctions, we suggest, is not likely to achieve internationally desired compliance. The bargaining dynamics of types 1 through 3 do not apply as the individuals are not in a position to bargain, and types 6 and 7 affect only those not listed. Thus, types 4 and 5 become dominant: sanctions appear as punishments rather than as instruments for change for individuals in categories of administrators and supporters.

Thus we suggest a fourth conclusion, this time focusing on the UN uses of sanctions over time: although the top leadership is the one that can effect change, the Security Council has become more cautious in actually targeting such individuals. This caution, we surmise, may make individually targeted sanctions less likely to achieve compliance, thus suggesting that a bolder approach may be more effective.[24]

Thus far we have commented on only the categories of leaders, administrators, and supporters. Matters may, in fact, be different when moving to the level of traders. Traders are the individuals that actually pursue actions that may involve violations of sanctions. . . .

[T]he Liberia case suggests strongly the utility of financial sanctions and possibly also the travel ban when meticulously monitored and when key individuals are clearly identified. The full evidence from the panel reports is compelling. Thus, another of our conclusions is that identifying traders may be a most promising avenue for strengthening sanctions regimes. The argument is somewhat different, but relates to the ability to deprive the target of resources or to shifting the balance of power (logics types 4 and 5 in Table 8.1). These individuals will not be able to influence the policies pursued by the government, but their services may be strategically crucial for the ability of the regime to continue war or maintain its policy or itself in power. They may also be few in number and often appear in several conflict situations. They are thus identifiable, but possibly difficult to bring to court. Sanctions may make their business more difficult. . . . Sanctions and criminal procedures may go hand in hand in such cases.

The case of the Democratic Republic of Congo (DRC) also illustrates that the naming and shaming of being listed can make individuals more vulnerable and put pressure on governments to act according to the sanction. . . .

Evidence of Political Compliance

The next step in our investigation was to understand the degree of compliance with the sanctions measure and with the political demands. This can be studied on two levels. One is to see if the individuals do change their views as they are exposed to the sanctions. A second, and most significant, level is to see if target government policies are changed. . . .

In our data there were nineteen individuals with whom we could record a change of political behavior, sixteen relating to Liberia, two to

Côte d'Ivoire, and one to the DRC. As we have seen, there were changes in policy by the leadership taking place in Liberia in 2003. . . .

On the individual level, the compliance rate is indeed low. In fact, if the number of individuals who have changed their behavior is less than 20 out of the 112 for which we have information in our dataset, that suggests a "success rate" below 20 percent. In relation to the total targeted number of actors (446), this is even more apparent, although we cannot know the situation for the total sample. This leads to a serious challenge on how the targeting is done. Obviously it can have an impact, but the targeting policies may not be optimal.

Among the eight cases, we may venture to suggest that individual sanctions played some role in ending the conflict in Liberia. However, in many accounts on the ending of the war in 2003 the sanctions are seldom cited even as a contributing factor.[25] In the case of Sierra Leone, there is an interesting statement to the International Court on Sierra Leone on 29 August 2009, where Charles Taylor argued that he actually had complied with the sanctions of 2000 by trying to foster a peace agreement, thus implying a degree of effect.[26]

The sanctions may have made negotiations more likely in the cases of Iran and North Korea; so far, however, without lasting and credible agreements. Developments in Angola were largely a result of the death of two top personalities in the UNITA leadership. The case of the DRC illustrates some effectiveness of the sanctions tool. Four listed individuals have been arrested, two of them by the Congolese government and two of them outside the country. Laurent Nkunda was arrested in Rwanda in 2009 and replaced as the commander of National Congress for the People's Defense in North Kivu. One administrator was promoted to leader despite being on the sanctions list only a month after being listed in 2008. He came under an arrest warrant by the International Criminal Court the same year for having committed war crimes.[27] These actions may have helped to reduce warfare in the DRC. In the case of the Sudan, there is little evidence of compliance with the individual sanctions and little evidence that the incumbent regimes or targeted actors have shifted their positions.

The compliance ratio for individually targeted sanctions appears not to be higher than is the case for other types of sanctions. It has regularly been estimated to be between 20 percent and 34 percent.[28] The central argument for targeted sanctions has been that they are smarter in the sense that they bring the same result as more comprehensive sanctions, but at lower cost. The success ratio suggests that this claim may be supported. However, these types of sanctions could be improved beyond the present compliance ratios. Thus, we need to draw conclusions for the future of these sanctions.

A Future for Individual Sanctions?

In this study of the individually targeted sanctions, we found that the impact may be more limited than anticipated when the concept was first developed. However, the different types of logic behind the targeting may still be valid, if the right individuals are targeted. The initial arguments were to directly focus on the top leadership. This was also what was done in the first situations: Angola (in this case the leadership of UNITA), Liberia (Charles Taylor and all other high-level officials), and Sierra Leone (some of the leaders). In addition these sanctions also included measures against the traders, the individuals that could be instrumental in violating the sanctions. Taking a bird's-eye view, these are also the three conflicts that are no longer among the most urgent world problems. The cases where the international community instead avoided confronting top leaders (Iran, North Korea, Côte d'Ivoire, and Sudan) are much further from a peaceful closure. Instead, these situations have become protracted. Particularly in the cases of Iran and North Korea, we found that the targeting is directed at administrators, not the policymakers. There are strong reasons why such individuals will not be able to affect the policies pursued. In fact, we suggest that the sanctions may make them more loyal to the regime.

The pattern of individual targeting may say something about the international commitment to achieving change. When leaders are directly targeted, it suggests that the international community has resorted to effects covered by types 4 through 7 in Table 8.1. There is a determination to bring about drastic political change. In cases where the targeting is different, the expectation may instead be one of negotiations. The sanctions are operating as inducements, according to types 1 through 3 in Table 8.1. The type of targeting strategy used tells us something about international attention and international political will.

The outcomes of these conflicts, of course, depend on a host of factors. The way regional actors respond is important for the possibilities of implementation. If the targeted individuals can move in their own region with minimal impediment, that serves to undermine the sanctions. However, major banking centers are further away and still out of reach. Strong regional support may be more important for effective arms embargoes, for instance.[29]

The sanctions on individuals are only part of the explanation. However, our analysis gives significant input to developing a more coherent UN targeting strategy. Sanctions should primarily target the top leaders. They are the ones that can effect changes and the different logics we identified may affect them, even if they do not hold financial assets abroad or travel widely for pleasure (as may be the case for both Iranian and North Korean leaders). The individual sanctions, however, serve to annoy them and stigmatize them. If the demands for change from the international community are not too high, it is more possible for them to shift policies, particularly if this can be seen to be part of a larger arrangement. In neither of these two cases is the international community demanding a change of government, only a change of nuclear policy.

The same argument applies to leaders in countries of civil war (here meaning Sudan, Côte d'Ivoire, and the DRC). These are situations where in fact international travel and foreign financial resources may be directly significant to the leadership. The cases that have been terminated belong to this group of cases.

In addition, our study suggests that the traders are very important. They are necessary for sustaining a war effort and they may play the same role in the cases of nuclear proliferation. There is a need for import of weapons in both cases (e.g., small arms, such as Kalashnikovs, in the civil wars and complex missiles in the nuclear proliferation cases). Such deliveries are likely to be banned and, thus, experts in embargo evasion are valuable. Targeting such individuals makes the deliveries even more difficult and less attractive. As they are operating on a market they may turn to other, less risky businesses, and in that way contribute to the sanctions. As can be seen from Table 8.3, so far only a few individuals in this category have been targeted. It may suggest that the traders, in fact, are not that many. It could also be that little effort has gone into identifying them. Either way, they will be significant in future sanctions regimes; if they are few they can be identified, sanctioned, and possibly brought to court. If they are presently unknown, it is important to identify them, their companies, and their networks. Of course, the traders in themselves cannot change policy, but they provide the necessary resources for many leaders to maintain power. Furthermore, they are calculating the profitability of different operations. Thus, they are likely to stay out of situations that are closely monitored and where the gains are in danger. They follow an economic logic that might not be so easily captured in the seven types we have identified. Their role as secondary actors may also require a different type of analysis. This we see as an important next step in sanctions research. . . .

Notes

1. David Cortright and George Lopez, *Smart Sanctions: Targeting Economic Statecraft* (Lanham, MD: Rowman & Littlefield, 2002); Peter Wallensteen, "A Century of Economic Sanctions: A Field Revisited," in Peter Wallensteen, *Peace Research: Theory and Practice* (New York: Routledge, 2011), pp. 183–205; Aaron Griffiths with Catherine Barnes, eds., *Power of Persuasion: Incentives, Sanctions and Conditionality in Peacemaking Accord* (London: Conciliation Resources, 2008).

2. T. J. Bierstecker, S. E. Eckert, A. Halegua, N. Reid, and P. Romaniuk, *Targeted Financial Sanctions: A Manual for Design and Implementation—Contributions from the Interlaken Process* (Providence: Watson Institute for International Studies, Brown University, 2001); Michael Brzoska, ed., *Design and Implementation of Arms Embargoes and Travel and Aviation Related Sanctions: Results of the "Bonn-Berlin Process"* (Bonn: International Center for Conversion, 2001); Peter Wallensteen, Carina Staibano, and Mikael Eriksson, "Making Targeted Sanctions Effective: Guidelines for the Implementation of UN Policy Options," report from the Stockholm Process (Uppsala, Uppsala University: Department of Peace and Conflict Research, Elanders Gotab, 2003); Peter Wallensteen and Carina Staibano, eds., *International Sanctions: Between Words and Wars in the Global System* (New York: Routledge; London: Frank Cass, 2005).

3. David Cortright, "Patterns of Implementation: Do Listing Practices Impede Compliance with UN Sanctions? A Critical Assessment," Policy Brief SSRP 0912-01 (Sanctions and Security Research Program, Fourth Freedom Foundation and Kroc Institute of International Peace Studies, University of Notre Dame, 2009).

4. Ibid.

5. G. Hogg and M. A. Vaughan, *Introduction to Social Psychology* (French Forest, New South Wales, Australia: Pearson Education Australia, 2005); B. S. Frey, *Dealing with Terrorism: Stick or Carrot?* (Cheltenham, UK: Edward Elgar, 2004).

6. Johan Galtung, "On the Effects of International Economic Sanctions: With Examples from the Case of Rhodesia," *World Politics* 19, no. 3 (1967): 378–416; Tom R. Tyler, *Why People Obey the Law* (Princeton: Princeton University Press, 1990); Soren C. Winter and Peter J. May, "Motivation for Compliance with Environmental Regulations," *Journal of Policy Analysis and Management* 20, no. 4 (2001): 675–698.

7. Peter Verboon and Marius van Dijke, "When Do Severe Sanctions Enhance Compliance? The Role of Procedural Fairness," *Journal of Economic Psychology* 32 (2011): 120–130; Tom R. Tyler, "Psychological Perspectives on Legitimacy and Legitimation," *Annual Review of Psychology* 57 (2006): 375–400.

8. Douglas D. Heckathorn, "Collective Sanctions and Compliance Norms: A Formal Theory of Group-Mediated Formal Control," *American Sociological Review* 55 (June 1990): 366–384.

9. Erica Cosgrove, "Examining Targeted Sanctions: Are Travel Bans Effective?" in Peter Wallensteen and Carina Staibano, eds., *International Sanctions* (New York: Routledge; London: Frank Cass, 2005), pp. 207–228.

10. Peter Wallensteen, Mikael Eriksson, and Daniel Strandow, *Sanctions for Conflict Prevention and Peacebuilding: Lessons Learned from Côte d'Ivoire*

and Liberia (Uppsala: Uppsala University, Department of Peace and Conflict Research, 2006); Mikael Eriksson, *Targeting Peace: Understanding UN and EU Targeted Sanctions* (Farnham, UK: Ashgate, 2011); Mikael Eriksson, *Targeting the Leadership of Zimbabwe: A Path to Democracy and Normalization?* (Uppsala: Uppsala University, SPITS, 2007). See also www.smartsanctions.se.

11. "Grave 'Injustice': Women Press for Sanctions Lift on Taylor's Ex, Jewel," *Frontline*, 23 June 2010, www.frontpageafrica.com/newsmanager /anmviewer.asp?a=11038.

12. Charles Taylor's gift of a large diamond to a celebrity has created a lot of media attention, but does not illustrate how the sanctions affected him while in power as the event took place before the sanctions were imposed.

13. Cosgrove, "Examining Targeted Sanctions."

14. Peter Wallensteen, Mikael Eriksson, and Daniel Strandow, *Sanctions for Conflict Prevention and Peace Building: Lessons Learned from Côte d'Ivoire and Liberia* (Uppsala: Uppsala University, Department of Peace and Conflict Research, 2006); UN Security Council Sanction Committees, www.un.org /sc/committees.

15. Winter and May, "Motivation for Compliance with Environmental Regulations."

16. UN Security Council Document S/2000/1195.

17. Cosgrove, "Examining Targeted Sanctions," and Wallensteen, Eriksson, and Strandow, *Sanctions for Conflict Prevention and Peacebuilding*, provide examples of this.

18. UN Security Council Document S/2006/735.

19. Wallensteen, Eriksson, and Strandow, *Sanctions for Conflict Prevention and Peacekeeping*.

20. In March 2011, the Security Council imposed sanctions on President Laurent Gbagbo together with four others, but by then the situation had already deteriorated into an armed conflict. UN Security Council Resolution, 30 March 2011, No. 1975, www.un.org/docs/sc.

21. Peter Wallensteen, Erik Melander, and Frida Möller, "Preventing Genocide: The International Response," in Mark Anstey, Paul Meerts, and I. William Zartman, eds., *The Slippery Slope to Genocide: Reducing Identity Conflicts and Preventing Mass Murder* (Oxford: Oxford University Press, 2011).

22. Cosgrove, "Examining Targeted Sanctions."

23. There are continuous rumors around this person. See, for instance, http://allafrica.com/stories/200809110844.html.

24. The targeting of President Gbagbo in March 2011 does not change this trend, as the sanctions were imposed at a time when his standing was already severely undermined.

25. In a recent account of these events, Desirée Nilsson does not give emphasis to this. For instance, see Desirée Nilsson, *Crafting a Secure Peace: Evaluating Liberia's Comprehensive Peace Agreement 2003* (Uppsala: Uppsala University, Department of Peace and Conflict Research, 2009).

26. See www.charlestaylortrial.org/2009/08/29.

27. See www.un.org/sc/committees/1533/pdf/1533_list.pdf S/2008/772.

28. Peter Wallensteen, "Characteristics of Economic Sanctions," *Journal of Peace Research* 5, no. 3 (1968): 248–267; Kimberly Ann Elliott, "Trends in Economic Sanctions Policy: Challenges to Conventional Wisdom," in Peter

Wallensteen and Carina Staibano, eds., *International Sanctions: Between Words and Wars in the Global System* (New York: Routledge; London: Frank Cass, 2005), pp. 3–14.

29. Damien Fruchart, Paul Holtom, Siemon T. Wezeman, Daniel Strandow, and Peter Wallensteen, *United Nations Arms Embargoes: Their Impact on Arms Flows and Target Behaviour* (Solna: Stockholm International Peace Research Institute and Uppsala University, 2007), www.smartsanctions.se.

9

A Tale of Two Institutions: The United Nations Security Council and the International Criminal Court

Rosa Aloisi

The International Criminal Court (ICC) is a judicial body created as a politically independent judicial institution to prosecute the most serious international crimes, including genocide, war crimes, and crimes against humanity. In the words of former ICC Chief Prosecutor Luis Moreno Ocampo, the job of the ICC is "to conduct investigations [concerning the most serious violations of international humanitarian law] fairly, impartially, and present it to the judges."[1] According to Article 13 of the ICC statute, the Court can initiate an investigation if

- A situation . . . is referred to the Prosecutor by a State Party . . . ;
- A situation . . . is referred to the Prosecutor by the UNSC acting under Chapter VII of the Charter of the United Nations; or
- The Prosecutor has initiated an investigation. . . .[2]

The negotiations preceding the formulation of Article 13 of the ICC Statute were surrounded by considerable controversies. The final version was the result of profound compromises and intense bargaining between those that wanted a judicial body completely independent from any political influence, and those espousing the idea of a judicial institution subordinated to some form of political control.

[One] of the key issues . . . was the role the UNSC would play in the initiation, development, and enforcement of ICC investigations. . . . The initial negotiations for the creation of a permanent international criminal court taking place within the UN International Law Commission (ILC) had envisioned a court that was perfectly subordinated to the UNSC and operating within the Charter of the United Nations. [The]

Reprinted from *International Criminal Law Review*, vol. 13, no. 1: 147–168. © 2013 by Brill Publishing. Reprinted by permission of the publisher. Edited for length.

five permanent members of the UNSC had envisioned a strong role for the UNSC . . . and a considerably circumscribed jurisdiction of the Court.[3] Opposed to this vision were all the other countries that were extremely suspicious of the intentions of the UNSC, whose record of being an impartial and fair institution was, to say the least, questionable.[4] . . . [The ILC opted for a compromise:] the Rome Treaty, while recognizing the power of the UNSC to refer a situation to the Court, and leaving the evaluation of the admissibility of the case to the investigation of the Prosecutor, gives to the UNSC the power to defer investigations . . . for twelve months, given the presence of peace talks, peace operations, and security concerns. . . . On the deferral power, the strict vote requirements for a resolution of the UNSC to pass—[a] nine vote majority and the concurrence of the five permanent members of the UNSC—was a considerable guarantee that the power to defer a situation was not going to be abused.[5] On the referral power, the political authority of the UNSC could empower international justice, by de facto extending [the ICC's] jurisdiction to non-member states.

[However, this compromise has created operational problems.] . . . The UNSC referral power extends the court's jurisdiction over states that are not members to the ICC statute. . . . In reality the UNSC referrals have been less than adequate in supporting the investigations of the ICC. [Referrals are] particularly difficult because of the UNSC's political composition; technical and financial support to the Court has been non-existent; and the UNSC has been accused of dispensing referrals selectively. These considerations require a thorough assessment and reconsideration of . . . [the UNSC referral power and] the political influence that the UNSC has over the ICC.

I argue that the referral power given to the UNSC has come at a high cost for the legitimacy and functioning of international justice. I will first give a brief overview of the relationship between the UNSC and ICC as established in the Rome Treaty. Then, I will specifically address two aspects of the UNSC referral procedures: 1) the type of enforcement mechanisms and cooperation requirements that the UNSC referral triggers and whether these enforcement mechanisms have been fully implemented; and 2) the political aspects of the referrals, which have to some extent politicized the work of the ICC. I argue that in analyzing the relationship between the UNSC and ICC as it has unfolded in the past decade, it is evident that clashing political and judicial interests have done a disservice to the implementation of international justice. I will focus on the two instances of referrals so far approved by the UNSC and highlight some of the political aspects that seem to be hindering and delaying, in spite of international pressures for UNSC attention, a referral of the situation in Syria. Lastly, I will address some of the solutions that could improve the relationship between the ICC and the UNSC, as well as create enforcement mechanisms that might provide a better system of international justice.

The UNSC in the ICC Treaty

[The] ICC Statute [includes two provisions] that deal with the relationship between the UNSC and the ICC. . . . Article 13(b) establishes that the UNSC may refer to the ICC a situation in which crimes that are under the jurisdiction of the ICC have been committed. . . .

Article 16 . . . establishes that [the UNSC may defer an ICC investigation for up to 12 months and may continue to renew that deferral.] . . . [T]he UNSC seems to be something in between a "triggering institution" and a "gatekeeper institution." On the one hand, it promotes investigations and, on the other, can stop them based on concerns of security. The deferral power, in particular, was based on the need to reconcile peace and justice in situations in which the presence of peace talks or security concerns makes justice a secondary goal to the international community. . . .

. . . There are two major concerns that Articles 13(b) and 16 present to the international community. First, the UNSC referral under Chapter VII of the Charter has the power to impose obligations on all member states of the Charter, regardless of their status as members of the ICC. However, once the UNSC refers a situation of a non-member state to the ICC, [the Court] has no power to enforce the cooperation of that state.[6] . . . [Second,] the practice of referral and deferral by the UNSC has been governed by political motives, thus diminishing in the eyes of the international community the legitimacy of the ICC's work. The questions to examine are two: 1) how has the UNSC fared in helping the ICC to enforce cooperation on non-member states? and 2) how much have the UNSC referrals (Darfur and Libya) and the decision not to yet discuss the situation in Syria been dictated by political concerns rather than the magnitude of the crimes? I suggest that the UNSC has not been particularly helpful in enabling the ICC to dispense international justice and that the ICC has willingly compromised some important requirements which characterized the legitimacy of law, in order to achieve that little international political support it could gather from the UNSC. . . .

. . . [The] UNSC has referred two cases to the ICC (Sudan on Darfur and Libya). . . . However, given the enormous difficulties faced by the ICC in accessing the countries under investigation, the lack of arrests of major criminals indicted, and the lengthy proceedings through which cases are built, . . . we need to assess the UNSC performance on three different grounds: 1) the amount of actual cooperation the UNSC has requested from relevant states; 2) the amount of cooperation given to the ICC following the referral; and 3) the technical and financial support necessary to the ICC to perform its investigations.

[The UNSC Resolutions authorizing these referrals (UNSC 1593 and 1970) limit] the subjects that can fall under the attention of the ICC and [restrict the] activities investigators can embark upon while performing their duties.

. . . [Both resolutions] clearly recognize that other non-state parties have no obligations under the statute, and invite organizations or other parties involved in the conflict to only "cooperate." . . . [The UNSC] limited the ICC jurisdiction to the relevant state under investigation, thus jeopardizing the achievement of universal justice and suggesting a hierarchy of crimes based on the individuals that perpetrated them. . . . In spite of approving the referral in order to let the ICC exercise its jurisdiction on the cases, Argentina and Brazil manifested their disapproval of the limitation of jurisdiction. . . . [The] UNSC resolutions considerably diminish the potential effectiveness of the referral as a mandatory enforcement mechanism. . . .

[There are considerable differences between the practices of the UNSC regarding the ICC] and the support given by the UNSC to the ad hoc tribunals for the former Yugoslavia and Rwanda. Under the statutes of the ad hoc tribunals, the UNSC imposed a general obligation of cooperation upon all member states. Ultimately this led to considerable facilitation in the execution of arrest warrants for those indicted by the two ad hoc tribunals. [The] ICC is still facing considerable difficulties in arresting President Al-Bashir of [the] Sudan in spite of the fact that he has travelled extensively through Africa and to countries that are members of the ICC. . . .

[The African Union has not interpreted] the referral of the UNSC as lifting President Bashir's [sovereign] immunity. The absence of such specification in the UNSC referral and the tentative terms with which it delimited the ICC jurisdiction weakened considerably the position of the ICC and its personnel in trying to access the country and asking other state members to the ICC to arrest Al-Bashir. President Al-Bashir has been travelling freely throughout Africa and each and every country, including Malawi, Chad, and Kenya, [has] adamantly refused to arrest him, suggesting that the UNSC referral or its request of cooperation with the ICC does not in any way mean that Al-Bashir['s] immunities have been lifted. . . . This is an example showing how the lack of specifications regarding the exact terms of the obligations imposed by the referral creates enormous difficulties for the exercise of the ICC jurisdiction. . . .

[The UNSC has also been passive] in giving support to the ICC after the referral of a specific situation. The relationship between the ICC and the UNSC has been limited to the periodic reports the Chief Prosecutor has presented concerning the evolution of the investigation. [The] UNSC has done little to support the investigations launched following its referrals, . . . even following instances of non-cooperation duly reported by the Prosecutors. The UNSC . . . has not threatened enforcement mechanisms under Charter VII of the UN Charter following clear instances of non-cooperation. . . .

There is also little cooperation when it comes to the imposition of sanctions against individuals indicted by the Court. The UNSC has at its disposal a lengthy list of sanctions that run from the freezing of foreign assets, to travel bans that could help the ICC. [For example, the] Court has been having problems collecting evidence [in Libya], accessing sites where crimes have been committed, and even talking to those indicted. . . . The UNSC has not exerted any kind influence, remaining mostly silent on the consequences its referral is having on the implementation of justice. . . .

[The ICC has many difficulties due to a lack of resources. The UNSC referrals say that ICC member states bear the costs of the investigations. They expressly prohibit the use of UN funds for ICC investigations.] The obstacles the ICC faces in embarking upon complex investigations with limited financial support have been additionally complicated by the lack of any technical or administrative support by the UNSC. . . .

[The Rome Statute does not address such questions as:] What happens after the UNSC refers a situation outside the jurisdiction of the ICC? How much involvement and responsibility should the UNSC have in the case? . . .

. . . [The Sudan and Libya examples show that a successful international judicial body requires] political, technical and financial support, together with the enforcement of arrest warrants. . . . [The politics of the UNSC permanent members make additional support unlikely. China and Russia place] great emphasis on non-interference in the affairs of other states due in part to both sovereignty concerns and fear of external interference in their own affairs. The economic and political interests that China and Russia have in the region create considerable protection against any infringement of Al-Bashir's immunity. . . .

Politics vs. Justice

. . . The political dimension of international justice is undeniable. The creation of international criminal courts, ad hoc and special tribunals has been the result of political will and, whether they have been more or less successful, has depended upon political support. International judicial institutions do not possess their own enforcement mechanisms; they do not have a police force to arrest indicted individuals and must rely either on the cooperation of sovereign states or on . . . the UNSC. The political and legal compromises [are evident not only] in the referrals, but especially in the non-referrals of situations by the UNSC to the ICC. Many feared that the legal functions of the ICC could interfere with the political functions of the UNSC. The UNSC feared that an investigation might interfere with ongoing efforts of conflict resolution, while the ICC feared that situations could remain pending before the UNSC . . . without ever being resolved.[7]

There is a paradox affecting the relationship between the ICC and the UNSC. [In] order for international justice to be legitimate, independence from political will is necessary. However, the ability of the UNSC referral to extend the jurisdiction of the Court has been considered an important aspect of the achievement of universal justice. In the absence of the UNSC referrals some of the worst cases of international humanitarian law could go unpunished. Given [this paradox, we need to analyze] a) whether the ICC can maintain fairness and impartiality in situations referred by the UNSC; [and] b) whether the UNSC can debate and refer situations based on the gravity of crimes, rather than on the political considerations of its permanent members. These points can be analyzed by assessing the two referrals of the UNSC on Sudan and Libya, but also by looking into other cases, such as Yemen, Sri Lanka, and more recently Syria, which, in spite of international pressures for UNSC referral, have not received the attention of the UNSC. . . .

When the UNSC [in 2005] referred the Sudan case on Darfur to the ICC . . . [many considered it] a breakthrough in the relationship between the two institutions. [The referral went through due to abstentions from] China and the United States, which could have vetoed the decision. The abstentions [followed a] report of the Commission of Inquiry into the situation, which unveiled dramatic events taking place in Darfur. . . . The need to avoid a veto . . . prompted some [UNSC members] to tailor a referral that made . . . concessions to the US and China. . . . The US wanted certain guarantees to protect US nationals from prosecution and to shield the UN from the costs associated with the operation of the ICC. [The US also wanted to limit ICC jurisdiction regarding non-member states, as discussed in the section above.] . . .

China also abstained [despite] considerable political and economic interests [in the Sudan].[8] From oil extracting firms, to the export of arms, China had been a close ally of the Sudanese government since the early 1990s. . . . While the UNSC could have played a firmer role in imposing sanctions, introducing economic embargos, and enforcing travel bans, it [was thwarted by] the political interests and veto threats [of] China. Lastly and more generally the UNSC made another statement that substantially limits the support the ICC would receive in its investigation of the Darfur situation. [Both China and the United States wanted] Paragraph 2 of the UNSC 1593, [establishing] that "States not party to the Rome Statute have no obligation under the Statute. . . ."

. . . [The limitation undermines] the legitimacy of the Court in the eyes of non-member states. . . . If a judicial institution cannot ask for the full support of the international community to perform its duties, and this situation is also enabled by the organ of the UN that has the power to enforce such cooperation, then the ICC seems to be doomed to be a weak institution facing insurmountable challenges . . . to its jurisdiction.

All these considerations are a clear indication that, although welcomed as [a] sign that the world would not tolerate heinous crimes going unpunished, the referral of the Darfur situation was de facto approved because of specific political compromises that have been limiting the power of the investigation of the ICC and level of collaboration of the UNSC in securing information, access to sites, and arrest warrants. . . . Sudan has consistently questioned, together with the African Union, the legitimacy of the ICC actions following the UNSC referral, by refusing to arrest President Bashir. However, the UNSC has also failed to [enforce its referral by] choosing not to impose sanctions and restrictions . . . on those countries that have hosted Bashir and that should be cooperating with the ICC as state parties to the ICC Treaty.

[The Libya referral] reflected many of the shortcomings of the Sudan referral, [but also includes additional problems].[9] In an attempt to quickly respond to the violence escalating in Benghazi and to the failure of Gaddafi's government to protect its population, the UNSC resolution was approved with an unprecedented unanimous decision. . . . The referral occurred before the International Commission of Inquiry into the escalation of violence in Libya had concluded its work and before a solid ground for prosecution had been established. Certainly there was widespread evidence of violations of humanitarian law and crimes against humanity being committed in Libya. . . . The ICC immediately issued an arrest warrant for Gaddafi, one of his sons, Saif Al-Islam Gaddafi, and a senior member of its government Abdullah Al-Senussi. The African Union quickly reacted by asking African countries to not cooperate with the Court, while some of the non-permanent members of the UNSC, although voting in favor of the referral, manifested their concerns regarding the possibility that the ICC investigation could hinder attempts at finding a negotiated exit from power by Gaddafi and his supporters.

[The Libya referral] was better structured than the Sudan referral and . . . better supported by the UNSC's [additional] actions.[10] The resolution imposed an arms embargo, travel bans, and froze the assets of Gaddafi and his supporters. However, the rapidity of its approval created two different sets of problems for . . . the ICC. First, there was a general problem of information about the facts that had justified the referral. The ICC stepped into a conflict situation without adequate knowledge of the events that had unfolded up to February 2011 and, although the Pre-Trial Chamber issued the arrest warrants only a week after the referral, there was a long list of Gaddafi's supporters who were simply unknown to the ICC investigators. Second, Resolution 1970 did not provide any bargaining strategy with Gaddafi's government and its supporters signaling that, in spite of a long list of sanctions intended to shape Gaddafi's behaviour, the real intention of the Resolution was to force Gaddafi out of power and create a new regime. This situation most likely triggered an additional escalation of violence, which then prompted the UNSC to approve Resolution 1973 asking all UN member states to discuss measures, including the use of force, to enforce security in Libya.

[The UNSC referral also contains provisions that limit ICC jurisdiction.] Like the Sudan resolution, [it excludes non-ICC] parties from the possibility of cooperation or prosecution by the Court. . . . [It also limits] the temporal jurisdiction of the Court, asking the ICC to investigate crimes under its jurisdiction that occurred after February 11, 2011. Although the Court jurisdiction on state members to the ICC is limited from the date they have ratified the Rome Treaty, one of the advantages of the UNSC referrals is its ability to tailor such resolutions in a way that would provide the most encompassing form of justice. . . . [However, given this limitation,] Western countries [with] long-term political and economic relationships with Gaddafi's regime . . . will never come under the scrutiny of the ICC investigation. Lastly, the referral . . . mentions Article 16 with regard to the deferral power of the UNSC. Given the approval of Resolution 1973, after which NATO forces were deployed in Libyan air space to enforce security and protect humanitarian interests, the reference to Article 16 in Resolution 1970 looms as a potential hindrance to the ICC investigation that could happen at any time when peace talks or security concerns rise.

[The] above considerations lead to the conclusion that Resolution 1970 is as much political as was Resolution 1593. Although welcomed as an opportunity for the ICC to investigate crimes that would have otherwise remained outside its jurisdiction, the UNSC referral helped create the basis for . . . selective justice—one in which individuals may not be indicted, states may not cooperate, and crimes may not be investigated. . . . The ICC has already been attacked as an institution in the hands of [W]estern powers. The limitations imposed on the investigations by the UNSC resolutions, which practically shield UN member states and nationals from the ICC prosecution, are a clear signal of political power working through a judicial institution. Under these conditions the ICC is not only limited in the impact that it may have on the promotion of justice, deterrence of crimes, and establishment of peace, but its legitimate standing as an impartial and fair judicial institution may also be questioned.

. . . [The] political nature of the referrals of the Darfur and Libya situations is evident in that the gravity of the crimes committed in those situations are not any greater than violations of humanitarian law occurring elsewhere, but overlooked by the UNSC.[11] . . .

. . . In 2009 the UNSC failed to take into serious consideration crimes against civilians in Sri Lanka. [A UN report showed] that tens of thousands of civilians had lost their lives between January and May 2009 in the fight between the government of [Sri Lanka] and Tamil rebels, with crimes committed . . . by both sides to the conflict.[12] More recently a report by Amnesty International to . . . the UN Human Rights Council established that . . . Sri Lanka has failed to account for the crimes committed by government and rebels thereby creating a climate of impunity "where arbitrary detentions, torture and other ill-treatment, enforced disappearances, and custodial killings continue unchecked."[13] [Despite the nature of this conflict, the UNSC will never refer this situation] given Russia's firm opposition to even discuss the case and China's strong support for the Sri Lankan government.

The "Arab Spring" [provides more examples]. The events unfolding in Yemen, violations of human rights in Bahrain of unarmed protesters asking for the end of Al Khalifa regime's brutality, and the [civil war] in Syria have not been addressed by the UNSC [regarding] international justice. Although adopting various resolutions . . . condemning human rights violations by Yemeni authorities and urging . . . investigations according to international standards, the UNSC never mentioned the Rome Treaty or the ICC. The close ties of the Yemeni regime to . . . the US [are] primary obstacles to a UNSC referral. While Bahrain protesters and human rights organizations have asked the ICC to intervene by issuing arrest warrants for the regime leaders inflicting torture and persecution on civilians, the UNSC has remained mostly silent. There are significant political interests in maintaining a friendly regime in a strategic section of the Middle East rather than seeing the rise to power [of a] Shiite-led government which . . . "could increase Iran's influence and lead to the loss of U.S. use of Bahrain's military facilities."[14]

[The UNSC has also failed to refer] the current situation in Syria [to the ICC]. In August 2011 the Human Rights Council . . . urged the UNSC to refer the situation to the ICC.[15] When states on the UNSC started drafting a referral it was done with a clear reference to the ICC jurisdiction over the crimes committed, but the reference was removed given the immediate reaction of China and Russia, which feared an escalation of events as in Libya. Following many reports of the Human Rights Council and the Office of the High Commissioner for Human Rights, the UNSC was repeatedly briefed to take action so that international criminal responsibility could be addressed. . . .

. . . [However, the] ties that Russia and China have with the Bashar al-Assad government make a referral of the UNSC to the ICC unlikely. Furthermore, it is feared that a veto by Russia and China regarding ICC intervention could be interpreted by the Syrian regime as a source of impunity. . . .

Discussion

As the analysis above shows, the lack of commitment to ICC operations following referrals, the heavily politicized language of the UNSC Resolutions 1593 and 1970, and the "power politics" discourses surrounding talks of future referrals of situations to the ICC, severely compromises the pursuit of international justice. It seems unlikely we will be seeing a referral by the UNSC in the near future. The Resolutions on Sudan and Libya were surrounded by extraordinary circumstances in which an unusual and united international support on Libya and strong indignation over the humanitarian crises in Darfur made the UNSC more willing to muster the political will to refer the situations. However, even those referrals are affected by the political games played at the UNSC. The limitation of jurisdiction, the lack of economic and technical support, and recognition of privileges for special categories of individuals seems to indicate a biased justice, which the ICC has accepted in the name of advancing universal jurisdiction.

The solutions to such a situation might be hard to find and even harder to enforce given the resistance of the UNSC to recognize the complete independence of the Court and the desire of the ICC to investigate cases that would not otherwise fall under its jurisdiction. The preferable solution would be that of pressuring states into accepting the jurisdiction of the Court, eliminating therefore a need for the referral of the UNSC. However, it is doubtful that leaders who could fall under the scrutiny of the ICC investigation will willingly submit their nations to the Court's jurisdiction. An enlargement of the ICC membership, including countries whose humanitarian crises have made headlines, is unlikely.

[What] is most needed is a redesign of the relationship between the UNSC and the ICC, including increasing pressures by the ICC members on the UNSC to align the aims of its resolutions with its behaviour, and a reconsideration of the way the UNSC addresses issues of international justice. In order to improve the relationship between these institutions it is necessary to reach a mutual understanding of the role each one of them plays in the international arena. Political interests are paramount to the UNSC and the implementation of international justice is of pivotal importance for the growing influence of the ICC. However, resolutions and acceptance of referrals must be driven by coordination and cooperation of the two different paramount interests governing these institutions. The UNSC should recognize that international justice cannot always bow to political considerations and that, if its ultimate goal is that of enforcing peace and security throughout the world, then the ICC could be an additional instrument in doing so. The ICC's mission to promote universal international justice does not comport well with the desire to accept constraints that ultimately do more harm than good to justice. The extension of its jurisdiction following the referral of the UNSC may damage what is more important—the legitimacy and fairness of its operations. Ultimately, what is important is the perception that justice delivered by the ICC is fair, impartial, and legitimate. . . .

Member states to the UN should also be more active in pressuring the UNSC to stop the evaluation of situations to be referred to the ICC based on the political relationships with leaders, rather than the gravity of the crimes committed. Aside from a general condemnation of the inertia of the UNSC, leaders sitting at the UN have done little to determine specific criteria through which the UNSC should assess the cases and then make a decision to refer it to the ICC. The UNSC has no responsibility to justify or explain its decisions and it is mostly immune from criticisms. It has no criteria to follow and it assesses each situation according to the country under scrutiny. Ideally, in the absence of consensus, the Permanent Members of the UNSC should abstain from vetoing resolutions referring cases, rather than becoming accomplices in the bloodshed of rampant human rights violations and humanitarian crises. . . .

Notes

1. Louis Moreno Ocampo, Al-Arabiya News, 4 November, http://english .alarabiya.net/articles/zou/u/04/175443.

2. Mahnoush H. Arsanjani, "The Rome Statute of the International Criminal Court," *The American Journal of International Law* (1999) 22–43. William A. Schabas, "United States Hostility to the International Criminal Court: It's All about the Security Council," *European Journal of International Law* (2004) 701–720.

3. Philippe Kirsch and John T. Holmes, "The Rome Conference on an International Criminal Court: The Negotiating Process," *The American Journal of International Law* (1999) 2–12.

4. Cherif Bassiouni, "Where Is the ICC Heading?" *Journal of International Criminal Justice* (1999) 4:421–427.

5. Schabas, *supra* note 2.

6. Dapo Akande, "The Effects of Security Council Resolutions and Domestic Proceedings on State Obligations to Cooperate with the ICC," *Journal of International Criminal Justice* (2012) 299–324. Carsten Stahn, "Libya, the International Criminal Court and Complementarity: A Test for Shared Responsibility," *Journal of International Criminal Justice* (2012) 325–349. Lawrence Moss, "The UN Security Council and the International Criminal Court— Towards a More Principled Relationship," *UN Security Council in Focus* (March, 2012) 1–13.

7. Arsanjani, *supra* note 2

8. Paul D. Williams and Alex J. Bellamy, "The Responsibility to Protect and the Crisis in Darfur," *Security Dialogue* (2008) 27–47. Erica Downs, "The Fact and Fiction of Sino-Africa Energy Relations," *China Security* (2007) 42–68.

9. Canadian International Council, May 6, 2012. http://www.opencanada.org /features/leslie-vinjamuri. Report of the International Commission of Inquiry to Investigate All Alleged Violations of International Law in the Libyan Arab Jamahiriya. UN Doc. A/HRC/17/44, 1 June, 2011.

10. Ivo H. Daalder and James G. Stavridis, "Nato's Victory in Libya: The Right Way to Run an Intervention," *Foreign Policy* (2012) 2–7.

11. Bassiouni, *supra* note 4; Simon Jennings, "Playing Politics with the ICC: The Security Council's Referral of Libya to The Hague Court Highlights the Limitations of International Justice," *Institute for War and Peace Reporting.* http://iwpr.net/report-news/playing-politics-icc.

12. Report of the Secretary General's Panel of Experts on Accountability in Sri Lanka. 31 March, 2011. http:/www.un.org/News/dh/infocus/Sri_Lanka /POE_Report_Full.pdf.

13. Amnesty International. "No Real Will to Account: Shortcomings in Sri Lanka's National Plan of Action to Implement the Recommendation of the LLRC," 21st session of the UN Human Rights Council (10–28 September 2012). http://www.amnesty.org/en/libraryasset/ASA37 I010I2012Ien/bza6ass 8-1da8-4de7-agao-6soefs73zbgcbIasa370102 o12en.pdf.

14. Kenneth Katzman, "Bahrain: Reform, Security, and U.S. Policy," *Congressional Research Service Report* (2012) p. 16.

15. UN Human Rights Council Special Report 19th special session on the "Deteriorating Human Rights Situation in the Syrian Arab Republic and the Recent Killings in El-Houleh," 1 June 2012. http://www.ohchr.org/Documents /HRBodies/HRCouncil/SpecialSession/Session/A-HRC-RES-S-1g-1_en.pdf.

Part 4

Economic Issues

Brian Frederking and Paul F. Diehl

International organizations have greatly influenced the maintenance of global economic stability since World War II. The current international economic system is built around the pillars of the World Trade Organization (WTO), the International Monetary Fund, and the World Bank. These institutions are largely controlled by Western states, either through formal voting procedures or sheer economic power. Developing countries argue that the current system is at best not designed to meet their needs and at worst designed to perpetuate the dominance of the Western states. The debates between developed countries of the North and the developing countries of the South dominate the agendas of international economic organizations.

The United Nations Millennium Development Goals (MDGs) provide an example of a significant attempt at global governance, which must reconcile the interests of the North and the South. In Chapter 10, Sakiko Fukuda-Parr and David Hulme argue that poverty reduction has emerged as a new transnational development goal embodied in the MDGs. Poverty reduction as a "supernorm" has replaced earlier economic objectives of industrialization, economic liberalization, and institutional/governance reforms. They show the life cycle of an international norm: (1) norm emergence, in which norm entrepreneurs use organizational platforms to persuade important actors; (2) norm cascade, in which states and international organizations institutionalize the norm in order to enhance reputation and legitimacy; and (3) norm internalization, in which bureaucracies adopt the norm through habit and demonstration. The authors argue that this process explains the development of poverty reduction as an institutionalized MDG.

The WTO has received considerable attention since its inception, hailed as an important vehicle for promoting open markets and vilified by protestors for hurting the interests of the world's poor. Developing rules to reverse current trends of increasing global hunger is another important global governance issue area illustrating tensions between the interests of northern and southern countries. In Chapter 11, Matias Margulis argues that the international food security regime has evolved into a "regime complex" for food security with divergent rules and norms across agriculture, trade, and human rights organizations about the appropriate role of states and markets in addressing food insecurity. The WTO includes rules outlining which policies states can pursue to achieve food security within the larger context of open trade. The international human rights regime has also aggressively asserted the human right to food, and there is considerable debate regarding the influence of WTO rules on food security and the appropriate policies necessary to offset any negative consequences. This dispute over whether WTO rules should accommodate food security norms is a major source of conflict in global trade negotiations.

Another controversial aspect of the WTO is its dispute settlement mechanism. Both the United States and China have initiated many cases against each other. In Chapter 12, Kennan Castel-Fodor argues that this is a positive trend: rather than the large number of cases representing the potential for a future trade war, we should interpret this as an indication that both countries view the dispute settlement mechanism as a legitimate path to resolve such disputes. The author analyzes two cases between the United States and China regarding US poultry and intellectual property rights and emphasizes the significance of the losing party complying with the WTO ruling. Such compliance illustrates the legitimacy of the institution and the willingness of both countries to use the WTO as a third-party intermediary to resolve trade disputes.

Not all trends can be construed as "positive" norm developments. In Chapter 13, Ronald Deibert and Masashi Crete-Nishihata characterize the recent development of global cyberspace rules as "norm regression": practices that make cyberspace less likely to be an open source of information and communication. States are engaging in traditional "security dilemma" practices in cyberspace, as they develop capabilities to fight and win wars in that domain. The authors discuss the information controls states use in cyberspace and how they contradict the constitutive rules of an open Internet. These information controls are spreading internationally and put the Internet at risk of changing from an open commons to one of controlled access. This is an important example of the possible emergence of norms and rules that directly undermine the norms and rules of a prior regime.

Few recent events were more important than the 2008 financial crisis and the ensuing global recession. In Chapter 14, Oliver Stuenkel argues that the financial crisis among developed countries caused a legitimacy crisis of the international financial order. The crisis encouraged unprecedented cooperation among the emerging BRIC powers (Brazil, Russia, India, and China), and they emerged in many ways relatively more stable than the Western powers. The author suggests two implications from this episode. First, the current governance structures regarding international finance are not stable, and future financial crises will continue to reduce their legitimacy and possibly lead to important changes. Second, the BRIC cooperation in finance may spill over into other types of cooperation—confidence-building measures, currency contingency funds, development banks, etc. The common theme across all these measures is to reduce global dependence on the dollar, a major source of US hegemony.

The global financial crisis had a particularly significant influence on the economic growth and monetary policy within the European Union. In Chapter 15, Wallace Thies puts the current debate in historical context: there have always been discussions about whether the European Union has finally encountered an obstacle that will end the historic experiment in economic integration. He argues that this historical perspective provides the appropriate context to understand the EU as a transformational project. EU members transitioned from a group of states that regularly declared war on each other to a security community in which war is not an option. Thies argues that the EU has been an unqualified success in these terms and that EU countries will find a way to make "Europe" work.

10

International Norm Dynamics and the "End of Poverty": Understanding the Millennium Development Goals

Sakiko Fukuda-Parr and David Hulme

The purpose of development as a global objective requiring international cooperation can and has been defined in many ways. Such definitions depend on how political leaders envision important normative goals for the world; how economists, philosophers, and political scientists theorize the process of development; and how these ideas are utilized and adopted by key stakeholders. A significant evolution in recent years has been the emergence of a broad consensus on ending poverty as the overarching objective of development. This consensus is institutionalized in the UN Millennium Declaration adopted in 2000 and in the widespread use of the global targets that have become known as the Millennium Development Goals (MDGs).

In previous decades, international development objectives were not so clearly defined nor did they focus on poverty and poor people. Although concern with widespread poverty has been a major factor for keeping development on the international agenda since the 1950s, strategies have been dominated by economic objectives ranging from building infrastructure, human capital, and an industrial base in the 1960s and 1970s, to economic liberalization in the 1980s and 1990s, to institutional and governance reforms since the 1990s.[1] Civil society advocates and academics have consistently criticized these national and international strategies for their neglect of poverty and the human dimension.[2]

This new consensus has important implications for the international political economy of development. As Charles Gore argues, the consensus was achieved at the expense of replacing the prioritization of building

Reprinted from *Global Governance*, vol. 17, no. 1: 17–36. © 2011 by Lynne Rienner Publishers. Reprinted by permission of the publisher. Edited for length.

national capacities for development.[3] While the MDGs are usually seen as desirable, Ashwani Saith points out that "the MDG phenomenon carries the potential for distorting meaningful intellectual and research agendas, and could function as the catalyst and vehicle for a fundamental realignment of the political economy of development at the global level."[4]

How did this normative shift take place? Was it driven by ethical considerations? What was the role of key individuals and institutional stakeholders? What were the strategic instruments deployed? The aim of this article is to explain how the MDGs emerged and became established and to analyze the trajectory of the antipoverty norm itself. We draw on documentary material and interviews conducted with over 100 individuals who were involved in the framing and implementation phases of the Millennium Declaration and MDGs. We use the model of international norm dynamics set out by Martha Finnemore and Kathryn Sikkink.[5] But we propose elements to extend and refine that model in this context. We argue that the MDGs brought specificity and concreteness to the idea of ending global poverty, and explain the dynamics of that process by extending the conceptual apparatus of Finnemore and Sikkink. We introduce two new concepts: the "supernorm," a cluster of interrelated norms grouped into a unified and coherent framework, and the "message entrepreneur," as distinct from the "norm entrepreneur."[6]

The Supernorm of Ending Global Poverty

In this article, we treat the MDGs as a vehicle to communicate and promote the objective of ending global poverty. Legislatively the MDGs originated in goals set in the Millennium Declaration, a political declaration signed by 189 countries, including 145 heads of state or governments, that commits to ending poverty as a key goal for the twenty-first century along with peace, human rights, and democracy. The development chapter of the Millennium Declaration is entirely focused on poverty rather than other dimensions of development. It starts with the statement: "We will spare no effort to free our fellow men, women and children from the abject and dehumanizing conditions of extreme poverty, to which more than a billion of them are currently subjected."[7] While the Millennium Declaration included clearly defined objectives and specific quantitative goals, these were further clarified into a form that could be monitored more effectively in the Road Map presented by the UN Secretary-General a year later.[8] These were presented in the Annex as Millennium Development Goals, including eight goals, encompassing eighteen targets and forty-eight indicators.

Conceptually, the MDGs constitute a single package; although each of the eight MDGs is important as an individual norm, they are strategic components of the broader supernorm that extreme, dehumanizing poverty is morally unacceptable and should be eradicated. The MDGs are interrelated both as normative ends and instrumental means. As ends, each is a necessary part of human dignity. As means, they reflect the findings of research since the 1980s showing the synergies among them; for example, education contributes to reducing child mortality and better health contributes to improving worker productivity.[9] An important conceptual advance in development thinking over the 1990s, reflected in both the academic literature[10] and policy of major agencies,[11] is the idea that poverty is multidimensional, and that ending poverty requires addressing different dimensions simultaneously.

Until the 1990s global poverty eradication was, at best, only a nascent global development norm promoted by activists, politicians, scholars, and international commissions,[12] and, at times, by major international organizations. But it was not until the 1990s that it began to be crafted into a supernorm. This took place through a series of separate initiatives. At the core of this process was the series of UN summits and conferences starting with the 1990 World Summit for Children. Though each event had specific origins and purposes, a common theme that emerged by the mid-1990s was an agenda for inclusive globalization and ending poverty and promoting equality.[13] Each event adopted declarations that are agendas for action, including quantitative targets. The Copenhagen Declaration from the World Social Summit in 1995 was a milestone in integrating various sectoral goals into the poverty umbrella.[14] This was the first UN conference focused on poverty that emphasized its multiple human dimensions. Next came the 1996 policy document, *Shaping the 21st Century,* by the Development Assistance Committee (DAC) of the Organization for Economic Co-operation and Development (OECD), the grouping of twenty-three major bilateral donors.[15] This document defined reducing poverty as the DAC members' common overarching purpose and set six International Development Goals (IDGs), including income poverty, education, gender disparity, maternal and child deaths, reproductive health, and environmental sustainability. Finally came the Millennium Declaration in 2000, followed by the MDGs published in 2001 that assembled a wide range of individual goals into a single supernorm.

The Life Cycle of the Antipoverty Supernorm

In this section, we analyze the process by which an antipoverty supernorm emerged and gained momentum. We apply Finnemore and Sikkink's model, which has examined norm changes such as the abolition of slavery and votes for women. This proposes a three-stage life cycle: (1) "norm emergence" in which a norm begins to receive domestic and international attention that culminates in a "tipping point" when a critical mass of states adopt the norm; (2) "norm cascade" when the norm diffuses throughout the international community; and (3) "norm internalization" when the norm changes behaviors.[16] Each stage is characterized by a particular set of actors, motives, and mechanisms of influence (Table 10.1).

Norm Emergence: Eradicating Poverty as a Global Responsibility

As Finnemore and Sikkink's model would predict, individuals with organizational platforms played key roles in this stage. These were people who had dedicated their professional lives to particular causes and found themselves with potentially important organizational platforms—as leaders of UN agencies, advocacy nongovernmental organizations (NGOs), and social movements. They commissioned studies and reports, collated and synthesized scientific evidence, formulated organizational priorities, and engaged in public advocacy and media campaigns to promote the specific norms to which they were committed.

A leading norm entrepreneur was Jim Grant, executive director of the UN Children's Fund (UNICEF), who spent decades researching, writing, and campaigning to end poverty. He mounted the World Summit

Table 10.1 The Life Cycle of an International Norm

	Stage 1 Norm Emergence	Stage 2 Norm Cascade	Stage 3 Norm Internalization
Actors	Norm entrepreneurs with organizational platforms	States, international organizations, networks	Law, professions, bureaucracy
Motives	Altruism, empathy, ideational commitment	Legitimacy, reputation, esteem	Conformity
Dominant mechanisms	Persuasion	Socialization, institutionalization, demonstration	Habit, institutionalization

Source: Martha Finnemore and Kathryn Sikkink, "International Norm Dynamics and Political Change," *International Organization* 52, no. 4 (1998): 887–917.

for Children in 1990 against considerable opposition and set an example of a high-profile event with wide participation.[17] In the end, an unprecedented number of countries (159) and heads of state or government (71) attended the summit. The declaration and plan of action adopted by the summit included a number of goals related to infant and maternal mortality, child malnutrition and illiteracy, access to basic services for health and family planning, education, and water and sanitation.[18] Subsequently, Grant used these goals to mobilize action, using the UNICEF headquarters and field offices as an organizational platform. He traveled the world persuading national leaders to finance and implement plans for immunization, iodized salt, and a number of other concrete targets.[19]

Another leading example is Nafis Sadik, a physician from Pakistan who spent all of her professional life advocating and advancing family planning programs. As executive director of the UN Population Fund (UNFPA) and secretary-general of the 1994 International Conference on Population and Development, she waged numerous diplomatic battles to include important, but controversial, issues in the agenda and conclusions.[20] Issues such as women's empowerment, reproductive rights, and even abortion could not be ignored when these were the cause of so many deaths. She won over the Vatican and conservative states in incorporating these issues as health and reproductive rights into the agenda of the conference.

International NGOs and NGO networks also played a major role, often working unofficially beside official delegates to the conferences. For example, the International Women's Health Coalition (IWHC) was a significant actor at Cairo and promoted the evolution of an accessible evidence base and an epistemic community for reproductive health. The women's movement played a strategic role at several summits by carefully deploying its members to lobby key audiences on key issues at key moments.[21] While this involved the efforts of thousands of organizations, there was a group of norm entrepreneurs who played leading roles in mobilizing networks of NGOs from around the world that undertook coordinated campaigns focused on key international poverty issues. These included, for example, Ann Pettifor of the Jubilee 2000 campaign on debt relief, Martin Khor of Third World Network advocacy on international economic policies, Adrienne Germain of IWHC on reproductive rights, and Roberto Bissio of Social Watch on aid and social investments.

The 1990s UN conferences were high-energy events with widespread participation and strategic coalition building across government and nongovernment actors.[22] There were preparatory processes that brought together technocrats and advocates from the substantive ministries, international and national NGOs, donor agencies, and the media in protracted dialogues to formulate national and regional positions. The content of these declarations reflected the broader participation and the critical positions and analyses of civil society and UN agencies on poverty, inequality, marginalization, and global governance.

Another source for the emergence of a poverty supernorm was the group that formulated the DAC's IDGs. This was the collective effort of a group of individuals representing France, Japan, the UK, United States, and other countries who met over the course of a year in different parts of the world to work out a future policy direction for aid. This process was driven partly by institutional interests. With the end of the Cold War had come a decline in political support for development aid, and foreign aid budgets had dropped dramatically.[23] The DAC selected six goals from the UN conferences of the early 1990s[24] in an effort to communicate a vision of what donors were striving to achieve in their development work for the twenty-first century. As Colin Bradford, who represented the United States in these negotiations, explains, "We needed a new post-post-war discourse for aid," one that could communicate with the "parliaments and publics."[25] In the formulation process, one of the major arguments was over how many goals to include, with all recognizing that fewer would be better, and some arguing for only one goal: the income poverty goal. Others argued that several goals were needed to appeal to different political constituencies such as women's groups, education groups, and health groups.

Among bilateral donors, four development ministers played particularly active roles as both domestic and international norm entrepreneurs. They used the IDGs to focus their countries' aid programs on poverty reduction goals. Clare Short (UK), Evelyn Herfkens (Netherlands), Hilde Johnson (Norway), and Heidemarie Wieczorek-Zeul (Germany) formed the informal Utstein Group. They strategized collectively, and used the IDGs to advocate increased aid commitments; a refocusing of aid on human development and poverty reduction; and reforms to trade, debt, and other policy areas.[26] Under the leadership of James Wolfensohn, the World Bank also became more active in promoting an antipoverty agenda.[27]

These norm entrepreneurs were a diverse group with diverse motivations operating from many different organizational platforms. Ideational commitments to ending poverty as an ethical imperative and to the broader principles of human dignity, equality, and social justice were important motivations for most of them and all had a deep personal commitment to reducing poverty. Many advocated a broader human-centered development paradigm and analytical frameworks such as basic needs, human development, capabilities, and feminism that differed from and critiqued mainstream economic analyses.

Toward the Global Tipping Point: Message Entrepreneurs, the Millennium Declaration, and the MDGs

By the late 1990s the vast number of goals being promoted by influential norm entrepreneurs, NGOs, and social movements, alongside the Copenhagen summit follow-up process and unrolling of the DAC's IDGs, presented Kofi Annan, the new Secretary-General of the UN, with a problem. These communicated a confusing message without any clear sense of priorities while Annan wanted to assert UN leadership over a coherent international development agenda. As the year 2000 approached, the Millennium Assembly needed to have a major impact. Just as the IDGs had served the donors, the MDGs turned out to be a solution to this problem in leading the world by their articulation of a unified, coherent, and simple message on the supernorm of global poverty eradication. The MDGs were a formulation of the antipoverty message, deliberately crafted to communicate more effectively than earlier specifications. The core strategy was: (1) to use quantitative goals because that spoke directly to results for which governments would be held accountable; and (2) to build on the momentum of the IDGs that had political traction, but lacked legitimacy because they were created by a donor group.

Finnemore and Sikkink argue that "norms that are clear and specific, rather than ambiguous or complex and those that have been around for a while . . . are more likely to be effective."[28] In addition, norms that are "widely accepted . . . in diplomatic discussions and treaties" are more likely to be effective.[29] The MDGs are a case in point. They were specifically designed to meet such conditions. The MDGs powerfully communicated the global antipoverty agenda because they delivered a concrete and simple message in three particular ways. First, they referred directly to concrete human conditions with which people could empathize rather than the abstract term "poverty" that was open to interpretation. Second, they had quantified time-bound targets and could be monitored. This made it clear that these were concrete objectives, not abstract aspirations. Third, the list was relatively short with only eight goals, not dozens, and could therefore be remembered and presented as a single PowerPoint slide. Keeping the list short was a key consideration in the formulation of the Millennium Declaration. It also was significant in the earlier IDGs.

The aims of the message entrepreneurs who drafted and negotiated the Millennium Declaration and MDGs were different from the norm entrepreneurs who had driven the UN conference agendas. They were institutionally embedded individuals who were motivated by organizational mandates. This is not to doubt their personal commitment to global poverty eradication, but their actions were not driven by these ideals in the same way. As already stated above, similar motivations had influenced the individuals who framed the IDGs. As those involved in the Office of the Secretary-General explain, the Millennium Summit was an opportunity for the UN and the Secretary-General to demonstrate global leadership. They aimed for a powerful declaration and prepared for this through the Secretary-General's report, *We the Peoples*. According to Ambassador Gert Rosenthal of Guatemala who co-chaired the intergovernmental negotiations on the Millennium Summit declaration, *We the Peoples* was a powerful document with clear prose and coherence that reflected the fact that it was not written by committee as most UN documents are, but by a single author—John Ruggie—with help from two collaborators.

Achieving the Global Tipping Point: The MDGs

As soon as the Millennium Declaration was adopted by the General Assembly in September 2000, the significance of the nascent goals as the message was recognized. Lord Mark Malloch Brown, then administrator of the UN Development Programme (UNDP), was one of the first to do so and he rushed to publish an editorial in the *International Herald Tribune*.[30] He then began to promote the goals in the declaration not yet packaged and labeled MDGs as the global development framework. This was not easy because he met with some resistance from political leaders who were taking other initiatives to mobilize support through other frameworks such as Gordon Brown on child poverty. The World Bank was also quick to see the potential and called a meeting to develop a more robust (and final) set of indicators for the goals.

This brought the UN, the World Bank, and the DAC secretariat into the process of forging a follow-up process. Inevitably, questions arose about leadership, and whether the goals would continue to be named IDGs. Ultimately, the Office of the Secretary-General undertook to lead the work of developing an implementation plan (the "Road Map") for the Millennium Declaration, including the final set of indicators. This work became a major task for Michael Doyle, who had succeeded Ruggie in the Secretary-General's office. Such a response to a General Assembly declaration is exceptional, given that the typical shelf life of a UN declaration is in days or weeks after adoption. An interagency group of technocrats—the core of whom had worked on the IDGs including the OECD's Brian Hammond, World Bank's Eric Swanson, and UNDP's Jan Vandemoortele—was formed to convert the list in the Millennium Declaration into a more robust set of goals with targets and indicators that could be monitored systematically. Malloch Brown also began to lobby and negotiate for these goals—yet to be labeled MDGs—with influential leaders such as Short.

The individuals who drove the process converting the Millennium Declaration's list into the MDGs were message entrepreneurs with characteristics quite distinct from norm entrepreneurs. They were less motivated by an ideational commitment to ending poverty and driven more by an organizational imperative. Ruggie and Doyle in the Office of the Secretary-General and Malloch Brown at UNDP were committed to making the UN a more effective organization. They had neither led nor engaged in the battles that had converted international development into poverty eradication over the 1990s. Malloch Brown sought to achieve more consensual relationships across the fractious development community that was divided by ideology and pitted the World Bank and International Monetary Fund (IMF) against NGOs with the UN caught in the middle. His view was shared by others in the development community who wanted more effective coordination of development strategies and activities, particularly World Bank president Wolfensohn, who made a point of personally reaching out to the UN as his predecessors had never done. They sought a more unified international community for development, which meant creating a shared vision and more constructive relationships among the World Bank, IMF, UN, bilateral agencies, and NGOs. As diplomats skilled in negotiations among organizations and governments, they had been trained mainly in history and political science rather than economics or practical work in development. They negotiated an agreement across the 189 UN delegations and also brought on board the three other sets of actors who were leading parallel efforts: the bilateral aid agencies (DAC of the OECD); the World Bank and IMF; and the UN specialized agencies.

To illustrate the tensions of the time, in June 2000 when the UN jointly published with the World Bank, IMF, and OECD the report *A Better World for All* on progress in meeting the DAC IDGs, an uproar went up from NGO networks.[31] They were shocked that the UN Secretary-General would sign a document with the heads of the World Bank, IMF, and OECD. This was seen as a betrayal. The antiglobalization debates behind much NGO thinking were often framed in antimarket ideology and portrayed the World Bank and IMF as the enemy. To communicate a coherent international agenda, which could be accepted by these fractious groups, required a message that would finesse the "market is best . . . market is worst" positions of the international financial institutions and antiglobalization NGOs. The MDGs achieved this through focusing on people and the ends of development around which a common vision could be established rather than the means to get there, which was fiercely contested.

The supernorm of global poverty eradication approached a global tipping point in September 2000 with the adoption of the Millennium Declaration, which won the unanimous approval of the General Assembly. With the publication of the MDGs in September 2001, and the mobilization to implement them, the tipping point was reached.

Cascading the MDGs: Old Obstacles and New Organizational Platforms

As Finnemore and Sikkink's model would predict, the key actors involved in the cascade process for the MDGs were states and international organizations that adopted the MDGs to comply with international standards and, for some, to enhance their international standing. The process of norm cascade for the MDGs can appear both simple and complex. At one level, arguably, the MDGs had an extraordinarily rapid and simple cascade process. Because they derived from the unanimous approval of the Millennium Declaration by the General Assembly, and most particularly by the majority of the world's heads of state, it could be argued that all governments of the world adopted them at the same time. But as Richard Jolly concludes in his analysis of UN goals, the effectiveness of these goals in mobilizing genuine action depends on institutional follow-up.[32] In this respect, the UN invested heavily through three major programs: (1) research to develop technical strategy; (2) a campaign to publicize the goals and mobilize support; and (3) support to national governments. In their policy statements, almost all national governments, multilateral organizations, and bilateral agencies started to refer to the MDGs as a central element of their strategy. But there were obstacles.

First, the United States was initially ambivalent and then later opposed to the MDGs. While President William J. Clinton stood alongside other heads of state at the September 2000 Millennium Summit to adopt the Millennium Declaration, the incoming George W. Bush administration turned hostile toward the MDGs. This position came to a head at the 2005 UN Millennium +5 Summit, when the incoming US ambassador John Bolton arrived during the final days of the preparations and objected to the use of the term "MDGs" in the draft declaration. The United States ultimately gave in since it was overwhelmingly isolated in its position.

A second challenge came from international NGO networks. NGO networks had confrontational meetings with the UN; for example, at the 2002 UNDP's Civil Society Advisory Board meeting with Malloch Brown. They argued that the MDGs were not democratically formulated but put together by bureaucrats and agreed on among governments without wider consultation.[33] The NGO networks were also critical of the content (see below) of the MDGs because: (1) important goals, especially reproductive health goals, were excluded; (2) the goals and targets were not ambitious enough, especially for countries that had already achieved them; (3) the Goal 8 partnership goals and targets were weak and lacked quantitative targets; and (4) systemic reforms of global governance structures and policies were excluded. Underpinning these specific criticisms was the deeply felt suspicion that the MDGs had co-opted the UN and NGOs into a consensus position with the World Bank and IMF—the systemic antiliberalization reform agendas for which many NGO networks had been campaigning were not advanced by the MDGs.

Third, most developing country governments gave only lukewarm support to the MDGs because they feared that they would be used as another set of donor conditions, and because they could see little value added. There was nothing new or innovative for the Global South in these goals: reducing poverty, freedom from hunger, education for all, and other goals had been part of national development plans for decades.

In the end, these objections did not prevent the international norm cascade process. The United States was marginalized. The NGOs could complain, but they could not persuade UN member states to block the MDGs. For the developing countries, fighting the MDGs would have undermined their interest in keeping social and economic development issues at the forefront of UN debates. And anyway, for most delegations, their country's president or prime minister had approved the Millennium Declaration, so how would their opposition to the MDGs be handled? For all stakeholders, the danger of appearing to object to pulling people out of abject poverty was a position to be avoided.

From their launch in September 2001, the MDGs began to command center stage in international development events: the 2002 Monterrey Finance for Development Conference sought ways to finance MDG implementation; Gordon Brown and Tony Blair used them to lead the G8 2005 summit at Gleneagles that secured a number of rich country commitments for action; celebrities (Bono, Bob Geldof, and Angelina Jolie) have mobilized popular support and raised public awareness about global poverty in the rich world. These were all effective mechanisms of persuasion in the MDG cascade process.

Omissions and Self-censorship

Five content omissions in the Millennium Declaration and the original MDG listing adopted in 2001 have continued to attract criticisms, particularly from their respective constituencies encompassing individuals from national governments, donor agencies, UN agencies, NGOs, academics, and specialists. Each argues that the omission did not reflect state-of-the-art thinking in development economics, human development, or best practice in international development. The 2001 list was a compromise finalized by an expert group seeking to keep the list as short as possible. As data professionals, they considered only objectives for which reasonably robust internationally comparable data series were available, dating back to 1990. But they also were sensitive to the demands of political expediency: to come up with a list that would be accepted by nearly 200 governments.

The most controversial omission was reproductive health services for all. This omission was no accident, but the result of pressure from the "unholy alliance" of the Holy See and a handful of conservative Islamic states that persuaded the G-77 to block this goal.[34] The message entrepreneurs who framed the Millennium Declaration and the MDGs did not want to fail in developing an umbrella listing of poverty goals around which consensus could be achieved. For these message entrepreneurs, reproductive health was a quibble over details. They tended to argue that it did not matter whether these specific goals were included or not because, in any case, they would be part of any reasonable implementation strategy.

The second omission relates to governance, human rights, and democracy. By the late 1990s, many leading researchers argued that poor people remained poor because they lacked power and were politically excluded. At a time when the World Bank's flagship *World Development Report 2000–2001* on poverty concluded that empowerment was one of the three key strategies for ending poverty, along with opportunity and security, it was surprising that the MDGs did not include governance to empower the poor.[35] It would have raised controversy with national governments as infringement on sovereignty.

The third omission was gender empowerment, which had only the target of eliminating inequalities in schooling in the original formulation. The women's movement had moved far beyond its early focus on educational disparities to issues that were as much or more fundamental to women's disempowerment: gender-based violence, lack of property rights, economic discrimination, and political exclusion. Goal 3 of the MDGs took the agenda back to the priorities of the 1970s.

The fourth omission was the limiting of the decent work target to youth employment. Reportedly, the top management of the International Labour Organization (ILO) was dismissive of the IDG and MDG exercises. They advised staff that such lists were "a passing fad, we don't need to get mixed up with them . . . this is not the only game in town."[36] The ILO position changed in the early 2000s and, by 2005, it was effectively advocating for decent work to become an MDG target.

The fifth omission was in Goal 8, which lacks quantitative, time-bound targets. While the results-based management principle of having SMART [stretching, measurable, agreed, realistic, and time-limited goals] targeting was rigorously pursued for Goals 1 through 6, and partially applied to Goal 7, it was systematically avoided for Goal 8. Because Goal 8 was not a quantitative goal in the Millennium Declaration, there was a limit to what the framers of the MDGs felt they could negotiate; the expert group engaged in self-censorship. By 2001, the lack of support for the MDGs in the George W. Bush administration was understood. And there was little to be gained by raising the likelihood of US withdrawal from this process by pushing for SMART goals for rich countries.

In 2005 some of these omissions were corrected with the addition of targets for reproductive health, women's political representation, and decent work, along with more detailed environmental targets. The belated inclusion of reproductive health targets was a result of energetic lobbying led by norm entrepreneurs—the head of the UN Population Fund and a group of countries that were committed to women's reproductive health rights. They acted politically and mobilized much of the UN membership to support the inclusion of this target, overturning the self-censorship exercised by the original framers of the Millennium Declaration and MDGs.

Norm Internalization

The internalization of the MDGs has made rapid progress at the level of policy statements, documentation, and reporting. The MDGs have become internalized as the meta-goal of virtually all international development efforts. The term "Millennium Development Goals" has entered the language of international development as a synonym for "poverty reduction." The goals are regularly referred to in policy documents of donor agencies and in national development planning documents such as the Poverty Reduction Strategy Papers.[37] They also are mentioned by NGOs, think tanks, and the media.

Monitoring MDG progress continues to command the highest profile at the General Assembly. The MDGs were the centerpiece of the 2005 Millennium +5 Summit at which the MDGs were officially affirmed and at a special high-level event in 2008. The 2010 General Assembly was an "MDG Summit" that reviewed progress and renewed commitment to accelerate progress toward achieving the goals.[38] Such events are significant for countries; for example, the prime ministers of both India and China have personally presented their national MDG reports at the UN. Conformity to international standards has clearly been a driving motive for using the MDG framework in monitoring development.

The MDGs have also been used to mobilize action across many different communities; private corporations,[39] municipalities,[40] national governments, schools, and NGOs have framed their activities in terms of contributions to MDG achievement. The Stand-Up Against Poverty campaign has mobilized ever-increasing numbers to make personal commitments to fight for MDGs, reaching 117 million in 2009. In effect, these instances show that the MDGs have become a habit, and reflect internalization as predicted by Finnemore and Sikkink's model.

Norm Content: Contestation and Consensus

The great strength of the MDGs as a supernorm, communicating a complex set of norms underpinned by a more abstract idea (global responsibility for eradicating extreme poverty) in concrete and unambiguous terms, is also their great weakness. They skirted around, and did not resolve, the ideational divides within the international community. The present form of the MDGs reflects many compromises to create a consensus on which the major stakeholders could agree. The tension continues between the many norm entrepreneurs (and their organizational platforms) who have pushed to get their norm included in the MDG supernorm framework and the message entrepreneurs who have striven to keep the MDG list as short and simple as possible. The message entrepreneurs either have argued that proposed additional goals are covered by existing goals, or have negotiated proposals for additional goals down to the target level (as with water and sanitation, decent work, and reproductive health) or the indicator level. The debates that emerged in the immediate aftermath of the Millennium Declaration continue in many formal and informal debates.[41]

Ideational Trajectory

The norm entrepreneurs who mobilized and energized the UN conferences and summits often were reacting against the Washington Consensus. But the message entrepreneurs wanted to avoid these divides within the international development community and achieve a broader consensus around poverty reduction. This meant attempting to create a cease-fire and moving beyond the contests over debt relief, structural adjustment, and many other issues because the MDGs had to be championed not only by the UN, but also by the World Bank and IMF. The leading message entrepreneurs, like Malloch Brown and Doyle, wanted a unified front. They were also seeking a "new bargain" between the aid donor countries and developing country governments to expand total aid flows. Reaching a consensus was critical. . . .

But the ideational divides were strong and entrenched. So when NGOs protested against the UN Secretary-General joining the heads of the World Bank, IMF, and OECD in signing *Building a Better World,* the 2000 progress report on the DAC's IDGs, Annan had to stand firm, writing back that the report was not a policy document and IDGs were goals and targets originated in UN conferences.[42] In the formulation of the MDGs and the Millennium Declaration, the message entrepreneurs consciously laid out the objectives that were shared among the dissenting parties and avoided the more contentious issue of the economic strategies, and other hot topics such as reproductive health, needed to achieve them. The lukewarm support for the MDGs from NGOs and developing country governments reflected their unease in endorsing a consensus with the Bretton Woods organizations.

It is no accident that the MDGs are headed by the goal of reducing the proportion of people living in extreme income poverty (Goal 1 and Target 1). That was the preference of the OECD. And by ensuring this goal was at the top of the list, the message entrepreneurs sought to make it clear that the shift from a focus on national development to global poverty reduction did not suggest that economic growth, based on globalization, was to be marginalized. This meant that the MDGs had a significant degree of continuity with earlier ideas about dealing with mass poverty. It also meant that the message entrepreneurs could disguise the complexity of the MDGs through the simple shorthand of Goal 1, to eradicate extreme poverty and hunger, and Target 1A, to halve the proportion of people whose income is less than $1 a day.

The MDGs are a grand simplification of the many goals and targets identified by the norm entrepreneurs of the 1990s. The goals and priorities of the 1990s UN conference processes had in common emphases on equality and human rights as well as partnerships across state, business, and civil society and across poor and rich countries. The vision of the Millennium Declaration was driven by the principles of human dignity, equality, and solidarity that reflect international human rights principles.[43] But the MDGs barely reflected these human rights principles.[44] While the MDGs adopted a human development conceptualization of poverty, approved by many opponents of neoliberalism and structural adjustment, they took a relatively conservative "basic needs" position.[45] This was taken instead of a more assertive human rights perspective that the meeting of basic needs is a global responsibility.[46]

Whether the supernorm that the MDGs represent is to be seen as a great advance, as a missed opportunity, or as a regression depends on the ideational framework applied. From a neoliberal growth perspective, the MDGs have shifted attention to social policy and may slow down the economic growth that is needed to reduce poverty. The MDGs neglected the centrality of growth and the private sector for poverty reduction and dangerously exaggerated the role and capacity of the state. But for critics of the neoliberal growth strategies of the late twentieth century, the MDGs are not progressive enough. The MDGs middle-of-the-road and post–Washington Consensus stance promoted by the message entrepreneurs opened them to criticisms from the left. For feminists (Peggy Antrobus and Rosalind Eyben) and the more radical left (Saith), the MDGs were seen as only a minor shift in the status quo, perhaps merely pretence.[47] The MDGs accepted that global capitalism should be the engine for achieving poverty reduction; failed to recognize the need for redistribution (both materially and in terms of political power); and conceptualized poverty reduction as a lack of goods and services rather than as a relational problem.[48] With the exception of gender equality within nations, the MDGs avoided directly promoting the reduction of social and economic inequality (between and within countries) or the achievement of human rights for all.

Conclusion

In this article, we have analyzed the evolution of a complex international supernorm to eradicate extreme poverty as a global responsibility. Finnemore and Sikkink's model has proved valuable in understanding these processes. But we have also extended the conceptual apparatus in four particular ways. First, complex, multiple goal norms are best understood as supernorms—carefully structured sets of interrelated norms that pursue a grand prescriptive goal. Second, while our analysis confirms the centrality of altruistically motivated individuals as norm entrepreneurs for the emergence of international norms, it also identifies a significant role for a different set of actors, the message entrepreneurs. Message entrepreneurs have personal normative positions, but their primary function is to achieve consensus, which is the purpose of an intergovernmental organization. The detailed content of the supernorm is of secondary importance for them. They use self-censorship to minimize confrontation. While a norm entrepreneur can be expected to stick to his or her principles, a message entrepreneur must mix principles with pragmatism to achieve a deal. The role of message entrepreneurs therefore is essential in making the transition from norm emergence to norm cascade and internalization. It also explains why ideas commonly become distorted when taken up by international organizations.[49]

The message entrepreneurs not only are essential in achieving norm cascade and internationalization, but they also influence—or reshape—the content of the norms. The poverty eradication supernorm emerged in the context of a fractious international community divided by ideological battles over structural adjustment. The MDGs came on the scene as a useful communication device and a means of coordination. They argued for a shift away from structural adjustment, but did not refute a market-based approach to development. This was only a partial solution to creating a larger and more coordinated attack on poverty since it brought with it several contradictions. First, while the motivations and intent of the norm entrepreneurs were to change policies they believed were obstacles to eradicating poverty, the key motivations of the message entrepreneurs were to avoid controversies, which they perceived to be driven by the ideologies of earlier eras, and achieve a pragmatic consensus to increase resources and efforts for poverty reduction. As a consequence, the institutionalization of the norm did not really lead to substantial change in policy approaches. Second, the norm entrepreneurs sought behavioral change in policymakers while the message entrepreneurs targeted the public at large who might support policies for poverty reduction.

The recent evolution of the agenda for international development, and especially its reworking as global poverty eradication, can be only partially explained by norm dynamics. Ideas count but when it comes to global altruism, the economic and political interests of states, and the elites who manage national affairs, take priority. A realist analytical perspective must lie alongside our constructivist approach. The slow movement on implementation of the supernorm through behavior change contrasts with the fast spread of the MDGs in policy statements: only limited evidence for specific countries and for specific targets suggests that poverty reduction is being accelerated; the development round in trade talks has been stymied; after an initial increase in the late 1990s, aid flows have stagnated; and progress has been slow in finding alternative approaches to manage intellectual property regimes to allow for increased access to technology. Moreover, the origins and trajectory of the MDG supernorm have to be seen in terms of the political and economic interests of corporations and rich states who want to maintain a neoliberal economic agenda of market globalization and, thus, seek to accommodate the challenge of global poverty through a third-way framework.

Notes

1. Alastair Greig, David Hulme, and Mark Turner, *Challenging Global Inequality: Development Theory and Practice in the 21st Century* (New York: Palgrave Macmillan, 2007).

2. For a review of poverty in the policy agenda, see UNDP, *Human Development Report* (New York: Oxford University Press, 1996), pp. 43–65.

3. Charles Gore, "The MDG Paradigm, Productive Capacities and the Future of Poverty Reduction," *IDS Bulletin* 41, no. 1 (2010): 70–79.

4. Ashwani Saith, "From Universal Values to Millennium Development Goals: Lost in Translation," *Development and Change* 37, no. 6 (2006): 1167.

5. Martha Finnemore and Kathryn Sikkink, "International Norm Dynamics and Political Change," *International Organization* 52, no. 4 (1998): 887–917.

6. Ibid.

7. UN, *Millennium Declaration* (2000). Resolution adopted by the General Assembly A/55/L.2, par. 11, www.un.org/millennium/declaration/ares552e.htm.

8. *Road Map Towards the Implementation of the United Nations Millennium Declaration: Report of the Secretary-General* (New York: UN, 2001).

9. UN Millennium Project, *Investing in Development: A Practical Plan to Achieve the Millennium Development Goals* (London: Earthscan, 2005).

10. For good summary reviews of these approaches, see David Clark, ed., *The Elgar Companion to Development Studies* (Cheltenham, UK: Edward Elgar, 2006).

11. Richard Jolly, Louis Emmerij, Dharam Ghai, and Frédéric Lapeyre, *UN Contributions to Development Thinking and Practice* (Bloomington: Indiana University Press, 2004).

12. Andrew Shonfield, *The Attack on World Poverty* (London: Chatto & Windus, 1960); Gunnar Myrdal, *The Challenge of World Poverty: A World Antipoverty Program in Outline* (London: Penguin, 1970).

13. UN, *The United Nations Development Agenda: Development for All* (New York: UN, 2007).

14. *Copenhagen Declaration on Social Development*, www.un.org/esa/socdev/wssd/copenhagen_declaration.html.

15. Development Assistance Committee, *Shaping the 21st Century: The Contribution of Development Co-operation*, OECD, Paris, May 1996, www.oecd.org/dataoecd/23/35/2508761.pdf.

16. Finnemore and Sikkink, "International Norm Dynamics and Political Change."

17. Peter Adamson and Richard Jolly, *Jim Grant: UNICEF Visionary* (Florence: Innocenti, 2007).

18. UNICEF, "World Declaration and Plan of Action on the Survival, Protection and Development of Children," 30 September 1990, www.un.org/gen info/bp/child.html.

19. Ibid.

20. Nafis Sadik, former executive director of UN Population Fund, interviewed by the first author, New York, 26 January 2009.

21. Martha Chen, "Engendering World Conferences: The International Women's Movement and the United Nations," *Third World Quarterly* 16, no. 4 (1995): 477–493.

22. UN, *The United Nations Development Agenda: Development for All* (New York: UN, 2007).

23. OECD, *Statistical Annex of the 2010 Development Co-operation Report*, table 9, www.oecd.org/document/9/0,3343,en_2649_34447_1893129_1_1_1 _1,00.html.

24. David Hulme, "The Making of the Millennium Development Goals: Human Development Meets Results-based Management in an Imperfect World," Brooks World Poverty Institute Working Paper No. 16 (Manchester: University of Manchester, 2008).

25. Interviews with key players in the DAC IDG process: Colin Bradford, interviewed by the first author, New York, 16 October 2008; Richard Carey, interviewed by the first author, New York, 16 October 2008; Richard Manning, personal communication with the first author, January 2009.

26. Hulme, "The Making of the Millennium Development Goals."

27. Sebastian Mallaby, *The World's Banker: A Story of Failed States, Financial Crisis, and the Poverty of Nations* (London: Penguin Books, 2004).

28. Finnemore and Sikkink, "International Norm Dynamics," pp. 906–907.

29. Jeffrey W. Legro, "Which Norms Matter? Revisiting the Failure of Internationalism," *International Organization* 51, no. 1 (1997): 31–63.

30. Lord Mark Malloch Brown, former Administrator of UNDP and former UN Deputy Secretary-General, interviewed by the first author, London, 27 June 2008; Mark Suzman, former staff of UNDP Administrator's office and former staff of UN Secretary-General's office, personal communication with the first author, 20 October 2008; Mark Malloch Brown, "Halving World's Poor Is Realistic Goal," *International Herald Tribune,* 21 September 2000, www.iht .com/articles/2000/09/21/edbrown.t_0.php.

31. See letter from the World Council of Churches, 28 June 2000, www.wcc -coe.org/wcc/news/press/00/22pu.html.

32. Richard Jolly, "Global Development Goals: The United Nations Experience," *Journal of Human Development* 5, no. 1 (2004): 69–95.

33. See Roberto Bissio, "Civil Society and the MDGs," *Development Policy* 3 (2003): 151–160.

34. David Hulme, "Politics, Ethics and the Millennium Development Goals: The Case of Reproductive Health," Brooks World Poverty Institute Working Paper No. 104 (Manchester: University of Manchester, 2009).

35. World Bank, *World Development Report 2000–2001: Attacking Poverty* (Washington, DC: World Bank, 2000), http://web.worldbank.org/wbsite/external /topics /extpoverty/0,,contentmdk:20194762~pagepk:148956~pipk:216618~the sitepk:336992,00.html.

36. A. Sylvester Young, director of statistics, International Labour Organization, interviewed by the second author, Geneva, 30 May 2007.

37. Sakiko Fukuda-Parr, "Reducing Inequality—The Missing MDG: A Content Review of PRSPs and Bilateral Donor Policy Statements," *IDS Bulletin* 41, no. 1 (2010): 26–35.

38. For a report on this summit, see the UNDP website, www.undp.org/mdg /summit.shtml.

39. Brookings Institution, *Brookings Blum Roundtable: The Private Sector in the Fight Against Global Poverty*, Aspen, Colorado, August 2005, www3 .brookings.edu /global/200508blum_agenda.pdf.

40. Millennium Campaign 2009, "European Local Authorities Unite to Call for Achievement of Millennium Development Goals," 23 April 2009, www.end poverty2015.org/europe/news/european-local-authorities-unite-call-achievement -millennium-development-goals/28/apr/09; David Hulme, Global Poverty (London: Routledge, 2010), chap. 4.

41. See, for example, the collection of articles in the special issue of *IDS Bulletin* 41, no. 1, edited by Andy Sumner and Clare Melamed, "The MDGs and Beyond."

42. Chakravarthi Raghavan, "Annan Replies to WCC over Better World for All Report," *Third World Network*, 4 July 2000, www.twnside.org.sg/title /wcc.htm. See also 28 June 2000 letter from World Council of Churches to the Secretary-General and response, www.wcc-coe.org/wcc/news/press/00/22pu.html.

43. UNDP, *Human Development Report* (New York: Oxford University Press, 2003); Philip Alston, "A Human Rights Perspective on the Millennium Development Goals," Background Paper for the Work of the Millennium Project Task Force on Poverty and Economic Development, 2004, www.hurilink .org/tools/HRsPerspectives_on_the_MDGs--Alston.pdf; UN, *The United Nations Development Agenda*.

44. UN OHCHR, *Claiming the MDGs: A Human Rights Approach* (Geneva: United Nations, 2008).

45. Hulme, "The Making of the Millennium Development Goals."

46. See, for example, UN OHCHR, *Claiming the MDGs*, for a detailed critique of the MDGs from this perspective.

47. Peggy Antrobus, "Critiquing MDGs from a Caribbean Perspective," *Gender and Development* 13, no. 1 (March 2005): 94–104; Rosalind Eyben, "The Road Not Taken: International Aid's Choice of Copenhagen over Beijing," *Third World Quarterly* 27, no. 4 (2006): 595–608; Saith, "From Universal Values."

48. Maia Green and David Hulme, "From Correlates and Characteristics to Causes: Thinking About Poverty from a Chronic Poverty Perspective," *World Development* 33, no. 6 (2005): 867–879.

49. Morten Bøås and Desmond McNeill, *Multilateral Institutions: A Critical Introduction* (London: Pluto, 2003).

11

The Regime Complex for Food Security: Implications for the Global Hunger Challenge

Matias E. Margulis

Food security has reemerged as a major issue in global governance. The perfect storm of surging energy prices, bio-fuel policies, food trade bans, and speculation on commodities markets that drove food prices to historical peaks in 2008 swelled the number of hungry people worldwide to an unprecedented 1 billion. Although the number of hungry persons has fallen slightly since then, food prices spiked sharply again in 2010 and 2011 and uncertainty about the availability of the world food supply continues to send jitters across global markets. Polities have also felt the repercussions of volatile and rising food prices. Let us not forget that the calls for "bread *and* freedom" became the rallying cry for the political movements in Egypt and Tunisia that toppled long-standing autocratic regimes. Chinese and Indian authorities have declared rising food prices a major macroeconomic concern that threatens both economic growth and social stability.

The recent food price crises exacerbated an already deteriorating world food security situation. Following a steady decline in the number of hungry people worldwide between 1970 and 1995, the global trend has since reversed, with world hunger continuously on the rise ever since.[1] This backward movement was unexpected and has surprised most policymakers. Current trends indicate that the first Millennium Development Goal (MDG)—to reduce the number of hungry people worldwide by half between 1990 and 2015—will not be met. A further concern is the domino effect of rising food insecurity; higher levels of

Reprinted from *Global Governance*, vol. 19, no. 1: 53–67. © 2013 by Lynne Rienner Publishers. Reprinted by permission of the publisher.

under-nutrition and malnutrition will undermine progress on other MDGs such as global health and social and human development.

There is now a wide acceptance among policymakers of the pressing need to reform the global governance of food security in order to address rising world hunger and improve the efficacy of existing food security interventions. It is widely acknowledged that the global scale, drivers, and complexity of food insecurity are beyond the capacity of individual states to manage alone. The current global reform drive includes increasing cooperation and policy coherence across the UN system, the Bretton Woods Institutions, regional bodies, and the Group of 20 (G-20) leaders. However, the hunger problem cannot be simply reduced to issues of poverty and food supply, which is the focus of current policymaking. World poverty has been constant—and even declined slightly—during the period in which hunger grew.[2] Rising hunger has occurred alongside constant growth in world food production in both absolute and per capita terms. While poverty reduction remains an important factor, there are other factors that need to be taken into account. As the recent food price crises have demonstrated, the drivers of food insecurity are increasingly complex and tied to structural changes in the global food economy.[3] Demand for international cooperation will only increase. Climate change is predicted to exacerbate food insecurity in developing countries and will further intensify the challenge of sustainably feeding a world population of 9 billion by 2050.[4]

The study of regime complexes is significant to the current debates about reform of the global governance of food security. There has been a transition from an international food security regime to a regime complex for food security, and this has major implications for efforts to improve policy coherence and the institutional architecture to address world hunger. Diverging rules and norms across the elemental regimes of agriculture and food, international trade, and human rights concerning the appropriate role of states and markets in addressing food insecurity produced a simmering transnational political conflict prior to the recent food price crisis. Understanding this conflict is critical because it is unresolved and therefore is a latent tension forestalling efforts to reform the global governance of food security.

The Construction of the International Food Security Regime

A major research program in international relations has explored the role of the intersubjective dimension of human action in constructing the global polity.[5] Norms, ideas, and identities play a critical role in structuring international relations alongside material factors. Norms are the underlying cognitive frameworks that shape actors' identities and preferences and construct the principles, rules, and institutions that constitute the international system.[6] Drawing from these insights, I trace how food security has been constructed as an issue area requiring international cooperation and the consolidation of an international food security regime over time. This historical narrative is critical to understanding the continuous evolution of international food security governance and its current historical juncture.

Eradicating hunger was one of the principal objectives of the postwar international system. Alongside the desire for peace and prosperity, the architects of the postwar system, led by the United States, held a belief about the international community's collective responsibility to fight hunger and the vast potential for advances in nutrition and agricultural science to achieve this end. This belief drove the creation of the Food and Agriculture Organization (FAO) in 1945, the first UN specialized agency tasked to raise world nutrition levels, improve food production and distribution, and ensure humanity's freedom from hunger.[7] Early FAO efforts sought to address the food problem through the international coordination of grain production and trade to redistribute surplus food produced in the West to meet the needs of the hungry in the developing world. However, the United States and other major grain producers, who enjoyed unique positions at that time as the world's granaries and preferred expanding agricultural trade, did not fully support international coordination and instead steered the FAO to focus its work on strengthening food supply management within developing countries.

In the 1960s, rapid population growth, combined with lagging food production in developing countries, prompted Malthusian fears of an impending world food shortage. It was during this period that the UN World Food Programme (WFP) was created under the umbrella of the FAO to provide food assistance to developing countries. While this development served multiple humanitarian, trade, and domestic farm policy objectives of the main aid donors, such as the United States, the European Community, Canada, and Australia (also the major grain-producing countries), the evolving practice of international food assistance further concretized the norm and expectations of international cooperation on hunger.[8] The creation of the WFP was quickly followed by the major grain-producing countries agreeing to a new international food aid burden-sharing system under the Food Aid Convention (FAC). In addition to food aid, these countries scaled up bilateral and multilateral assistance to foster food production in developing countries by financing technological transfers and the introduction of higher-yield seed varieties, fertilizers, and pesticides (i.e., the Green Revolution).

The term *food security* was first incorporated into international policy during the early 1970s. An unexpected shortage of wheat caused panic on international food markets that drove grain prices skyward. Food-importing countries—the vast majority of states—desperately scrambled to secure food supplies. This was the first recognized world food crisis and it led to severe hunger in many countries. The crisis revealed a new driver of hunger to policymakers: price volatility and the unreliability of food supply on international markets.[9] The events of 1972–1974 challenged assumptions about how world food markets worked and led to political consensus about the need for new instruments of international cooperation to eradicate hunger. Several new international institutions came out of the 1974 FAO World Food Conference, including multilateral forums for interstate cooperation and an international financial institution, the International Fund for Agricultural Development (IFAD), to address the new drivers of food insecurity.[10] Although the conference produced political consensus about the need to address food security, the return of stability on international food markets soon after it was held diminished the sense of urgency for major international market reform.

The concept of food security continued to evolve, incorporating advances in the understanding of the causes of hunger. In particular the work of Nobel Prize–winning economist Amartya Sen, which demonstrated that access to food and not just food supply was critical to averting famine, reoriented international policies to look beyond traditional food production and supply issues.[11] Sen's theory of entitlements recognized that there were multiple causes of hunger, including food supply, availability, utilization, and access.[12] This new idea prompted a major rethinking of international food security policies away from the emphasis on bulk food transfers toward incorporating a set of interventions that target various dimensions and scales. This multifaceted understanding of hunger became the basis of the international consensus definition of food security negotiated by states at the 1996 World Food Summit.[13] This definition remains the accepted basis for international and national food security policymaking.

Taken together, these developments shaped the construction of food security as an issue area and the formation of an international regime around it. The desire to eradicate hunger alongside an evolving understanding of food security was reflected in the institutional arrangements and practices of international society. At the core of the international food security regime, and what differentiated this regime from the agricultural policy regime's focus on expanding consumption, production, and trade, was the widely accepted principle of international collective action to eradicate hunger and reduce the number of persons who suffer and die from hunger and malnutrition. The institutionalization of this regime is most commonly associated with the Rome-based UN food agencies: the FAO and its offshoots, the WFP and IFAD. The work of these institutions was grounded on shared principles and understandings of food security, with each institution performing a unique function: the provision of interstate negotiation and an information clearinghouse, the delivery of and standard-setting for international food assistance, and the provision of long-term loans, respectively. Other international institutions were key parts of the international food security regime. However, they varied in centrality and type, ranging from the short-lived World Food Council (1974–1994), a ministerial-level body tasked with keeping food security on the political agenda, to the Standing Committee on Food and Nutrition, which continues to ensure policy coherence across the UN system. Institutions outside of the UN system were also embedded in the regime, such as the FAC and the Consultative Group on International Agricultural Research, a network of international agriculture and food research centers nominally under the World Bank. While these latter institutions had variegated linkages to the UN institutions, there was a shared understanding among them about what food security meant and an underlying principle—eradicating hunger—that girded their work.

From International Food Security Regime to a Regime Complex for Food Security

There has been a shift from an international food security regime to a regime complex for food security. This shift occurred in the 1990s when institutional proliferation resulted in overlapping authority among the international food security, international trade, and human rights regimes. This has assembled a set of institutions with diverging norms and rules into a regime complex formation.

The creation of the World Trade Organization (WTO) in 1995 was a decisive moment in the emergence of a regime complex for food security. In particular, the Agreement on Agriculture (AA) and the Agreement on the Application of Sanitary and Phytosanitary Measures (SPS) brought agriculture and food governance under the binding international law of the WTO. The AA encompasses specific rules that determine the policies that states are permitted to undertake in order to achieve food security.[14] This includes, for example, domestic food subsidies and direct food assistance, types of border protection and financial support permitted to strategic food security commodities, export bans, and the operation of food reserves. The AA also contains rules on the provision of international food aid.

From the onset, the WTO acknowledged that international trade rules could have consequences for world food security. A key objective of the AA was to reduce agricultural overproduction in developed countries that was seen widely as the cause of a vicious cycle of low food prices, farm crises, and a transatlantic agricultural subsidy war.[15] During the negotiations of the AA, developed countries sought to boost the price of agricultural goods, reduce the burden of farm subsidies on national budgets, and maintain protection for domestic agricultural interests. It was recognized that success in achieving these objectives could carry negative food security implications such as higher food import bills for net food-importing developing countries. Therefore, the AA's framework explicitly charges the WTO and its members with continuously monitoring the impact of trade reforms on world food security and, if necessary, with providing assistance to countries that experience difficulties in financing food imports.[16] The SPS also governs food security because it sets the international standards for food safety. It provides the framework and conditions under which states may implement trade restrictions, such as on the import of foodstuffs that pose risks to human health. Presently, the AA and SPS are under renegotiation as part of the Doha Round (2001–present) of multilateral trade negotiations.

The WTO's binding rules and strong dispute settlement system give it significant authority in governing food security. Its broad coverage of food security in the AA and SPS created new linkages with the international food security regime. It introduced to the complex a very different normative orientation to the global governance of food security than had previously existed. The WTO's objective is to liberalize world agriculture along market-oriented principles, including rules that seek to limit state intervention that is perceived to distort self-regulating markets. At the WTO, trade officials argue that agricultural liberalization is key to increasing global food trade, which they associate with enhancing world food security.

The international human rights regime also has taken on greater authority in the global governance of food security by promoting the human right to food. The human right to food is not a new concept. It was first articulated in the 1948 Universal Declaration of Human Rights and then given legal character in the 1966 International Convention on Economic, Social, and Cultural Rights, which obligated parties to progressively realize the right to food and ensure an equitable distribution of world food supplies in relation to need. The right to food took on greater salience when states agreed to clarify the definition and the rights and obligations implicit in this human right as an outcome of the 1996 World Food Summit. The obligation of states to respect, protect, and fulfill the right to food is now an accepted international norm. Moreover, the right to food is becoming ever more institutionalized. International guidelines on the right to food were negotiated by states in 2003. While these guidelines are not legally binding, they further specified states' obligations and devised a framework for national legislation and international cooperation on agriculture, development, and international trade issues.[17] The monitoring and enforcement capacity on the right to food has been significantly strengthened under the work of the Office of the High Commissioner for Human Rights; the Committee on Economic, Social and Cultural Rights; and the Human Rights Council. The latter has developed enhanced processes to receive and respond to violations of the right to food and, thus, there are greater reputational costs for states and nonstate actors that violate this right.

An increasing number of states, such as South Africa, Brazil, and India, have created constitutional frameworks to protect the right to food. Admittedly, not all state actors fully support the expansion of the human rights regime's authority and the spilling over of human rights into the food security debate. Nevertheless, there is growing international consensus that the right to food is a critical dimension of food security because it defines the obligations of states to ensure that access to food is not diminished by other policies, particularly for the most vulnerable groups in society. Food as a human right, a right implicit with national and international legal obligations, is a new and important norm in the regime complex for food security. The linkage between food security and the right to food creates new expectations among citizens and other actors for state action to promote food security.

Global food security governance has the characteristics of a regime complex. In the regime complex for food security, there is an overlap of three elemental regimes—agriculture and food, international trade, and human rights—characterized by different norms that deal with a common issue, food security. These elemental regimes exhibit overlapping memberships as most states are members of the FAO and WTO or have signed on to the relevant international human rights treaties.

Overlapping Rules for Food Security

Scholars of regime complexes alert us to the impacts of overlapping rules on international cooperation and the myriad strategies employed by states and other actors in response to such situations.[18] Overlapping rules can introduce uncertainty, cause coordination problems by altering the incentives for international cooperation, and encourage forum-shopping and forum-shifting behavior among participants.[19] On the other hand, overlapping rules, once acknowledged by states as a constraint on cooperation, may in fact prompt direct efforts to increase coherence across the elemental regimes. Overlapping rules in the regime complex for food security increase uncertainty for policy actors and have been a source of transnational conflict between states and international organizations.

Consider the case of international food aid rules. Historically, international food aid rules rested with the original international food security regime, specifically under the FAO and FAC, that over time established best practices for international food aid, including minimizing potential negative impacts on food trade. This situation changed when authority over food aid rules was rescaled with the creation of the WTO. The AA linked trade and food aid in a new way; it included explicit references to the existing FAO and FAC food aid rules as criteria for determining if a WTO member's food aid policies were legitimate aid or a disguised farm subsidy. This particular development, which broke with the long-standing preference by most developed countries to keep food aid issues out of the General Agreement on Tariffs and Trade and the World Trade Organization, was the result of trade tensions and not humanitarian concerns. Having the AA cover food aid was viewed by many grain-producing countries as a means to keep questionable US food aid practices in check, such as the use of food aid to gain a commercial foothold in foreign markets. As a result, food aid became deeply entangled in the politics of international trade.[20]

The linkage between the food security and trade regimes has led to greater interaction among international and transnational policy actors. And this includes greater political friction among these actors. For example, when the current FAC expired in 2002 and was due to be renegotiated, states agreed to postpone renegotiating it until the WTO negotiations were finalized. This outcome was imposed by the trade ministries of the advanced economies on their international aid counterparts. Trade officials feared that renegotiating the FAC concurrently with the AA could result in forum shopping and the potential watering down of international food aid rules. Development officials hoped the renegotiation of the FAC would provide the opportunity to finally update the rules to reflect new best practices for international aid. Suspending the FAC renegotiation was publicly criticized by nongovernmental organizations (NGOs) active in humanitarian assistance, which cited this as further evidence of the WTO's "chilling effect" on other policy fields.[21] Development officials were similarly disconcerted about trade politics apparently trumping development issues. Food aid policy experts argue that freezing the FAC renegotiation for reasons related to trade policy derailed the political momentum that had been building among international development agencies to modernize the FAC to address rising global food insecurity.[22]

Overlapping rules and negotiations of food aid rules at the WTO also impacted the WFP. While the WFP is not involved in formal food aid rule making, nor is it formally linked to the WTO under the AA, this institution plays a key role in food aid delivery (it delivers the majority of multilateral food aid) and as a key forum for developing best practices. During the early years of the Doha Round, WFP officials expressed strong reservations about some WTO members' proposals that would increase the WTO's authority over international food aid. For example, one 2003 proposal supported by most WTO members envisaged the multilateral trade regime as the final arbiter of what is legitimate (and, by extension, legal) international food assistance. Given a lack of formal capacity to intervene in the state-based negotiations at the WTO, WFP officials resorted to launching an international media campaign critical of the WTO food aid proposal on the eve of the 2003 WTO ministerial meeting in Hong Kong.[23] The WFP's forceful and highly public critique of the WTO proposal came as an unexpected shock to many trade negotiators and prompted reconsideration by WTO members of the content and implications of future WTO food aid rules. The case of the WFP and WTO food aid rules illustrates that regime complexes can produce transnational political conflicts related to actors' perceptions of hierarchy, even when there are no formal overlapping rules or institutional linkages.

Norm-based Conflicts and Food Security Governance

Norm-based conflicts are evident in the regime complex for food security. There is considerable transnational political contestation surrounding the impacts of trade liberalization on food security and the appropriate global policies required to mitigate any negative consequences. This contest is played out within the regime complex for food security, with the WTO and UN institutions being influential actors. Diverging norms between the WTO and the UN institutions over the state-market relationship and its role in world food security frame this conflict. The WTO views free trade as being supportive of world food security; this position is the official view of the WTO secretariat and also of the powerful proponents of agricultural trade liberalization (e.g., the United States, European Union, Brazil, Canada, and Australia).[24] The FAO and UN human rights systems acknowledge the potential of trade liberalization to improve rural livelihoods.

However, these institutions' support for international trade is tempered by the recognition of asymmetrical power relations where powerful food-exporting countries and several transnational agri-food companies disproportionately shape market outcomes. The UN institutions are mandated to address the needs of food-insecure people and they contend that free trade does not necessarily enhance access to adequate food. UN institutions target the WTO negotiations because trade rules are binding on states, especially food-insecure ones, and this creates uncertainty for states on how to reconcile potential trade and human rights obligations. Norm-based conflicts have prompted the UN institutions to seek to influence international trade rules so that states have recourse to a wide set of policy measures to regulate national and international markets to achieve food insecurity objectives, including the obligation of states to protect the right to food under international law. In short, the UN monitors (and seeks to influence) trade negotiations with an eye toward ensuring that food security concerns are not lost to horse trading in the final deal.

It would be a mistake to equate these divergent readings of trade and food security as symptoms of bureaucratic turf wars. For example, the FAO strongly supported the creation of the WTO and provided developing countries technical support during negotiations of the AA. Since 1995, the FAO has cooperated closely with the WTO on many policy and technical issues. The FAO has never sought authority over agricultural trade negotiations. Instead, conflict between these institutions arises from the FAO's assessment that the AA is unbalanced and favors Northern agriculture interests. This view is shared by most developing countries, which make up the vast majority of WTO member states.

Diverging norms also engender problems of trust among actors. For example, international trade and human rights officials remain skeptical about each other's intentions, in large part because there is a concern that efforts to reconcile international trade and the right to food will lead to the weakening of one system at the expense of the other. Recent discourse about aligning trade and human rights is encouraging; however, scholars have noted the necessity for social learning and cultural change among international and national officials to bridge the current normative chasm.[25]

A new political dynamic in the regime complex for food security is heightened disagreement among old and new powers over food security and the role of international trade. Developing countries at the WTO—in particular the Group of 20, a Southern bargaining coalition on agriculture—with the support of the Group of 33 (G-33) coalition of developing countries with agricultural sensitivities, have pushed for new trade provisions to support food security that would protect key basic food staples and other crops produced by resource-poor farmers from being subject to further liberalization. One measure, the so-called Special Safeguard Mechanism (SSM), is intended to provide developing countries with the right to raise import tariffs on a temporary basis for sensitive food security crops. In theory, the SSM would prevent the rapid inflow of foreign, subsidized food imports, which cause food prices to bottom out and can wipe out small farmers. Another measure under consideration at the WTO, the "special products" proposal, would permit most developing countries to negotiate for a lower overall cut to the tariffs on products designated as critical to food security.

Developing countries claim these measures are vital to promote world food security. FAO officials have long supported these types of measures, including providing technical support to the WTO and developing countries during the development of these measures. More recently, the UN special rapporteur on the right to food, Olivier De Schutter, has recommended that WTO member states adopt these instruments, suggesting that these are consistent with states' obligations to protect the right to food. Developed countries claim these two instruments are protectionist and contrary to the spirit of the WTO's agenda of progressive trade liberalization. By extension, there is a concern that the SSM and special products may further expand the WTO's authority into food security.

The conflict over the extent to which the WTO and the AA should accommodate food security has proved to be a major source of political deadlock in the Doha Round. Breaking the WTO deadlock will likely require that new trade-related food security instruments be accepted; this is even truer after the recent global food crisis. By implication, this will require greater permissiveness by WTO members to support more, not less, state intervention in agricultural markets. The actual political economy implications of this are unclear; however, it does suggest potentially less market access for the major agricultural exporters. The normative tensions are profound here because what is at stake is tacit recognition that the WTO's mandate to reform agricultural trade along market lines needs to be reevaluated in light of global food security concerns. The WTO secretariat and many WTO members recognize and are disconcerted by such an outcome because they fear this may unravel not just the agricultural negotiations, but the entire Doha Round of negotiations, and thereby endanger liberalization on industrial goods and services.

While the WTO has significant regulatory authority in the regime complex, the moral authority continues to rest with the UN institutions rooted normatively in the international food security and human rights regimes. As such, there is no clear solution to addressing norm-based conflicts in the regime complex for food security. Centralization is an unlikely outcome. Increasing the authority of the WTO over food security will be strongly opposed by the UN system, the WTO, most states, and NGOs. At the same time, most states will continue to value the strong rule-based system of the WTO in spite of the current difficulties in the Doha Round. As such, states are unlikely to delegate responsibility for agriculture trade policy to the UN system. This would undermine the authority of the WTO and require states to recalculate the benefits and costs under all of the existing WTO trade agreements without agriculture on the table. Indeed, that option could cause further breakdown of the multilateral trade regime.

Implications for the Twenty-First-Century Food Security Challenge

The global governance of food security is at a crossroads. On the one hand, international efforts to reduce world food insecurity have fallen considerably short of expectations and commitments. There is a broad agreement that the current levels of world food insecurity are unacceptable morally and ethically as well as from a social and economic development policy perspective. The current state of world food insecurity is a dark stain on the record of international cooperation given that the tools and technologies to mitigate food insecurity among the most vulnerable are well proven, widely available, and inexpensive. On the other hand, there are signals that herald measured optimism. Food insecurity is a now a priority issue in global governance. This is evident in the recent work programs on food security, including the Group of 8 (G8) 2008 L'Aquila Food Security Initiative and the 2012 New Alliance for Food

Security and Nutrition programs to support agricultural production, technology, and research; and the establishment of the Global Agriculture and Food Security Program, a multi-donor fund to support private and public investment in agriculture, managed by the World Bank. It is also evident in the deepening transnational food security policy network at the UN High-Level Task Force on the Global Food Security Crisis and Committee on World Food Security. Greater cooperation at the regional level on food security is also promising, such as efforts by the African Union to increase the share of the national budget devoted to agriculture and the near completion of the Association of Southeast Asian Nations (ASEAN) Plus Three Emergency Rice Reserve.

Returning to the present multilateral efforts to address global food insecurity, we can observe many of the conflicts latent in the regime complex already at play. Diverging norms over trade liberalization are visible in the current debate on food export bans by major grain producers such as Russia and Ukraine. The WTO, World Bank, and G8 blame unilateral export bans for high food prices and call for trade rules to prohibit states from using them in the future. By comparison, the UN institutions are aware that many poor countries also resort to bans in times of uncertainty and they have called for greater transparency and coordination of international food supplies, but have not fully endorsed an outright prohibition on export bans. If there is agreement on disciplining export bans, this is likely to require granting greater authority to the WTO given that its rules cover agricultural export bans. WTO rules are likely to be limited to reducing the negative impacts of export bans on international market actors. However, WTO rules are unlikely to be crafted in a manner to directly minimize the negative impacts of price swings on particular groups of food-insecure individuals, which is precisely what would be demanded by the norms of the international food security and human rights regimes. Another example is the resistance by the G8, WTO, and World Bank to the UN's attempts to mainstream the right to food as a central pillar of the multilateral response to the food crises. The former are major proponents of trade liberalization and are concerned that a rights-based framework may encourage developing countries to decrease their reliance on international markets and place a greater emphasis on food self-sufficiency.[26]

The recent appearance of the G8, G-20, and World Bank as key actors in global food security governance is notable, and it is evidence of the increasing density in the regime complex for food security. Even more significant is the emergence of a potential new and fourth elemental regime in the complex, international finance. There is now a consensus that financial speculation is a major driver of rising and volatile food prices. The G-20 finance ministers and international organizations are working on regulatory options to reduce food price volatility and this may cover financial speculation in agricultural commodities. Similar to international trade, a nascent conflict can be observed within the regime complex: there is a strong divergence of views between the United States, international financial institutions, and private actors (which are resistant to new public forms of regulation of commodities trading) and France, most net food-importing developing countries, the UN system, and global civil society (which strongly support greater regulation of financial markets). It is premature to speculate on the longer-term implications of this possible expansion of the regime complex for food security. However, it is clear that the linkages between food security and international finance are recognized by actors as significant and warranting international cooperation.

Going forward, diverging norms and rules are likely to remain a source of conflict and fragmentation in ongoing efforts to strengthen the global governance of food security. It is essential that policymakers recognize the existence and characteristics of the regime complex for food security and seek new ways of forging consensus among multiple and conflicting norms and rules. A failure to recognize the interlocking relationship among the elemental regimes of agriculture and food, international trade, and human rights is likely to impede international cooperation to reduce world hunger.

Notes

1. Food and Agriculture Organization, *The State of World Food Insecurity* (Rome: FAO, 2010).

2. World Bank, "Poverty Trends," http://web.worldbank.org/wbsite/external /topics/extpoverty/O,contentMDK:22569498-pagePK:148956-piPK:216618-the SitePK:336992,00.html.

3. Food and Agriculture Organization, *The State of Food and Agriculture. Biofuels: Prospects, Risks and Opportunities* (Rome: FAO, 2009).

4. See Jennifer Clapp, "The Global Food Crisis and International Agricultural Policy: Which Way Forward?" *Global Governance* 15, no. 2 (2009): 299–312; Food and Agriculture Organization, *How to Feed the World in 2050* (Rome: FAO, 2009).

5. John G. Ruggie, *Constructing the World Polity: Essays on International Institutionalisation* (London: Routledge, 1998).

6. Martha Finnemore and Kathryn Sikkink, "Taking Stock: The Constructivist Research Program in International Relations and Comparative Politics," *Annual Review of Political Science* 4 (2001): 391–416.

7. Food and Agriculture Organization, *Constitution of the Food and Agriculture Organization* (Rome: FAO, 1965).

8. D. John Shaw, *World Food Security: A History Since 1945* (Basingstoke: Palgrave Macmillan, 2007).

9. Matias E. Margulis, "Global Food Governance: The Committee for World Food Security, the Comprehensive Framework for Action and the G8/G20," in Rosemary Rayfuse and Nicole Wiesfelt, eds., *The Challenge of Food Security* (Cheltenham: Edward Elgar Publishers, 2012), pp. 231–254.

10. United Nations, *Report of the World Food Conference, 5–16 November 1974* (Rome: Food and Agriculture Organization, 1974).

11. Food and Agriculture Organization, *Trade Reforms and Food Security: Conceptualizing the Linkages* (Rome: FAO, 2002); Shaw, *World Food Security.*

12. Amartya Sen, "Ingredients of Famine Analysis: Availability and Entitlements," *Quarterly Journal of Economics* 96, no. 3 (1981): 433–464.

13. The current definition is: "Food security exists when all people, at all times, have physical, social and economic access to sufficient, safe and nutritious food which meets their dietary needs and food preferences for an active and healthy life." Cited in Rome Declaration on World Food Security (Rome: FAO, 1996), www.fao.org/docrep/003/w3613e/w3613e00.htm.

14. Carmen G. Gonzalez, "Institutionalizing Inequality: The WTO Agreement on Agriculture, Food Security, and Developing Countries," *Columbia Journal of Environmental Law* 27 (2002): 431–487; Harmon Thomas, ed., *Trade Reforms and Food Security: Country Case Studies and Synthesis* (Rome: FAO, 2006).

15. Robert Wolfe, *Farm Wars: The Political Economy of Agriculture and the International Trade Regime* (London: Macmillan, 1998).

16. World Trade Organization, *Decision on Measures Concerning the Possible Negative Effects of the Reform Programme on Least-Developed and Net Food-importing Developing Countries* (Geneva: WTO, 1995).

17. Food and Agriculture Organization, *Constitutional and Legal Protection of the Right to Food Around the World* (Rome: FAO, 2010).

18. Kal Raustiala and David Victor, "The Regime Complex for Plant Genetic Resources," *International Organization* 58, no. 2 (2004): 277–309.

19. See ibid.; Karen Alter and Sophie Meunier, "The Politics of Regime Complexity," *Perspectives on Politics* 7, no. 1 (2009): 13–24.

20. Jennifer Clapp, *Hunger in the Balance: The New Politics of International Food Aid* (Ithaca: Cornell University Press, 2012).

21. Robyn Eckerseley, "The Big Chill: The WTO and Multilateral Environmental Agreements," *Global Environmental Politics* 4, no. 2 (2004): 24–50; Mark Axelrod, "Savings Clauses and the 'Chilling Effect': Regime Interplay as Constraints on International Governance/Law," in Sebastian Oberthiir and Olav Schram Stokke, eds., *Managing Institutional Complexity: Regime Interplay and Global Environmental Change* (Cambridge: MIT Press, 2011), pp. 87–114.

22. John Hoddinott, Marc Cohen, and Christopher Barrett, "Renegotiating the Food Aid Convention: Background, Context, and Issues," *Global Governance* 18, no. 3 (2008): 283–304.

23. World Food Program, "Don't Play with Our Food," *Financial Times*, 14 December 2005; Simone Heri and Christian Haberli, "Can the World Trade Organization Ensure That Food Aid Is Genuine?" NCCR Trade Working Paper Series 2009/19 (Bern: World Trade Institute, 2009).

24. WTO Director General Pascal Lamy, "Doha Round Can Help Lift Africa's Agriculture," 21 February 2011, www.wto.org/english/news_e/sppl_e /sppl188_e.htm.

25. See Robert Howse and Ruti Teitel, *Beyond the Divide: The Covenant on Economic, Social and Cultural Rights and the World Trade Organization* (Geneva: Friedrich-Ebert-Stiftung, 2007); Susan Aaronson, "Seeping in Slowly: How Human Rights Concerns Are Penetrating the WTO," *World Trade Review* 6, no. 3 (2007): 413–449.

26. See Robert Zoellick, "Free Markets Can Still Feed the World," *Financial Times*, 5 January 2011; Pascal Lamy, "Trade Is Part of the Answer, Not Part of the Problem," speech given at Berlin Agriculture Ministers' Summit, 22 January 2011, www.wto.org/english/news_e/sppl_e/sppl183_e.htm.

12

Providing a Release Valve:
The US-China Experience with the
WTO Dispute Settlement System

Kennan J. Castel-Fodor

The sounds of saber rattling seem to emanate from the delicate relationship between the United States and China. Observers and media alike have proclaimed the possibility of a trade war looming on the horizon. While trade frictions between Washington and Beijing occur in nearly every facet of the relationship, the latest trends in World Trade Organization (WTO) litigation have garnered intense scrutiny. In recent years, both countries have initiated an increasingly higher volume of cases against one other. While many view this trend as a harbinger of a potential trade war, [we] present an alternative interpretation of this trend in US-Chinese WTO litigation. The litigation-intensive focus between the United States and China within the WTO's Dispute Settlement Body (DSB) [illustrates] the efficacy of the institution and the willingness of both countries to utilize the DSB as a viable trade-friction intermediary.

[This article includes four parts.] Part I . . . introduces the process and operation of the DSB, the unique historical context of China's accession to the WTO, and the early interactions between the United States and the People's Republic in the DSB. [This] provides the necessary framework within which to analyze the relational developments between the two parties in the DSB as a rule-oriented international dispute settlement system.

. . . The components of the DSB that make it both a suitable forum for resolving contentious US-Sino disputes are presented in [Part II].

Reprinted from *Case Western Reserve Law Review*, vol. 64, no. 1: 201–238. © 2013 by Case Western Reserve University. Reprinted by permission of the publisher. Edited for length.

These components will be analyzed through the characteristics that induce both China and the United States to utilize the DSB as a legal forum. [This section introduces] the direct institutional benefits and indirect benefits that members are able to accrue. . . . [Part III] analyzes two DSB cases between the United States and China [regarding US poultry and intellectual property rights]. These cases illustrate the willingness of both countries to submit important issues to the DSB. [They also show] the importance of compliance by the losing parties and the implications of compliance as acceptance of the DSB's legitimacy. . . .

Finally, [the conclusion offers] suggestions about the future of the DSB as a viable mechanism for addressing burgeoning trade frictions between Beijing and Washington. . . .

I. The WTO Dispute Settlement Body

The DSB stands as one of the achievements of the Uruguay Round of Negotiations in 1995 that resulted in the creation of the World Trade Organization. The DSB was designed to remedy a number of the weaknesses and failures of its predecessor, the General Agreement on Tariffs and Trade (GATT). . . . The efficacy of the GATT dispute settlement system was frustrated by the consensus requirement for decision making. This allowed nations whose measures were challenged to constructively block the establishment of a panel or the implementation of an adverse ruling. The flaws inherent in the GATT system prompted the desire for change when forming the WTO. Positive change was accomplished through an adherence to binding panel and Appellate Body determinations whose adoption requirement was changed to [avoid] consensus. This transformation in decision-making requirements greatly diminished the role of politics within international trade dispute settlement in favor of a rule-oriented, legal forum. At the center of the WTO's newly created dispute settlement system is the Dispute Settlement Body, entrusted with the responsibility of resolving trade disputes under the WTO covered agreements. . . .

Unlike the previous GATT regime, the WTO dispute settlement system is compulsory for all WTO members. This commitment conveys the willingness of all members to bind themselves in advance to the adjudicatory powers of the DSB. The system is designed to compel losing respondents to bring any offending measure(s) into conformity with WTO obligations rather than to render punitive damages. One innovative feature of the DSB is the Appellate Body, which allows the losing party to appeal an adverse judgment from the panel determination. Other features include the framework of process deadlines and compliance-monitoring mechanisms that generate an "integrated dispute settlement" whereby the same rules apply to all disputes leveled under the covered agreements, unless specifically provided for under an agreement. . . . In doing so, the DSB occupies a unique legal position within the international community as its utilization provides a novel legalized structure with which to protect the concessions and expected benefits of all members. . . .

The process of negotiating China's membership in the WTO was long and arduous. In negotiating its accession, China made a number of unique concessions on issues of trade in both goods and services that far exceeded the obligations of other WTO members. Despite the myriad unique obligations in China's Accession Protocol, China still viewed WTO membership as a vital component of its long-term economic prosperity. China even accepted the mandatory jurisdiction of the DSB—a monumental step in Beijing's affirmation of the role of the international system. China [instituted] extensive measures to bring its economy into conformity with accession obligations. Throughout China's negotiations, the United States consistently advocated for China's membership in the WTO. The United States had a particular interest in bringing China into a rule-oriented, formalized system that allowed for compulsory adjudication of trade frictions and violations of economic commitments. Despite the difficult accession negotiations, both China and the United States recognized the long-term benefits of WTO membership for the People's Republic. . . .

In order to fully appreciate the recent trends in WTO litigation between Beijing and Washington, it is necessary to examine the dynamic between the two powers during the first five years of China's WTO membership (2001–06). The initial years were relatively calm in terms of litigation as China became acclimated to the new system. [Numerous] explanations for China's reticence to utilize the DSB [include] its "non-litigious legal traditions," a lack of internal legal capacity, and limitations imposed within China's accession protocol. In fact, China did not have to defend itself as a respondent until three years after its accession in 2004 and defended against only one other complaint in the first five years. During this period, China brought only one case against the United States. Some believed that the rhetoric emanating from Beijing in 2005 indicated that China would not actively utilize the DSB to resolve trade frictions. Beijing's official stance began to change in 2006 when it proclaimed that China would utilize the WTO and the DSB to properly handle trade frictions.

A juxtaposition of the inactivity during the initial five-year period with interactions since 2006 demonstrates the trend toward an increasing utilization of DSB litigation by both China and the United States. For example, the United States brought thirteen WTO cases against China between 2007 and 2012—three in 2007, two in 2008, one in 2009, three in 2010, one in 2011, and three in 2012. The United States went from initiating two cases over five years against China to thirteen cases over six years. Similarly, China has initiated a higher volume of cases against the US since 2006—one in 2007, one in 2008, two in 2009, one in 2011, and two in 2012. China's altered reliance on the DSB to resolve trade frictions with the United States is evident considering that China utilized the dispute settlement system once in the first five years and seven times in the subsequent six years. The statistical variations in litigation reliance within the WTO intimate a marked shift in both countries' strategies for resolving trade frictions. In fact, litigation between Beijing and Washington accounts for a significant portion of both countries' overall DSB interactions. Both parties' drastic changes in the usage of the DSB continue to garner significant discourse on the trend's motivations and implications, particularly whether these changes symbolize a positive or negative development for the international trading system. . . .

II. Positive Characteristics of the Dispute Settlement Body

The DSB provides a number of direct benefits through its organizational structure and rule-based system. Membership in the WTO assumes that nations will fulfill trade-related commitments and realize expected benefits. The WTO deals broadly with the rules of trade between nations, encompassing a host of responsibilities both globally and intergovernmentally. The DSB stands as the forum through which WTO rules and obligations are protected. Serving as a crucial component to the WTO's operation, the DSB attempts to promote stability within the international trading system. When a member abrogates its WTO obligation, the DSB provides a dispute settlement process for aggrieved parties to seek remedy.

First, the remedies available within the DSB structure provide a direct benefit to both the complainant and respondent. For the complainant, a favorable outcome from a panel ruling results in a judgment ordering the removal of the respondent's disputed measure. Retaliation, as a permissible remedy, is allowed only as a "last resort" and is subject to a number of institutional limitations when a member fails to [comply]. The complainant's retaliatory measures are only "temporary" and can consist of a suspension of concessions at a level "equivalent" to the harm. Given the various remedy measures, the complainant is provided some way to mitigate the harmful effects of the offending member's measure.

Even when faced with an unfavorable verdict, the respondent is able to directly benefit from the structured remedy system within the DSB. The limitations surrounding retaliation ensure that the respondent is confronted by temporary measures that the DSB determines are equivalent to the respondent's offending measure. This remedy application mitigates the prospect of punitive damages that are meant to punish offending nations beyond the actual harm incurred. These limitations also prevent escalation of a "tit-for-tat" trade war. Even when a complainant is permitted to retaliate, such actions are narrowly tailored to minimize the disturbance in liberalizing trade.

These benefits provided by the DSB incentivize member nations, such as the United States and China, to utilize the formal forum rather than to engage in potentially volatile bilateral negotiations, especially considering the lack of limitations on national action outside a formal international organization. This instills a confidence within both countries that a loss in the DSB will not result in exorbitant penalties that ultimately dwarf the initial harm. The guarantee of proportionality allows both the United States and China to conduct a cost-benefit analysis concerning the maintenance of a measure, particularly when the removal of a WTO inconsistent measure is not politically feasible at the time of the panel determination. Furthermore, both the United States and China can feel assured that taking sensitive topics to the DSB will not result in the imposition of additional obligations other than those agreed to and enumerated in the covered WTO agreements. This ensures that no outcome from the DSB can burden either country with obligations that have not been fully negotiated and from which they could not opt out. These measures operate as safeguards that build faith in the efficacy of the WTO as an international organization entrusted with a mandatory dispute settlement system.

Second, the advent of the appellate process within the international trading system allows for review of panel decisions, providing a higher level of scrutiny and consistency. The Appellate Body is designed to provide legitimacy to the economic dispute settlement system through a focus on the composition, scope of review, and structured deadlines. For composition, the Dispute Settlement Understanding (DSU) provides specific qualifications for persons serving on the Appellate Body in order to bolster the validity and legitimacy of appellate review determinations. The scope of the appellate review does not include fact finding, which is the role specifically delegated to the panel. Instead, the design of the DSB appellate process reduces appealable issues to those of law that are "covered in the panel report and legal interpretations developed by the panel." Furthermore, the deadlines enumerated within the DSU for appellate decisions provide participants with a clearly defined timetable for the resolution of disputes.

The Appellate Body quickly demonstrated its efficacy as it resolved a number of high-profile, controversial cases that had been holdovers from the previous GATT era. The establishment and success of the appellate review within the WTO system provides China and the United States assurance that DSB litigation is not subject to a single panel determination, allowing either nation to target specific issues of law or legal interpretations thought to be incorrectly determined under the covered agreements. This feature instills confidence that the ultimate outcome of a contentious trade dispute between the United States and China will be properly adjudicated.

Third, the myriad issues presented in each case allow the DSB to render determinations that are "win-win" rather than merely a "winner-take-all" system. The DSB can achieve a mutually beneficial process through the application of independent review for resolving disputes. Impartiality, as a hallmark of the DSB, allows panelists to divorce trade issues from the typical state-centric political rhetoric. The ability to separate and resolve multiple issues through a trade-forum intermediary provides the United States and China benefits in dealing with trade frictions. The political connections that complicate complex trade issues can be disassociated from the appropriate adjudication under the WTO covered agreements.

This positive development in the resolution of complex trade issues is evident in the contentious dispute between Beijing and Washington over intellectual property protections within China. The United States brought three claims against China under the Trade-Related Aspects of Intellectual Property Rights (TRIPS): the threshold for criminal procedures and penalties, the disposal of infringing goods, and the copyright protection for censored works. While the Panel ruled favorably for the United States on the issues of the disposal of infringing goods and the copyright protection for censored works, the United States lost on the important issue of the threshold for criminal procedures and penalties. The Panel's mixed ruling allowed both sides to claim a successful outcome in the case. The DSB was able to independently assess the complex, but related, claims and adjudicate each claim on its legal merit under the TRIPS agreement. Had these issues been subject to bilateral negotiations, the resolution of the trade friction may have been impossible due to political intermingling of all the issues into one "winner-take-all" scenario. This mentality may very well have escalated the trade frictions between Beijing and Washington into a full-blown trade war.

The institutional characteristics of the DSB encourage the United States and China to utilize the dispute settlement forum to resolve contentious trade issues. As the WTO remedies a number of the inherent flaws that plagued the GATT system, members gain a greater confidence in the adjudicatory powers of the trade dispute settlement system. The features of the rule-based organization that have augmented its efficacy and the members' willingness to use the DSB include its neutrality and legitimacy. The DSB provides members with a rule-oriented dispute settlement system with which to address trade frictions. The DSB provides tangible benefits through its remedy-limiting mechanisms, its appellate process, and its ability to adjudicate mutually beneficial situations. These benefits induce both the United States and China to continuously employ the DSB to mitigate trade frictions. . . .

While the direct benefits from the DSB institutional characteristics help to explain the rationale underlying the United States' and China's decisions to join and use the WTO and its dispute settlement system, the indirect benefits accrued by both nations may illuminate why both powers have drastically increased their utilization of the litigation feature. One indirect benefit of advancing national ends through WTO litigation is the mollification of domestic anxiety in both the People's Republic and the United States. Another benefit is the channeling of an individual nation's behavior so as to produce a more cooperative international trading environment. The continuous usage of the DSB as a forum for trade dispute settlement instills a long-term investment for both nations in the longevity and ultimate viability of the organization. Additionally, the litigation focus through the DSB allows both Beijing and Washington to project "soft power" throughout the international system. Finally, experience with DSB litigation bolsters China's internal legal capacity, which can generate positive benefits for both China and the international system.

The Sino-American relationship remains a salient political issue within the United States, with the People's Republic often vilified. A number of subjects tend to ignite the ire of the American public and Congress, including human rights, currency manipulation, and trade frictions. The US administration's engagement of China through DSB litigation conveys a strong political stance in instances of perceived violations of China's international obligations. This litigation strategy toward China helps to placate the American public's anger as well as the calls for tougher legislation from Congress. The saber rattling from Congress can prove potentially catastrophic for US-Chinese relations as protectionist trade legislation can spark damaging retaliatory policies from China. The US administration can use WTO litigation to address issues preemptively before protectionist elements in Congress can act. For the American government, WTO litigation provides a unique ability to diffuse political tensions that could have deleterious ramifications for the long-term benefit of the Sino-American relationship.

While the Chinese government is not subject to the same democratic undulations, domestic pressure within China is of great concern to the Chinese Communist Party's (CCP) political stability. Economic concerns are always at the forefront of the CCP domestic and foreign policy, as demonstrated through the maintenance of the currency policy that has caused much contention. Sometimes, China's initiation of WTO litigation is the direct result of domestic concerns toward particularly prominent trading partners. Like the United States, the Chinese government can utilize DSB determinations to implement or speed up reforms that may not be particularly popular domestically. This is particularly true in situations in China where reform, without DSB determinations, would be untenable. The prospect of WTO litigation and the permeation of DSB norms throughout China can provide the CCP domestic credibility for instituting reformist policies. Increasing WTO litigation and improving Chinese legal savvy can also provide the indirect benefit of bolstering the Chinese public's faith in not only the WTO and DSB but also other international organizations. This provides the CCP with a stronger trade dispute mechanism that would have more support from the Chinese domestic populace. . . .

Another characteristic of the DSB, which may also characterize international organizations on a broader scale, is the ability to channel the behavior of member states. While realists may posit that states will always act with purely self-interested motives, within the legal framework of the DSB, such behavior may ultimately contribute to the long-term success of the dispute settlement body. The compulsory jurisdiction of the DSB assures members that involvement in the dispute settlement system will involve repeat participation, as both a complainant and respondent. This knowledge is bolstered through the explicit DSU requirement that all recourse concerning perceived violations of the WTO covered agreements be settled through the DSB mechanisms. The knowledge of recurring involvement in the DSB instills within both the United States and China an investment in the long-term success of the organization. This commitment means that both countries will be willing to comply with an adverse ruling in hopes that the other will comply the next time it faces an adverse ruling. The understanding that future cases will be brought means neither nation will self-destruct the entire system. The DSB provides stability for conducting bilateral negotiations knowing that there is a formal, predictable system to resort to if negotiations collapse or if promises are broken.

The WTO exemplifies the economic reality that all nations have interdependent economic systems. Accordingly, the appearance of trade frictions will not be an anomaly but rather a signature of a growing economic order in which interactions between members are ever-more prevalent and routine. The DSB's legal functioning as the mechanism through which to resolve these trade frictions assures members of the reoccurrence of WTO disputes. In doing so, it establishes a significantly high threshold for measuring the importance of any one individual case or issue in the broader scheme of future DSB interactions as well as the enjoyment of other expected benefits provided under the covered agreements. The existence of this high threshold dissuades losing parties from persistent [noncompliance] or calling into question the legitimacy of the DSB itself. In the rule-oriented dispute settlement structure of the DSB, all participants, whether a developed or a less developed country, have an interest in preserving the legitimacy of the dispute settlement system in order to accrue perceived benefits. As such, the behavior of member states is channeled so as to preserve the longevity of the DSB. Both the United States and China thus have a sufficient vested interest in the DSB beyond any single dispute, with behavioral responses skewed toward compliance as well as an instilled reticence to indict any one DSB determination as perversely flawed or illegitimate.

As China attempts to project its brand as an international power on a "peaceful rise," it must employ tools other than its military might to advance this image. . . . The DSB is a forum from which the Chinese government can project both its legal acumen and willingness to engage international organizations. . . . As a component of the peaceful-rise strategy, China is better able to protect its interests from within the WTO than challenging its legitimacy. [It] has demonstrated that it is making a good faith effort to adhere to the rules of the international system and to provide more transparency for its actions. Even when China loses an argument in the DSB, it continues to hone its litigation skills and demonstrates an investment in the long-term viability of the DSB. This is particularly important when China complies with an adverse ruling, demonstrating the validity of the DSB and projecting to other trading partners that compliance is required. This ensures that China can utilize the DSB in order to advance its own interests and to get other trading partners, like the United States, to alter policies that are unfavorable to the Chinese economic system.

[One effect of] active participation in DSB litigation [is] the development of China's legal institution[s], both specifically within WTO disputes as well as the spillover effect to other Chinese legal forums. When China entered the WTO in 2001, its domestic legal capabilities were brought under harsher scrutiny. China was obligated to reform its legal system as a prerequisite to WTO accessions, demonstrated through the promulgation of myriad laws that aimed to bolster an anemic legal system. At that time, China's legal profession was woefully underdeveloped in both experience and domestic reverence, having nearly nonexistent exposure to international dispute settlement systems. Beijing was faced with the daunting task of confronting the WTO system's sharp learning curve. . . . China recognized that the shortcomings of its legal system were jeopardizing its ability to effectively protect its trade interests through utilization of the DSB. The prospect of DSB litigation serves as a catalyst for China to implement measures to bolster its legal institutional capabilities.

These measures focus on cooperation between the Chinese government and other individuals and organizations with legal knowledge beneficial for dealing with WTO dispute settlement. For example, in expanding the government's ability to account for WTO accession, the Chinese State Council established a Division of WTO Law that retains in-house lawyers with specialized knowledge of international law and the WTO system. In addition, the Chinese government created a Permanent Mission in Geneva specifically for providing a more effective management of its DSB disputes. Another feature is China's adamancy in seeking out scholars, legal experts, and professionals from around the world to instruct and disseminate WTO legal expertise within the Chinese government, legal profession, and universities across China. Similarly, China has sent its legal experts abroad to study and practice international and WTO law at foreign universities and other world trade forums. China has also fostered internal mechanisms for rapidly developing the legal acumen necessary for effective usage of the DSB, particularly through the generation of Chinese think tanks specialized in WTO law. Finally, China built its legal experience within the WTO through participation in WTO disputes as an interested third-party member. In doing so, China was able to observe the process without being directly involved as a complainant or respondent. The extent to which China is dedicating human capital and financial resources to honing its WTO litigation capacity demonstrates its commitment to a high-quality legal framework. . . .

These indirect benefits provide both the United States and China with hefty incentives for maintaining a strategy of using DSB litigation to resolve trade frictions. First, the DSB serves as an outlet through which the governments in both countries can vent domestic frustration. Being a legal intermediary aids in bolstering the legitimacy of reform efforts in China while also diffusing the political frustrations surrounding such reforms. Second, the DSB helps to stymie the desire to engage in tit-for-tat trade battles through the use of channeled behaviors as both nations realize that future litigation means a routinized compliance system. Third, accepting the DSB's compulsory jurisdiction as an international dispute settlement body helps China project its soft-power presence within the global community. Finally, China's involvement within DSB litigation fosters the development of Beijing's legal capacity in regard to WTO litigation, the legal profession in China, and other multilateral regimes in which China is engaged.

III. *US-Poultry* and *China–Intellectual Property Rights*

The comprehensive compliance features of the DSB are one of the most important innovations of the WTO system, providing an enforcement mechanism within the international trading sphere. . . . [Compliance] with DSB determinations through implementation is an indicator of a state's willingness to accept the . . . underlying principles of the DSB, and the implementation reaffirms the state's dedication to the long-term sustainability of the dispute settlement system. Thus, a state's compliance record on adverse rulings serves as an effective mechanism for evaluating a state's commitment to resolving trade frictions through the DSB.

In terms of compliance records for disputes between the United States and the People's Republic, the record of cases reaching either panel or appellate determinations is relatively limited. As of April 2013, five of the eight disputes China initiated as complainant had reached some determinative level. The limited scope is more apparent in the number of disputes reaching panel or appellate determination when the United States initiates as a complainant—seven out of fifteen cases. Since China's accession to the WTO in 2001, the Chinese government has often preferred to negotiate a settlement to the WTO dispute prior to the submission of the DSB determination. . . . [An] analysis of two representative disputes in which both countries faced adverse rulings provides a beneficial insight into the United States and China's approaches to DSB compliance.

In *US-Poultry*, China requested a panel determination to challenge the United States' measure concerning China's access to the US market for poultry. . . . The provision . . . prevented Chinese poultry from being reimported into the United States after the US Department of Agriculture (USDA) had determined that China was once again eligible to export poultry product to the United States. This USDA determination removed the total ban on Chinese poultry that was imposed in response to the avian flu epidemic in 2004.

China put forward a number of claims under various WTO-covered agreements, including Articles I and XI of the 1994 GATT Agreement on Agriculture and the Sanitary and Phytosanitary (SPS) Agreement. The panel in *US-Poultry* held, with regard to the most important issues, that [the US law] was inconsistent with US obligations under GATT and the SPS Agreement. Furthermore, the panel rejected the United States' assertion . . . that claimed the measure was enacted in order to "protect human and animal life and health from the risk posed by the importation of poultry products from China." Despite the dispute involving an important national issue—health and safety—the United States did not appeal the determination. In fact, as the Panel noted, the measure in contest expired two days after China submitted its first written submission. Although the measure expired prior to the Panel report, the dispute still provides a valuable insight into the United States' approach to compliance with adverse DSB rulings involving China. . . . While this dispute did not require the United States to take any proactive step in removing the offending measure, the DSB determination established the inconsistency of such a provision in future legislation. The United States demonstrated its willingness to comply with the panel's determination through the continued omission of a similar provision in subsequent appropriations legislation.

Similarly, China was faced with an adverse panel ruling in 2008 over intellectual property rights protections. The Panel analyzed . . . claims the United States brought against China under the TRIPS Agreement. The United States challenged . . . [a lack of criminal procedures and penalties within China for trademark counterfeiting or copyright piracy]. . . . The Panel found in favor of the United States . . . concerning customs measures and [copyright law]. . . .

In response to the Panel's determination, China informed the DSB that it would comply. . . . Here, as with the United States in *US-Poultry*, China did not appeal the Panel's ruling. China . . . [instead amended the copyright law] to bring the measure into conformity. . . . This case indicates China's willingness to comply with the adverse rulings and bring its inconsistent measures into conformity with its WTO obligations.

While [these cases] demonstrate a good record on DSB compliance from the United States and China, [they] represent a small body of available DSB-compliance cases between the two nations. Many allege that the United States is a notoriously noncompliant state within the WTO because the United States has repeatedly been accused of delaying compliance. However, when faced with adverse rulings in disputes with China, the United States has maintained a better compliance record, although not always through routine means of implementation. For China, many scholars laud its compliance record within the DSB as one demonstrating a "responsible attitude toward its international obligations." In terms of additional compliance instances, both nations have notified the DSB of the implementation of . . . adverse panel determinations in 2013. . . . In both cases, the losing party informed the DSB that it intends to comply with the determination, implementing the recommendations within the negotiated [deadline]. If the trend toward increased usage of the DSB to resolve US-Sino trade frictions continues, the record of disputes reaching either panel or appellate determinations should increase in frequency. Ultimately, this will provide a greater sample size for determining the degree to which the United States and China are willing to implement adverse rulings. If either nation consistently fails to implement determinations in the future, the viability of the DSB to resolve trade frictions may be jeopardized because noncompliance may instigate reciprocal noncompliance from the other nation. . . .

IV. Conclusion

Ever-expanding global trade relations have spawned highly contentious disputes between the United States and China, two of the world's most powerful economic juggernauts. The volatility of these disputes has caused numerous observers to opine that trade frictions could devolve into an outright trade war. The United States and China have demonstrated a willingness to utilize the DSB and its rule-oriented structure to mitigate the harmful effects of possible trade warfare. While the design of the DSB is not perfect, its institutional structure provides a number of direct benefits that induce member participation. This [article] examined how these direct benefits ensure a stable economic environment through a highly regulated remedy structure, an appellate system to serve as a legal safeguard, and an independent quasi-judicial body to diminish political unpredictability on issue determination. Aside from these institutional benefits, the indirect benefits that both Washington and Beijing accrue help explain the surge in desire to resort to DSB litigation. For one, both the US and Chinese governments can garner political protection from utilizing the DSB as an intermediary through which to release domestic frustrations. Additionally, the DSB also assists in channeling member behavior toward a long-term investment in the international economic system, projecting soft power, and building the Chinese legal capacity. The attractiveness of DSB litigation continues to grow as other mechanisms for resolving trade frictions fail to provide suitable resolution, including both bilateral and multilateral negotiations. . . . In both *US-Poultry* and *China–Intellectual Property Rights,* the countries accepted the recommendations of the DSB and brought the offending measures into conformity with WTO obligations.

Ultimately, both the United States and China must devote great care and attention to the management of DSB litigation. The United States must be wary of vilifying China when trade frictions arise; such a perception can foster anti-Chinese sentiment which can lead to protectionist measures. The growth in protectionist measures predicated on domestic ire will frustrate the effective operation of the DSB and diminish the direct and indirect benefits that the organization provides. The United States should recognize the significance of China's willingness to resolve trade frictions through a compulsory, third-party intermediary. Although litigation is adversarial in nature, the United States would benefit from a stronger Chinese confidence in international dispute settlement systems.

While the DSB is providing a means of resolving tense trade issues, the efficacy and legitimacy of the system is predicated on the United States' and China's perceptions of the DSB's fairness, impartiality, and legal quality. . . . With responsible management of DSB litigation, the countries are able to benefit from the existence of a highly functioning international legal forum. As illustrated by DSB interactions since China's accession to the WTO, the United States and the People's Republic have much to gain from the usage of the DSB to resolve contentious trade frictions and would do well to maintain such an advantageous system.

13

Global Governance and the Spread of Cyberspace Controls

Ronald J. Deibert and Masashi Crete-Nishihata

Cyberspace encompasses the global digital communications environment that is embedded in political, economic, and social activity. One of the burgeoning areas of cyberspace research is the study of information controls: actions conducted in and through cyberspace that seek to deny, disrupt, manipulate, and shape information and communications for strategic and political ends. Whereas once it was popularly assumed that cyberspace was immune to government regulation due to its dynamic nature and distributed architecture, a growing body of scholarship has shown convincingly how governments can shape and constrain access to information, freedom of speech, and other elements of cyberspace within their jurisdictions.

Today, more than thirty countries engage in Internet filtering, not all of them authoritarian regimes.[1] Internet surveillance policies are now widespread and bearing down on the private sector companies that own and operate the infrastructure of cyberspace, including Internet service providers (ISPs). Likewise, a new generation of second- and third-order controls complement filtering and surveillance, creating a climate of self-censorship.[2] There is a very real arms race in cyberspace that threatens to subvert the Internet's core characteristics and positive network effects.

The study of cyberspace controls has tended to focus on the nation-state as the primary unit of analysis and has examined the deepening and widening of these controls within domestic contexts. But largely unexamined so far are the *international* and *global* dynamics by which such controls grow and spread. The dynamics and mechanisms at these

Reprinted from *Global Governance*, vol. 18, no. 3: 339–361. © 2012 by Lynne Rienner Publishers. Reprinted by permission of the publisher. Edited for length.

levels are important to consider because states do not operate in a vacuum; they are part of a global social order that has important implications for how they are constituted (constitutive norms), and what they do and how they behave (regulative norms).[3] This can have both "positive" and "negative" dynamic characteristics. In a positive sense, states learn from and imitate each other. They borrow and share best practices, skills, and technologies. They take a cue from what like-minded states are doing and implement policies accordingly.

There are also negative international dynamics that shape the character of global relations. States compete against each other. Their perceptions of adversarial intentions and threats can impact the decisions they make. This dynamic has been characterized in the international relations literature as the logic of the "security dilemma."[4] One can see this logic playing itself out clearly today in cyberspace with the development of national armed forces capabilities to fight and win wars in that domain.

Government policies and behavior are also impacted by the activities of transnational actors—namely, civil society networks and the private sector—that function as a conduit and propagator of ideas and policies. Civil society networks educate users within countries about best practices and networking strategies, lobby governments, and operate largely irrespective of national boundaries.[5] The networks that tend to get the most attention are those for the promotion of human rights such as access to information, freedom of speech, and privacy. These networks come in a variety of shapes and sizes. Some are independent and largely grassroots in origin; others have been drawn into a support structure synchronized to the foreign policy goals of major governments such as the United States and the European Union. But few of them, especially the more important ones, operate only in a domestic policy setting.

Private sector actors are responsive to and seek to develop commercial opportunities across national boundaries and are increasingly a part of the global system's mechanisms and dynamics of cyberspace controls. Particularly relevant in this respect is the cyber-security market, estimated to be on the order of $80 billion to $140 billion dollars annually. Commercial providers of networking technology have a stake in the securitization of cyberspace and can inflate threats to serve their more parochial market interests. Private actors also own and operate the vast majority of the infrastructure and services that we call cyberspace. For that reason alone, their decisions can have major consequences for the character of cyberspace and are examples of the growing exercise of private authority in world politics.[6] It is not too far a stretch to argue that some companies have the equivalent of "foreign policies" for cyberspace, in some ways going beyond individual governments in terms of scope and influence.

In this article, we present an overview of information controls exercised in cyberspace as they have emerged over the past several decades, contrasting those controls with the constitutive rules, norms, and principles they are displacing. We then lay out a research framework for the study of global dynamics and mechanisms of the growth of cyberspace controls. Typically, international relations research on the spread of norms in global governance focuses on what might be construed as "positive" norm development: the spread of human rights, democracy, or the end of slavery, to give just a few examples. As Paul Kowert and Jeffrey Legro have pointed out, there is a bias in the study of norm propagation toward what might be considered good norms:

> A related bias in the study of norms is the "good norms" problem. Analysts tend to focus on those issues that are normatively desirable—e.g., the spread of democracy, the rise of human rights, the integration of world society, and prohibitions against the use of force. Yet undesirable norms are equally possible. Examples include norms of military autonomy and the use of force, economic domination, the acceptability of intrastate violence (e.g., civil war), and the disintegrative tendencies that exist in international politics (e.g., nationalism, religious exclusivity). These issues too deserve attention from the emerging sociological approach. But "bad" or threatening norms remain understudied.[7]

In contrast, we analyze what might be considered "norm regression" in global governance: the growth and spread of practices that degrade cyberspace as an open commons of information and communication.[8] The aim is not to provide an exhaustive analysis of these dynamics and mechanisms as much as it is to sketch out a conceptual and analytical framework for further research. Drawing primarily from constructivist theories, we lay out several areas where such dynamics and mechanisms might be found and investigated further. In the conclusion, we consider some of the reasons why research in this area is important for the study and policy of global cyberspace governance and practice.

From Open Commons to Controlled Access

In the early period of the Internet's development, it was widely assumed that the distributed and highly decentralized technology would be difficult, even impossible, for governments to regulate. The Internet's founding architects designed a set of technological and normative principles that laid the foundations for the network and guided how it should be accessed and operated. One of the most important design principles of the Internet is the end-to-end argument (e2e) formulated by Jerome H. Saltzer, David P. Reed, and David D. Clark (in 1984), which organizes the placement of functions in a distributed computing network sharing a basic common protocol (TCP/IP). It states that access to and use of applications on the network should be nondiscriminatory, meaning that users on the edge of the network should freely control applications and services and be enabled to develop new applications to distribute over the network as long as they conform to the principle.[9] The e2e formed one of the central principles of the Internet for technological reasons. However, beyond its technological importance, e2e has had economic, political, and social effects, and has been advocated as a key driver for innovation.[10] An associated principle stemming from e2e is *network neutrality,* which can be defined as the "right of users to access content, services and applications on the Internet without interference from network operators or government," and the "right of network operators to be reasonably free of liability for transmitting content and applications deemed illegal or undesirable by third parties."[11]

The foundational principles of Internet communications would have remained limited and largely experimental were it not for important conscious policy decisions made by the United States and other Western countries to "keep the state out" of Internet governance. Recognizing at the time that this new mode of communication would help trigger new forms of ingenuity and economic growth, key policy decisions were made in the 1990s to separate out institutions of Internet governance from the direct oversight of states—in particular, the United States. Although the latter still wielded important indirect and structural controls, operating and other decisions were made primarily by the Internet's engineers following a model of consensus building and request for comments more familiar to the university-based computer science and engineering community that gave birth to the Internet than to political parliaments and assemblies. These decisions were paradigmatic in the short term and set a framework for other countries to follow suit.

The combination of the technological and normative aspects of the Internet in this period frame the Internet as an "open commons" in which the domain was considered a separate space resistant to state regulation and control.[12] Over time, however, these assumptions have been called into question as governments, often operating in coordination with the private sector, have erected a variety of information controls and once-disparate technological ecosystems and new technologies have begun to converge around the Internet, sometimes bringing with them alternative modes of governance that do not conform with the Internet's foundational principles. The resulting communications environment, which we call cyberspace, exhibits a tension between older norms, rules, and principles and those that are gradually displacing them. From the starting point of an open commons of information and communication, these new practices can be described as a form of "normative regression" because they revert back to traditional state-based forms of control that are typical of the pre-Internet days of territorialized regimes of communications.

We define *information controls* broadly as actions conducted in and through cyberspace that seek to deny, disrupt, manipulate, and shape information and communications for strategic and political ends. Information controls include an array of technologies, regulatory measures, laws, policies, and tactics. These can include media regulation, licensing regimes, content removal, libel and slander laws, and content filtering. Countries vary widely in terms of their transparency and accountability around such practices and in terms of the methods by which they carry out information controls. Invariably, the private sector actors who own and operate the vast majority of cyberspace infrastructure are being compelled or coerced to implement controls on behalf of states.

Perhaps the most basic form of state control in cyberspace is *Internet filtering* or censorship, which is the prevention of access to information online within territorial boundaries. Rationales for national filtering regimes vary. Some states justify Internet filtering to control access to content that violates copyright, concerns the sexual exploitation of children, or promotes hatred and violence. Other countries filter access to content related to minority rights, religious movements, political opposition, and human rights groups. The Open Net Initiative (ONI) has been studying national Internet filtering since 2003 and, through a combination of technical interrogation, field research, and data analysis methods, conducts tests to verify the presence of Internet filtering in more than sixty countries on an annual basis. The reports of ONI provide a "snapshot" of accessibility at the point of time of testing from the perspective of national information environments. When ONI started documenting Internet filtering in 2003, only a handful of governments engaged in the practice. The latest reports of ONI indicate that more than forty countries engage in some form of Internet filtering, a growing number of them being democratic industrialized countries. Some of the nondemocratic regimes that engage in Internet filtering do so using commercial filtering products developed in the United States and Canada.[13] Others have developed more homegrown solutions. Some states provide "block pages" for banned content that explain the rationale and legal basis for the blocking; others provide only error pages, some of which are misleading and meant to misdirect users from the states' intentions. It is now fair to say that there is a growing norm worldwide for national Internet filtering, although the rationale for implementing filtering varies widely from country to country.

The trajectory of greater government intervention into cyberspace has developed beyond Internet filtering. Governments have shown a greater willingness to employ a broader range of regulatory, legal, covert, and offensive means to shape cyberspace in their strategic interests. For example, there have been a growing number of incidents where states have disrupted or tampered with communication networks for political purposes, including around elections and public demonstrations. ONI calls these actions *just-in-time blocking*—a phenomenon in which access to information is denied during important political moments when the content may have the greatest potential impact such as elections, protests, or anniversaries of social unrest.[14] In 2011 both Egypt and Libya severed all Internet access for brief periods of time during the Arab Spring. Similar tactics have been employed in Nepal (2005), Burma (2007), and China (2009). During the Green Revolution in Iran, the government was suspected of ordering ISPs to tamper or "throttle" bandwidth and the use of certain protocols associated with censorship circumvention and anonymity tools as a means to control opposition movements. Disruptions of access to communications in response to protest and social unrest have also been called for, and in some cases implemented, in democratic states. In response to the 2011 UK riots, Prime Minister David Cameron made a speech to the House of Commons in which he stated, "We are working with the police, the intelligence services and industry to look at whether it would be right to stop people communicating via [social media] when we know they are plotting violence, disorder and criminality."[15] In the summer of 2011, the Bay Area Rapid Transit System (BART) shut down cell phone service to four stations in San Francisco in reaction to a planned protest in an effort to disrupt its organization.[16] These and numerous other similar cases are examples of the sea change that has occurred over the past decade in terms of government approaches to cyberspace.

One important element of growing cyberspace controls is the downloading of responsibilities to the private sector, a phenomenon known as *intermediary liability*.[17] For example, both industrialized and developing governments have begun to legislate greater responsibilities on ISPs, telecommunications companies, and mobile operators to "police the Internet." These companies are being required by law to retain and archive user data, and share that data with law enforcement and intelligence agencies, in some cases without judicial oversight. As these requirements grow, the functions of network operators have incrementally changed toward a more fine-grained inspection and manipulation of the flow of traffic in ways that begin to impinge on e2e and network neutrality. Some large-scale network operators have even begun to take more offensive measures to police the Internet on their own. The concept of *active defense,* for example, which is now gaining widespread currency, describes actions taken by private sector network operators to take down and neutralize offending network nodes and traffic at their source, regardless of their geographic origin.[18]

The spectrum of information controls and their growing emergence across democratic and authoritarian states that we outlined above shows that, whereas once the dominant metaphor of state involvement in cyberspace was hands off, today the dominant metaphor is one of control. But how did these control norms spread internationally?

International and Global Mechanisms and Dynamics

Awareness and documentation of growing cyberspace controls on a per-nation basis is on the rise. Missing, however, is a consideration of the international and global mechanisms and dynamics of growing cyberspace controls. The field of international relations is premised on the notion that there are factors that affect state identity and behavior operating at an international systemic or global level. To put it simply, states are embedded in a global order that affects who they are (constitutive norms), what they do, and how they do it (regulative norms).

Although some of this scholarship has been rightly criticized in the past for reifying the international system and ignoring domestic level processes, it nonetheless identifies an important dimension of political behavior that needs to be considered.[19] States' policies are formed in interaction with other states in the international system and through interactions with transnational actors like civil society and the private sector.[20] However much domestic struggles and local threats motivate what states do, their interactions with each other, their perceptions of adversarial actions and intentions, and their involvement in institutions at a global level matter as well.

In the following section, we draw primarily from social constructivist approaches to illuminate where mechanisms and dynamics can be found in cyberspace practices and governance. Our aim is not to test or advance social constructivism as a body of theory per se. Rather, it is to use fairly well-established insights from international relations theory to help understand how information controls are spreading internationally. That said, cyberspace practice and governance may present an interesting case of "norm regression" for further research by international relations theorists since what we are describing is the emergence of norms, rules, and principles that undermine those related to a prior regime of shared practices. To be sure, what distinguishes good from bad norms is always in the eye of the beholder. But because the practices we trace diminish cyberspace as a global commons, and hold out the prospect of reinstituting a state-based governance regime that preceded it, we believe they can be accurately characterized as an example of norm regression.

Formal Organizations and Mechanisms

Norm Promotion Through International Institutions

The most obvious place to look for such international dynamics are the main forums of Internet governance: the International Corporation for Assigned Names and Numbers (ICANN), the International Telecommunication Union (ITU), the Internet Governance Forum (IGF), and others. These international institutions are important touchstones for the identification of the mechanisms and dynamics in which we are interested here.[21] Scholars of Internet governance have examined the stakeholders, processes, and policy outputs of these various institutions in detail for many years.[22] They are observing that these institutions are under new pressures as governments assert themselves more forcefully in cyberspace. As a consequence, the main issues that are addressed in some of these forums are changing; in technical governance forums, for example, previously nonpoliticized or mostly technical issues are becoming the objects of intense political competition. Institutions such as the Internet Engineering Task Force (IETF) or the Regional Internet Registries (RIRs), which may have been overlooked in the past as overly technical and functional in nature, deserve renewed attention by scholars if only for the fact that some governments are now taking them seriously as vectors of policy formation and propagation.

For example, a loose coalition of like-minded countries have begun to develop strategic engagements with international institutions, like the ITU and the IGF, in ways that are quite novel and unlike previous engagements. Most strikingly, Russia and the Russian-speaking countries of the former Soviet Union have adopted a wide-ranging engagement with these forums to promote policies that synchronize with national-level laws around information security.[23] China has also recently explicitly stated not only its belief in the sovereign control over national information space, but that global cyberspace should be governed by international institutions operating under the United Nations.[24] Not surprisingly, their policies have been vocally supported by the secretary general of the ITU, Hamadoun Toure, who has called for, among other initiatives, a state-based cyber-arms control treaty that would imply significant renationalization of the Internet. He has also been a vocal supporter of the United Arab Emirates, Indonesia, India, and others who have pressured companies like Research In Motion (RIM) to share encrypted data under the rubric of national security protections.[25] Every year since 1998, Russia has put forward resolutions at the United Nations to prohibit "information aggression," which is widely interpreted to mean ideological attempts, or the use of ideas, to undermine regime stability. At least twenty-three countries now openly support Russia's interpretation of information security.

Sometimes engagement at these forums is intended to stifle or stonewall rather than promote certain policies. For example, Chinese delegations have been quite prominent at the IGF meetings, ironically as a means to stall the forum from gaining credibility and to undermine the broadening of Internet governance to civil society and other non-state stakeholders. At the November 2009 IGF meeting in Egypt, for example, a book launch of an ONI volume, *Access Controlled,* was disrupted by UN security officials because of a poster to which the Chinese delegation objected that contained a reference to the "Great Firewall of China."[26] The propagation of norms internationally can be facilitated not only by promotion, but also by obstruction of contrary tendencies.

What is perhaps most interesting is that the international institutions whose missions are primarily focused around technical coordination of the Internet—the Internet Assigned Numbers Authority (IANA), ICANN, the IETF, and RIRs—have become increasingly politicized and subject to securitization pressures. As Brenden Kuerbis and Milton Mueller note, while Internet authority is highly distributed, "elements of hierarchy do exist, especially around critical resource allocation, and it is likely that security and other concerns will lead to continuing efforts to leverage those hierarchies into more powerful governance arrangements."[27] The securitization pressures are evident in the direct presence of law enforcement agencies (LEAs) in ICANN and RIR engagements. Examples include continuing efforts of LEAs to influence domain-name search (WHOIS) policy and more recent negotiations on the Registrar Accreditation Agreement where LEAs have imposed demands that circumvent the bottom-up policymaking process to push for identity checks on domain name registrants and challenge the use of identity-shielding registration services.[28] Military, intelligence, and civilian agencies from the US government have also had a presence in key Internet governance bodies (especially in the IETF) and have pushed agendas to secure Internet resources. These interactions are sometimes done directly, but more often through contractors. These agencies have typically participated in these forums as peers among other stakeholders that are present. As demands for secure Internet resources mount, the desire for LEAs and other agencies in both democratic and non-democratic regimes to seek influence in Internet governance bodies and agendas will continue.

Governments whose strategic interests are oriented around legitimization of national controls are viewing these cyberspace governance forums as important components of a broader, more comprehensive international policy engagement. For example, a coalition of Russian-speaking countries supported by China and India, have put forward a proposal through a submeeting of the ITU to give governments veto power over ICANN decisions. Generally speaking, engagement in these various international forums is an attempt by some countries to reassert the legitimacy of national sovereign control over cyberspace by promoting such a norm at international venues. Ironically, in other words, international institutions are perceived by policymakers of these countries as vehicles of nationalization. Such a strategic perception of international institutions has been characterized by Amitav Acharya as "norm subsidiarity," whereby marginal states promote norms through international institutions to "preserve their autonomy from dominance, neglect, violation or abuse by more powerful central actors."[29]

Policy Coordination Through Regional Organizations

Although international institutions are important conduits of norm propagation and legitimization, they can also be unwieldy and diffuse. As a consequence, coalitions of like-minded states are increasingly operating through more manageable lower-level organizations such as regional institutions. Some of these forums attract little attention, meet in relative obscurity, and thus take actions that rarely see the light of day and are ignored or overlooked by activists and others concerned with Internet freedom and cyberspace governance. But the actors who comprise them treat them seriously and use them as vehicles of policy coordination and information sharing.

One example is the Shanghai Cooperation Organization (SCO), which is a regional organization made up of China, Kyrgyzstan, Kazakhstan, Russia, Tajikistan, and Uzbekistan. India, Iran, Mongolia, Afghanistan, and Pakistan have observer status, and Belarus, Turkey, and Sri Lanka are considered dialogue partners. Iran is engaged in the SCO, but prevented from formally joining because of UN sanctions. However, it is considered an active participant in the SCO summits, which have been held regularly throughout the region since the early 2000s. The SCO aims to share information and coordinate policies around a broad spectrum of cultural, economic, and security concerns, among them cyberspace policies. Generally speaking, experts see the SCO as a regional vehicle of "protective integration" against international norms of democracy and regime change, with shared information policies being seen as critical to that end.[30] Recently, the SCO issued a statement on "information terrorism," which drew attention to the way in which the countries have a shared and distinct perspective on Internet security policy. The SCO has also engaged in joint military exercises and missions as simulations of how to reverse color-style revolutions and popular uprisings. Unfortunately, the SCO's meetings tend to be highly secretive affairs and therefore not easily subject to outside scrutiny. But they are likely to become important vehicles of policy coordination, giving unity, normative coherence, and strength to the individual countries beyond the sum of their parts.

Norm Diffusion Through Bilateral Cooperation

Norms can diffuse internationally in the most direct way by governments sharing resources and expertise with each other in bilateral relationships. There has been long-standing speculation that China and Chinese companies are selling technology to regimes that export its filtering and surveillance system. For example, information technology experts from China's Military Intelligence Division recently visited Sri Lanka, ostensibly to offer advice on how to filter the Internet.[31] . . . However, these discussions and arrangements are rarely transparent, typically shrouded in the type of secrecy that accompanies matters of national security, law enforcement, and intelligence matters. They are likely to become more important vehicles for the promotion of these states' strategic interests as they seek to propagate practices internationally that are supportive of their own domestic policies.

Informal Mechanisms

Although these forums and bilateral relations are important, they do not exhaust by any means the dynamics and mechanisms of cyberspace controls at play at the international level. Here, it is important to underline the many different means by which norms, behaviors, and policies are propagated globally. Although formal sites of governance, such as those described above, are important, norms can propagate through the global order in a variety of ways. *Norm diffusion* is the process through which norms are socialized and shared, and then become internalized, accepted, and implemented by national actors. This process is uneven and mixed, and can vary in different contexts depending on the depth by which the norm penetrates societies. Norms enter into and are accepted into national contexts depending on preexisting belief systems of a national society that support or constrain their acceptance. Norms can be propagated internationally by norm entrepreneurs (transnational actors, nongovernmental organizations [NGOs], and businesses acting as conveyor belts or conduits) or through imitation, learning, socialization, and competition.[32] The latter processes are often difficult to document empirically because of their epistemic or cognitive foundations. But they are important factors in explaining the spread and adoption of policies like Internet filtering. To understand the growth of cyberspace controls over the past decade, we need to better understand the mechanisms and dynamics of this diffusion internationally.

Imitation and Learning

Among theories of international relations of all stripes, there is a basic understanding that government policies are formed on the basis of the dynamic relations with other states in the international system. Governments are outward looking as much as they are inward looking. When one government sees another doing something, the pressures may build to do likewise or risk being left behind. Studies of learning and imitation in international relations offer up a number of hypotheses that can be collected and imported into the study of cyberspace controls.[33] A number of anecdotes suggest that this is a potentially fruitful area of inquiry.

In the most elemental sense, states learn from and imitate each other's behaviors, speech acts, and policies. They borrow and share best practices, skills, and technologies. They take a cue from what like-minded states are doing and implement policies accordingly. Fear and "self-help" are among the most important and perennial drivers of imitation and learning. States implement policies based on reactions to what other governments are doing for fear of being left behind or overtaken by adversaries. This dynamic may be particularly acute around cyberspace given the pace of technological change. As David Dolowitz and David Marsh explain, "Technology can also push governments into policy transfer because of the speed with which it forces change. Governments, not knowing how to deal with the issues technological advances create, turn to each other for precedents and ideas."[34] A current example of such a dynamic can be seen clearly in the rush by many countries to pressure RIM, the Canadian maker of BlackBerry products, to cooperate with local law enforcement and intelligence. After the United Arab Emirates went public with its concerns that RIM might have made an arrangement with the US National Security Agency that it wanted extended to its own security services, numerous other governments chimed in and joined the line, including India, Bahrain, Indonesia, and Saudi Arabia.

The most intense forms of imitation and learning occur around national security issues because of the high stakes and urgency involved. For example, in reaction to revelations of Chinese-based cyber-espionage against US companies and government agencies, former US director of national intelligence Dennis Blair asserted that the United States needs to be more aggressive in stealing other country's secrets. After reports surfaced of major compromises of the Indian national security and defense establishment traced back to the Chinese criminal underground, some members of the Indian government proposed legislation to give immunity and a stamp of approval for Indian hackers to do the same to China.[35] India also blocked imports of Chinese telecommunications equipment and moved swiftly to establish cyber-warfare capabilities within its armed forces.[36]

In what will be familiar to international relations theorists, we are now entering into a classic "security dilemma" arms race spiral in cyberspace as dozens of governments look to other states' actions and perceived intentions to justify the need to bolster offensive cyber-warfare capabilities. Cyberspace has many of the characteristics identified by international relations theorists as associated with exacerbating the logic of the security dilemma: offense is considered to be overwhelmingly dominant; deterrence is difficult to implement because of problems around attributing the source of cyber-attacks; there is a lack of transparency around many cyberspace information operations, which are typically undertaken behind a veil of secrecy; and, finally, the barriers to entry are low, to the point where even individuals can participate in consequential cyber-attacks.[37]

The imitation and learning process is not uniform, but mixes with national interests and local culture to create a warp and woof. Governments can look to other states in the international system to lend legitimacy to slightly modified or even altogether different policies. For example, after the United States and other industrialized countries adopted antiterror legislation, many countries of the Commonwealth of Independent States (CIS) did likewise. However, their policies were much more far-reaching and oriented more toward the stifling of minority independence and political opposition movements and the shoring up of regime stability than fighting international terrorism. This process of normative reshaping around local circumstances and interests in this case conforms to Acharya's argument that a norm will more likely be adopted if it will enhance the legitimacy and authority of extant institutions and practices.[38]

A similar process can be seen in the spread of cybercrime and copyright protection legislation. Under the umbrella of an international norm intended for one purpose, states can justify policies and actions that serve more parochial aims. For example, Russia and other authoritarian regimes have used the excuse of policing copyright to seize opposition and NGO computers, in at least one case with the assistance of companies like Microsoft. Similarly, the now widespread belief that it is legitimate to remove videos from websites that contain "offensive" information can be interpreted broadly in various national contexts. For example, Pakistani authorities have repeatedly pressured video hosting services to remove embarrassing or politically inflammatory videos under this rubric.

Some authoritarian and competitive authoritarian regimes that are otherwise geographically remote appear to be learning from each other's "best practices" when it comes to dealing with cyberspace controls over opposition groups. For example, a growing list of countries have banned short message services (SMS) and instant messaging services prior to national crises or significant events like elections or public demonstrations. Although it is possible that each of these countries is doing so in isolation, it seems more likely that inspiration is drawn from other countries' actions. India, Cambodia, China, Mozambique, Turkmenistan, Egypt, and Iran have all disabled SMS and text messaging during or leading up to recent elections, events, or public demonstrations as a way to control social mobilization.

Imitation and learning are major components of normative propagation, but they are processes that are difficult to document empirically. Unless government representatives or policymakers specifically point to an instance or act from which they are drawing inspiration, imitation and learning processes can be obscure and have to be deduced from behavior or practices.

Commercial Conduits

Norms can spread internationally, carried by private actors and, in particular, by companies offering a service that supports the norm. For example, a major market for cyber-security tools and technologies has exploded in recent years in response to pressing cyber-security issues and the growing cyber-arms race. Companies are naturally gravitating to this exploding market in response to commercial opportunities. But they can also influence the market itself by the creation of products and tools that present new opportunities for states. There are, for example, a wide range of new products that offer deep packet inspection and traffic shaping capabilities in spite of the fact that such activities are contrary to fading norms around network neutrality at the heart of cyberspace governance. There are also companies that offer services and products designed for offensive cyber-network attack operations. For example, during the events of the Arab Spring, Egyptian protesters broke into the headquarters of the Egyptian security services and discovered what appeared to be a contract between a German-UK company and the Egyptian security services for computer network exploitation products and services. Naturally, the principals of these companies have a vested interest in ensuring the market continues to expand, which can in turn influence government policies.

The market for surveillance and offensive computer operations that has emerged in recent years was preceded and is supplemented by a market for Internet filtering technologies. The latter were developed initially to serve business environments, but quickly spread to governments looking for solutions for Internet censorship demands. ONI research throughout the 2000s was able to document a growing number of authoritarian countries using US-based commercial filtering products, including Smartfilter in Iran and Tunisia, Websense in Yemen, and Fortinet in Burma. More recent ONI reports document a Canadian company's products being used in Yemen, Qatar, and the United Arab Emirates.[39] Some of these products appear to have been tailored to meet the unique requirements of authoritarian regimes. For example, the Websense product had built-in options for filtering categories that included human rights and NGOs. In one case, a Power-Point presentation by the company Cisco (the maker of telecommunications routing equipment) surfaced in which the argument was made that a market opportunity presented itself for the company working in collusion with China's security services. Commercial solutions such as these can help structure the realm of the possible for governments. Whereas in the past it might have been difficult or even inconceivable to engage in deep packet inspection or keyword-based filtering on a national scale, commercial solutions open up opportunities for policymakers looking to deal with vexing political problems on a fine-grained scale.

International Vacuums (*Horror Vacui*)

Absence of Restraints

One of the least obvious mechanisms of norm propagation is the absence of restraints. Policies, practices, and behaviors can spread internationally when there are no countervailing safeguards or checks. Norm diffusion through the absence of restraints might be likened to the principle of nature abhorring a vacuum. Practices and behaviors fill a void in the policy arena. This mechanism is perhaps the most difficult to pin down empirically because it lacks any identifiable source or location. Yet it may be among the most important global dynamics of the spread of cyberspace controls.

One might hypothesize that norm diffusion via the absence of restraints is most amenable to the diffusion of bad norms precisely because there are no countervailing restraints. For example, the spread of cybercrime, and the blurring of cybercrime and espionage, can be explained in part because of the ways in which these actors are able to exploit fissures in the international system. Bad actors act globally and hide locally in jurisdictions where state capacity is weak and beyond the reach of law enforcement where the victims are located. Some governments may even be deliberating cultivating a climate favorable for crime and espionage to flourish by their inaction. For example, major cyber-espionage networks and acts of cybercrime have been traced back to China, Russia, and other countries that take little or only symbolic measures against perpetrators, in part because of the strategic benefits that accrue to these countries by the flourishing of those activities. These governments can reap the windfalls of the ecology of crime and espionage through the black market while maintaining a relatively credible position of plausible deniability. The same logic might be applied to the market for offensive computer network exploitation and attack capabilities: in the absence of restraints to the contrary, businesspeople will seek out and exploit commercial opportunities of a growing cyber-arms race.

Conclusion

Consideration of the international dynamics and mechanisms of cyberspace controls is important for several theoretical and practical reasons. First, there are unique processes that occur at the international level distinct from what happens domestically. These dynamics and mechanisms help explain why a growing norm around Internet filtering and surveillance is spreading internationally. States do not operate in isolation, but are part of a dense network of relations that influences their decisions and actions. Without considering these dynamics and mechanisms, we may be missing some of the more important explanations for growing cyberspace controls that, up until now, have been primarily attributed to domestic-level causes. The framework that we provide in this article is meant to be a first step in identifying some of the most important sources of those dynamics and mechanisms.

[Second, the] focus on the spread of cyberspace controls, as we outlined, may offer an important contribution to the study of international norm diffusion. Up until now, scholarship in this area has been focused predominantly on the propagation and diffusion of good norms such as landmines and chemical weapons bans, the abolition of slavery, and the spread of democratic values.[40] The examples we described show that propagation and diffusion of (what may be considered by some as) bad norms can happen along the same lines and employ some of the same dynamics and mechanisms. Further research into the spread of cyberspace controls may shed light on some unique dynamics and mechanisms employed by authoritarian or democratically challenged regimes. It is sometimes assumed that these governments are, by definition, inward looking and have an aversion to internationalism and multilateralism. Some of the examples we pointed out show, to the contrary, that these regimes have active international and regional engagements that are likely going to continue to grow.

Third, a focus on international dynamics and mechanisms underscores the iterative and relational quality of state behavior. States' actions and behaviors are formed very much in response to other states' decisions, often in unintended ways. This observation has important policy implications for democratic industrialized countries. The policies that domestic governments implement may be picked up on by authoritarian regimes to legitimize their actions at home in ways considerably different than their original intent. Unfortunately, there is not a lot that can be done to guard against this dynamic. But it is important to be alert to it and recognize it when it occurs. General statements about the war on terror or copyright controls can be turned into excuses for a broad spectrum of otherwise nefarious actions by authoritarian regimes. These dynamics also underscore the importance of consistency, transparency, and accountability in democratic regimes. For example, shortly after Secretary of State Hillary Clinton admonished governments for pressuring RIM to collude with security services, the Barack Obama administration introduced legislation that would put in place precisely the same procedures as those requested by Saudi Arabia, the United Arab Emirates, India, and others. Governments are embedded in an international system and, thus, a dense network of social relations. One cannot understand the spread of cyberspace controls without understanding their international dynamics and mechanisms.

Finally, interpreting these developments through a constructivist lens at the international level can help clarify where those with aims to mitigate norm regression in cyberspace might direct their efforts. One of the principal characteristics of constructivism is the contingent and open-ended nature of international politics. While the trends we described here are powerful and reflect deep-seated dynamics and interests of major powers, they are not irreversible. A large and distributed social movement, which cuts across civil society, the private sector, and governments, exists with aims to protect and preserve cyberspace as an open commons of global information. While this movement faces an uphill struggle, the multiple ways in which cyberspace controls spread internationally can give a more detailed and precise road map for points of legal, regulatory, and discursive intervention and robust checks and balances.

Notes

1. R. Deibert, J. Palfrey, R. Rohozinksi, and J. Zittrain, eds., *Access Denied: The Practice and Policy of Global Internet Filtering* (Cambridge: MIT Press, 2008).

2. R. Deibert, J. Palfrey, R. Rohozinksi, and J. Zittrain, eds., *Access Controlled: The Shaping of Power, Rights, and Rule in Cyberspace* (Cambridge: MIT Press, 2010).

3. T. Hopf, "The Promise of Constructivism in International Relations Theory," *International Security* 23, no. 1 (Summer 1998): 171–200.

4. J. H. Herz, "Idealist Internationalism and the Security Dilemma," *World Politics* 2, no. 2 (1950): 157–180.

5. Margaret E. Keck and Kathryn Sikkink, *Activists Beyond Borders: Advocacy Networks in International Politics* (Ithaca: Cornell University Press, 1998).

6. R. Abrahamsen and M. Williams, *Security Beyond the State: Private Security in International Politics* (Cambridge: Cambridge University Press, 2011).

7. Paul Kowert and Jeffrey Legro, "Norms, Identity, and Their Limits: A Theoretical Reprise," in Peter Katzenstein, ed., *The Culture of National Security: Norms and Identity in World Politics* (New York: Columbia University Press, 1996), pp. 485–486.

8. R. McKeown, "Norm Regress: US Revisionism and the Slow Death of the Torture Norm," *International Relations* 23, no. 5 (2009): 5–25.

9. J. H. Saltzer, D. P. Reed, and D. D. Clark, "End-to-End Arguments in System Design," *ACM Transactions on Computer Systems* 2, no. 2 (1984): 277–288.

10. M. A. Lemley and L. Lessig, "The End of End-to-End: Preserving the Architecture of the Internet in the Broadband Era," *UCLA Law Review* 48 (2001): 925–972.

11. M. L. Mueller, "Net Neutrality as Global Principles for Internet Governance," Internet Governance Project, School of Information Studies, Syracuse University, http://internetgovernance.org/pdf/NetNeutralityGlobalPrinciple.pdf.

12. R. Deibert, J. Palfrey, R. Rohozinski, and J. Zittrain, "Access Contested: Toward the Fourth Phase of Cyberspace Controls," in R. Deihert, J. Palfrey, R. Rohozinski, and J. Zittrain, eds., *Access Contested: Security, Identity, and Resistance in Asian Cyberspace* (Cambridge: MIT Press, 2011).

13. H. Noman and J. C. York, "West Censoring East: The Use of Western Technologies by Middle East Censors, 2010–2011," Open Net Initiative, March 2011, http://opennet.net/west-censoring-east-the-use-western-technologies-middle-east-censors-2010-2011.

14. R. Deibert and R. Rohozinski, "Good for Liberty, Bad for Security? Global Civil Society and the Securitization of the Internet," in R. Deibert, J. Palfrey, R. Rohozinski, and J. Zittrain, eds., *Access Denied: The Practice and Policy of Global Internet Filtering* (Cambridge: MIT Press, 2008), pp. 123–149.

15. British Prime Minister's Office, "PM Statement on Disorder in England," 11 August 2011, www.number10.gov.uk/news/pm-statement-on-disorder-in-england.

16. Bay Area Rapid Transit, "Statement on Temporary Wireless Service Interruption in Select BART Stations on Aug. 11," 12 August 2011, www.bart.gov/news/articles/2011/news20110812.aspx.

17. E. Zuckerman, "Intermediary Censorship," in R. Deibert, J. Palfrey, R. Rohozinski, and J. Zittrain, eds., *Access Controlled: The Shaping of Power, Rights, and Rule in Cyberspace* (Cambridge: MIT Press, 2010).

18. J. P. Kesan and C. M. Hayes, "Mitigative Counterstriking: Self-Defense and Deterrence in Cyberspace," Illinois Public Law Research Paper No. 10-35, http://papers.ssrn.com/sol3/papers.cfm?abstract_id=1805163; US Department of Defense, Strategy for Operating in Cyberspace, July 2011, www.defense.gov/news/d20110714cyber.pdf.

19. Robert O. Keohane, ed., *Neorealism and Its Critics* (New York: Columbia University Press, 1986).

20. Alexander Wendt, *Social Theory of International Politics* (Cambridge: Cambridge University Press, 1999); Alexander Wendt, "Anarchy Is What States Make of It: The Social Construction of Power Politics," *International Organization* 46, no. 2 (1992): 391–425.

21. M. Barnett and M. Finnemore, "The Politics, Power, and Pathologies of International Organizations," *International Organization* 53, no. 4 (1999): 699–732.

22. R. Deibert and R. Rohozinski, "International Organization and Cyber-governance," in Robert A. Denemark, ed., *The International Studies Encyclopedia*, vol. 7 (West Sussex: Wiley-Blackwell, 2010), pp. 4203–4218; M. L. Mueller, "Internet Governance," in Robert A. Denemark, ed., *The International Studies Encyclopedia*, vol. 7 (West Sussex: Wiley-Blackwell, 2010), pp. 4610–4627.

23. "Policy Statement by Igor Shchegolev, Minister of Telecom and Mass Communications of the Russian Federation," International Telecommunication Union plenipotentiary conference, Guadalajara, Mexico, 4 October 2010, www.itu.int/plenipotentiary/2010/statements/russian_federation/shchegolev -ru.html.

24. B. Kuerbis, "Reading Tea Leaves: China Statement on Internet Policy," Internet Governance Project, 8 June 2010, http://blog.internetgovernance.org /blog/_archives/2010/6/8/4548091.html.

25. "RIM Should Open Up User Data: UN Agency," *CBC News*, 2 September 2010, www.cbc.ca/news/technology/story/2010/09/02/rim-user-data-un.html.

26. Jonathan Fildes, "UN Slated for Stifling Net Debate," *BBC News*, 16 November 2009, http://news.bbc.co.Uk/2/hi/technology/8361849.stm.

27. B. Kuerbis and M. Mueller, "Negotiating a New Governance Hierarchy: An Analysis of the Conflicting Incentives to Secure Internet Routing," *Communications and Strategies* 81 (2011): 125–142, http://papers.ssrn.com/sol3 /papers.cfm7abstract_id=2021835.

28. M. L. Mueller and M. Chango, "Disrupting Global Governance: The Internet WHOIS Service, ICANN, and Privacy," *Journal of Information Technology and Politics* 5, no. 3 (2008).

29. A. Acharya, "Norm Subsidiarity and Regional Orders: Sovereignty, Regionalism, and Rule Making in the Third World," *International Studies Quarterly* 55, no. 1 (2011): 95–123.

30. R. Allison, "Virtual Regionalism, Regional Structures and Regime Security in Central Asia," *Central Asian Survey* 27, no. 2 (2008): 185–202; R. Weitz, "China, Russia, and the Challenge to the Global Commons," *Pacific Focus* 24, no. 3 (December 2009): 271–297.

31. S. Sirimanna, "Chinese Here for Cyber Censorship," *Sunday Times*, 14 February 2010, www.sundaytimes.lk/100214/News/nws_02.html.

32. M. Finnemore and K. Sikkink, "International Norm Dynamics and Political Change," *International Organization* 2, no. 4 (Autumn 1998): 887–917.

33. B. Goldstein, "Imitation in International Relations: Analogies, Vicarious Learning, and Foreign Policy," *International Interactions* 29, no. 3 (2003): 237–267.

34. D. Dolowitz and D. Marsh, "Who Learns What from Whom: A Review of the Policy Transfer Literature," *Political Studies* 44, no. 2 (1996): 343–357.

35. J. T. Philip and H. Singh, "Spy Game: India Readies Cyber Army to Hack into Hostile Nations' Computer Systems," *Economic Times*, 6 August

2010, http://economictimes.indiatimes.com/news/news-by-industry/et-cetera /Spy-Game-India-readies-cyber-army-to-hack-into-hostile-nations-computer -systems/articleshow/6258977.cms.

36. R. Blakely, "India Blocks Deals with Chinese Telecoms Companies over Cyber-spy Fears," *The Times* (London), 10 May 2010, http://business.timesonline .co.uk/tol/business/markets/china/article7121521.ece.

37. We are grateful to Eli Jellens of iDefense for suggesting these characteristics in an unpublished 2011 brief shared with us. See also R. Deibert, R. Rohozinski, and M. Grete-Nishihata, "Cyclones in Cyberspace: Information Shaping and Denial in the 2008 Russia-Georgia War," *Security Dialogue* 43, no. 1 (2012): 3–24.

38. A. Acharya, "How Ideas Spread: Whose Norms Matter? Norm Localization and Institutional Change in Asian Regionalism," *International Organization* 58, no. 2 (2007): 239–275.

39. H. Noman and J. G. York, "West Censoring East: The Use of Western Technologies by Middle East Censors," Open Net Initiative, March 2011, http://opennet.net/west-censoring-east-the-use-western-technologies-middle -east-censors-2010-2011.

40. One exception is R. McKeown, "Norm Regress: US Revisionism and the Slow Death of the Torture Norm," *International Relations* 23, no. 5 (2009): 5–25.

14

The Financial Crisis, Contested Legitimacy, and the Genesis of Intra-BRICS Cooperation

Oliver Stuenkel

> It is time to start reorganizing the world in the direction that the over-whelming majority of mankind expects and needs.
> —Celso Amorim, "BRICs and the Reorganization of the World"[1]

When the finance ministers and central bankers of the BRIC countries (Brazil, Russia, India, and China) met on 7 November 2008 in Brazil, less than two months had passed since Lehman Brothers' bankruptcy. The financial crisis seemed to make things so unpredictable that the Brazilian government had decided, at the last minute, to change the location of the summit from Brasília to São Paulo, close to the international airport to allow the participants to quickly return to their home countries to monitor the crisis. In times of globalization, the financial crisis at the heart of the global economic core was widely thought to have profound consequences for all countries that participated in the international market.

Yet as *The Economist* wrote at the time, the largest emerging markets were "recovering fast and starting to think the recession may mark another milestone in a worldwide shift of economic power away from the West."[2] As the BRIC finance ministers stated, "We recognized that the crisis has to some extent affected all of our countries. We stress however, that BRIC countries have shown significant resilience."[3] As the meeting in São Paulo made clear, the BRIC countries not only had discussed ways to protect themselves against the crisis, but also how they could use it as an opportunity to adapt global structures in their favor. Within the following four months, BRIC finance ministers and central bankers met four times—in contrast to their weak ties prior to

Reprinted from *Global Governance*, vol. 19, no. 4: 611–630. © 2013 by Lynne Rienner Publishers. Reprinted by permission of the publisher. Edited for length.

the crisis. The results were palpable: prior to the Group of 20 (G-20) summit in London in April 2009, the BRIC countries were able to act as agenda setters and considerably influence the final G-20 declaration— all by making use of the BRIC grouping, a vehicle that had, in its political dimension, barely existed before the crisis.

The rise of the BRIC grouping is one of the most commented on phenomena in international politics of recent years. Yet little is known about how and why institutionalized cooperation between the BRIC countries began. In this article, I make two arguments. First, I contend that an unprecedented combination in 2008—a profound financial crisis among developed countries, paired with relative economic stability among emerging powers—caused a legitimacy crisis of the international financial order, which led to equally unprecedented cooperation between emerging powers in the context of the BRIC grouping. The Group of 20 leaders' endorsement at the London summit of almost all of the substantive recommendations put forward before by BRIC countries' finance ministers also shows that these countries were able to use their temporarily increased bargaining power to turn into agenda setters at the time—culminating in the International Monetary Fund (IMF) quota reforms agreed on in 2010.[4] This shows that even short periods of reduced legitimacy in global governance can quickly lead to the rise of alternative institutions such as, in the case of the crisis that began in 2008, the BRIC platform that now forms part of the landscape of global governance. Current governance structures thus may be far less stable than is usually assumed—and future financial crises may very well reduce their legitimacy further and lead to additional, more profound alterations.

Second, I argue that intra-BRIC cooperation in the area of international finance was the starting point of a broader type of cooperation in many other areas, suggesting the occurrence of spillover effects of cooperation. In addition to confidence building between the BRICS (Brazil, Russia, India, China, South Africa) countries, the fact that the BRICS grouping is setting up institutionalized structures—such as a BRICS currency contingency fund and a BRICS development bank in 2013—helps explain why institutionalized cooperation is likely to continue even when the initially propitious conditions to do so are no longer present.

No Motley Crew: From São Paulo to Horsham

Why did the finance ministers and central bankers of four seemingly disparate countries with diverging interests decide to meet in Brazil and issue a joint communiqué at the height of the financial crisis, a week prior to the first G-20 summit in Washington, DC (November 2008)? And how were these four countries able to turn into such an influential grouping only several months later, during the G-20 summit in London in April 2009?

A Look Back

In 2001 Jim O'Neill, recently appointed head of global economic research at Goldman Sachs, sought to create a category for the large, fast-growing developing countries that he thought could symbolize the current global economic transformation. As an economist, O'Neill did not take any political aspects into account and devised the group based on economic indicators, focusing on gross domestic product (GDP) growth rates, GDP per capita, and population size. . . . O'Neill predicted that "over the next 10 years, the weight of the BRICs and especially China in world GDP will grow, raising important issues about the global economic impact of fiscal and monetary policy in the BRICs."[5]

Yet while O'Neill did not expect the grouping to develop politically, he created the *BRIC* term with the momentous political developments at the time. As he later argued,

> Imagine the situation in which I came up with that idea. This was shortly after 9/11. The terrorist attacks on New York and Washington strengthened my belief that the dominance of the western countries needed to be superseded, or at least complemented, by something else. If globalization were to continue to be successful, it should not sail under the US flag. It seemed to me that because of their sheer size and their populations, China, India, Russia and Brazil had the economic potential. What emerging markets have in common—in addition to their distrust of the West—is their bright future.[6]

Initially, the term's impact was limited to the financial world. The aftermath of the September 11 terrorist attacks and the subsequent US military mobilization and invasion of Afghanistan dominated the geopolitical debate in 2002.

In October 2003, Goldman Sachs . . . predicted that, by 2050, the BRIC economies would be larger in terms of US dollars than the Group of 6 (G6), which consists of the United States, Germany, Japan, the United Kingdom, France, and Italy.[7] The 2003 paper's influence surpassed the limits of the financial world, helping the *BRIC* term turn, in the following years, into a buzzword in international politics.

Window of Opportunity

BRIC did not become a household name because of its conceptual novelty; rather, it was because the grouping powerfully symbolized a narrative that seemed distant in the 1990s, but appeared to make sense in 2008. A momentous shift of power from the United States and Europe toward emerging powers such as China, India, and Brazil was taking place, making the world less Western and more ideologically diverse. Economic liberalization in emerging market economies began to pay off, resulting in consistently higher growth rates than in the developed world. In contrast, the United States' hitherto unlimited power seemed to reach its limits in costly and potentially ill-conceived military engagements in Iraq and Afghanistan and a challenging war on terrorism, which seemed to reduce US legitimacy, opening a window of opportunity for emerging countries to gain greater visibility. At a remarkable speed, unipolarity seemed to turn into a mere transition phase on the way toward a multipolar age. As Randall Schweller and Xiayou Pu argue, "Unipolarity, which seemed strangely durable only a few years ago," appears today as a "passing moment." They continue that the United States "is no longer a hyper-power towering over potential contenders. The rest of the world is catching up."[8]

While the US National Intelligence Council's 2005 Global Trends report predicted that the United States would remain the "single most powerful actor economically, technologically and militarily,"[9] the 2009 report foresaw "a world in which the US plays a prominent role in global events, but . . . as one among many global actors."[10] . . .

In short, the financial crisis that erupted in the United States in 2008 led to a legitimacy crisis of the international financial system. Legitimacy matters because it is a fundamental element of order. As the normative basis of political order, legitimacy sustains the recognized authority to rule in a community. Current order must be accepted by all relevant actors and its rule must be deemed legitimate by the rest of the world to be stable. A legitimacy crisis, as a consequence, increases the risk of international political change.

Describing the years prior to the first BRIC summit, Matias Spektor states: "The US went to war in the Middle East, Europe faltered, Asia rose, and the institutions that governed the world were evidently no longer up to the task. Unsettling as they were, these transformations opened up a new world of opportunities."[11]

Seeking to make use of these dynamics, the first informal encounter in the context of the BRIC grouping took place in 2006, when the foreign ministers of Brazil, Russia, India, and China met on the sidelines of the sixty-first UN General Assembly in New York. They met again a year later, at Brazil's initiative, still with the aim of identifying areas where they could cooperate. In May 2008 in Yekaterinburg, Russia, the foreign ministers held their first stand-alone meeting, after which they issued the first joint BRIC communiqué. . . .

In their search for a common denominator, the BRIC foreign ministers quickly realized that the economic crisis in the United States provided emerging powers with a unique opportunity to rally around an issue of great importance: the necessity to reform the international financial order. In the communiqué issued in São Paulo, the BRIC countries stated their dissatisfaction clearly:

> We called for the reform of multilateral institutions in order that they reflect the structural changes in the world economy and the increasingly central role that emerging markets now play. We agreed that international bodies should review their structures, rules and instruments in respect of aspects like representation, legitimacy and effectiveness and also to strengthen their capacity in addressing global issues. Reform of the International Monetary Fund and of the World Bank Group should move forward and be guided towards more equitable voice and participation balance between advanced and developing countries. The Financial Stability Forum must immediately broaden its membership to include a significant representation of emerging economies.[12]

The G-20 seemed to be the ideal platform for this endeavor—a powerful grouping that included the four BRIC countries. It thus is no coincidence that intra-BRIC cooperation began in earnest in the realm of international finance—an area that seemed particularly ripe for change during the first two years of the crisis. The decision to cooperate in a more structured way was made when the BRIC heads of government met on the sidelines of the Group of 8 (G8) summit on 9 July 2008.

Amorim captures the spirit of the time when he argues that "the BRICS have contributed to keeping the global economy on track . . . now, they seek to strengthen themselves as a bloc that helps balance and democratize the international order at the beginning of the century."[13] Touching on a theme that would eventually become the rallying cry for the BRIC countries, Amorim argues that "we should continue to promote reform . . . of the international financial institutions, a topic we will discuss in November, when the Ministers of Finance of the BRIC countries will meet in São Paulo."[14]

BRIC Summitry: Generating Trust

Four months later, the finance ministers and central bankers came together in Brazil, in a move that gave further impetus to intra-BRIC cooperation. In the first paragraph of their communiqué, after a brief mention of the international crisis, the BRIC countries reported that "we . . . discussed proposals put forward by the countries on reforming the global financial architecture."[15]

Yet far more important than the actual content of the communiqué was the fact that Brazil, Russia, India, and China used the BRIC platform to initiate preparatory meetings prior to the G-20—reflecting their strong belief in the benefits of cooperation between them. While actual cooperation between emerging powers was still incipient at the time, and mutual knowledge relatively low, the São Paulo communiqué made clear that the BRIC platform was more than a mere ad hoc grouping. . . .

In late November 2008, during a bilateral meeting in Rio de Janeiro, Russia's president Dmitry Medvedev and Brazil's president Luiz Inácio Lula da Silva announced that the heads of state of the BRIC countries would hold their first-ever summit in Russia in 2009. After the meeting, Lula argued that the financial crisis offered opportunities for emerging powers to strengthen cooperation between themselves and their position in global affairs as a whole. According to a Brazilian policymaker, "cooperation in the field of international finance would generate trust between the BRICs' governments, allowing for broader cooperation further down the road."[16] The BRIC finance ministers and central bankers, for their part, announced in São Paulo that they would hold their next meeting in Washington, DC, in late April 2009. Yet rather than wait until then, they gathered again on 13 March in Horsham, a day before the G-20 finance ministers and central bankers met there, and two weeks prior to the next G-20 leaders summit in London on 2 April.

In Horsham, the BRIC countries' commitment to governance reform was reiterated, this time in more explicit terms:

> We draw our special attention to the reform of international financial institutions. We stand for reviewing the IMF role and mandate so as to adapt it to a new global monetary and financial architecture. We emphasize the importance of a strong commitment to governance reform with a clear timetable and roadmap. We consider that IMF resources are clearly inadequate and should be very significantly increased through various channels. Borrowing should be a temporary bridge to a permanent quota increase as the Fund is a quota-based institution. Hence we call for the completion of the next general review of quotas by January 2011.[17]

They further stated that

> we call for urgent action with regard to voice and representation in the IMF, in order that they better reflect their real economic weights. In the Fund, a significant realignment of quota should be completed not later than January 2011. This is necessary to enable members more equitable and fuller participation in the Fund's efforts to play its man-

date role. A rebalancing of representation on the Executive Board . . . would lead to a more equitable representation of the membership.[18]

A similar request was made by the BRIC countries regarding the World Bank. They asked for "the speeding up of the second phase of voice and representation reform in the World Bank Group, which should be completed by April 2010," and called it "imperative" that the next heads of the IMF and the World Bank be selected through "open merit-based" processes, irrespective of nationality or regional considerations.[19]

While the idea that the BRIC grouping could align some of their positions was met with profound skepticism from the beginning, the G-20 leaders' endorsement at the London summit in 2009 of several of the substantive recommendations put forward before by BRIC countries' finance ministers in Horsham also shows that the BRIC grouping may significantly increase emerging powers' bargaining power and, therefore, prove to be more sustainable than its relatively low level of institutionalization suggests. Specifically, the recommendations made in the BRIC countries' communiqué in Horsham found their way into the G-20 declaration on various levels; for example, the leaders of the G-20 supported the threefold increase of resources available to the IMF and allowed the issuance of new special drawing rights (SDRs). In addition, they promised to "build a stronger, more globally consistent, supervisory and regulatory framework for the future financial sector."[20] The G-20 leaders also announced that the heads of international financial institutions "should be appointed through an open, transparent, and merit-based selection process."[21] All of these demands had been articulated by the BRIC finance ministers and central bankers prior to the G-20 summit. In the same way, the term "reform" appears over ten times in the G-20 declaration, reflecting pressure from emerging powers to provide them with more space.[22]

The BRIC countries' push for reform culminated in 2010, when a significant quota reform was agreed on—including a quota shift by more than 6 percent in favor of large emerging countries. China became the third-largest shareholder and overtook Germany while Russia, India, and Brazil entered the list of ten most important shareholders. The IMF hailed these steps as "historic" and pointed out that they represented "a major realignment in the ranking of quota shares that better reflects global economic realities, and a strengthening in the Fund's legitimacy and effectiveness."[23] It thus can be argued that, in the realm of international finance, the BRIC countries were briefly able to act as agenda setters, bringing together countries that otherwise may not have found a common cause.

Spillover Effects of Cooperation

The meetings of finance ministers and central bankers in São Paulo in November 2007 and Horsham in March 2008 can be seen as the starting point of far broader cooperation. From then on, intra-BRIC cooperation expanded to other areas.

Shortly after the G-20 summit in London (April 2009), the BRIC countries' national security advisors met for the first time, reflecting a dramatic expansion in the scope of their activities. At that meeting, participants discussed possibilities to join forces in the combat against terrorism, illegal migration, and drug and arms trafficking. In addition to the ties between the finance ministries and central banks of the BRIC countries, this encounter established a common platform for the countries' security communities. Since 2009, the national security advisors have met on a yearly basis.

On 16 June 2009, Russia hosted the first BRIC leaders summit in Yekaterinburg, which was attended by Brazil's president Lula, Russia's president Medvedev, India's prime minister Manmohan Singh, and China's president Hu Jintao. . . .

The theme of reforming international financial institutions initially continued to be the leitmotif of the encounter. As Medvedev pointed out, there was a "need to put in place a fairer decision-making process regarding the economic, foreign policy and security issues on the international agenda" and that "the BRIC summit aims to create the conditions [for] this new order."[24] Particular emphasis was laid on ending the informal agreement that the United States and Europe could appoint the World Bank president and IMF director, respectively.

Yet new issues were added to the agenda. Aside from seeking to reform international institutions, reducing global dependence on the dollar was one of the key themes of the conversations at the summit. Prior to the summit, Medvedev proposed that countries use a mix of regional reserve currencies to reduce reliance on the dollar. Russia said it would reduce the share of US Treasuries in its $400 billion reserves. This echoed China's and Brazil's decisions to invest $40 billion and $10 billion respectively in IMF bonds, a move to diversify their dollar-heavy currency reserves. While the BRIC leaders discussed how to reduce dollar assets in their existing reserves, the Russian government also sought to discuss ways to limit the use of the dollar in bilateral intra-BRIC trades. China, which has the strongest trade ties with the other BRIC countries, had already signed a deal with Brazil in May

2009, to allow some bilateral trade transactions to be conducted in Brazilian real and Chinese yuan. . . .

After the 2009 leaders summit, the frequency and breadth of intra-BRIC cooperation increased markedly. In the second half of 2009, the BRIC countries' finance ministers and central bankers met again in preparation for the G-20 summit in Pittsburgh. The BRIC foreign ministers again met on the sidelines of the General Assembly in New York (September 2009). In February 2010, the heads of national statistics institutes of the BRIC countries organized the first meeting at the sidelines of the UN Statistics Committee in New York. A month later, the first BRIC exchange program for judges was organized in Brasilia. Two weeks later, the BRIC agriculture ministers held their first meeting in Moscow. In April 2010, the heads of BRIC development banks met for the first time—an encounter that marked the beginning of wide-ranging cooperation that eventually led to India's proposal to create a BRICS development bank in 2012.

The second BRIC leaders summit followed in April 2010 in Brasília, during which heads of government again agreed to increase "intra-BRIC cooperation" in an attempt to strengthen ties on different levels of government and civil society. On 14 April, the Institute for Applied Economic Research, a Brazilian think-tank, hosted the first BRIC academic forum in Brasília, which brought academics and policy analysts from the four member countries together to develop joint ideas about how to strengthen cooperation. On the same day, in Rio de Janeiro, the first BRIC business forum took place. Finally, the second meeting of BRIC national security advisors occurred in Brasília on 15 April. Since Brazil had also hosted the India, Brazil, South Africa (IBSA) summit a day earlier, South Africa's president Jacob Zuma was able to hold bilateral meetings with all BRIC leaders in an—ultimately successful—attempt to include his country in the grouping. By then, the BRIC grouping had already received formal and informal membership requests by several other countries such as Mexico, Indonesia, and Turkey.

The third leaders summit in Sanya, China, in March 2011 saw the entry of South Africa, which symbolized the BRICS (now with a capital S) countries' taking full ownership of the term. Shortly after the summit, representatives of the cities of Rio de Janeiro, St. Petersburg, Mumbai, and Qingdao met to sign the Qingdao Protocol, which called for greater cooperation between the cities. During the fourth BRICS summit in New Delhi in 2012, leaders declared they would study the viability of a BRICS development bank, which would in fact be the first step toward institutionalizing the BRICS grouping.

Criticism

Throughout this process of institutionalization, the vast majority of observers in the United States and Europe argue that the category was inadequate for a more rigorous analysis, given that the differences between the BRIC countries far outweigh their commonalities.[25] One common argument is that, in economic terms, Russia and Brazil are large commodity exporters whereas China is a large commodity importer; China is a proponent of the Doha Round, India a skeptic. This matters because the countries generate growth in different and often opposing ways; while Brazil and Russia benefit from high energy prices, India, as a major energy consumer, suffers from them.[26] Another common argument against the grouping is that, from a political perspective, Brazil's and India's vibrant democracies contrast China's and Russia's more authoritarian governments. Brazil is nonnuclear while Russia, India, and China possess nuclear weapons, and India is a nonsignatory of the Nuclear Nonproliferation Treaty. Russia remains highly suspicious of Chinese encroachment in its demographically declining Far East. More importantly, critics say, is that an unresolved border conflict between China and India as well as overlapping spheres of interest in the Indian Ocean are often cited as proof that the BRIC grouping is an impossible alliance. On a more general level, however, it is argued that the BRIC countries do not constitute a coherent group because their positions in the global political order differ strongly.[27]

While Brazil and India are pushing for a more fundamental redistribution of institutional power in today's global governance structures, Russia and China—both permanent members of the UN Security Council—are essentially status quo powers, reluctant to change a system that has served them well during the past decades. Finally, bilateral ties between some of the BRIC countries—for example, between Russia and Brazil—are largely insignificant. In sum, for many observers, the BRIC countries are too disparate to be a meaningful category. . . . Several of these arguments are indeed valid. The structural differences between the BRICS members make cooperation more difficult today. In addition, lower growth figures in the emerging world may further dampen hopes to increase cooperation and position the BRICS grouping as a relevant and unified actor in some aspects of international politics.

Yet countering such criticism, and partly to address the problems described above, the number of issues debated at the summits has continually broadened, now ranging from geopolitics and the crisis in Syria, to the economic crisis, to domestic challenges such as education and health care. In addition to the yearly summits, numerous working groups and regular ministerial-level meetings in areas such as defense, health, education, finance, trade, agriculture, and science and technology have been established over the past two years, creating an unprecedented degree of interaction—more than fifty official meetings between the BRICS countries. In addition, BRICS competition authorities, summit sherpas, central bank heads, urbanization experts, think-thank representatives, and businesspeople have convened regularly. The BRICS grouping has thus established a system that one could call "transgovernmentalism," which implies that groups make contact with similar groups in other countries and departments of state to forge links with their counterparts in other states.[28]

. . . [At] the fifth BRICS summit in Durban in 2013 [the leaders] decided to establish two important structures. First of all, they agreed on creating a currency contingency fund to protect members' economies in times of crisis. More importantly, however, they decided to set up a BRICS development bank. These two decisions transformed the BRICS grouping from an ad hoc grouping into a more institutionalized structure, assuring unprecedented cooperation between the countries' finance ministries and central banks.

Regarding the development bank, however, fundamental questions remain. For example, will there be a physical secretariat or will it be a "virtual bank," akin to a network among the BRICS's national development banks? Will each country contribute the same amount (the talk is currently of $10 billion), or will members contribute according to the size of their economy? South Africa is said to prefer the latter and India the former as it fears China's dominance. Will the bank be controlled by emerging powers alone or will established powers be allowed to have a minority stake? Will the bank invest only within BRICS countries or also outside of the grouping (i.e., in Africa)? India is said to prefer the former, as it requires massive infrastructure investment, and it would be far more comfortable taking loans from a BRICS development bank than a Chinese-controlled bank. Will the bank develop lending paradigms that differ from those created by the World Bank and other established banks? This last question is perhaps the most important one of all. Some say that the development bank will avoid the conditions that the World Bank and the IMF attach to their loans. This could lead Western observers to accuse the BRICS development bank of providing rogue loans and undermine the West's attempts to promote good governance in the developing world. Particularly in times of lower economic dynamism, setting up the institution may take longer than initially expected.

The question regarding conditionality points to a larger uncertainty about the future of global governance. Will emerging powers' projects such as the BRICS development bank undermine existing institutions and the principles that sustain them? BRICS policymakers go out of their way to point out that the BRICS development bank will complement existing institutions. Yet why then, skeptics may ask, do they not hand over the money to the World Bank, the IMF, or other institutions that are already in place? Why go through the hassle of creating a new institution?

The answer, clearly, is that while emerging powers seek a larger role within the existing framework, they do not feel that established powers are willing to provide them with the adequate power and responsibility. Reforms at the World Bank and the IMF have been too slow and not far-reaching enough. The World Bank remains, despite its name, essentially a Western-dominated institution in the eyes of emerging powers. It is difficult to read the creation of the BRICS development bank as anything other than that.

It can thus be said that the early cooperation in the realm of international finance, which began in earnest during meetings in São Paulo and Horsham in late 2008 and early 2009, served as a confidence-building mechanism that had a spillover effect that made possible a much wider range of interaction in other, unrelated areas. This is particularly noteworthy as several bilateral government-to-government relations between BRIC countries were underdeveloped prior to the international financial crisis—now, on the other hand, government departments in the BRICS countries have direct contact with each other.

Post-crisis BRICS Cooperation

Realist theory is capable of explaining the cooperation between the BRIC countries during the financial crisis. After having identified a common interest, they began to cooperate and jointly press for change—and quite successfully so, as the results of the G-20 summit in London in 2009 attest. According to realist thought, however, this issue-based cooperation would have ended after the most intense period of the crisis—in the same way that realists at the end of the Cold War had expected NATO to disband.

Yet while early intra-BRIC cooperation was strongly tied to the theme of the international financial crisis until 2009, it then moved into areas that were not related to financial issues or global governance at all. Rather, close cooperation in the area of finance had created the trust that allowed ties to expand into fields such as education, science and technology, and defense. This type of cooperation no longer depends on the collective high growth that led to cooperation in the first place. It would thus be wrong to assume that lower growth figures in the BRICS economies—a phenomenon clearly visible since 2012—will reduce their interest in stronger intra-BRICS cooperation.

Why did this proliferation of cooperative behavior take place? Principally used by scholars who studied the phenomenon of regional integration in Europe, the concept of spillover may have some relevance to explain the growth of intra-BRICS cooperation.[29] According to Leon N. Lindberg, a "spillover" implies that political cooperation, once initiated, is extended over time in a way that was not necessarily intended at the outset.[30] Philippe C. Schmitter writes that "spillover refers . . . to the process whereby members of an integration scheme—agreed on some collective goals for a variety of motives but unequally satisfied with their attainment of these goals—attempt to resolve their dissatisfaction by resorting to collaboration in another, related sector (expanding the scope of mutual commitment) or by intensifying their commitment to the original sector (increasing the level of mutual commitment), or both."[31]

. . . Intra-BRICS cooperation, of course, differs strongly from that seen in the early days of European integration, and the BRICS grouping is unlikely to ever develop into anything similar to the European Union. The BRICS platform does not yet involve making binding decisions or jointly managing any aspect of countries' economic or political affairs; neither is their sovereignty pooled. However, intra-BRICS cooperation has developed to a degree that requires a more sophisticated answer than merely pointing to increased bargaining power during the financial crisis.

Rather than functional spillover, which describes the effects of advanced economic integration, the spillover seen among BRICS countries is of a more simple and incipient type. It relates to the effects of confidence building between government bureaucracies, which—upon a positive experience in one area—decide to cooperate in additional, but not necessarily related fields. Contrary to functional or political spillover effects seen in Europe, the potential spillover effects seen among the BRICS countries do not involve interest groups outside of government, but relate entirely to intra-governmental activities. Intra-BRICS cooperation remains, to this day, a state-driven process, so one could also liken it to "elite socialization" among BRICS governments.

After successful cooperation in the area of international financial negotiations, largely coordinated by the finance ministry and foreign ministry in each country, leading policymakers decided that cooperation in other areas—such as security—could be similarly beneficial. Individuals who have dealt with BRICS issues are more likely to seek closer ties to BRICS countries even when they have moved into other areas of the administration. Amorim, for example, one of the decisive figures in promoting the political dimension of the original BRIC grouping, stepped down as Brazil's foreign minister in late 2010 and later became minister of defense and continues to foster intra-BRICS ties in that capacity. This process can be expected to continue as a function of the growing number of policymakers involved in activities that form part of the wider universe of intra-BRICS cooperation.

According to interviews with policymakers from the four countries involved, government bureaucracies began, in 2008 and 2009, to engage widely and frequently in a rather unprecedented way. Brazil's finance minister Mantega, for example, met with his BRIC counterparts more frequently than any other group outside of South America, underlining the importance of the grouping to the Brazilian government. This development of elite socialization is described by Carsten Stroby-Jensen in the case of the European Union:

> Over time, people involved on a regular basis . . . will tend to develop European loyalties and preferences. . . . We can imagine how participants in an intensive and ongoing decision-making process, which may well extend over several years and bring them into frequent and close personal contact, and which engages them in a joint problem-solving and policy-generating exercise, might develop a special orientation to that process and to those interactions, especially if they are rewarding. . . . This elite would try to convince national elites of . . . cooperation. At the same time . . . negotiations would become less politicized and more technocratic. As a result, it was expected that the agenda would tend to shift towards more technical problems upon which it was possible to forge agreement.[32]

While the parallels between the European Union and the BRICS grouping are, as mentioned above, limited, intra-BRICS cooperation is clearly becoming less political and more technical as more and more bureaucrats from different ministries get involved in the process—further indicating that intra-BRICS cooperation is likely to be more sustainable than generally thought. A natural by-product of growing intra-BRICS cooperation is stronger bilateral ties among BRICS members. A 2008 visa-free travel agreement between Russia and Brazil came into effect in 2010. Easing visa rules is part of a more far-reaching attempt by both governments to strengthen ties, which includes high-level deals to build up cooperation in areas such as energy, space, and military technologies. It will also contribute to increasing not only business contacts, but tourism, which should help broaden the BRICS countries' mutual understanding on a societal level—a vital element in reducing the "trust deficit" between the countries.

Since the financial crisis that began in 2008, the global scenario has changed. Brazil symbolizes this best. GDP grew less than 2 percent in 2012, and its performance in 2013 can no longer be compared to that of the past decade. While Europe still struggles, the US economy is slowly beginning to recover and it may very well grow faster than Brazil's over the next years. A more confident United States, no longer tied down in Iraq and Afghanistan is unlikely to provide rising powers with the space that the BRICS so skillfully used over the past years. In addition to lower growth, Brazil's forays into the world's top league—marked by Lula's attempt to negotiate with Iran in 2010 and its stint as a nonpermanent Security Council member—were far from smooth.

Yet it should come as no surprise that slower growth in the BRICS economies in 2012 and 2013 has had little impact on the BRICS countries' willingness to strengthen cooperation even further. Irrespective of current growth figures, policymakers in emerging countries are convinced that the BRICS meetings serve as a useful vehicle to promote South-South cooperation, which has grown considerably over the past two decades. Slow growth alone cannot undo the desire to diversify emerging powers' partnerships—after all, South-South cooperation is one of emerging powers' key elements in an attempt to democratize global affairs and reduce the disproportional weight that the Global North has had in the global conversation until now.

Conclusion

In this analysis, I have argued that an unprecedented combination in 2008—a profound financial crisis among developed countries, paired with relative economic stability among emerging powers—led to a systemic legitimacy crisis, and then equally unprecedented cooperation between emerging powers in the context of the BRIC grouping. It is notable how quickly the four BRIC countries identified themselves as potential partners in this endeavor, and how the call for reform turned out to be the fundament of a much more sophisticated process of cooperation. Rather than being limited merely to the yearly leaders summits, intra-BRICS cooperation today is defined by ample, increasingly technical cooperation between a growing number of ministries such as education, science and technology, agriculture, finance, and health.

The financial crisis, and the temporarily reduced legitimacy of the international financial system, can thus be said to have been the determining factor in the creation of the BRIC grouping. Based on cooperation that began in earnest in 2008 (with separate meetings by the foreign ministers, presidents, finance ministers, and central bankers), the BRICS countries decided to explore opportunities to cooperate in other areas as well. Cooperation in the area of international finance was the starting point for a broader type of cooperation in many other areas, suggesting the occurrence of spillover effects of cooperation. In 2013, for example, the BRICS countries began their cycle of cooperation in early January, when the five countries' national security advisors met in Delhi to discuss issues ranging from cyber-security, terrorism, piracy, and other threats to international security.

Shivshankar Menon, India's national security advisor, argues that "there was a high level of congruence in our discussion of these issues. We found it very useful, in fact useful enough that at the end everyone said we must do this again. That gives you an idea of how successful the participants thought it was."[33] In the same month, BRICS health ministers met in New Delhi, followed by the annual meeting of BRICS competition authorities whose self-proclaimed goal is to curb anticompetitive practices at all levels, and contribute towards evolving transparent mechanisms and processes in its markets.[34] And also in January, BRICS revenue department heads met and signed a communiqué, identifying seven areas of cooperation, including sharing of anti-tax evasion and noncompliance practices, and a BRICS mechanism to facilitate countering abusive tax avoidance transactions. Soon afterward, the third BRICS academic forum took place in Durban, bringing together academics and policy analysts from the five countries. In the forum's final declaration, it created the BRICS Think Tanks Council "for the exchange of ideas among researchers, academia and think tanks."[35] A little later, at the fifth BRICS leaders summit in Durban, national leaders along with representatives of their cabinets, including foreign ministers and ministers of finance, trade, education, and science and technology, discussed ways to enhance cooperation. Most of the issues discussed were no longer related to the financial crisis that had helped the BRIC leaders meet in the first place five years earlier. Intra-BRICS cooperation is thus likely to continue, even after the conditions that facilitated its genesis—the financial crisis in the West—have disappeared.

Notes

1. Celso Amorim, "Brics e a reorganização do mundo," *Folha de S. Paulo*, 8 June 2008, wwwl.folha.uol.com.br.

2. "Not Just Straw Men: The Biggest Emerging Economies Are Rebounding, Even Without Recovery in the West," *The Economist*, 18 June 2009.

3. "Brazil, Russia, India and China First Meeting of BRIC Finance Ministries Joint Communiqué," 7 November 2008, par. 4, www.brics5.co.za /about-brics/sectorial-declaration/financial-ministers-meeting/first-meeting-of -finance-ministers.

4. Dante Mendes Aldrighi, "Cooperation and Coordination Among BRIC Countries: Potential and Constraints," Pre-BRIC Summit Preparatory Meeting (São Paulo: Fundaçâo Instituto de Pesquisas Económicas, June 2009). See the declaration at "London Summit—Leaders' Statement," Government of Canada, 3 April 2009, www.canadainternational.gc.ca/g20/summit-sommet/g20 /declaration_010209.aspx.

5. Jim O'Neill, "Building Better Global Economic BRICs," Goldman Sachs Global Economics Paper No. 66 (London: Goldman Sachs, 30 November 2001), p. 1.

6. Erich Follath, "Goldman Sachs' Jim O'Neill: BRICS Have Exceeded All Expectations," Spiegel Online, 21 March 2013, www.spiegel.de/international.

7. Dominic Wilson and Roopa Purushothaman, "Dreaming with BRICs: The Path to 2050," Goldman Sachs Global Economics Paper No. 99 (London: Goldman Sachs, 1 October 2003), p. 1.

8. Randall Schweller and Xiaoyu Pu, "After Unipolarity: China's Vision of International Order in an Era of US Decline," *International Security* 36, no. 1 (2011): 41.

9. "Mapping the Global Future. Report of the National Intelligence Council's 2020 Project" (December 2004), National Security Council, p. 8, www.au.af.mil /au/awc/awcgate/dni/global_trends_mapping_the_global_future _2020.pdf.

10. "Global Trends 2025: A Transformed World" (November 2008), National Intelligence Council, p. 2, www.aicpa.org/research/cpahorizons2025 /globalforces/downloadabledocuments/globaltrends.pdf.

11. Matias Spektor, "A Place at the Top of the Tree," *Financial Times Magazine*, 22 February 2013.

12. "Brazil, Russia, India and China First Meeting of BRIC Finance Ministries Joint Communiqué," 7 November 2008, par. 4, www.brics5.co.za/about -brics/sectorial-declaration/financial-ministers-meeting/first-meeting-of-finance -ministers/.

13. Amorim, "Os Brics e a reorganizaçâo do mundo."

14. Ibid.

15. "Brazil, Russia, India and China First Meeting of BRIC Finance Ministries Joint Communiqué."

16. Interview with a Brazilian diplomat, Brasília, 20 March 2013.

17. "BRICS Finance Communiqué," par. 9, BRICS Information Center, University of Toronto, 14 March 2009, www.brics.utoronto.ca/docs/090314-finance.html.

18. Ibid., par. 9.

19. Ibid.

20. "London Summit—Leaders' Statement," Government of Canada, 3 April 2009, www.canadainternational.gc.ca/g20/summit-sommet/g20/declaration _010209.aspx.

21. Oliver Stuenkel, Daniel Gros, Nikita Maslennikov, and Pradumna B. Rana, "The Case for IMF Quota Reform," Council on Foreign Relations, 11

October 2012, www.cfr.org/international-organizations-and-alliances/case -imf-quota-reform/p29248.

22. Oliver Stuenkel, "Can the BRICS Cooperate in the G-20? A View from Brazil," Occasional Paper No. 123 (Johannesburg: South African Institute of International Affairs, December 2012).

23. Stuenkel, Gros, Maslennikov, and Rana, "The Case for IMF Quota Reform."

24. Dmitry Medvedev, "Opening Address at Restricted Format Meeting of BRIC Leaders," President of Russia, 16 June 2009, www.kremlin.ru/eng/text /speeches/2009/06/16/2230_type82914_217934.shtml.

25. Andrew Hurrell, "Hegemony, Liberalism and Global Power: What Space for Would-Be Great Powers?" *International Affairs* 82, no. 1 (2006): 2.

26. Ruchir Sharma, "Broken BRICs: Why the Rest Stopped Rising," *Foreign Affairs* (November/December 2012), www.foreignaffairs.com/articles /138219/ruchir-sharma/broken-bdcs.

27. Philip Stephens, "A Story of Brics Without Mortar," *Financial Times*, 24 November 2011.

28. Ian Bache, Stephen George, and Simon Bulmer, "Theories of European Integration," in Ian Bache, Stephen George, Simon Bulmer, *Politics in the European Union* (Oxford: Oxford University Press, 2011), pp. 3–20, at 9.

29. Carsten Stroby-Jensen, "Neo-functionalism," in Michelle Cini, ed., *European Union Politics* (Oxford: Oxford University Press, 2007), p. 89.

30. Leon N. Lindberg, *The Political Dynamics of European Economic Integration* (Stanford: Stanford University Press, 1963).

31. Philippe C. Schmitter, "Three Neofunctional Hypotheses About International Integration," *International Organization* 23, no. 1 (1969).

32. Stroby-Jensen, "Neo-functionalism," pp. 91–92.

33. Rajeev Sharma, "BRICS NSAs Thrash Out Security Agenda for Durban Summit," http://indrus.in/articles/2013/01/H/brics_nsas_thrash_out_security _agenda_for_durban_summit_21597.html.

34. "The Beijing Consensus of the Second BRICS International Competition Conference Between Competition Authorities of the Federative Republic of Brazil, the Russian Federation, the Republic of India, the People's Republic of China and the Republic of South Africa," BRICS Leaders Meeting, 21 September 2011, Beijing, www.cade.gov.br/upload/The%20Beijing%20Consensus%2021 %20Sept%202011.pdf.

35. "Declaration on the Establishment of the BRICS Think Tanks Council," www.safpi.org/sites/default/files/publications/brics_think_tanks_council _declaration_201303.pdf.

15

Is the EU Collapsing?

Wallace J. Thies

Is the European Union (EU) on the verge of collapse? Recent events suggest the answer is so self-evident that the question itself is hardly worth posing. With each passing day, the news from Europe seems mostly to get worse, rarely better. Normally cautious politicians strive to show that they "get it" by issuing gloomy statements on Europe's future. Commentators of all sorts weigh in with their own versions of gloom and doom. "This is about the future of Europe now," said Peter Bofinger, a German economist. "If Italy blows apart, the [Eurozone] blows apart."[1] "Europe," Fareed Zakaria wrote in October 2011, "is facing its most severe challenge since 1945."[2]

Saying that Europe is facing its "biggest crisis since World War II" may be a handy attention-getter, but it is hardly an original claim. Even a cursory review of the history of the EU will likely reveal that a self-selected group of policymakers, pundits, and professors is always proclaiming the EU to be "in crisis" or even on the brink of collapse. . . .

[E]very decade since the creation of the Common Market in the 1950s has witnessed repeated claims that the EU (or one of its predecessors) was either dying or about to collapse. None of these claims has been proven true, at least not yet. . . .

To explain how and why this came to be, this paper proceeds in three steps: first, an overview of what I call the "EU-is-collapsing" literature; second, a review of the strengths of democracies, which make them better partners than the conventional wisdom on the EU might suggest; third, a discussion of why these issues matter and what to do about them.

Reprinted from *International Studies Review*, vol. 14: 225–239. © 2012 by Wiley Publishing. Reprinted by permission of the publisher. Edited for length.

In the rest of the paper, I focus on the EU and its predecessors as instruments of political and economic integration in Europe, with two qualifications. First, I support my claims by drawing on the whole history of the EU, not just current or recent events. I do so to show that repeated and exaggerated claims of imminent disaster have been a feature of politics within the EU ever since the Common Market was formed in the 1950s. In effect, even if there had been no Euro-zone debt crisis, there would still be an energetic corps of policymakers, pundits, and professors, dedicated to the proposition that there is something terribly wrong with the EU, and they know how to fix it. For this group, EU "crises" are a fact of life and an opportunity. If they didn't have the debt problem to write about, they likely would find some other reason to proclaim the EU in deep trouble or even on the brink of collapse.

Second, I view the EU, the EC, and the EEC as tools created to transform Europe from a collection of warring states to a security community within which war would be unthinkable. Because Germany's economic size and strength has grown relative to its partners in recent years, I expect that France, Britain, and Germany too will go to great lengths to keep the EU, and its security-assuring role, in place. I recognize that this will not be easy, especially if each passing year brings with it a torrent of inaccurate and misleading claims that the EU (or the EC or the EEC) is once again on the brink of collapse or even, for all practical purposes, already dead. I challenge this decades-old conventional wisdom about the EU, and I offer reasons for believing that an international organization made up entirely of liberal democratic states will exhibit great resilience and impressive staying power. International politics is full of surprises, so we can never say never when discussing the possibility of an EU collapse. We can, however, make a strong case that the democracies that comprise the EU are better partners than is generally realized, and that they will continue to find ways to make "Europe" work, as they always have done in the past.

The EU-Is-Collapsing Literature

"The history of Europe," French President Jacques Chirac once told an American journalist, "is a history of crises overcome."[3] What exactly does it mean to say that the EU is "in crisis"? In the case of the Atlantic Alliance, claims that yet another NATO-shattering crisis is at hand have been both frequent and consistently wrong.[4] Is the EU literature following the same mistaken path? I argue that the answer to that question is "yes." Much like the NATO case, the EU literature is filled with so-called crises, many of which were promptly labeled the EU's worst ever. Because EU crises have occurred so often and then faded from view so quickly, observers and policymakers straining to make their views known have resorted to the same means as their counterparts writing about NATO—namely, exaggerated claims based on unexamined premises and backed by superficial comparisons drawn from the history of the EU. These three elements are found together so often that they can usefully be viewed as a coherent school of thought.

In the absence of any widely accepted indicators that would allow observers to track changes in the health and well-being of a complex organization like the EU, those authors who write professionally about the EU have often resorted to shrillness or even hype to draw attention to their views. Instead of mere "crises" within the EU, observers have taken as their subject a "full-scale crisis," an "acute crisis," a "survival crisis," a "major crisis," a "serious crisis," and even "tonight's crisis."[5] Still others have described the EU as "trapped in a political and civilizational crisis," undergoing "one of its most profound crises ever," facing "the deepest institutional crisis of its 43-year history," or "facing an identity crisis and [thus] the risk of gradually disintegrating."[6] There are, however, at least three problems with this approach.

First, claims that the EU is once again "in crisis" are common rather than rare. Insiders and outsiders alike have been warning of fatal crises and/or catastrophic splits within the EU and its predecessor organizations at least since the early 1960s. These predictions have never come true, at least not yet. This has not, however, dissuaded new generations of authors from continuing to predict that the EU is doomed. The greater the resort to overstatement, however, the more skeptical the target audience is likely to become. The more cynical the target audience's views might appear, the greater the temptation to resort to inflated language to make the case that this time the fatal crisis really is at hand. . . . One of the more interesting issues raised by claims that this time the fatal crisis really is at hand is why sophisticated observers on both sides of the Atlantic continue to traffic in predictions that have about as much credibility as claims to know what the stock market will do tomorrow.

Second, consider the relationship between policy-making insiders and journalist/academic outsiders regarding the health and well-being of the EU. Insiders use claims of an actual or impending EU crisis as a rhetorical shot across the bow—in other words, a warning that trouble is brewing and something should be done about it soon, preferably in the form of other members acquiescing to the demands being made by whoever fired the (verbal) warning shot. Speaking in the aftermath of a December 1983 EEC summit that was said to have ended in "total deadlock," British Prime Minister Margaret Thatcher warned, "Nothing was settled at this summit. We are coming up to a crisis."[7] Europeans should not, French Foreign Minister Claude Cheysson warned a month later, "minimize the importance" of the "crisis" within the Common Market "because if it continues the consequences for the Community may be fatal."[8] EC President Jacques Delors used the same tactic in December 1990, when he warned that if certain countries (read: Britain) attempted to reopen discussions regarding monetary union, "it will provoke a political crisis."[9]

Why do high-ranking officials issue these sorts of veiled, and sometimes not so veiled, threats? Because they know they have willing accomplices in the press and the academic world. Journalists accord great weight to complaints—anonymous or otherwise—made by officials from EU members' foreign, finance, and trade ministries. Observers from the academic world take note of these complaints and write books and articles that analyze the causes of the EU's distress and prescribe needed changes. The potential for self-fulfilling prophecies is very great.

Third, judgments about the EU's health and well-being are typically based on evidence that is little more than impressions formed by observers as they watch, sometimes on a day-to-day basis, the latest intra-EU spat unfold. The effect of this reliance on impressionistic judgments is to make the "EU-is-collapsing" literature inherently subjective and imprecise, but with a built-in bias toward discovering and then publicizing conflicts between and among EU members. Their awareness that journalists are taking note of everything they say and do in public gives officials a powerful incentive to make intemperate comments in the hope that these will become the lead story on the evening news programs, and then appear again the next day, this time on the front pages of important newspapers. Journalists are inherently conflicted when it comes to deciding what is newsworthy and what is not. If they faithfully report what insiders are saying, they improve their chances of leading the TV news broadcasts or placing their byline on the front page, but at the cost of becoming the insiders' publicists. If they ignore or even downplay whatever line insiders are pushing, they risk being shut out entirely, and maybe moved to a less prestigious beat.

The inherently subjective and imprecise nature of the EU-is-collapsing literature was neatly captured in a series of articles that appeared in the *New York Times* within about a 7-month span in 1983 and 1984. In December 1983, the *Times'* Paul Lewis described the EC as "facing the most difficult political crisis of its 26-year history."[10] Three months later, on the eve of another EC summit meeting, Lewis described the EC as "pushed to the brink of bankruptcy and disintegration by disputes over soaring farm subsidies. . . . Another failure this week, conference sources agree, risks a deepening of the crisis to the point where the Common Market could start to break up."[11] And then in July 1984, Lewis described the EC as having been "pushed into a new final crisis today, barely a month after its leaders said they have resolved its internal quarrels over money."[12] For those keeping score, the tally would read: 7 months, three crises, each of which was said to be a threat to the EC's very existence. . . .

Unexamined Premises

The frequency with which insiders and outsiders have resorted to rhetorical warning shots and exaggerated claims as a way of making their voices heard has meant that important issues regarding the EU and its predecessors have often gone overlooked. Assessments of the EU, or the EC and the EEC before it, typically begin with the claim that it is once again "in crisis," followed by a discussion of causes, consequences, and possible fixes. None of the many writers who have contributed to this literature have defined their terms in a way that would allow a disinterested observer to know with confidence when the EU is in crisis and when it is not. So how do we know that the EU is once again in crisis or even on the verge of collapse?

Many writers base their claims in this regard on personal observation, and sometimes participation, in the latest EU food fight. Insiders and outsiders may not be able to define an EU crisis with scientific precision, but they do not need to because they know it when they see it. Specifically, when the representatives of EU member states (i) find it difficult to agree on some important matter; (ii) make veiled threats of dire consequences if others don't quickly grasp the rightness of their position; (iii) grow angry with one another; and (iv) vilify or even insult one another in public, something must be terribly wrong with the EU. The more numerous and/or vehement the complaints made by those on the inside, outsiders often assume, the more perilous the EU's situation must be. In effect, the EU-is-collapsing literature assumes that the greater the number of unresolved issues within the EU, the worse its overall condition must be. Once again, there are at least three problems with this approach.

First, while it might seem self-evident that the greater the number of disputed issues (alternatively, the more heated the disagreements within the EU), the worse its condition must be, this is not necessarily so. Simply counting the number and/or estimating the intensity of disagreements within the EU or its predecessors are not reliable measures of the EU's health and well-being. Disagreements over policy do more than strain relations among EU members. They also activate the EU's supporters (of whom there are many) and those who, while not necessarily enamored of the EU, see it as still the best chance to achieve the decades-long dream of greater integration in Europe. Crises are more than just political theater. They offer opportunities for ambitious politicians—to trumpet their own views, to mediate, to ingratiate themselves to one side or the other, to score points at a rival's expense, or to reconcile with those from whom they have been estranged.

Second, consider the reasons offered by an American journalist for the apparent breakdown of negotiations at the EC's Athens summit in December 1983: "First, the disagreement at Athens over finances was fundamental. The talks broke down because Britain and West Germany want to change the direction that European economic policy should take in the 1980s and 1990s. Second, there seems no practical alternative to the route that Britain and Germany have proposed, even though it scares their partners."[13] The problem with this view is that money issues—who pays how much for what—are always in dispute within the EU. Each member's contribution to the EU budget consumes resources that members could otherwise use to pay for the various entitlements that modern welfare states are expected to provide to their citizens. Because money issues are so fundamental, they usually cannot be resolved by technocrats or even by cabinet ministers, so they are bumped up to summits. EU summits are not convened to deal with trivialities. Summits are where heads of government are expected to earn their pay, by negotiating with their peers over issues of great concern to them all. When EU heads of government meet, "the agenda is always too long and the mood is often uncomfortably tense. Only if thorough and skillful preparatory staff work has been done do the national leaders have much chance of success, and even then they sometimes fail."[14]

Third, as the examples cited thus far suggest, the 1980s was a decade when EC members seemed to have great difficulty working together effectively. A "bitter internal dispute" over agricultural policy required multiple summits to resolve during 1983 and 1984.[15] Then toward the end of the decade, discussion of the integration issue started a "noisy and potentially destructive squabble with the 12-member group." What concerns the Europeans these days "is whether they will even be speaking to each other by 1992."[16] The 1980s may have been an exhausting experience, but it was also a time when multiple European states were clamoring to join the EC, which was soon to become the EU. Statesmen rarely scramble to jump onto a sinking ship, which suggests that the leaders of those aspiring new members must have seen something quite different about the EC/EU than did the doomsayers.

Superficial Comparisons

There is one striking difference between the "NATO in crisis" literature and its "EU is collapsing" counterpart. Concerning the former, observers discussing the latest NATO crisis often go to great lengths to distinguish their crisis from all those that came before. They do so in part to buttress their claim that their crisis really is serious and even potentially fatal, and in part to anticipate objections from others that there is nothing particularly distinctive about this latest NATO crisis, thus making it unworthy of space on a widely read op-ed page or in a prestigious scholarly journal. Contributors to the "EU is collapsing" literature usually dispense with these comparisons, instead taking it as self-evident that today's crisis is not just serious but potentially a storm that the EU might not survive. And when they do make the case that today's crisis is different from and thus more perilous than previous crises, they have often fallen victim to impressionistic judgments based on highly subjective evidence. Why is this latest crisis different from all the rest? The answer, all too often, is that the authors of this literature say so.

Again, there are at least three problems with this approach. First, reliance on even seasoned observers to assess what is going on means that judgments regarding the EU's health and well-being are essentially impressionistic and thus vulnerable to dramatic reversals based on little more than atmospherics. In December 1983, the EEC was widely said to be facing its greatest crisis ever; by March 1984 this assessment had been downgraded to just another "Common Market crisis." What was the reason for this downgrade? The "atmosphere at the meeting," it was subsequently reported, "is better and more businesslike than at the session held in Athens 3 months ago."[17]

Second, the heavy reliance on impressionistic evidence means there is no reliable way to relate variations in the severity of so-called EU crises to variations in political behavior, processes, and outcomes. Presumably once the threshold that separates crises from non-crisis situations is crossed, the behavior of EU members should change, political processes should change, and so too should political outcomes. But what kinds of changes should be expected once the crisis threshold has been crossed, besides diplomats behaving badly in public? Consider in this regard the "near crisis" of February 1988, which was accompanied by public name-calling. "British Prime Minister Margaret Thatcher called the French 'crazy.' French Prime Minister Jacques Chirac called Mrs. Thatcher a vulgar name that British diplomats could not find in their French-English dictionaries."[18] By the standards of the EU-is-collapsing literature, this behavior should have triggered a sky-is-falling, head-for-the-hills kind of crisis, except it did not. This was a "near crisis," nothing more.

Third, why do EU members even bother to hold the various conferences and summit meetings at which disagreements (often heated) are aired for all to see, thereby setting the stage for another round of predictions that the EC is about to fail? One answer that is often given is that "the EU is constantly outgrowing its old treaties as it goes on adding new members and new functions."[19] An organization that constantly outgrows its treaty-based legal foundation as it adds new members and new responsibilities seems an unlikely candidate for verge-of-collapse status. This is one reason why it is short-sighted to focus on the latest intra-EU disagreements. Doing so diverts attention from noticing that the EU has been phenomenally successful: in Andrew Moravcsik's words, "the most ambitious and most successful example of peaceful international cooperation in world history."[20]

The Strengths of Democracies

The EU-is-collapsing literature suggests that disputes among EU members grow more debilitating over time, in part because the EU grows weaker and more feeble as it absorbs the wounds inflicted by each new crisis, in part because EU members' behavior worsens as they push the limits of what they can get away with for the sake of greater leverage over their partners. But if EU crises are both frequent and debilitating, why has it not collapsed by now? How can an organization absorb, almost annually, grave new wounds inflicted by its unruly members, only to revive itself and take on new challenges, and not just once but many times? And if the damage from these so-called crises does indeed cumulate over time, leaving the EU weaker and worse off, why have so many Central and East European states tried so hard to join in recent years? Conversely, why have a few or even one current member not left the EU?

The EU-is-collapsing literature has no good answers for these questions, so we should consider an alternative explanation—namely, that the EU, an organization made up entirely of liberal democratic states, has innate strengths not found in other organizations that include non-democracies. Contrary to the conventional wisdom, the EU is not yet on the brink of collapse, although even its strongest supporters must recognize that this could change very quickly, depending on how the various rescue plans for its most indebted members play out. But in the meantime, the EU continues to do what it was created to do—namely, denationalize defense and security issues, accept new members, and continue broadening and deepening the range of issues that come within its purview. This is not an accident. There are several reasons why the EU is likely to exhibit great resilience and impressive staying power despite seemingly endless disputes among its members.

First, in democracies, governments that raise expectations and then fail to meet them can expect to be punished by the voters when the next election is held. The Euro-zone debt issue is a good reminder in this regard. Since January 2011, governments in Ireland, Portugal, Spain, Greece, and Italy have all changed hands. This has two salutary effects. First, a change of administration brings to power new leaders with new ideas and new solutions to the problems their predecessors failed to solve. Second, a change of government in several EU members encourages other governments to work harder, to avoid the fate of those who have already been ousted from their posts.

Second, in democracies, perhaps the surest path to higher office— either elective or appointive—is to identify problems as they arise and offer solutions to them. Democracies are filled with would-be office holders on the lookout for issues that fit well with whatever ideas they have to offer. Incumbents and their would-be successors constantly study the electorate's mood and make adjustments to their policies and/or their positions on the issues of the day. This means that problems are often identified and solutions proposed early on, as ambitious problem-solvers stake their claims to issues for which they believe they have a solution.

Third, in democracies, holding high office is a reward for doing things, not just complaining about the shortcomings of others. This means that policymaking in democracies is strongly oriented toward the future rather than the past, Instead of wallowing in blame and recriminations, politicians in democracies prefer to look forward, toward the next election and/or the next compromise, which helps explain why EU "crises" are generally short-lived and transient in their effects. And they have good reasons for overweighting the future relative to the past. Wallowing in the past is a tacit admission of a problem left unsolved. And if incumbents do lose sight of their mandate to solve problems as they arise, there are always new cohorts of would-be office-holders eager to challenge them on this point.

Fourth, democracies are better than is generally realized at coping with new and/or unexpected challenges. In the democracies that make up the EU, electorates want governments that work. And since economic, environmental, and regulatory issues are not at all respectful of national boundaries, solving problems in practice means cutting deals with other EU members. Politicians born and raised in the EU countries are likely to instinctively grasp that they can do little on their own. The only way for ambitious politicians to get things done is by cultivating friends and supporters wherever they can be found, even people or parties that they do not particularly like.

Fifth, it is not the absence of stress that makes for a successful organization; it is how an organization responds to stress that determines whether it will succeed or not. Politics is never stress free, but democracies—either singly or working collectively—are likely to be especially good at managing and containing the stresses and strains of political life. "Constitutional democracies achieve their internal unity not by eliminating all their contentious political forces, but by providing a rational framework for competition among them." In similar fashion, "the nascent EEC could not expect to eliminate struggles among its member states. But it could hope to provide them with a moral and institutional framework to protect individual national rights and accentuate common national interests."[21] Hindsight suggests that the EU and its predecessor organizations have done just that. Writing about the pre-Maastricht treaty negotiations aimed at making the leap from EC to EU, an American journalist noted that, "after a year of painstaking negotiations, the stakes at Maastricht loom so great that pressure to compromise on lingering points of discord seems irresistible."[22] It is hardly a surprise that EU members would find themselves facing "irresistible" pressures to compromise. In democracies, compromise is the life-blood of politics. Politicians in democracies are not just masters of the theatrical arts, they are also expert risk-takers. Even as they exchange epithets and barbed comments, they retain an instinctive grasp of how hard they can push for a certain outcome without going too far, thereby bringing down on themselves the opprobrium for allowing a promising initiative to collapse.

Sixth, liberal democracies work best when they have the support and approval of other liberal democracies. Working collectively with other democracies confers legitimacy on one's policies—otherwise, why would other liberal states be willing to discuss them and agree on them? Working collectively also builds momentum that can carry over to future agreements. And if winning the support of other liberal states requires a change of rhetoric or even policy, politicians in democracies have repeatedly demonstrated their determination not to let foolish consistency stand in the way of compromise and even reconciliation with their political foes.[23]

The bitterly contested EC summits of 1983 and 1984 illustrate this last point quite nicely. Those summits were followed almost immediately by conciliatory gestures and promises to keep searching for a solution that would be acceptable to all. And in this case, conciliation worked. Less than a decade after the rancorous disputes of the early 1980s, the very same members who for years had vilified each other and warned of dire consequences if their views were not taken more seriously signed the Maastricht Treaty, thereby completing the transition from EC to EU as well as laying the foundation for what would become the European Monetary Union. The EU-is-collapsing literature, particularly that portion that suggests the EU grows weaker with every new crisis, cannot explain why this turnaround occurred. Indeed, that literature strongly suggests that the Maastricht Treaty should never have been signed.

Taken as a group, these points suggest that an organization like the EU will be both conflict-prone but also in possession of strong self-healing tendencies that make compromise possible, and not just once but again and again. Because the EU depends on member contributions to fund its operations, there will be a never-ending argument among those members over who should pay what share of the cost of keeping the EU in business. On the other hand, precisely because the EU is the most successful supranational organization ever created, it offers an institutionalized channel that EU members can use to line up support for their own positions and thus gain leverage in their disputes with one another—leverage that would be lost forever if EU members were as reckless and as short-sighted as the EU-is-collapsing literature suggests.

In addition, a multi-state organization like the EU will likely have multiple lines of cleavage and agreement running through it. Just because some members disagree on some issues does not mean that all members disagree about everything, or even a lot of things. Hence, EU members caught up in one or more disagreements are unlikely to push those disagreements too far because they do not want to jeopardize their relations with those members that are not much involved in today's disagreement, nor do they want to jeopardize the uncontroversial parts of their relationship with those with whom they, for the moment at least, disagree. The EU-is-collapsing literature by and large overlooks these self-healing tendencies because of its fixation on misleading indicators like veiled threats and/or public name-calling. But these self-healing tendencies are important because they help us understand how and why the EU survives despite repeated strident warnings that collapse is imminent. If we are to better understand how and why the EU not just survives but, indeed, thrives, we need to know more not only about how these EU crises begin, but also what happens as they intensify, wane, and then fade away.

Why These Issues Matter

Viewed in retrospect, claims that the EU is "in crisis" or even on the brink of collapse might seem to be little more than harmless clichés. These claims are not harmless. Clichés obscure much more than they clarify. They constitute budding self-fulfilling prophecies just waiting for an audience naïve enough to believe them. Paying for the EU consumes resources that politicians in democracies can always find other uses for. The more that elites and electorates hear that the EU is failing, the greater the temptation to spend that money on something else.

Far from being a collection of harmless clichés, the EU-is-collapsing literature is fundamentally misleading in its assessments of the EU, in four ways. First, "Since Maastricht, the EU has been trying to widen its scope, extend its membership, and streamline its institutions, all at the same time."[24] An EU doing little or nothing to further the cause of European integration would indeed be a candidate for collapse, since the benefits of membership would likely fall short of the costs involved. The EU and its members have been trying to do a great deal, and they have been more successful than generally realized. Writing in December 2011, an American journalist noted that, "already Italy has implemented austerity measures, Spain has passed a constitutional amendment to limit its debt, and Greece has sworn to crack down on tax scofflaws—changes that seemed unthinkable just a year ago."[25] The EU-is-collapsing literature obscures these accomplishments, thereby making it seem as if the EU is a bad bargain, when in fact it is not.

Second, the EU-is-collapsing literature offers no reliable way of knowing when the EU is "in crisis" and when it is not. Instead, that literature takes it as self-evident that the EU is "in crisis" whenever its members argue heatedly, grow exasperated with each other, criticize each other, reject each other' proposals, and so on. This is a wholly unsatisfactory situation, the reason being that EU members are always disputing something. When they shout at each other in public, it is called a crisis. When they shout at each other in private, it is called diplomacy.

Third, the EU-is-collapsing literature has little to say about how and why the EU has become the longest lasting and by far the most accomplished case of political and economic integration, with the exception of the formation of the United States at the end of the eighteenth century. Indeed, the EU-is-collapsing literature strongly suggests that the EU's accomplishments should not have occurred and that the organization itself should have broken apart years ago.

Fourth, the EU-is-collapsing literature highlights essentially transient phenomena—bad language, petty behavior—while neglecting more interesting possibilities such as the ability of democracies to compromise, to reconcile, and to innovate. These self-healing tendencies, which are found within liberal democracies but not in other kinds of states, have allowed the EU to overcome disputes among its members, and not just once but again and again. In effect, the EU-is-collapsing literature directs our attention to relatively unimportant phenomena while neglecting more important and more interesting aspects of the integration process.

If we are to overcome the conceptual weakness of the EU-is-collapsing literature, there are three lines of inquiry that we should follow. First, a scholarly concept like "crisis" is valuable provided it contributes to new knowledge about an important subject, like integration in general and the EU in particular. It can do so in three ways: first, by identifying a class of situations that have enough in common that they can be reliably distinguished from situations that fall outside the class; second, by making possible comparisons among items that fall within the class, like the relative severity of EU crises; and third, by contributing to the development of empirically verifiable hypotheses that relate variations in situational context (crisis versus non-crisis—the independent variable) to variations in political behavior, political processes, and political outcomes (the dependent variables). An unavoidable prerequisite for doing these things in practice is to rework the concept of an EU crisis so that a disinterested observer could 1) know when the EU is in crisis, and when it is not; and 2) be able to determine the relative severity of EU crises. These are essential if we aspire to test whether changes in context (crisis versus non-crisis) really do co-vary with changes in behavior, processes, and outcomes. Similarly, we need to be able to measure the relative severity of EU crises in order to relate variations in the intensity and duration of these crises to variations in the way political actors behave and interact. Indeed, our goal should be to construct a database of so-called EU crises, ranked according to their relative severity.

Second, how might our disinterested observer determine whether and when the EU is "in crisis" and when it is not? An international organization like the EU (or NATO too) is truly "in crisis" when one or more of its members are indifferent between leaving the organization and making the changes in policy and/or expenditures necessary to resolve whatever caused the alleged crisis. Viewed this way, has any member of the EU and its predecessor organizations ever crossed the crisis threshold, in the sense of becoming indifferent between staying in and getting out? EU members have often warned of dire consequences if their views were not accorded greater respect and responsiveness by other members, but credible threats to leave are conspicuous by their absence.

Third, the EU-is-collapsing literature devotes almost all of its attention to how EU crises begin, while under-weighting or outright ignoring (i) what is happening with those EU programs that are not closely connected to whatever issue allegedly touched off the latest crisis; and (ii) the ways in which the various activities that the EU pursues have over the long term produced some remarkable accomplishments. One way to illustrate the point is by posing the counterfactual question: would the Europe of today be better off or worse off if there had been no Maastricht Treaty and thus no EU hard at work on issues like downsizing and restructuring Europe's defense industries, providing peacekeeping forces for the Balkans, transitioning to the euro, helping to spread democracy to Eastern Europe, and undertaking multiple rounds of enlargement? The EU-is-collapsing literature largely ignores these long-term accomplishments, because they don't fit very well with chasing down the latest rumor regarding who insulted whom during yesterday's shouting match.

Put differently, despite decades of claims that the EU is on the brink of collapse, we know little more about what this brink looks like, and what it means for political behavior and political outcomes, than we did when warnings that the EU's predecessors were about to collapse first circulated during the 1960s. In effect, observers writing about the EU in the twenty-first century continue to use the same tired clichés and strained metaphors as did generations of their predecessors. It is this absence of cumulative knowledge that is the EU-is-collapsing literature's defining characteristic.

These three lines of inquiry are essentially a suggestion for treating the concept of an EU crisis as a social science concept rather than a rhetorical shot across the bow. There is, of course, no guarantee that this research strategy will prove any better or more productive than what is available now, but in view of the dismal results produced by the EU-is-collapsing literature it can hardly hurt to try something new.

Notes

1. Faiola, Anthony. (2011) Italy Unveils Budget Plan as Debt Fears Intensify, *Washington Post*, August 6: A8.
2. Zakaria, Fareed. (2011) Europe's Growth Problem, *Washington Post*, A21.
3. Hoagland, Jim. (2004) Europe's Growing Pains, *Washington Post*, February 8: B7.
4. Thies, Wallace J. (2007) "Was the US Invasion of Iraq NATOs Worst Crisis Ever? How Would We Know? Why Should We Care?" *European Security* 16 (1): 29–50. Thies, Wallace J. (2009) *Why NATO Endures*. Cambridge: Cambridge University Press.
5. Richburg, Keith. (2003a) EU Unity on Iraq Proves Short-Lived, *Washington Post*, February 19: A24; Drozdiak, William. (1997) Unity Drive Is Faltering in W. Europe, *Washington Post*, July 4: A26; Frankel, Glenn. (2005) Summit Collapse Leaves E.U. Adrift, *Washington Post*, June 18: A12; Swardson, Anne. (1998) Europeans Overcome Dispute to Launch Euro, *Washington Post*, May 3: A1.
6. Giuliani, Jean Dominique. (2006) "Borders Challenge Europe," in *Changing Identities and Evolving Values: Is There Still a Transatlantic Community?* edited by E. Brimmer. Washington, DC: Johns Hopkins University; Center for Transatlantic Relations, p. 38; Swardson, Anne. (1999) EU Executive Body to Resign in Fraud Probe, *Washington Post*, March 16: A1; Lamassoure, Alain. (2006) "Europe Needs a New Approach to a New Project," in *Changing Identities and Evolving Values: Is There Still a Transatlantic Community?* edited by E. Brimmer. Washington, DC: Johns Hopkins University; Center for Transatlantic Studies, p. 27.
7. Lewis, Paul. (1983) Common Market Ends Summit Talks in Total Deadlock, *New York Times*. December 7: 1.
8. Lewis, Paul. (1984) Crisis in Common Market Could Ruin It, French Warn, *New York Times*, January 19:1.
9. Drozdiak, William. (1990) Europeans Closer to Single Currency, *Washington Post*, December 16: A38.
10. Lewis, Paul. (1983) Common Market Ends Summit Talks in Total Deadlock, *New York Times,* December 7: 1.
11. Lewis, Paul. (1984) Difficulties Rise for Europeans as Talks Begin, *New York Times*, March 20: 1.
12. Lewis, Paul. (1984) Common Market Reopens Dispute on Budget Shares, *New York Times*, July 28:1.
13. Lewis, Paul. (1983) Common Market: Gravest Crisis Yet, *New York Times*, December 8: 33.
14. Apple, R. W. (1984) Amid Babel in Brussels, Tough Talk by Leaders, *New York Times*, March 20: 6.
15. Lewis, Paul. (1983) Common Market Chiefs in Crucial Parley Today, *New York Times*, December 4: 3.
16. DeYoung, Karen. (1988) Europeans Squabble as Integration Deadline Draws Close, *Washington Post*, October 31: A13.
17. Lewis, 1984: 6.

18. Revzin, Philip. (1988) Despite Difficulties, Moves to Strengthen Common Market Gain, *Wall Street Journal*, February 23: 1.

19. The Economist. (2000) The Union Pauses for Breath, February 12: 49.

20. Moravcsik, Andrew. (2001) Despotism in Brussels? *Foreign Affairs*, 80 (3): 114–122.

21. Calleo, David. (2001) *Rethinking Europe's Future*. Princeton: Princeton University Press.

22. Drozdiak, William. (1991) Member Countries Gather to Forge Pan-European Union, *Washington Post*, December 8: A33.

23. Baun, Michael. (1995–1996) The Maastricht Treaty as High Politics: Germany, France, and European Integration. *Political Science Quarterly*, 110 (4): 605–624.

24. Calleo, 2001: 294.

25. Birnbaum, Michael. (2011) Pressure Builds for Merkel to Change Slow Euro-Zone Approach, *Washington Post*, December 5: A8.

Part 5

Social and Humanitarian Issues

Brian Frederking and Paul F. Diehl

International organizations are increasingly active in social and humanitarian issue areas. Many goals within this issue area (literacy, nutrition, health care, sanitation) are widely shared. Pursuing these objectives is less controversial than those in security or economic issue areas, and therefore support for these efforts is generally high. For example, the World Health Organization is almost universally applauded for is efforts at eradicating disease. The UN High Commissioner for Refugees has twice been awarded the Nobel Peace Prize. Some of the most effective work of international organizations takes place in this issue area. Of course, some disagreements exist: whether to include abortion services in a global plan to reduce population growth, differing cultural perspectives about the status of women, and whether to use war crimes tribunals to punish violations of humanitarian international law are some examples of global discord in this issue area.

Social and humanitarian issues are also ones in which nongovernmental organizations (NGOs) have a more prominent role. NGOs do not have the military capacity or economic strength to be major actors in security or economic affairs. In this area, however, NGOs may have the expertise or legitimacy that many international organizations lack. NGOs may be able to operate without all the political constraints on international organizations, which exist in sensitive areas like human rights. NGOs also may be able to operate more effectively on the ground to provide aid during a wide range of humanitarian emergencies.

The 2014 Ebola outbreak illustrates the importance of developing global rules to minimize threats from disease. Global governance in such a technical issue area often requires cooperation between the public sector, the private sector, and civil society. In Chapter 16, Chris

Ansell, Egbert Sondorp, and Robert Hartley Stevens argue that global public policy networks that bridge these sectors are often crucial mechanisms to facilitate the spread of knowledge and to encourage coordination. They argue that networks are helpful when there are limits on the capacity to direct coordination among many different groups. They analyze the Global Outbreak Alert and Response Network and conclude that it is a "relative success story" by helping the international community to respond to over seventy global outbreaks in over forty countries.

Climate change is another global public policy area requiring cooperation between public and private actors. In Chapter 17, Jessica Green emphasizes the importance of "private authority" in the development of the climate change regime complex. Green examines the proliferation of privately created standards to measure and manage greenhouse gas emissions and shows that there is a surprising amount of policy convergence around the public rules established by the Kyoto Protocol. Even though many states have not formally ratified Kyoto, the presence of these private standards suggests the centrality of the protocol within the climate change regime. The high level of recognition of public authority by private standards suggests that the public norms embodied in the protocol will likely endure regardless of the treaty ratification process. While analysts who focus on the public production of rules conclude that Kyoto is largely a failure, Green's analysis of private rules and private authority shows that the norms embedded in Kyoto are indeed operating.

Human rights is another central area of global governance, and one crucial issue is monitoring—how can we evaluate whether countries are in compliance with human rights norms? In Chapter 18, Philip Alston and Colin Gillespie explore the difficulties of human rights monitoring by examining extrajudicial executions. To what extent are such killings accurately reported? The authors analyze the reports of four important organizations: Human Rights Watch; Amnesty International; the UN Special Rapporteur on Extrajudicial, Summary, or Arbitrary Executions; and the United States Department of State. They explain why the reporting of each institution is incomplete and discuss the implications of such incomplete reporting for the human rights regime.

A growing global governance issue is the trafficking of women. Despite increased attention to and awareness of the issue, the problem continues to grow in scope. In Chapter 19, Rashida Manjoo examines the legal frameworks for the protection for women trafficked for sexual exploitation. She discusses the many challenges that remain as obstacles against effective governance in this area. She argues that in order to understand the complicated issues surrounding human trafficking, we should view it within the context of economic realities, globalization, the feminization of migration, armed conflict, the breakdown of the state, and the transformation of political boundaries.

16

The Promise and Challenge of Global Network Governance: The Global Outbreak Alert and Response Network

Chris Ansell, Egbert Sondorp, and Robert Hartley Stevens

Networks, it has been argued, offer a promising solution to the challenges of global governance. "Trisectoral" global public policy networks, for example, have been advanced as an important bridge between the public sector, the private sector, and civil society. Through this bridging role, they may facilitate management of knowledge, encourage coordination between institutions, and enhance civic participation.[1] Thorsten Benner, Wolfang Reinicke, and Jan Witte argue that such networks contribute to global governance in at least three ways: (1) they can provide a negotiating forum for standard setting; (2) they can facilitate international coordination; and (3) they can provide a flexible institutional mechanism for treaty implementation.[2]

Perhaps the most elaborated argument for global network governance is advanced by Anne-Marie Slaughter, who argues that "networked threats require a networked response."[3] She champions transgovernmental networks—networks of government officials—as an appropriate networked response to these threats. She argues that intergovernmental networks can expand the reach of regulation, build trust and cooperation among governments, facilitate intergovernmental information sharing, and establish global standards of practice and performance. Networks, she argues, offer "a flexible and relatively fast way to conduct the business of global governance, coordinating and even harmonizing national government action while initiating and monitoring the different solutions to global problems."[4] Not surprisingly, the promise of transgovernmental networks has been widely appreciated in the context of the European Union.[5]

Reprinted from *Global Governance*, vol. 18, no. 3: 317–337. © 2012 by Lynne Rienner Publishers. Reprinted by permission of the publisher.

Like many social science concepts, the term *global governance network* is an elastic one and often interchangeable with related terms like "transnational public-private partnership."[6] For the purposes of this article, a *governance network* is a more or less formal association whose members retain their independence of action while agreeing to work together on common enterprises that produce collective goods.[7] Networks typically have an independent extragovernmental status, though in some cases they may be incorporated into formal governing frameworks.[8] They typically are not official governing bodies, though they may be associations of government bodies or government officials. A *global governance network* is a network whose members come from (but do not necessarily represent) different nations or are themselves transnational institutions.

Networks are commonly seen as an attractive approach to governance in situations where problem solving requires coordination among many different stakeholders, but where there are limits on the capacity to centrally direct this coordination. This is, of course, the archetypical situation of international politics. The traditional response to international "anarchy" has been to create multilateral organizations or treaties to manage global problems. Although these institutions may themselves have network-like qualities (e.g., associations of independent members), they are generally recognized as official government organizations or regimes. What can independent extragovernmental associations add to this traditional approach to global governance? The answers are varied, but networks are frequently invoked as governance solutions when an institutional framework for coordination or a forum for discussion or negotiation is desired between: (1) public and private stakeholders; (2) multiple international organizations or regimes; or (3) private stakeholders operating outside of or in the absence of international organizations or regimes.

There is now also an extensive literature on local or regional (domestic) network governance. Although the territorial scale of these networks is smaller, they are often created in response to the same kinds of challenges that global networks face—situations where interjurisdictional or interorganizational cooperation is valued, but where central authority to steer this cooperation is limited. This literature also finds virtues (and vices) in networks as flexible modes of governance. Some scholars of domestic network governance have been intrigued with its democratic and deliberative potential while others have been concerned about the democratic accountability of networks.[9] Others emphasize the way that networks are able to address "wicked" public problems.[10] Scholars of domestic network governance have also begun to identify the factors that shape the success or failure of network governance and have discussed strategies for network management.[11]

In this article, we drill down to the operational level of one global network organization, the Global Outbreak Alert and Response Network (GOARN), to investigate the promises and challenges of network governance. GOARN was established in April 2000 as a mechanism for coordinating international responses to infectious disease outbreaks. Partners include government agencies, universities, laboratories, nongovernmental health organizations, and other public health networks, leading GOARN to explicitly think of itself as a "network of networks."[12] Housed and supported by the World Health Organization (WHO), GOARN serves as a coordinating mechanism for rapid response to disease outbreaks of international concern. A typical GOARN mission assembles teams of infectious disease experts drawn from different partner institutions. The emphasis is on rapid and early response since diseases can spread rapidly and quick response can help to limit the overall spread of the disease. GOARN teams are therefore rapidly deployed to assist affected countries or regions to effectively diagnose and respond to disease outbreaks.

As a form of global network governance, GOARN is a relative success story. Since it was created, GOARN has played an important role in responding to over seventy global disease outbreaks in over forty countries, including many hemorrhagic fever outbreaks in sub-Saharan Africa (Ebola, Marburg, Rift Valley fever, etc.), the 2003 severe acute respiratory syndrome (SARS) outbreak, numerous clusters of human cases of avian influenza (H5N1), and the recent swine influenza (H1N1) pandemic.[13] GOARN's remit includes rapid alert and response to disease outbreaks that have the potential for global impacts. By continuously monitoring outbreaks around the world, GOARN assesses this potential and alerts GOARN members as necessary. GOARN missions are typically deployed in response to requests for aid from countries where a globally relevant outbreak is occurring. A few missions, however, have been deployed for purposes of risk assessment or to aid countries with more localized outbreaks of endemic and recurrent diseases (e.g., cholera).

GOARN's positive role in the SARS outbreak was particularly notable and illustrates the way that it operates as a "network of networks." The earliest cases of SARS were picked up in media reports in February 2003 by two GOARN partners, the Global Public Health Intelligence Network and the US Global Emerging Infections Surveillance and Response System, which then placed another GOARN partner, the WHO Global Influenza Surveillance Network, on alert. GOARN served as a coordinating node between these networks. The WHO also mobilized GOARN to send response teams to Hong Kong, Singapore, Taiwan, and Vietnam to investigate the outbreak and to conduct contact tracing. These GOARN field teams deployed 115 experts representing 26 different partner institutions and 17 countries. Later, when the response moved into the containment phase, GOARN served as the hub for a "virtual network" of laboratories, clinicians, and epidemiologists responding to the outbreak.[14]

This record of activity makes GOARN an attractive case for examining both the potential and the limits of global network governance. A case study, of course, is not an ideal tool for making generalizations. However, case studies can be useful for calling attention to theoretical mechanisms and linkages that may be of more general importance. Our study was conducted in the spirit of Philip Selznick's naturalistic approach to the human sciences. Selznick argues that inquiry should be directed toward understanding how ideal forms—in this case, governance networks—work in practice and in distinctive contexts. We should strive, he argues, to understand the factors that enable or limit the realization of the values they promise.[15]

Figure 16.1 situates this case within a synthetic model of network governance derived from the case and from the literature on network governance. The shaded areas in the figure point to the mechanisms and linkages that the GOARN case particularly illuminates. As our study shows, one challenge of network governance arises from the management of performance imperatives—high priority objectives fostered by the design of the network and the goals of members. The management of these performance imperatives is both enabled and constrained by the wider institutional environment in which the network operates. The key insight of the case is that the struggle to successfully manage these performance imperatives may imperil the further development of the network itself, and thus the case calls particular attention to the linkages between network design, management, and development. To put the findings in Selznick's terms, the realization of the potential and value of networks can be self-limited by the challenge of achieving its own goals.

We drew the findings in this case study from several sources. In the summer of 2007, the first author conducted several preliminary interviews with GOARN's Occupational Support Team (OST) focused on the organizational challenges of rapid deployment. In early 2009, the first author joined the other two authors as members of an external review committee organized under the auspices of GOARN's Steering Committee (SCOM). As members of the external review committee, we traveled

Figure 16.1 Synthetic View of Network Governance

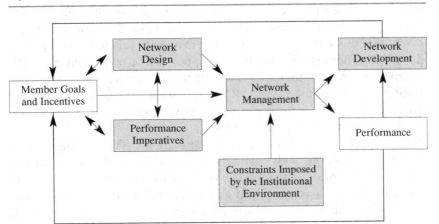

twice to the WHO headquarters in Geneva, where GOARN is based. On the first trip in February 2009, we participated in formal interviews with the OST and with relevant WHO officials, including a number of seasoned veterans of GOARN missions. After this meeting, the review committee conducted a survey of GOARN partners (described below) to ascertain their views of GOARN and its future. On the second trip in April 2009, we participated in a SCOM meeting and a GOARN partners meeting where we presented and received feedback on some of the findings from our survey. These meetings also provided the opportunity for many informal conversations with SCOM members and partners. On both visits, the external evaluation team was given access to GOARN records, including mission reports, financial data, and former SCOM meetings. Below, we report our findings as they pertain to the general issue of network governance while preserving the confidentiality of the institutions, people, and records to which we were given access.

Who Needs a Network for Global Alert and Response?

As a form of global network governance, GOARN is distinctive, though not exceptional. It is not primarily a policymaking body, like other global public policy networks. Nor does it set or enforce global standards. While some of its partners are nonstate actors, GOARN's role is not primarily to mobilize civil society, as do transnational networks of nongovernmental organizations (NGOs). In many respects, GOARN is similar to other "global public-private partnerships" that have proliferated in global governance and that have been extensively used in global health governance to respond to specific diseases.[16] However, to the extent that the term *partnership* suggests that the relationship to private donor institutions is primary, this description can be misleading. GOARN is primarily, though not exclusively, a network of public or quasi-public institutions. Nonetheless, GOARN is clearly a form of global network governance. Its role is to coordinate the rapid response of its partner institutions to infectious disease outbreaks.

GOARN held its first meeting in April 2000.[17] The meeting brought together sixty-seven WHO partners involved in global disease surveillance and response. The meeting laid out the founding principles of GOARN, which was conceived as a technical partnership that would help limit the spread of international diseases through rapid coordinated response. (See Figure 16.2 for a list of GOARN's general principles.) A key function of this technical partnership would be to rapidly mobilize necessary expertise and resources to assist affected states. In broad terms, the creation of GOARN can be seen as a response to the rising threat of global epidemics and to the recognition that some states, particularly in the developing world, do not have adequate capacity to respond to these threats. However, the immediate impetus to create GOARN came from the field experiences of both the WHO and partner institutions in combating specific disease outbreaks. During several outbreaks, problems arose because bilateral assistance to affected countries was poorly coordinated. In some cases, responders found themselves working at cross-purposes and providing less than optimal mixes of expertise and resources to affected countries.

As a governance network, GOARN has a hybrid design.[18] Formally, it is an "independent" network of partner institutions. However, it is housed and institutionally supported by the WHO. As an independent network, GOARN is guided by a steering committee, which consists of up to twenty representatives from participating institutions and networks. SCOM is supposed to provide GOARN with strategic direction. Day-to-day matters, however, are managed by a small secretariat, the Operational Support Team, which is based in the WHO headquarters in Geneva. The OST consists of a project manager, medical officer, communication officer, and two administrative staff. Within the WHO, the OST is integrated into the Alert and Response Operations Team in the Epidemic and Pandemic Alert and Response Branch (EPR). Although many partners have made in-kind contributions to GOARN in the form of people and resources for missions, only a few have made direct contributions to the

Figure 16.2 GOARN's General Principles

1. The WHO ensures outbreaks of potential international importance are rapidly verified and information is quickly shared within the Network.

2. There is a rapid response coordinated by the Operational Support Team to requests for assistance from affected state(s).

3. The most appropriate experts reach the field in the least possible time to carry out coordinated and effective outbreak control activities.

4. The international team integrates and coordinates activities to support national efforts and existing public health infrastructure.

5. There is a fair and equitable process for the participation of Network partners in international responses.

6. There is strong technical leadership and coordination in the field.

7. Partners make every effort to ensure the effective coordination of their participation and support of outbreak response.

8. There is recognition of the unique role of national and international NGOs in the area of health, including the control of outbreaks. NGOs [provide] support that would not otherwise be available, particularly in reaching poor populations. While striving for effective collaboration and coordination, the Network will respect the independence and objectivity of all partners.

9. Responses will be used as a mechanism to build global capacity by the involvement of participants from field-based training programs in applied epidemiology and public health practice, for example, Field Epidemiology Training Programs (FETPs).

10. There is a commitment to national and regional capacity building as a follow up to international outbreak responses to improve preparedness and reduce future vulnerability to epidemic prone diseases.

11. All Network responses will proceed with full respect for ethical standards, human rights, national and local laws, and cultural sensitivities and traditions.

Source: World Health Organization, Department of Communicable Disease Surveillance and Response, n.d., "Guiding Principles for International Outbreak Alert and Response: Global Outbreak Alert and Response Network," http://whothailand.healthrepository.org.

institutional costs of supporting GOARN itself. The costs of operating GOARN, staffing the OST, and holding SCOM and partner meetings largely fall to the WHO.

GOARN partner institutions are diverse in structure, role, and geographical location, but share a strong interest in infectious disease response. Many of them have operational responsibilities for response. These include the major national response institutions, such as the US Centers for Disease Control and Prevention and the China Center for Disease Control and Prevention. Partners also represent surveillance systems, like the Mekong Basin Disease Surveillance Unit and the East African Disease Surveillance Group. Infectious disease laboratories (e.g., Australia's Burnet Institute for Medical Research) and public health and hospitals (e.g., Nepal's Sukra Raj Tropical and Infectious Disease Hospital) are also members. A number of universities with strong public health missions (e.g., Nagasaki University's Institute of Tropical Medicine) and a number of global health NGOs (e.g., Médecins Sans Frontières) are also partners. Finally, a number of partners represent units or networks from within the WHO or the UN system, such as the WHO clinical network. Overall, GOARN has more than 100 partner institutions, which are geographically distributed around the world. However, the majority of partner institutions are located in Europe, North America, and the Asia Pacific region.

In a general analysis of network design, Keith G. Provan and Patrick Kenis describe a range of types of networks.[19] A "shared governance" network is a decentralized association with dense horizontal interaction between members. They contrast this form of network with a "brokered" network, where network governance occurs through "a single organization, acting as a highly centralized network broker, or lead organization, regarding issues that are critical for overall network maintenance and survival."[20] They further distinguish between "participant-governed" and "lead-organization governed" brokered networks. These distinctions point to GOARN's hybrid nature. GOARN is largely a lead organization–brokered network that is coordinated and made possible by WHO sponsorship; however, GOARN is also managed by an independent secretariat that reports to an external board. We later discuss some of the tensions inherent in this hybrid form.

While the WHO and other partners obviously felt there was a need for a coordinating mechanism for global outbreak alert and response, the rationale for GOARN is not self-evident. Why is a network necessary to achieve this coordination? After all, the WHO has a formal responsibility for providing assistance to affected countries. The WHO already provides much of the logistical support, manpower, and financial resources for international response. Moreover, the WHO is already a mechanism for mobilizing member resources for international public health needs. If the WHO could directly play this coordinating role, what are the advantages of working through a network?

There are at least four interrelated answers to this question. The first answer has to do with the advantages to the WHO of mobilizing partners as a technical community. By mobilizing partner institutions directly as a technical community, GOARN facilitates rapid coordination. Direct and sustained contact with partner institutions contributes to the speed and quality of coordination in subtle but important ways. Expert rosters, for example, tend to become quickly outdated; as a network, GOARN deepens communication links for regular and rapid updating of relevant contacts and expertise. Through training and meetings, GOARN also helps to prepare member institutions for effective integration into multilateral missions.

A second answer has to do with the reverse flow of influence. The relationship between the WHO and GOARN partners would be ineffective if it were just a matter of the WHO mobilizing this technical community for its own ends. GOARN also enables technical partners to directly influence multilateral operations. While the WHO is the lead organization, GOARN is technically an independent network, creating opportunities for its member institutions to provide input into the shape of missions. As a multilateral mechanism, GOARN helps partners to ensure that their contributions to response efforts will be efficient and effective.

A third rationale for GOARN is related to the fact that some important technical institutions are quasi-public or even private. On the one hand, these institutions may have resources and expertise they are willing to contribute (they often gain experience, skill, and knowledge through participation in international responses), but little capacity (logistical, diplomatic, etc.) for placing their people in the field. On the other hand, working through formal multilateral channels, the WHO would find it difficult to integrate many of these institutions into response operations; nor do quasi-public and private institutions necessarily relish subordinating themselves to control by the WHO. As an independent network, GOARN provides a framework for direct integration of these quasi-public and private partners.

GOARN's fourth benefit is its capability to manage the contributions between multilateral, regional, and bilateral response. The WHO has lead responsibility for managing multilateral response. However, as mentioned above, nations often have an interest and desire to send bilateral aid during an outbreak. There are also many regional institutions that have an interest in providing assistance. GOARN creates a mechanism for bilateral and regional contributions to be coordinated under the umbrella of multilateral operations.

Taken together, network governance creates an institutional space for the orchestration of different kinds of transactions necessary for rapid and effective response.[21] A close examination of GOARN operations reveals that they bring at least four types of coordination into alignment for the purposes of rapid response. GOARN:

1. locates and mobilizes available and relevant expertise and resources from within the WHO and partner institutions;

2. communicates (through the WHO regional and country offices) with Ministries of Health about their needs and negotiates the terms of reference for GOARN teams;
3. deploys multilateral resources and experts as field teams and coordinates these teams in the field;
4. provides a two-way flow of information and communication between the WHO headquarters and field teams during operations.

Arguably, the WHO could perform each of these coordination tasks directly without working through a network. But by creating an institutional interface for these four types of transactions, GOARN facilitates a relatively seamless and rapid integration across these four different coordination tasks.

This description of GOARN as a form of network governance is an idealized one. As we explore in the next several sections, GOARN faces many challenges as it tries to play this intermediary role.

Why Global Network Governance Is Challenging

To gauge the effectiveness of GOARN and to collect feedback on how members envisioned the network's future, our evaluation team conducted a survey of partners. The survey was sent to 103 partner institutions and we received responses from 81 different partners.[22] This survey found significant support for GOARN and its continued role. A strong majority (78 percent) of partners surveyed believed that GOARN was at least somewhat successful in achieving what they regarded as its most important function—mobilizing special expertise for outbreaks. Thirty-four percent of respondents believed that GOARN was "very successful" and 43 percent thought GOARN was "somewhat successful" in mobilizing expertise that would not have been available otherwise during outbreaks. A strong majority (70 percent) also believed that GOARN was at least somewhat successful in achieving what they regarded as its second most important function—providing back-up response capacity during outbreaks. Twenty-four percent thought GOARN was "very successful" and 46 percent thought GOARN was "somewhat successful" in providing this capacity.

The survey, however, also found that GOARN was less successful in increasing coordination and reducing competition that results from bilateral response. Only 44 percent of respondents felt that GOARN was somewhat or very successful in managing this bilateral "chaos."

This modest success is not surprising. Multilateral coordination during outbreaks is an extremely challenging process and tendencies toward bilateral deployment continue.

This problem of multilateral coordination is related to another problem that GOARN faces, which can be described as a problem of "branding." During outbreak responses, there is sometimes confusion about GOARN and its status. Some local officials and institutions do not discriminate between the WHO and GOARN. Others do not fully understand GOARN's role as a multilateral coordinating body. In general, GOARN's visibility is not particularly high. This problem can make it difficult for GOARN to establish its authority during field missions. Although this problem of branding and visibility has multiple sources, it is in part associated with the ambiguous status of GOARN as a network. On the one hand, local officials and institutions have established relationships with WHO country and regional offices and naturally utilize these relationships as needs arise. For some, GOARN appears to be just a fancy acronym to describe the support arriving from the WHO. On the other hand, GOARN missions are composed of representatives of partner institutions. Local officials and institutions may try to deal directly with these representatives in a bilateral fashion. Thus, as a coordinating network, GOARN sometimes faces difficulty in distinguishing itself from its lead organization and from its individual members.

Another area that reveals the challenge of network governance is in information sharing. Information is, to put it mildly, a "lumpy" commodity in global disease governance. Many will recall China's delay in sharing information about the SARS outbreak or Indonesia's refusal to share information on avian influenza strains. But these are only the most dramatic examples of a universal tendency to act with great reserve when it comes to sharing information about a disease outbreak. Since outbreaks can have serious political, economic, and social consequences, national governments and their public health agencies are naturally cautious about sharing such information, particularly before it has been validated. As mentioned above, it is critical to respond to outbreaks in a timely way. Therefore, timely access to information is essential for effective response.

Beyond its role in coordinating multilateral response missions, GOARN aspires to be a mechanism for international information sharing. GOARN primarily seeks to accomplish this "alert" function through a secure website that it has established to share information with partners about outbreaks. One source of GOARN's information comes from the Global Public Health Information Network (GPHIN), a

Canadian-based Web-trawling system for early identification of disease outbreaks (along with other information systems, like Promed). Another source of GOARN information is the WHO itself, which is informed by its members of outbreaks. A third potential source of information is GOARN's own partners.

Despite this range of sources, GOARN often has difficulty providing unique information to partners, which has undermined, to some degree, its usefulness as a mechanism of information sharing. Our external evaluation survey of partners found that 31.8 percent of respondents used the website frequently, while 37.6 percent used it only sometimes, and 22.4 percent used it rarely. The survey also found that 36.9 percent of respondents believed that they received information from GOARN "at the earliest possible moment" while 34.5 percent believed they received information from GOARN "after it had been verified." In open-ended responses to the evaluation survey, several partners noted that GOARN's website does not often provide much unique information.

Ideally, GOARN would create rapid sharing of unique outbreak information within its technical community. GOARN, however, must itself exercise caution in sharing information, and the need for discretion may have increased with the implementation of the 2005 International Health Regulations (IHR).[23] These regulations were created in response to SARS and in the face of the threat of an avian flu pandemic and were designed to ensure that information about disease outbreak situations of international concern was reported to the WHO. While the new IHR are seen as a positive development for international disease governance, they may complicate GOARN's information-sharing role.[24] In open-ended responses to our evaluation survey, several partners highlighted the impact on GOARN caused by the new IHR. They pointed out that the IHR can constrain the early access to information through GOARN.

Until the implementation of the IHR on 15 June 2007, the information provided by GOARN to partners included what is known as the WHO Outbreak Verification List (OVL). Since June 2007, the OVL has been kept confidential within the WHO under an interpretation of Part II of the IHR, particularly Article 11, "Provision of Information by WHO." The article asserts that the WHO

> shall not make this information generally available to other States Parties, until such time as: (a) the event is determined to constitute a public health emergency of international concern . . . (b) information evidencing the international spread of infection . . . has been confirmed by WHO . . . (c) there is evidence that control measures . . . are unlikely to succeed . . . or the [affected] State Party lacks sufficient

operational capacity . . . to prevent further spread of disease, or (d) the nature and scope of international movement . . . requires immediate application of international control measures.[25]

While it is true that information shared with the WHO prior to the implementation of the new IHR may have also been held confidentially, several interviews within GOARN suggested that the new legal framework increased the WHO's caution in early sharing of information with GOARN partners.[26] In order to be granted access to critical IHR information, GOARN must also respect the WHO controls on information sharing. Readers should not conclude that GOARN was necessarily better off before the 2005 IHR came into effect; the net effect on information sharing may be quite positive. The main point is that GOARN must negotiate a complex information environment, with mixed incentives for keeping information confidential and for information sharing.

Managing Performance Imperatives

The WHO has a major responsibility for providing disease alert and response assistance for the international community. Since the WHO's founding in 1946, control of the international spread of infectious diseases has been one of its core responsibilities. The 2005 IHR reaffirmed and expanded these responsibilities. On request from a member state, the IHR instruct the WHO to provide technical guidance and assistance, including "the mobilization of international teams of experts for on-site assistance" (Article 13(3)). It may also offer to "mobilize international assistance in order to support the national authorities in conducting and coordinating on-site assessments" (Article 13(4)). GOARN is one of the WHO's major mechanisms for providing technical support and expertise to national governments who request assistance.

As a mechanism used to fulfill the WHO's international responsibilities, GOARN is closely integrated into the WHO's alert and response framework, and in many respects is treated as an operational arm of the WHO. Nominally, however, GOARN is also an independent network that reports to SCOM, which represents the network partners. In theory, this situation creates a potential conflict, with GOARN pulled between competing "principals" (the WHO and SCOM). While a few partners resent the WHO dominance, there is in practice little conflict. The WHO is clearly recognized as the dominant party in the relationship and most partners accept this arrangement. Our external evaluation team asked partners directly about this relationship. A large majority (64.8 percent) felt that the balance between integration into the WHO's operations and network independence was about right, and only 8 percent of partners felt that greater independence was desirable if it came at the cost of reduced integration into those operations.

Despite this general satisfaction with the status quo, the performance imperatives of meeting WHO responsibilities ultimately weaken the development of the network itself. The most obvious evidence of this comes from the relatively moribund state of SCOM, which has met infrequently over the past five years. SCOM's weakness can be traced to the OST's responsibility for day-to-day missions and operations. These responsibilities include managing the GOARN website, holding GOARN training programs, and monitoring potential outbreaks. In the event of a request for assistance, the OST is then responsible for managing each of the four tasks associated with organizing GOARN missions (mobilizing expertise and resources from partners, communicating with host country institutions, deploying GOARN missions, and remaining in communication with these missions during their deployment). This is a big job and the OST is a small group. In the face of these operational pressures, management of the wider network naturally becomes a secondary priority.[27] SCOM could (and should) play the role of network steward, but the organization of SCOM itself depends in part on the OST's capacity to facilitate SCOM meetings and communication.

Operational pressures are one explanation for a weakening of the network. But operations might also be seen as an opportunity for network development. GOARN missions are composed of representatives from the WHO and from GOARN partners, and are clearly therefore an opportunity to reinforce the partners' commitment to the network itself. Yet the operational and organizational imperatives of GOARN missions place rather significant limits on this opportunity. The first constraint is on the size of the missions. In many cases, affected countries are willing to accept only small GOARN missions, though this depends on the scope of the problem and the capacity of the affected country. The other constraint is that affected counties increasingly request only highly specialized expertise ("superexperts," as Mike Ryan, the former director of the WHO Alert and Response Operations, calls them). These constraints on size and skill level tend to skew participation on missions to a relatively small group of partners with strong capacity and access to these superexperts. The overall result is that a majority of partners have no experience of participating in GOARN missions. Over 50 percent of our respondents to the external evaluation survey reported that their institution had not participated in a GOARN mission while nearly 23 percent reported that their institution had participated in only a single mission. Approximately 8 percent of the respondents indicated that their institution had participated in six or more missions. Kent Buse and Andrew M. Harmer point to the unrepresentativeness of stakeholders as one of the "unhealthy habits" of global public-private health partnerships, but it is important to recognize that this skewed representation on missions is a product of the various demands and constraints imposed on missions.[28]

Despite this tendency for a few major partners to dominate missions, this is not the full story. There is also some evidence that GOARN makes it possible for some institutions to become involved that would not otherwise have the capacity to participate in international missions.

In their analysis of different kinds of network governance, Provan and Kenis suggest that networks—particularly those networks with strong lead organizations—often confront a tension between efficiency and inclusiveness.[29] A strong lead organization reduces the demands on members, facilitating efficient operations. However, the negative consequence of this efficiency can be the weakened commitment of the members to the network. GOARN faces a similar challenge. The WHO has important alert and response responsibilities that create operational pressures for the OST. These missions potentially create opportunities for network mobilization, but the organizational (and political) imperatives of GOARN missions work against the greater inclusiveness of members. The result reinforces a pattern of informal network coordination between the WHO operational staff and a few prominent GOARN partners. The broader network, however, suffers as a result from underdevelopment.

A related tension noted by Provan and Kenis is between network flexibility and stability. Networks like GOARN need to adapt flexibly to changing conditions, but they also need to provide a framework for long-term interaction and commitment. These needs can conflict when the need to respond to immediate concerns discourages attention to longer-term needs. The weakness of SCOM appears to be one symptom of this limited attention to longer-term development.

Finally, it is worth noting that some of the key founders of GOARN conceived that it could be a mechanism for peer-to-peer networking. Such peer-to-peer networking is clearly seen at partner meetings, which are organized as miniconferences, with breakout panels on topics of interest to the GOARN technical community. However, between infrequent partner meetings (which are expensive to hold), there is little evidence of peer-to-peer networking within the framework of GOARN. During this period, initiative and communication are centralized in Geneva. The strong lead role of the WHO makes the goal of a peer-to-peer community more of an aspiration than a reality.

Negotiating the Institutional
Minefield of Outbreak Response

Not only must GOARN navigate a balance between its role as an operational arm of the WHO and its status as an independent network, but it must also cope with the challenges posed by the wider institutional ecology in which it works. One of the major institutional complexities that GOARN must confront is the WHO's regionalized structure. In some respects, the WHO is actually a federation of regional health organizations, which in some cases even predate the formation of the WHO itself. These six regional offices are: Africa (AFRO), Eastern Mediterranean (EMRO), Europe (EURO), the Americas (AMRO), Southeast Asia (SEARO), and the Western Pacific (WPRO). They operate fairly independently and have their own relationships with donors. The WHO also has country offices, which cultivate strong ties to their corresponding Ministries of Health. These country offices often have closer relationships with the WHO regional offices than with the WHO headquarters in Geneva.

Many of GOARN's early missions were focused in Africa. Before the SARS outbreak occurred in 2003, GOARN and WPRO had little experience with each other. While GOARN's role in SARS was a positive one, it raised a set of questions about GOARN's relationship to the regional offices that still is not fully resolved. After SARS, for example, there was discussion within the regions, and notably within WPRO, about whether it should create its own regional version of GOARN. This issue, in turn, raised a question about the lead role of GOARN. Was GOARN in charge of response operations or was the regional office? Ultimately, GOARN acknowledged that it needed to work through regional offices in fielding missions.

This relationship with the regions has some potentially positive implications for GOARN. Post-SARS and in anticipation of an H5N1 pandemic, WPRO became highly active within GOARN, and this activity suggested the possibility of a synergistic relationship with the WHO regional offices. As WPRO became more active, institutions in the Western Pacific region also engaged more actively within GOARN. These institutions brought a somewhat different set of concerns to GOARN in comparison with partners activated earlier. The new institutions had a greater interest in capacity building, something that the founding GOARN meeting had anticipated as a role for GOARN (see Figure 16.2). But with the exception of its training program, GOARN has not been actively involved in capacity building. This lack of engagement in capacity building can again be partly traced back to the operational imperatives that GOARN faces. The OST conceives of its primary role as rapid response during the very early stages of an outbreak and regards later stages of response to be handled best by other institutions. Consequently, it is difficult to engage in capacity building with small teams operating in this rapid response mode.

Beyond the institutional complexities of the WHO itself, GOARN must interact with a range of other networks. From the beginning, GOARN considered itself a "network of networks." The minutes from the founding meeting in 2000 suggested that GOARN should work with existing networks and seek to play a complementary and supportive role with these networks. As suggested by the 2003 SARS example, in many respects this network of networks concept works quite well. The OST routinely works with other public health networks, such as the International Food Safety Authorities Network (INFOSAN). Both GOARN and INFOSAN are headquartered at the WHO headquarters in Geneva and are active networks with their own distinctive (though sometimes overlapping) technical communities.

GOARN is less certain about how it should partner with other networks, including some sponsored by the WHO. Some of these networks are only weakly developed and are less capable or willing to engage in active collaboration. The OST is not clear about whether network building is a good use of its energies. Should it take an active leadership role in trying to develop these networks? Or is this an inefficient and perhaps inappropriate role for GOARN? Again the issue is related to GOARN's operational imperatives. By facilitating the creation of specialized networks, GOARN would be encouraging greater peer-to-peer networking. Issue-specific and disease-specific networking has the potential to create operational efficiencies during outbreak responses as well as a potential to promote learning and benchmarking. If these networks are strong and self-maintaining, then GOARN can work with them during outbreaks. However, networks typically require significant inputs of organizing energy and often are not self-maintaining. If networks are weak, they may become irrelevant to outbreak response or may even hinder it. So GOARN is faced with a decision about whether it should promote networks and how much energy it should expend to catalyze them.

Conclusion

This study of the Global Outbreak Alert and Response Network demonstrates both the promise and the challenge of global network governance. Since April 2000, GOARN has been an active and important player in international disease governance. By assembling missions that rapidly provide critical expertise and resources to countries affected by disease outbreaks, GOARN serves a critical role in containing contagious disease and providing backup response capacity. This response function is valued both by GOARN's main sponsor, the World Health Organization, and by its members, response institutions and laboratories from around the world. GOARN's alert function is less unique and distinctive, but also has some value for the WHO and GOARN partners. Despite this success, GOARN is also clearly constrained by the imperatives that flow from meeting the WHO's operational responsibilities and from the challenges that arise from working in a complex institutional environment (not to mention the challenge of working in the hostile environments of global disease outbreaks). While a success story, GOARN is difficult to sustain as an institution that fully lives up to the promise of global network governance.

This is a "glass half full" story: global networks like GOARN do have the potential to address complex global problems, but we also have to appreciate that most networks will operate under fairly significant constraints. The main theoretical point of our analysis is that networks, as promising approaches to global governance, confront significant challenges in developing their full potential as networks. In the case of GOARN, the dominance of the WHO as the lead organization and the paramount importance of meeting the WHO's day-to-day operational responsibilities have led to fairly narrowly based participation by network partners. The design of the network (a lead organization–sponsored network) and the challenge of managing the network to meet its operational goals within the set of constraints it faces have ultimately made it difficult to develop the network into a vibrant, independent, and broad-based community.

Our study calls attention to the role of network managers in "squaring the circle"—juggling the various performance demands and constraints of network governance while maintaining the network itself. Other scholars of network governance have also noted this challenge. Witte, Reinicke, and Benner argue that "the ability of networks to innovate and produce sustainable results depends on the talent of network managers to keep the ties between actors loose but still close enough to be manageable."[30] They observe that it is often a challenge for network managers to find the right balance between consultation of partners and delivery of network objectives. In the GOARN case, delivery of network objectives has partially trumped the maintenance and development of the network itself.

If we try to generalize from this study, it suggests that global governance networks are likely to be self-limiting in various ways. In any institution, the pursuit of one set of objectives is likely to place limits on the pursuit of other objectives. But for global network governance, successfully meeting institutional and performance imperatives may place significant constraints on mobilizing and developing the wider network itself, tempering the promise of global networks as an ideal form of mobilizing broad-based participation and horizontal coordination. Governance networks with significant responsibilities are not easy or inexpensive to build or maintain. Unless members are highly motivated to maintain high levels of participation and peer-to-peer networking or unless performance imperatives themselves create incentives to mobilize the wider network community, global governance networks are likely to eventually confront the kinds of network development problems that even a successful network like GOARN now faces. Lead organizations and the network itself will confront questions of how much to invest in network maintenance and network building. Global governance networks may still perform well under these circumstances, but the network itself might become quite restricted in size and activation.

Notes

1. See Thorsten Benner, Wolfang H. Reinicke, and Jan Martin Witte, "Global Public Policy Networks," *Brookings Review* 21, no. 2 (2003): 18–21; Thorsten Benner, Wolfang H. Reinicke, and Jan Martin Witte, "Shaping Globalization: The Role of Global Public Policy Networks," in Bertelsmann Foundation, ed., *Transparency: A Basis for Responsibility and Cooperation* (Gütersloh, Germany: Bertelsmann Foundation, 2002); Wolfgang H. Reinicke, "The Other World Wide Web: Global Public Policy Networks," *Foreign Policy* 117 (Winter 1999–2000): 44–57; Jan Martin Witte, Wolfgang H. Reinicke, and Thorsten Benner, "Beyond Multilateralism: Global Public Policy Networks," in Alfred Pfaller and Marika Lerch, eds., *Challenges of Globalization: New Trends in International Politics and Society* (New Brunswick, NJ: Transaction, 2005). Witte, Reinicke, and Benner, "Beyond Multilateralism," suggest that global public policy networks can play at least six different roles: (1) agenda setting and advocacy; (2) standard setting; (3) knowledge collection and dissemination; (4) creation or deepening markets; (5) policy implementation; and (6) representation.

2. Benner, Reinicke, and Witte, "Global Public Policy Networks."

3. Anne-Marie Slaughter, *A New World Order* (Princeton: Princeton University Press, 2004).

4. Ibid., p. 10. Slaughter distinguishes between information, enforcement, and harmonization networks.

5. Paul Thurner and Martin Binder, "European Union Transgovernmental Networks: The Emergence of a New Political Space Beyond the Nation-State?" *European Journal of Political Research* 48, no. 1 (2009): 80–106; Burkard Eberlein and Abraham L. Newman, "Escaping the International Governance Dilemma? Incorporated Transnational Networks in the European Union," *Governance: An International Journal of Policy, Administration, and Institutions* 21, no. 1 (2008): 25–52.

6. Marco Schäferhoff, Sabine Campe, and Christopher Kaan, "Transnational Public-Private Partnerships in International Relations: Making Sense of Concepts, Research Frameworks, and Results," *International Studies Review* 11, no. 3 (2009): 451–474.

7. The term *partnership* is often used to describe an association composed of a few members while the term *network* is commonly reserved for associations with larger memberships.

8. Eberlein and Newman, "Escaping the International Governance Dilemma?"

9. Eva Sørenson and Jacob Torfing, *Theories of Democratic Network Governance* (London: Macmillan, 2007); Yannis Papadopoulos, "Problems of Democratic Accountability in Network and Multilevel Governance," *European Law Journal* 13, no. 4 (2007): 469–486; Peter Bogason and Juliet A. Musso, "The Democratic Prospects of Network Governance," *American Review of Public Administration* 36, no. 1 (2006): 3–18.

10. Nancy Roberts, "Wicked Problems and Network Approaches to Resolution," *International Public Management Review* 1, no. 1 (2000): 1–19; Ellen Van Bueren, Erik-Hans Klijn, and Joop F. M. Koppenjan, "Dealing with Wicked Problems in Networks: Analyzing an Environmental Debate from a Network Perspective," *Journal of Public Administration Research and Theory* 13, no. 2 (2003): 193–212.

11. Keith G. Provan and Patrick Kenis, "Modes of Network Governance: Structure, Management, and Effectiveness," *Journal of Public Administration Research and Theory* 18, no. 2 (2007): 229–252.

12. World Health Organization, "Global Outbreak Alert and Response: Report of a WHO Meeting," Geneva, Switzerland, 26–28 April 2000, Document No. WHO/CDS/CSR/2000.3.

13. For published accounts of GOARN's role in individual outbreaks, see David L. Heymann, Guénaël R. Rodier, and the WHO Operational Support Team to the Global Outbreak Alert and Response Network, "Hot Spots in a Wired World: WHO Surveillance of Emerging and Re-emerging Infectious Diseases," *The Lancet Infectious Diseases* 1, no. 5 (2001): 345–353; Mark Salter and Kande-Bure O'Bai Kamara, "Lassa Fever: The Role of the Global Outbreak Alert and Response Network (GOARN)," *Merlin: Health Care in Crises*, 1–2 February 2002, pp. 1–2.

14. On GOARN's role in the SARS outbreak, see David L. Heymann and Guénaël R. Rodier, "Global Surveillance, National Surveillance, and SARS," *Emerging Infectious Diseases* 10, no. 2 (2004): 173–175; David L. Heymann, "SARS and Emerging Infectious Diseases: A Challenge to Place Global Solidarity Above National Solidarity," *Annals Academy of Medicine Singapore* 35, no. 35 (2006): 350–353; Martin Eserink, "A Global Fire Brigade Responds to Disease Outbreaks," *Science* 303, no. 5664 (2004): 1605–1606; David L. Hey-

mann, "The International Response to the Outbreak of SARS in 2003," *Philosophical Transactions of the Royal Society B*, no. 1447 (2004): 1127–1129; US General Accounting Office, *Emerging Infectious Diseases: Asian SARS Outbreak Challenged International and National Responses*, Report No. GAO-04-564 (Washington, DC: US General Printing Office, 2004).

15. Philip Selznick, *A Humanist Science: Values and Ideals in Social Inquiry* (Palo Alto: Stanford University Press, 2008).

16. Nicole A. Szlezák, Barry R. Bloom, Dean T. Jamison, Gerald T. Keusch, Catherine M. Michaud, Suerie Moon, and William Clark, "The Global Health System: Actors, Norms, and Expectations in Transition," *PLoS Medicine* 7, no. 1 (2010): 1–4; Schäferhoff, Campe, and Kaan, "Transnational Public-Private Partnerships in International Relations"; Kent Buse and Andrew M. Harmer, "Seven Habits of Highly Effective Global Public-Private Health Partnerships: Practice and Potential," *Social Science and Medicine* 64, no. 2 (2007): 259–271; Kent Buse, "Governing Public-Private Infectious Disease Partnerships," *Brown Journal of World Affairs* 10, no. 2 (Winter–Spring 2004): 225–242; Kent Buse and Gill Walt, "Global Public-Private Partnerships: Part II—What Are the Health Issues for Global Governance?" *Bulletin of the World Health Organization* 78, no. 5 (2000): 699–709.

17. World Health Organization, "Global Outbreak Alert and Response: Report of a WHO Meeting," Geneva, Switzerland, 26–28 April 2000, Document No. WHO/CDS/CSR/2000.3.

18. Details of the structure of GOARN are set out in a working document, "Global Outbreak Alert and Response Network: Structure of the Network," produced by the World Health Organization, Department of Communicable Disease Surveillance and Response, no date.

19. Provan and Kenis, "Modes of Network Governance."

20. Ibid., p. 234.

21. Candace Jones, William S. Hesterly, and Stephen P. Borgatti suggest that four types of exchange conditions favor network governance: (1) demand uncertainty with stable supply; (2) customized exchanges high in asset specificity; (3) complex tasks under high time pressure; and (4) frequent exchanges among parties. In GOARN's case, the most salient factor appears to be that response missions require complex tasks under high time pressure. However, it may also be important that these missions are highly customized productions that rely heavily on specialized expertise (high asset specificity), respond to uncertain demand conditions, and often bring many of the same institutions and people together (frequent exchange). See Candace Jones, William S. Hesterly, and Stephen P. Borgatti, "A General Theory of Network Governance: Exchange Conditions and Social Mechanisms," *Academy of Management Review* 22, no. 4 (1997): 911–945.

22. Our survey was distributed using a commercially available online survey platform (Survey Monkey) using a list of GOARN contacts provided by the OST. The list included up to three contacts for each GOARN partner and was eventually sent to a total of 301 individuals. Through e-mail, all contacts were invited to respond to the survey. The e-mail provided a link to the survey, which was estimated to take no more than thirty minutes to complete. After the initial distribution, several further e-mails were sent to remind contacts to complete the survey. The invitation e-mail and the survey were written in English, but a

French version of the survey was made available on request. Responses were received from 81 partner institutions, with some institutions contributing more than one response. Twenty-two partner institutions did not respond to the survey. A total of 113 survey responses were received. However, the rate of response to most questions was lower. On closed-ended opinion questions, the number of responses ranged from a low of 84 to a high of 92, with an average of 87 responses. Open-ended questions allowed respondents to elaborate on closed-ended questions if they desired. As expected, fewer responses to open-ended questions were received, with a low of 16 responses to a high of 40 responses. Given the number of institutions that responded to the survey, we believe the response rate is adequate to draw conclusions from the survey. The geographical distribution of responses reflected the distribution of partners, with the best representation from Europe, North America, and the Asia Pacific region.

23. See www.who.int/csr/ihr.

24. Michael G. Baker and David P. Fidler, "Global Public Health Surveillance Under the New International Health Regulations," *Emerging Infectious Diseases* 12, no. 7 (2006): 1058–1065. Our survey asked partners whether they believed that the IHR improved information sharing: 27.4 percent responded that the IHR "strongly" enhance information sharing; 34.5 percent indicated that IHR "somewhat" enhance; and 10.7 percent indicated that they have "little effect." Slightly over 20 percent of respondents were "not sure."

25. World Health Organization, *International Health Regulations 2005*, 2nd edition (Geneva: World Health Organization Press, 2008), pp. 13–14.

26. One anonymous reviewer challenged this view of the effects of the new IHR, pointing out that the pre-2005 OVL was also held in confidence and noting that the current IHR make various provisions to increase the flow of information. We acknowledge that the situation is not clear-cut, but believe it is important to raise the issue.

27. Joaquín Herranz, Jr., characterizes the literature on network management as describing a spectrum that runs from "passive" to "active" management of the network. With respect to the day-to-day management of the network for the purposes of GOARN missions, the OST's management style is more active. But in terms of the long-range development of the network, OST's management style would probably be characterized as passive. See Joaquín Herranz, Jr., "Multisectoral Trilemma of Network Management," *Journal of Public Administration Research and Theory* 18, no. 1 (2008): 1–31.

28. Buse and Harmer, "Seven Habits of Highly Effective Global Public-Private Health Partnerships," pp. 262–264.

29. Provan and Kenis, "Modes of Network Governance."

30. Jan Martin Witte, Wolfang H. Reinicke, and Thorsten Benner, "Beyond Multilateralism: Global Public Policy Networks," *International Politik und Gesellschaft* 2 (2000): 176–188.

17

Order out of Chaos:
Public and Private Rules
for Managing Carbon

Jessica F. Green

In many respects, the Kyoto Protocol has been a policy failure. It has not achieved the necessary reductions to avoid the "dangerous anthropogenic interference with the climate system" identified in the 1992 Framework Convention. It created a market for carbon offsets of dubious efficacy. Although these less-than-ambitious targets for reduction were extended for a second commitment period at the Doha conference in December 2012, a number of developed nations refused to renew their commitments, leaving only 15 percent of global emissions covered by the Protocol. The Protocol is also waning in political importance: states are moving toward a number of different forums to pursue policy goals. Some of these are alternative intergovernmental forums, such as the Major Economies Forum or the World Bank. Others are forms of private authority: situations in which private actors (including firms and NGOs) are serving as both *de facto* and *de jure* global rule makers. The result is an increasingly complex institutional landscape, with hundreds (if not thousands) of institutions at global, national, and local levels that seek to address various facets of the climate change problem. Does this proliferation of institutions (i.e., institutional complexity) contribute to or undermine effective regulation?

This paper sheds light on the question of institutional complexity by inserting a factor often overlooked in research to date: the presence of private authority. Specifically, it examines the proliferation of privately created standards to measure and manage greenhouse gas (GHG) emissions within the "regime complex" for climate change, which can be under-

Reprinted from *Global Environmental Politics*, vol. 13, no. 2: 1–25. © 2013 by MIT Press. Reprinted by permission of the publisher. Edited for length.

stood as the group of loosely coupled and non-hierarchical institutions that address the problem of climate change.[1] Using a newly constructed dataset and employing network analysis, it shows that the case of carbon standards provides some surprising evidence of policy convergence—both around publicly created rules and a select subset of privately created rules. Drawing from theories of policy convergence, I offer an explanation for the observed variation.

The paper makes three arguments. First, in order to understand the regime complex for climate change, we must include all forms of governance, including those created by private forms of authority. Second, and more importantly, when we include private authority in the analysis, the presence of private standards affirms the centrality of the Kyoto Protocol within the broader regime complex. A network analysis of recognition among standards reveals that fully 79 percent of standards created by private actors recognize rules created under the Kyoto Protocol. This finding suggests an unintended consequence of private authority: it can serve as a venue for the embedding of public rules. Third, the order that emerges out of the seeming chaos within the regime complex can be explained by private regulators' desire to distinguish themselves from competitors and to minimize users' exposure to switching costs in the future.

The high level of recognition of public authority by private standards suggests an unanticipated consequence of public authority as embodied by Kyoto Protocol: its vestiges will likely remain, irrespective of the outcome of the inter-governmental process, perpetuated through private authority. This suggests the possibility of long-term residual effects of the Kyoto Protocol, even as its future legal form remains uncertain. In contrast to those who argue that Kyoto has been a failure, I suggest an unexpected way in which it has been a success. To borrow Sidney Tarrow's metaphor, the institutions created by the Kyoto Protocol have served as a kind of "coral reef." In Tarrow's version, activists are drawn to international institutions, which provide venues in which they may interact and "form horizontal connections" among themselves.[2] The Kyoto Protocol has served a similar "coral reef" function, attracting private rule makers whose governance activities come to form part of the regime complex. In this case, the reef serves not as a way for activists to organize, but rather for private authority to contribute to an orderly expansion of the regime complex.

The paper proceeds as follows. I first examine the literature on institutional complexity, highlighting the often overlooked role of private authority. I then turn to the literature on policy convergence for potential explanations of why we observe convergence under conditions of complexity. Second, using a new dataset, I systematically map and describe the proliferation of private authority in the regime complex for climate change. Third, I use network analysis to illustrate how order arises out of chaos. I show that public rules are the clear anchor for private rules on carbon management. I further demonstrate that not all private rules are created equally: there is hierarchy among them. The final section offers an explanation for the observed convergence among rules, based on the network analysis and supplemented by interviews with private standard setters.

Regime Complexity and Policy Convergence

This section briefly reviews the literature on private authority and focuses on two bodies of literature that seek to explain the effects of institutional complexity: regime complexity and policy convergence. The literature on regime complexity largely ignores the role of private actors; work on environmental governance and climate governance is much further along in this respect. Moreover, the work on regime complexity tends to emphasize the negative effects of complexity over causal explanations; the policy convergence literature, by contrast, offers clear explanations for convergence across competing sets of rules.

The role of private authority, understood as the ways that private actors make rules and set standards which others adopt, is well explored in the literature on climate change and on environmental governance more broadly.[3] Biermann and Pattberg point to the emergence of new types of actors, and thus, new institutional arrangements that permeate global environmental governance, calling for more research on the dynamics of institutional change.[4] Pattberg and Stripple lay out a reconceptualization of climate governance that moves beyond the simple dichotomy of public and private, and identify a similar need for better knowledge about the interactions among institutions in a densely populated landscape of diverse actors.[5] Recent work from Bernstein and colleagues is similarly cognizant of the growing importance of private authority, noting that the complex interactions between actors and practices in carbon markets blur the boundaries between "public" and "private" governance.[6] A number of additional works share an interest in the relationship between governments and markets, and provide a similar perspective on the fluid relationship between the public and private realms in carbon governance.[7] This analysis answers the call for further research, and to show in fine-grained detail the ways in which this "blurring" occurs.

The research presented here has an additional goal: to link explicitly the work on private authority in the realm of environmental governance with a broader set of works in international relations and public policy which takes up similar issues. The literature on regime complexity (RC) has recently evolved as a way to understand the causes and effects of the proliferation of international institutions. Because of the increasing number and density of institutions, Raustiala and Victor argue that one must study the ensemble of institutions working in a given issue area in their totality, rather than examining each individually. This group of institutions constitutes a regime complex: "an array of partially overlapping and nonhierarchical institutions governing a particular issue-area."[8] In short, RC theory is a way of understanding institutional complexity as constituted by a group of related institutions treated as a single unit.

Despite the widely held view that private actors are increasingly important in world politics, RC theory has largely overlooked their role. In their description of the regime complex for climate change, Keohane and Victor make only passing reference to initiatives undertaken by private actors, though interestingly, they note that the way private initiatives interact with bilateral and multilateral efforts will determine their future utility in addressing climate change.[9] In their excellent symposium on international regime complexity, Alter and Meunier consider the role of nonstate actors more carefully. They expect that "complexity contributes to making states and IOs [international organizations] more permeable, creating a heightened role for experts and non-state actors."[10] Nonetheless, when contemplating the effects of regime complexity on the fragmentation of international law, they only consider the preferences and actions of states. The "increased permeability" of states and IOs to private actors is therefore restricted to activities such as problem definition, strategic dissemination of information, and proposing solutions. Certainly, the authors identified the need to understand the role of private actors. However, their conceptualization of this role is still overly narrow. They do not consider the ways in which private actors may be exercising authority—that is, making rules—in the context of the regime complex. This paper contributes to this underexplored part of the literature.

Much of the RC literature outlines the ill effects of institutional complexity. Forum shopping, shifting, competition, and exploitation of legal ambiguities are all ways that actors can pick and choose among institutions to select the one most hospitable to their aims. There are fewer works that discuss the positive effects of complexity, which include innovation, experimentation, and the ability to avoid deadlock.[11] However, these works do not elaborate clear conditions under which we should expect to observe either set of effects, positive or negative. For this reason, I turn to work on regulatory harmonization, which provides a useful framework for understanding the effects of institutional complexity.

Studies of policy convergence can be viewed as another way to explain the effects of institutional complexity. Policy convergence can be understood as "any increase in the similarity between one or more characteristics of a certain policy across a given set of political jurisdictions."[12] The proliferation of rules across governance units (whether provinces, states, or other geographic units) has led scholars to ask, what factors contribute to their eventual convergence or continued divergence? Explanations for convergence are varied. Vogel famously described a "California effect," in which leaders set the bar high, and laggards must adjust if they wish to gain market access.[13] Simmons provides a slightly different explanation where harmonization of capital market regulation arises due to material incentives to emulate the hegemon, which has the freedom to set standards as it pleases.[14] Drezner has argued that effective, harmonized standards only emerge in global politics when Great Powers have shared preferences about regulatory outcome.[15] McNamara offers an ideational explanation in which shared normative and causal beliefs among leaders about neoliberal policies led to low rates of inflation across Europe, which in turn enabled nations to enact the domestic policies needed to promote further integration.[16] Still other explanations of convergence focus on a hierarchical process, where policies converge due to imposition via international law or international organizations.[17]

These explanations of policy convergence, while useful, do not explicitly consider the role of private regulation. A few scholars have begun to consider whether and how harmonization among private rules might occur.[18] One explanation is similar in logic to the California effect. When private standards certify environmental or social quality (such as fair trade or organic products), convergence on a stringent standard may occur to meet the demands of customers and suppliers and thus maintain market share. Consumers may demand standards that guarantee high quality, rather than those that engage in mere greenwashing. Suppliers may seek to insulate themselves from naming and shaming campaigns by activists. Governments (some of which support private environmental standards financially) may use certain standards in their procurement practices as a way to promote wider use.[19] Sabel et al. describe a similar process, whereby transparency about labor practices allows leading firms to "credibly document their accomplishments to the public in a way that compels emulation by laggards, and points the way to an enforceable regulatory regime."[20] At the same time, private rule makers have an incentive to distinguish themselves from other competitors, and demonstrate the quality of their "product."

A second explanation of convergence hinges on social and ideational factors. In this view, convergence occurs through interactions among private standard setters. Repeated interactions may facilitate learning, or a diffusion of norms about appropriate practices.[21] In other words, "process dynamics" are the key explanation of harmonized standards.[22] While this explanation makes intuitive sense, in practice, it is difficult to disentangle the effects of norms and ideas when strategic and material incentives are also present. For this reason, I acknowledge this potential explanation, but do not consider it in my empirical analysis below.

In sum, the literature policy convergence helps pick up where discussions of regime complexity end. The RC literature explains different effects of complexity, but not the conditions under which they occur. By contrast, the work on convergence offers a clear explanation for why convergence among private standards might occur: to ensure that standard setters are meeting the demands of their users for both environmental quality and reputational benefits.

Mapping Institutional Complexity: Private Standards for Carbon Measurement

Addressing climate change involves many different types of policies and actors. Generally, the focus has been on the complex landscape of public efforts, at the national and international levels.[23] In this section, I expand the notion of institutional complexity with respect to climate change by describing privately created standards to manage GHGs. Private actors include NGOs, private firms, and transnational networks. For clarity, I refer to the rules promulgated by these actors as private standards; these are distinct from the organizations that create them, which I refer to as private rule makers. I exclude IOs and national governments, while acknowledging that the boundaries between public and private are not always neatly drawn.

I also bring a new methodological approach to the literature on regime complexity. Most work to date has been qualitative, either mapping the constellation of governance activities that constitute the regime complex, or explaining the effects of complexity in a small number of intergovernmental agreements and/or organizations. I seek to map complexity in a different way, using social network analysis.[24] A network can be understood as "a finite set or sets of actors and the relation or relations defined on them."[25] The set of actors in this network is transnational carbon governance initiatives, both public and private. The relations are the ties that connect them (or do not), and are operationalized as recognition of others' rules. These ties show us the structure of the network, which in turn provides insight into the relative importance of individual nodes based on their position in the network.

Mitigation efforts are premised on the ability to measure emissions. We need to know either the amount of GHGs emitted, or be able to calculate the amount being "saved" (i.e., prevented from being emitted) due to some activity. Just as banks need robust ways to account for gains and losses, so too do states and other entities need credible, accepted procedures for calculating their emissions; these needs are distributed across many types of actors and levels of governance.

The tools for counting carbon are similarly diverse. Households will calculate their emissions differently from firms or states. Partially as a result of these different needs, different measurement tools, or standards, have emerged. Yet there is not a one-to-one correlation between the type of standard and its users. Instead, there are multiple tools for measurement at the transnational level, some created by governments. Yet, there is also a strong presence of privately created standards. I turn now to a description of this institutional complexity, focusing first on the private standards and then on analysis of the relationship among public and private standards.

The data presented here comprise all of the private transnational standards for carbon measurement currently in use. The transnational criterion means that the standard must function in at least two countries, so standards that operate in just one country are not included in the dataset. In this initial description of private standards, I exclude those created by governments or international organizations, though these are considered below. I include only those whose primary aim is carbon measurement and management. Those that apply more generally to energy efficiency, sustainability, or other environmental issues are not included.

I compiled this data by triangulating among several sources, updating the data as new sources have become available. Table 17.1 lists all the standards in the dataset. The dataset presents basic information on these standards: the year they were created, their organizational goal, and whether they require third-party verification. I gathered this information in three complementary ways. First, I used the website for each organization to see whether they self-identify as linked to any other standards in the dataset. Second, most of the websites contained one or more document that described the methodological details of the standard. If any other standard-setting organization was mentioned in that document, this was coded as recognition. Third, to ensure the robustness of my coding, I also conducted a brief email survey, sent to each organization included in Table 17.1. I asked about the basic data listed above and about which other standards and/or verification systems they recognized (if any). Positive answers to either of these questions were

Table 17.1 Private Carbon Standards

Name	Year
Cleaner and Greener Certification	2000
Climate Action Reserve	2001
Greenhouse Gas Protocol Corporate Standard	2001
Carbon Neutral	2002
Plan Vivo	2002
Chicago Climate Exchange (and offset standard)	2003
Gold Standard	2003
Carbon Disclosure Project	2003
Climate, Community and Biodiversity Standard	2005
Green Tick Carbon Neutral	2005
Greenhouse Gas Protocol Project Standard	2005
ISO 14064-2	2006
Voluntary Carbon Standard	2006
ISO 14064-1	2006
ISO 14064-3	2006
CarbonFix	2007
Certified CarbonFree	2007
Climate Change Action	2007
Green-e (climate)	2007
VER +	2007
ISO 14065	2007
The Climate Registry	2007
Planet Positive	2008
Social Carbon	2008
Sustainable Carbon	2008
Carbon Trust Standard	2008
CEMARS	2008
Good Climate	2008
American Carbon Registry	2008
GreenCircle	2009

coded as recognition. Additional interviews, in person and by Skype, were conducted with five organizations.

Figure 17.1 shows the cumulative number of private standards by year. There is a clear and steady increase in the creation of standards over time. The majority of standards, 73 percent, were created between 2005 and 2009, after the Kyoto Protocol entered into force. Although countries recently agreed to extend the Kyoto Protocol, its fate was unclear until December 2012. Considerable uncertainty about the status and permanence of the current regulatory arrangements remains; its end date remains undecided. The spike in private standards after 2005 provides preliminary evidence that private actors responded to the finite lifespan of the Kyoto Protocol by creating additional rules that could possibly outlast the Protocol.

Figure 17.2 shows the different types of standards, categorized by their functions. Standards have four different functions. First, offset standards provide rules for measuring avoided emissions (and in some cases, other environmental co-benefits) of carbon mitigation projects. The emphasis in offset standards is the methodology for calculating emissions reductions. Second, accounting standards provide a protocol for actors to measure their emissions, and focus on total emissions, rather than reductions. Third, transparency standards provide a centralized repository for users to report their emissions to others. Accounting and transparency standards differ in one important respect. Accounting

Figure 17.1   Creation of Climate Standards, Cumulative

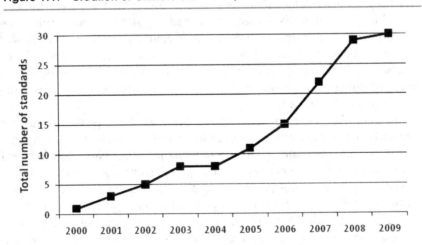

Figure 17.2　Private Climate Standards, by Function

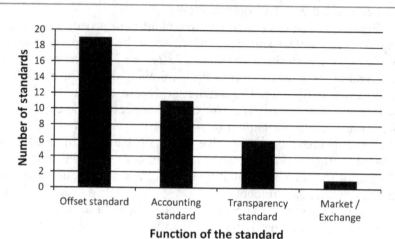

standards are first-party standards, often used by actors to catalogue information on their GHG emissions, with no requirement to make such information public.

Transparency standards are third-party standards because the information is made public by a third party. These are often emissions registries, where entities calculate their emissions and make them publicly available in one central place. As discussed below, some of these require verification, while others do not. The Climate Registry, for instance, provides a platform for participating entities to publicly report their GHG emissions. Fourth, there was one private standard that created a market: the Chicago Climate Exchange established a system for quantifying and trading carbon emissions. However, as of January 2011, the market was phased out and has been replaced with an offsets program. There is, of course, overlap among these different functions; the goal is to provide a sense of how institutional complexity manifests itself in terms of the different types of standards.

Figure 17.2 yields two interesting findings. First, private actors are typically not in the business of creating carbon markets, despite the fact that we tend to associate private actors with market activities. In their ideal form, markets are independent of the state.[26] Buyers and sellers interact based on quantities and prices. Here we find evidence of the opposite: those interactions are conditional upon states that have explicitly created those markets—the framework within which those transactions may occur. Thus, contrary to Strange's assertion that in the postwar period, markets "are the masters over the governments of states," this data shows that markets fall within the realm of states.[27] Figure 17.2 shows that private actors rarely create markets. Indeed, this has happened only once, and one could reasonably interpret the closure of the Chicago Climate Exchange as the failure to create a fully, self-sustaining private carbon market. In sum, creating markets for GHGs is almost exclusively the province of public authority.

Second, Figure 17.2 shows where private actors are especially active: they are in the business of creating offset standards. Offsets can exist without markets, but in such cases, must rely on altruistic consumers to purchase them. Coupled with markets however, they become an important tool for market participants to achieve compliance. As the discussion below shows, a very large proportion of private standards are linked to public markets, suggesting that altruism is not the dominant driver in the growth of private standards.

Fully 80 percent of private standards require third-party verification. This finding shows that most standard setters care about credibility and compliance, or at least wish to appear that they do. There is some helpful variation across organizational goals. The majority of offset standards require third-party verification (89 percent). By contrast, only 67 percent of transparency standards require third-party verification. This is unsurprising: transparency standards have the straightforward simple goal of getting emitters to report. This is a much shallower form of cooperation, where free-riding is not an issue. Thus, third-party verification is less important. Of course, verification of these reports is desirable; however, if the goal is incremental—to get organizations to begin thinking about and measuring their emissions—compulsory verification might scare off the more reluctant participants. In short, transparency standards aim to ensure broad participation, so cooperation is relatively shallow.

By contrast, since offsets are essentially creating a currency from an intangible good (the removal of emissions, vis-à-vis a previously established baseline), verification is a key element for credibility.[28] Without verification that offsets have been generated, the issuing of credits is akin to printing money—creating a commodity with no physical value. Unverified projects allow for the possibility that the offset credits . . . have no correlation to the actual physical reductions. This is not only inefficient in terms of combating climate change, but also has the effect of deflating the value of the "currency." Thus, third-party verification is an important signal in offset standards, to ensure the value of the commodity being purchased. Put another way, since free-riding is possible (which is not the case for transparency standards), verification is needed.

The Effects of Complexity

The general hypothesis put forward in this paper is that policy convergence among private standards will be demand driven: private rule makers seek to maximize the environmental and reputational benefits to those using their rules. Reputational benefits accrue when standard users can claim that they are responsible global citizens taking voluntary action to combat climate change. Reputational benefits are contingent on high environmental quality: if users choose low quality standards, they cannot make the same "green" claims. Thus, if the hypothesis holds, we should also expect private rule makers to be concerned about signaling the quality of their standards to potential users. A second benefit that private standards can provide is to minimize users' exposure to switching costs or future regulatory requirements. If this hypothesis holds, we should expect private rule makers to be concerned about the interoperability of their rules with others, particularly public rules.

There are two main observable implications of the hypothesis. First, we should expect these private standards to exhibit high amounts of compatibility. If private actors within the regime complex are concerned about their users' exposure to future regulatory costs, or about switching costs more generally, they will try to "hedge their bets" by maximizing their compatibility with other standards. Maximizing compatibility increases the likelihood that their rules will continue to be usable in a future regulatory regime. In particular, we should expect to see compatibility between private and public standards. Second, if private rule makers are concerned about providing reputational benefits to their users, they will try to maximize compatibility with those that they perceive as high quality. Thus, we should observe a race to the top, which eventually produces leaders among the myriad private standards. Conversely, if private actors are unconcerned about the quality of competing standards, then we should not see the emergence of particularly important private standards. In fact, the analysis below demonstrates that both predicted effects—high levels of compatibility and the emergence of private leaders—are observed.

To analyze the effects of complexity, I draw on two sources of data. First, I map the connections among standards through network analysis to show the degree of compatibility among them. The nodes represent each of the standards that meet the criteria described above. The ties represent whether there is recognition of the standards through the procedures detailed in the previous section. Second, I augment the network analysis with data gathered from semi-structured interviews with the standards organizations from which I asked basic questions about motivations for the creation of the standard and considerations about compatibility.

Figure 17.3 shows the network of carbon standards. The network is based on the original 30 private standards presented in the previous section; it then adds all of the other standards that these original 30 recognize. Whereas there are 30 private transnational standards measuring carbon, there are 41 standards in the network, including public standards.

Figure 17.3 suggests visually that a few standards are more important than others, given their number of ties. These include the Clean Development Mechanism (CDM), the Greenhouse Gas Protocol, the Verified Carbon Standard, the Climate Action Registry, and the family of ISO-14000 standards. As the discussion below indicates, while the visualization of the network provides a useful "first cut" at the key standards, more information, including the direction of these ties, is needed for a fuller interpretation.

Recognition operates in two ways. Standard A may accept Standard B. For example, the Carbon Neutral standard certifies entities that have offset 100 percent of their emissions. It accepts offsets from a variety of other private standards including the Gold Standard, the Chicago Climate Exchange, and the CDM. Alternatively, Standard A may appropri-

Figure 17.3 Network of Carbon Management Standards

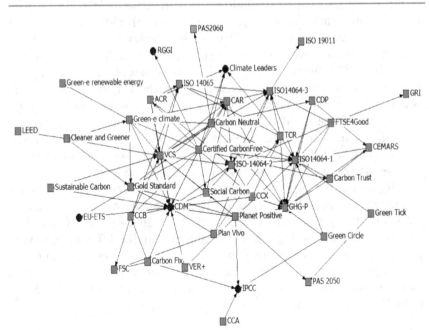

ate the rules and practices of Standard B. I operationalize recognition by examining the document(s), which outline the details of the standard. If this document specifically invokes the rules or practices of other standards or their verifiers, I code this as recognition. For example, the Climate, Community, and Biodiversity standard can be combined with a number of other offset standards to ensure that benefits beyond emissions reduction are achieved. Both acceptance of other standards and appropriation of parts of other standards constitute forms of recognition. It is important to note that this operationalization does not require mutual recognition. Standard A may recognize Standard B in one of the two specified ways, but Standard B may not recognize Standard A. Nonetheless, this one-way relationship is still coded as recognition. In the parlance of network analysis, this is a one-mode directed network.

Future Costs in the Regulatory Market

Descriptive analysis helps to understand the degree to which standards adopt a strategy of maximizing compatibility. A first cut at this hypothesis would predict a dense network, with high levels of recognition across all of the standards. In fact, the density of the network is rather low, at 14.2 percent. This means that only 14.2 percent of all possible ties among the offset standards are present. However, a more refined version of this hypothesis is that strategic actors will recognize the most important standards, rather than simply trying to recognize all of them. Indeed, this is the pattern we observe. Despite the low level of overall density, there are some standards in the network that are much better connected than others. The distribution of ties demonstrates a conscious strategy by private actors to connect to other specific standards in the network. This provides preliminary evidence that although there is an explosion in the number of private standards post-Kyoto, clearly some have emerged as more important—and indeed more credible—than others. In other words, to understand the strategic nature of compatibility, we must look beyond the overall density of the network to ties to specific actors.

To identify the important actors in the network, I turn to the centrality of individual standards. Because this is a directed network, we can examine who is being chosen by others (i.e., a measure of prestige) as well as who is doing the choosing. Choosers are important for diffusing regulatory practices, whereas those being chosen are important for the rules they create. I turn first to the prestigious actors—those who are chosen—and their characteristics. Table 17.2 shows normalized values for both indegree centrality (prestige) and outdegree centrality (diffusion).

Table 17.2 Centrality of All Standards in the Network

	Outdegree (normalized)		Indegree (normalized)
Certified CarbonFree	30	CDM	37.5
Carbon Neutral	25	ISO14064-1	30
Planet Positive	22.5	GHG-P	27.5
VCS	12.5	VCS	22.5
CAR	12.5	ISO-14064-2	20
Green-e climate	12.5	ISO14064-3	17.5
TCR	12.5	CAR	12.5
ACR	12.5	Gold Standard	12.5
FTSE4Good	12.5	ISO 14065	12.5
CCB	10	Climate Leaders	10
Social Carbon	10	IPCC	10
CCX	10	Green-e climate	7.5
Carbon Fix	10	FSC	7.5
Cleaner and Greener	10	TCR	5
Plan Vivo	10	CCB	5
ISO14064-1	7.5	Social Carbon	5
ISO14064-3	7.5	CEMARS	5
Carbon Trust	7.5	PAS 2050	5
CDP	7.5	ACR	2.5
Green Circle	7.5	CCX	2.5
ISO-14064-2	5	Carbon Trust	2.5
Gold Standard	5	CDP	2.5
CEMARS	5	VER+	2.5
Green Tick	5	EU-ETS	2.5
Sustainable Carbon	5	Green-e renewable energy	2.5
ISO 14065	2.5	GRI	2.5
VER+	2.5	ISO 19011	2.5
CCA	2.5	LEED	2.5
CDM	0	PAS2060	2.5
GHG-P	0	RGGI	2.5
Climate Leaders	0	Certified CarbonFree	0
IPCC	0	Carbon Neutral	0
FSC	0	Planet Positive	0
PAS 2050	0	FTSE4Good	0
EU-ETS	0	Carbon Fix	0
Green-e renewable energy	0	Cleaner and Greener	0
GRI	0	Plan Vivo	0
ISO 19011	0	Green Circle	0

Figure 17.3 shows that the CDM is a key node in the network. The CDM, which was created by the Kyoto Protocol, allows developed countries to fund offset activities in the developing world to help meet their emissions targets. Quantitatively, it also has the highest level of prestige, as measured by indegree centrality. Of all standards, 37.5 percent have chosen to recognize the CDM's standards. Moreover, if the population is restricted to only those standards that include offsetting as an organizational goal, the proportion rises to 79 percent. The CDM is prestigious in the sense that many other standards are choosing it. In general, public standards tend to be more prestigious than private ones (.233), as indicated in Table 17.3.

The high level of recognition of this public standard can be understood as a response to future costs of regulation. Since it is unclear whether the CDM will remain in effect after the expiry of the Kyoto Protocol, maintaining compatibility with its standards is a reasonable strategy to ensure the continued relevance of private standards in the event that the CDM continues to operate. Moreover, it is an important way to demonstrate to the users of these standards that their voluntary efforts may be consistent with future regulatory requirements.

Another interesting potential effect of the CDM's prestige is the likelihood that the standards set by the CDM will persist, even if the institution itself does not. This suggests the possibility of long-term residual effects of public rules within the seeming chaos of the regime complex. Even if the intergovernmental process continues to deteriorate, the strength of publicly created rules is being reaffirmed and embedded through private actors.[29]

Interestingly, although the CDM is the most prestigious of all the standards in the network, it is the anomaly among the public standards in the network. The dark circles in Figure 17.3 are national and international

Table 17.3 Similarity Matrix for Selected Network Attributes

	Age	Public?	Private?	Outdegree (normalized)	Indegree (normalized)
Age	1.000	0.221	−0.221	−0.289	0.173
Public?	0.221	1.000	−1.000	−0.363	0.233
Private?	−0.221	−1.000	1.000	0.363	−0.233
Outdegree (normalized)	−0.289	−0.363	0.363	1.000	−0.222
Indegree (normalized)	0.173	0.233	−0.233	−0.222	1.000

public carbon standards. There are only five named by the original thirty private standards: the CDM, the EU Emissions Trading Scheme, Climate Leaders (a voluntary program created by the US EPA), the Regional Greenhouse Gas Initiative (an emissions trading system in the Northeast of the US), and the Intergovernmental Panel on Climate Change. All except for Climate Leaders have prestige values below the mean.

The low level of prestige of the other public standards provides additional support for the regulatory uncertainty explanation. There is no need to hedge when the trajectory of these standards is clearly established. Put another way, there appears to be no demand for private authority in these instances. The EU-ETS, despite implementation challenges, is firmly established, as are the myriad accounting procedures established by the IPCC. Two other public standards are on their way out: Climate Leaders is being phased out, and the Chicago Climate Exchange is transitioning from a market to an offsets program. The Regional Greenhouse Gas Initiative was created in spite of the intransigence of the US federal government. Although it is pursuing links to other regional programs in the US, this process is still in its preliminary stages. Thus, it has yet to establish itself as a well-functioning and prominent set of rules. Hedging through recognition would be premature at this point.

Competition for Quality Among Private Standards

Private standards are seeking to maximize their flexibility with respect to public rules under the CDM. But this fact does not explain recognition among private rules. Surely, these private standards are unlikely to become public law. This raises the question: why recognize other private standards? The reason for recognition, I argue, stems from the need to demonstrate quality to standard users.

The explosion of private standards following the entry into force of the Kyoto Protocol created great variability among the quality of standards. Higher quality standards, concerned about establishing and maintaining their reputation, sought to associate themselves with other high quality standards—creating a club of standards that lead the pack in terms of prestige. An examination of the network shows that not all standards are created equal. Despite an overall low density of the network, there are several clear leaders among private standards, which enjoy high levels of prestige; they provide evidence for the concern about credibility. Interestingly, the most prestigious standards, both public and private, tend to be older; there is a small, positive correlation between the age of a standard and its level of prestige, or indegree centrality (0.173) as indicated in Table 17.3.

Along with the CDM, there are five other particularly prestigious standards (greater than one SD above the mean), as demonstrated by Table 17.2. Three ISO standards (for simplicity, referred to as the 14064 series) are very frequently recognized by others. Two of these are accounting standards (1 and 3), and the third is used for measuring offsets (2). The GHG Protocol was the basis for ISO 14064-1; hence many other standards recognize both ISO [14064-1] and the GHG Protocol, which are substantively very similar.[30] Finally, the Verified Carbon Standard, an offset standard that emphasizes its compatibility with the CDM, is also frequently selected by others—22.5 percent of all possible incoming ties are present. Together, these seven standards represent 40 percent of the total ties in the network. . . .

[Many] of those interviewed emphasized the importance of credibility, both for their own standards, and for those that they recognize. This translates most frequently into openness, transparency, widespread consultation with interested parties, and periodic review of the rules and their application. . . .

Thus, the rapid growth of carbon standards coupled with their individual concerns about maintaining credibility gave rise to an important effect: clear leaders have emerged among the patchwork of private carbon standards. Institutional complexity has produced some consensus about which carbon standards should be used: those that are transparent, have had an open drafting process, and have been (and continue to be) the subject of rigorous review. . . . High quality standards have emerged, and they are at the center of the network.

Diffusion of Leading Practices

High quality standards do not simply appear; they are made. One way they are made is through recognition by other standards. I turn now to the "choosers" of standards, as indicated by their outdegree centrality. These are important consumers of standards, enhancing the network effects of those with high prestige. Interestingly, the most outdegree central standards are all private: Certified CarbonFree, Carbon Neutral and Planet Positive. Certified CarbonFree, for example, recognizes 30 percent of all standards in the network. This provides additional support for the hypothesis: private standards are hedging by maximizing compatibility with other standards, both public and private. One effect of hedging is to reinforce the importance of public rules. A second effect, as indicated in this section, is to create leaders among private standards.

Indeed an analysis of the key players in the network shows that two private standards are the best connected: VCS and ISO 14064-1 reach 98 percent of the network via a maximum of one intermediary. The high prestige (as indicated in the previous section) and the impressive reach of these two standards provide additional evidence that quality standards occupy key positions in the network. Other standards are also recognized by public entities. The Australian government also recognizes the Gold Standard. The California cap and trade system is basing its offset standards on those created by the Climate Action Reserve.

By contrast, four of the five public standards have an outdegree centrality of zero. The CDM, RGGI, Climate Leaders and the IPCC have not chosen to recognize any other standards. The one exception is the EU-ETS, which accepts offsets generated under CDM standards. Again, this underscores the finding that private rules, rather than public ones, are serving as diffusers of authority. This is further evidenced by an observed correlation between private standards and outdegree centrality, illustrated in Table 17.3. Private rules are correlated with recognizing more standards (.363); by contrast, public rules are correlated with being recognized by more standards (.233).

In sum, the network analysis points to three drivers of convergence. First, private standards' desire to maintain relevance for their users in the face of future regulatory changes has led almost all offset standards to recognize the rules created under the CDM. Second, the need for credibility has given rise to a set of leading private standards, which are more prestigious (in the sense of network centrality) than other private standards in the network. The former "wild west" of carbon markets is consolidating around a clear set of leaders. Third, the fact that private standards tend to have higher outdegree centrality shows their important role as diffusers of leading standards—both public and private. By contrast, public standards virtually never choose to link themselves to other standards, with the one exception of the EU-ETS and the CDM. The interaction among public and private actors shows that private actors, not public ones, are reacting to the need to signal quality and minimize the costs of future regulatory changes. This has had the unanticipated effect of producing some convergence around what constitutes a good standard for measuring and managing carbon.

Conclusion

Complexity is not the same as chaos. This paper shows an emerging order in the complex institutional landscape that governs climate change. The mix of public and private actors and their accompanying standards for GHG management provides new spaces for interaction and unexpected effects. The presence of private actors, coupled with concerns about demonstrating credibility and providing benefits for users, has reaffirmed the importance of the CDM rules and produced clear leaders among private rules. Bumpus and Liverman argued that the private standards are "a network of often small private organizations and NGOs [which exist] without reference to national or supranational bodies or higher levels of administration."[31] Evidence here suggests otherwise. Rather, a distinct order—and even a hierarchy—has emerged out of the messy landscape of carbon standards. There is an order emerging from the chaos.

Three main arguments can be derived from the data. First, institutional complexity is, well, complex. It is incumbent upon scholars to recognize the full range of variation with respect to complexity, and this means including sources of private authority. To exclude private authority is to exclude a key form of variation. Second, when we include private authority, we observe public authority in a different light—as the hub for carbon rules within the broader regime complex. Third, the literature on regime complexity tends to emphasize the negative effects of complexity, as an engine for further chaos that fuels strategies of forum shopping, and opportunities for exploitation of ambiguities. However, this paper shows that it also provides an opportunity for convergence.

There are several broader implications of these findings both for theory and for policy. With respect to policy, the future of carbon markets remains uncertain. Decisions taken at Durban affirmed a second commitment period for Kyoto. However, this decision trades one type of uncertainty (whether the compliance market will persist) for another (whether or not there will be a gap between the two periods). Durban also created a new, yet-to-be-defined market mechanism, and reaffirmed a future role for REDD+. All of these developments suggest that private rule makers should continue to be concerned about future regulatory requirements, and by extension about interoperability with public standards as well as leading private standards. Moreover, the possibility of a future REDD market has led a number [of] private rule makers to develop standards for this potential market. Indeed, roughly one-third of all credits traded on the voluntary market in 2010 were REDD projects. Since the CDM explicitly excluded avoided deforestation as a source of credits, there are no public rules in place. It appears that private rule makers are leading the way in this regard.

In addition, there are three key theoretical implications of the analysis presented here. First, this paper demonstrates that convergence may have a distinct flavor under conditions of complexity. Clearly, it does not mean the consolidation of myriad institutions. Rather, convergence results in an emergence of some sense of order across these diverse sets of rules and actors. Much work remains to be done to elaborate both the mechanisms that produce order within complex institutions, and the conditions under which we might expect such order to emerge.

Second, despite harsh criticism and general pessimism about the Kyoto Protocol, there may yet be a silver lining. The offset standards created by the CDM are now well embedded in private standards operating in the voluntary market. Some of these standards are even recognized by governments. It is very likely that these rules are here to stay. Thus, it is reasonable to expect that the present rules on carbon will affect future ones. With private standards as faithful users and diffusers (and in some cases, improvers), CDM rules will likely provide a common baseline for future offsets.

Third, and related, the case of carbon standards is redefining the nature of "public." The interactions between public and private show the ways in which public goods—emissions reductions—are being created and provided through a complex network structure and heterogeneous actors. As politicians and scholars wrestle with ways to provide global public goods, they must keep this definitional shift in mind. Finally, studies of regulatory dynamics suggest conditions under which we can expect to upward or downward harmonization. This paper shows that we should include private regulation in the mix as one of the potential explanations.

Notes

1. Keohane, Robert O., and David G. Victor. 2011. The Regime Complex for Climate Change. *Perspectives on Politics* 9 (1): 7–23.

2. Tarrow, Sidney. 2001. Transnational Politics: Contention and Institutions in International Politics. *Annual Review of Political Science* 4: 1–20, p. 15. I am grateful to Bob Keohane for suggesting this metaphor.

3. Cashore, Benjamin. 2002. Legitimacy and the Privatization of Environmental Governance: How Non-State Market Driven Systems Gain Rule-Making Authority. *Governance* 15 (4): 508–529.

4. Biermann, Frank, and Philipp Pattberg. 2008. Global Environmental Governance: Taking Stock, Moving Forward. *Annual Review of Environment and Resources* 33 (1): 277–294.

5. Pattberg, Philipp, and Johannes Stripple. 2008. Beyond the Public and Private Divide: Remapping Transnational Climate Governance in the 21st Century. *International Environmental Agreements* 8 (4): 389–408.

6. Bernstein, Steven, Michele Betsill, Matthew Hoffmann, and Matthew Paterson. 2010. A Tale of Two Copenhagens: Carbon Markets and Climate Governance. *Millennium—Journal of International Studies* 39 (1): 161–173, p. 168.

7. Lövbrand, Eva, and Johannes Stripple. 2011. Making Climate Change Governable: Accounting for Carbon as Sinks, Credits and Personal Budgets. *Critical Policy Studies* 5 (2): 187–200; Lovell, Heather, and Diana Liverman. 2010. Understanding Carbon Offset Technologies. *New Political Economy* 15 (2): 255–273.

8. Raustiala, Kal, and David G. Victor. 2004. The Regime Complex for Plant Genetic Resources. *International Organization* 58 (2): 277–309, p. 279.

9. Keohane and Victor 2011, cited in note 1.

10. Alter, Karen J., and Sophie Meunier. 2009. The Politics of International Regime Complexity. *Perspectives on Politics* 7 (1): 13–24.

11. Hoffmann, Matthew J. 2011. *Climate Governance at the Crossroads.* Oxford: Oxford University Press.

12. Knill, Christoph. 2005. Cross-national Policy Convergence: Concepts, Approaches and Explanatory Factors. *Journal of European Public Policy* 12 (5): 764–774, p. 768.

13. Vogel, David. 1997. *Trading Up: Consumer and Environmental Regulation in a Global Economy.* Cambridge, MA: Harvard University Press.

14. Simmons, Beth A. 2001. The International Politics of Harmonization: The Case of Capital Market Regulation. *International Organization* 55 (3): 589–620.

15. Drezner, Daniel W. 2007. *All Politics Is Global: Explaining International Regulatory Regimes.* Princeton, NJ: Princeton University Press.

16. McNamara, Kathleen. 1999. Consensus and Constraint: Ideas and Capital Mobility in European Monetary Integration. *Journal of Common Market Studies* 37 (3): 455–476.

17. Knill 2005, cited in note 12.

18. Cashore, Benjamin, Graeme Auld, and Deanna Newsom. 2004. *Governing Through Markets: Forest Certification and the Emergence of Non-state Authority.* New Haven, CT: Yale University Press.

19. Bernstein, Steven, and Benjamin Cashore. 2007. Can Non-state Global Governance Be Legitimate? An Analytical Framework. *Regulation and Governance* 1 (1): 1–25.

20. Sabel, Charles F., Dara O'Rourke, and Archon Fung. 2000. Ratcheting Labor Standards: Regulation for Continuous Improvement in the Global Workplace. KSG Working Paper No. 00-010. Cambridge, MA: Harvard University, p. 2.

21. Ruggie, John Gerard. 2002. The Theory and Practice of Learning Networks: Corporate Social Responsibility and the Global Compact. *Journal of Corporate Citizenship* 5 (Spring): 27–36.

22. Fransen, Luc. 2011. Why Do Private Governance Organizations Not Converge? A Political-Institutional Analysis of Transnational Labor Standards Regulation. *Governance* 24 (2): 359–387, p. 361.

23. Michonski, Katherine, and Michael Levi. 2010. *Harnessing International Institutions to Address Climate Change.* New York: Council on Foreign Relations; for exceptions, see Bernstein et al. 2010, cited in note 6; Okereke, Chukwumerije, Harriet Bulkeley, and Heike Schroeder. 2008. Conceptualizing Climate Governance Beyond the International Regime. *Global Environmental Politics* 9 (1): 58–78.

24. Hafner-Burton, Emilie. 2009. The Power Politics of Regime Complexity: Human Rights Trade Conditionality in Europe. *Perspectives on Politics* 7 (1): 33–37.

25. Wasserman, Stanley, and Katherine Faust. 1994. *Social Network Analysis: Methods and Applications.* Cambridge: Cambridge University Press.

26. Gilpin, Robert. 1987. *The Political Economy of International Relations.* Princeton: Princeton University Press, p. 11.

27. Strange, Susan. 1996. *The Retreat of the State.* Cambridge: Cambridge University Press, p. 4.

28. Victor, David G., and Joshua C. House. 2004. A New Currency: Climate Change and Carbon Credits. *Harvard International Review* (2): 56–59.

29. Lovell, Heather C. 2010. Governing the Carbon Offset Market. *Wiley Interdisciplinary Reviews: Climate Change* 1 (3): 353–362.

30. Green, Jessica F. 2010. Private Standards in the Climate Regime: The Greenhouse Gas Protocol. *Business and Politics* 12 (3).

31. Bumpus, Adam G., and Diana Liverman. 2008. Accumulation by Decarbonization and the Governance of Carbon Offsets. *Economic Geography* 84 (2): 127–155, p. 141.

18

Global Human Rights Monitoring, New Technologies, and the Politics of Information

Philip Alston and Colin Gillespie

Antonio Cassese was a jurist of great vision and creative imagination.
. . . In his final work—*Realizing Utopia*—he took it upon himself to
spell out his vision for "a global community grounded in a core of
human rights." . . . [Cassese] was largely disillusioned with the ability
of the mass media to focus any sustained attention on human rights
issues, and he relied instead on international civil society to fulfill that
role. He saw that group as consisting mainly of "the most independent,
impartial, and proactive nongovernmental organizations" and emphasized their roles in: (i) "gathering and disseminating information"; (ii)
"drawing publicity to issues"; and (iii) "acting as the moral voice of the
international community."[1] . . . [He stressed] the importance of developing methods of fact finding that would enable international courts and
other bodies to respond more effectively to serious violations of human
rights. After highlighting the limitations of official bodies, including the
UN, to fulfill this role, and criticizing the International Committee of the
Red Cross for its policy of confidentiality, he placed Human Rights
Watch and Amnesty International at the forefront of the efforts to provide
the factual basis upon which the international community can act. . . .

[The] central role that Cassese saw for a very small number of international NGOs—and he generally referred specifically only to Amnesty
International and Human Rights Watch—raises a number of important
questions. Is it appropriate in the 21st century to rely so heavily upon
such a small group of actors? How effectively do these actors interact
with the human rights movement as a whole, and even with one another?

Reprinted from *The European Journal of International Law*, vol. 23, no. 4: 1089–
1123. © 2012 by Oxford University Press. Reprinted by permission of the publisher.
Edited for length.

Are the methods of work on which they rely sufficiently collaborative, transparent, and self-correcting as to warrant such weight being placed upon them? And are they making effective use of new information and communications technologies to reach out to broader constituencies and take full advantage of the opportunities available?

[In this article] we can do little more than highlight some of the deficiencies that currently exist and seek to start a more vibrant debate within the human rights community as to the ideal vision of information gathering and sharing for a 21st century. . . .

Our analysis begins with an effort to understand the strengths and weaknesses of the existing system in terms of how effectively it gathers information and how comprehensive is the resulting picture. Our analysis assumes that although the community of international human rights monitors consists of a large number of individual actors pursuing diverse goals and with widely varying mandates, it is also necessary to consider its results in overall or aggregate terms rather than just by focusing on its individual components. In other words, we want to know not only how comprehensive or systematic the monitoring undertaken by the leading NGOs is but also what the sum of the parts looks like. . . .

[In this article we seek] to provide a snapshot of the *status quo* by examining extrajudicial executions and the extent to which major incidents of such killings over the past decade or so have been reported upon by the entities which would be most likely to monitor such events. . . .

In order to generate the data necessary to provide a picture of the current situation, we analysed the reporting results of four of the key entities that systematically monitor significant incidents of extrajudicial killings. They include the two largest international NGOs in the human rights field, which are also the ones consistently invoked by Cassese—Human Rights Watch (HRW) and Amnesty International (AI). In addition, for reasons explained below, we also include the UN Special Rapporteur on extrajudicial, summary, or arbitrary executions (the SR) and the United States Department of State (the SD). Given that the definition of extrajudicial executions used by the UN and by human rights groups generally is very wide-ranging, it would be impossible to monitor all such killings that take place around the world and extremely difficult to identify the range of such killings which are subsequently taken up and reported on by the four entities. In order to make the research manageable, the focus of this article is on those incidents involving extrajudicial executions which reached a sufficient level of public concern or prominence within the relevant community as to warrant the creation of a Commission of Inquiry (CoI), which would most typically be under government auspices but entrusted to the judiciary or some other relatively independent body.

Assessing the Extent of Information Dispersal

[Global] information dispersal in relation to [a human rights] issue such as extrajudicial executions is problematic. [We focus on extrajudicial executions as a proxy to illustrate problems that occur] when groups (whether governments, corporations, or NGOs) fail to collect or incorporate directly relevant information possessed by other individuals or groups for use in their overall decision-making matrix. As a result, decisions are based on incomplete or partial information. In some situations, the resulting costs may be minimal, but in others they may well be significant.

In the human rights field, information can be considered dispersed when different organizations possess certain data relating to a given situation which they will generally . . . make more widely available, but where it is not straightforward, let alone routine, for the disparate information to be brought together. The argument is not, of course, that an interested party needs to consult the websites of Human Rights Watch, Amnesty International, and the US State Department in order to get a balanced picture, although the fragmented or partial picture that each of them presents in relation to a given situation is a concern. Rather it is that there is a much broader array of actors relevant to any given human rights situation who possess highly relevant information which is not able to be made available in a meaningful way and injected into the broader information database on which decisions are based. We argue that such dispersal is problematic, and in what follows we seek to explain why.

There have been various proposals to produce a single authoritative analysis of the human rights situation in any given country. When the SD reports were being honed and expanded in the early years of the Carter Administration, an idea was floated that those reports could become a single authoritative source by encouraging collaboration and taking account of other reports. But the human rights community gave the suggestion short shrift and the idea was promptly abandoned. Critics argued that there was no such thing as a single revealed truth, that the emphasis and even the information included would always reflect the values, interests, and perceptions of both the original fact-finder and the ultimate compiler. Others noted that there was value in diversity, in terms both of the information collected and of the interpretations placed upon it. In other words, despite the hallowed place accorded to what the human rights community called "fact-finding," there can be no such thing as neutral, objective "finding" of facts. . . .

So the question then is whether the insights gained from these earlier explorations of information centralizing approaches should lead us immediately to dismiss any suggestion that acknowledged problems of information dispersal should be considered a matter of concern today. Our . . . concern is to ensure that the diverse perspectives and approaches that are already available in relation to a given issue are more readily accessible and that the key entities undertaking information generation in relation to a given issue are more consistently aware of relevant information already available elsewhere.

What are the advantages of reducing information dispersal and encouraging better information sharing? The first is improved efficiency. Better information sharing can help to avoid replication of effort, and make it easier for each of the stakeholders to target their own inquiries and fact-finding efforts more effectively and efficiently. . . . The second is expanded participation. The involvement of a wider range of sources in the provision of information and making those diverse sources more accessible will help to increase the number and diversity of actors involved. The third is enhancing the reliability of the information by creating a more effective market place of ideas. The key actors would sometimes be challenged to reconcile their own fact-finding with different results emerging from other sources. The battle for accuracy would no longer rely essentially on the cut and thrust between governments and individual fact-finders, which is often so polarized and adversarial as to shed relatively little light on the disputed facts. Instead, the perspectives of the major entities would be contrasted and compared with the expected outcome of greater accuracy and fewer errors. In general, it seems that such aggregations of data are likely to produce a more accurate overall result. . . . The fourth advantage is to provide greater reinforcement in terms of the persuasiveness of the information generated and the message that is being promoted, although this will also depend very much on the methods that are used for collecting and aggregating the information, as we discuss below.

We next argue that the sample of comparative results analysed here constitutes a convincing proxy for illustrating the extent to which the human rights monitoring system in general is characterized by extensive information dispersal. We thus need to justify the focus on: (i) extrajudicial executions; (ii) CoIs as a relevant and convincing benchmark; (iii) the specific entities selected as being representative of the international regime in this context.

It is axiomatic in terms of international human rights law that there is no fixed, official hierarchy of rights. . . . We can, however, point to the centrality of the right to life in the overall human rights framework, its listing at the top of virtually any charter of human rights, and the comparative emphasis that is accorded to it in the jurisprudence of human rights courts and other forums. In addition, human rights implementation is also heavily focused on the other principal dimension of extrajudicial executions which is upholding the obligation of the state to investigate, prosecute, and punish all infringements of the right to life, whether carried out by state agents or others.[2] It is thus unsurprising that one of Amnesty International's major early campaigns, in the 1970s, focused specifically on this phenomenon, or that the first of the individual Special Rapporteurs appointed by the UN Commission on Human Rights to deal with a thematic mandate was mandated to examine "summary or arbitrary executions."[3]

The centrality of the phenomenon is also reflected in the fact that the Annual Report prepared by the State Department's Bureau of Democracy, Human Rights and Labor emphasizes efforts to prevent unlawful killings. Thus, every entry in the annual country reports on human rights begins with the thematic issue of unlawful killings.

In [the following] section we briefly examine the reasons for selecting the four representative monitoring entities and examine the extent to which each purports to undertake comprehensive, as opposed to selective, monitoring on an issue such as extrajudicial executions.

NGOs: Amnesty International and Human Rights Watch

In any given country there may be individual civil society groups which provide more detailed and extensive information about specific incidents or rights, but in terms of global reporting two organizations stand out: Amnesty International (AI) and Human Rights Watch (HRW). . . . AI and HRW are the most systematic NGO sources for global reporting on executions. Nevertheless, both acknowledge that their reporting is not comprehensive. . . . AI does not purport to be comprehensive and insists that silence on a given issue is not to be interpreted as implying that a state is respecting the right in question. HRW explicitly disavows any claim to be comprehensive, and adds that not all available information relating to the countries in which HRW is active is reflected in the report. But these annual reports by AI and HRW are supplemented by a great many stand-alone country or thematic reports. . . .

The United Nations: The Special Rapporteur on Extrajudicial Executions

Within the UN context, there are many potential sources of information about extrajudicial executions in a given country. The problem is that most of those sources do not publish reports on the matter, let alone compile statistics. It is clear that agencies and offices such as the Office of the High Commissioner for Human Rights (OHCHR), the Office of the UN High Commissioner for Refugees (UNHCR), the Office for the Coordination of Humanitarian Assistance (OCHA), and a range of others will be engaged in collecting information that will at least touch upon, even if only by way of background, major human rights violations, and that this would generally include significant instances of extrajudicial executions. But whether because they see human rights as extraneous to their specific mandates, they do not believe that they can adequately substantiate such reports, they fear the political fallout from exposing such information, or for diverse other reasons, none of these agencies undertake systematic, publicly available, monitoring of extrajudicial executions.

There is, however, one actor who is charged with an explicit responsibility in this regard, and that is the Special Rapporteur on extrajudicial, summary, or arbitrary executions appointed by the Human Rights Council. The first SR was appointed in 1982 and detailed annual reports have been submitted to the Council (or its predecessor, the Commission on Human Rights) every year since 1983. While these reports contain a wealth of information about allegations of extrajudicial executions on a global basis, the reports are nonetheless considerably less comprehensive than might be expected. Several restrictions account for this restricted coverage. First, there are severe resource constraints, which means that the SR can only act, and thus eventually report, upon a limited number of the cases actually drawn to his or her attention in any given year. Secondly, in theory the SR is supposed to react only to cases brought to his or her attention, rather than being pro-active. And, thirdly, because an unlawful killing constitutes a violation of human rights only in cases in which the government concerned has not taken the necessary action to investigate, prosecute, and punish, there is a presumption that the SR will only take up cases in which the government has demonstrably failed in its obligations, or seems likely to do so.

Governments: The US State Department Reports

While governments are important sources of human rights information, their contributions are all too often confined to defending their allies and criticizing those with whom they have generally poor relations. While various governments have sought to distance themselves from this stereo-type, only one has opted to publish a comprehensive report on the state of human rights in all countries in the world. The US State Department's annual volumes of *Country Reports on Human Rights* are the result of a congressional mandate, which began in the early 1970s as an effort to compel the executive to take greater account of human rights in both its foreign relations and its foreign aid policies. While the original focus was only on those states receiving US aid, the number of countries dealt with has since grown to encompass all member states of the UN. Although civil society groups have regularly criticized some aspects of the reports, especially in relation to highly controversial issues or to states with which the US has especially close or especially strained relations, the reports are considered by many to be reasonably balanced and accurate and to con-stitute an important source of additional information.[4] . . .

Nonetheless, it might reasonably be questioned whether the State Department reports are sufficiently objective or accurate to warrant being included as a major reference point in our study. There are grounds upon which their objectivity could be challenged, such as reluctance to be strongly critical of embattled allies. Their even-handedness could be questioned, in terms of the weight accorded to different issues, their thor-oughness in relation to some countries and not others, and the diversity of sources used in practice.[5] And, most importantly, their nature and scope have changed significantly over the years, making it dubious to rely upon them to undertake a close comparison between the situation in a given country in 2012 compared with some earlier period.

The principal response lies in the fact that these reports have consis-tently been relied upon by scholars undertaking empirical analyses in order to assess the impact of the human rights regimes.[6] . . .

Commissions of Inquiry as a Proxy for Reporting

CoIs to investigate killings are set up in relation to only a relatively small number of the extrajudicial executions committed in the world. But it is their relatively uncommon occurrence that makes them attrac-tive as a unit of analysis. In essence, they are generally set up only when the relevant domestic police and/or judicial processes have been shown to be inadequate to the task of conducting an effective and impartial investigation. In addition to the inability of the normal mech-anisms to deal with the problem, there would generally need to be sig-nificant domestic and/or international pressure upon the government to take steps to demonstrate that it is fighting against impunity. Although there may well be questions as to what exactly constitutes a CoI, the basic concept is well known to international human rights law and is dealt with at some length in important soft law instruments such as the UN Principles on the Effective Prevention and Investigation of Extralegal, Arbitrary, and Summary Executions. . . .

Given both the legal and other pressures upon governments to establish a CoI, and the propensity of many governments to follow that path, this becomes a valid and practical yardstick by which to measure the coverage achieved by different monitoring groups in relation to extrajudicial executions.

Processing the Data

We surveyed the materials that are available online in relation to each of the four monitoring groups and conducted searches for CoIs. Because of the different availability and structures of the relevant websites, this process involved much more than a straightforward electronic search for that term. By way of example, we searched also for references to inquiries that were not listed as CoIs *per se*, because they had been named after the individuals who were heading them. Wherever it seemed that a given monitoring group had omitted a reference to a CoI identified by one of the others we did an additional search using all likely alternative terminologies in order to confirm that the relevant CoI had not been acknowledged under a different nomenclature.

Although there are extensive searchable online records available from three of the four sources that date back prior to 1999, we took that year as our starting point because it marked the beginning of the SD reports being placed online. From that date onwards our search covered the following decade so that we included reports from all sources, including the SD, up to and including 2009.

Based on this methodology, we recorded reports of 81 CoIs into unlawful killings during the 10-year period. Those inquiries were conducted by 42 states and one non-state entity (Hamas) and they related to killings in an array of different contexts such as post-election violence, the unlawful use of police force, or the activities of death squads.

The most interesting findings concern the extent of crossover reporting from one source to another. Of the 81 reports of CoIs, only six are common to all four of the reporting sources; 16 are reported by three of the institutions, and 16 by two. Most surprisingly, however, fully 43 of the CoIs into unlawful killings, or more than half, are reported by only one of the institutions.

How might one account for the high number of "orphan" CoIs? One explanation would be that the different institutions have different mandates and use different *modus operandi*. The SR, for example, functions in more of a reactive way, seeking to intervene in situations in which appropriate action has not been taken by the governments concerned. Thus, where a CoI has been set up and is conducting an effective inquiry, there may be no compelling reason for the SR to become involved. This would help to explain why the SR's reports reflect, by a wide margin, the lowest count of CoIs—only 12 are mentioned during the period 1999–2009. Conversely, the SD's role is retrospective in the sense that it looks back after a year and takes note of all relevant developments. It is thus not surprising that it leads all the other institutions in reporting on 58 distinct CoIs during the decade. It is also in the best position to piggy-back on the work of the others. Although, of course, that raises the question why its reports do not track an even higher percentage of the total number of CoIs.

AI and HRW can be seen to be somewhere in the middle. Their responsiveness to relevant incidents will be significantly influenced by the severity of the violations alleged. Other occurrences might either go below their radar screens or be deemed not sufficiently significant to warrant being reported upon. This is also consistent with the high score achieved by the SD, since 15 of the 19 reports that were unique to its databases related to incidents in which the number of people alleged to have been unlawfully killed was small.

These suggested explanations for the differences or discrepancies do not, however, provide a comprehensive explanation. Take, for example, the reporting on CoIs in Ethiopia. HRW documented targeted killings by the military against members of the Anuak, a local ethnic group, in 2005, and the subsequent setting up of a CoI to look into these killings. The SD followed HRW's lead on this, reporting on the killings and also on the CoI, and couching its criticisms of the CoI in language nearly identical to that of HRW. In the same year, demonstrators were killed in post-election violence, and an additional CoI was set up to investigate these deaths. HRW did not, however, note this development despite the fact that it concerned a state in which it was already doing work and involved a significant number of killings. In contrast, the SD did report on the CoI. AI, for its part, seems to have recorded neither of these CoIs.

What conclusions may be drawn from this example? The first is simply that the reporting of each institution is incomplete. One response might be that this is not a problem since anyone interested in Ethiopia will be following and aggregating the reports of all of the institutions.

But if the institutions themselves are not taking account of relevant information publicly available elsewhere, it seems unlikely that most external and less well briefed observers are likely to do it, or even to know that such diligence would be needed. In this instance, the failure to share the information on the negative impact of one CoI—into killings of the Anuak—allows for an incomplete picture of CoIs in Ethiopia to emerge. As a result, international actors might continue to call for CoIs to be set up by this government, without the knowledge that two had failed in close proximity to one another. This is a good illustration of a situation in which an institution might make poor decisions based on what appears to be insufficient information.

An even more instructive example concerns CoIs in Nigeria. According to the databases, Nigeria established, at either the federal or state level, 13 CoIs into unlawful killings. Of these 13 CoIs, one was reported on by three organizations, three were reported on by two (though not the same two), and the remaining nine were orphans, with the SD picking up only one, HRW noting five, and AI reporting on three. The first report included in the data came from HRW in 2001, in a report about killings in Jos (in Plateau State). In the next year the two NGOs and the SD reported on a CoI created in Benue, AI reported on a CoI looking into violence between police and students, and the SD reported on a CoI into an investigation linked to deaths for wandering onto an oilfield. AI also reported on the CoI first noted by HRW into violence in Jos. The following year, 2003, HRW noted in two separate reports that CoIs had been established in 2000 and 2002.

Two issues emerge from the reconstruction of this timeline. The first is the problem of dispersed information and the failure to bring together diverse data sources available to one or other of the reporting institutions. The second is linked to this. None of the CoIs resulted in a public report, which most human rights experts would consider to be a fatal flaw in terms of the likelihood of having an impact on governmental policy or conduct. But because of the dispersal of the data this information was never brought to light at the time. As a result, it was neither surprising nor inappropriate for the SR and the NGOs to continue to endorse the validity of this technique in the Nigerian context. Should the information possessed by the various institutions have been brought together it seems probable that most actors would have raised questions about the value of such inquiries in Nigeria, and as a result have pursued a different, ideally more effective, strategy.

The preceding discussion only hopes to elucidate three main points that can be gleaned from a purely quantitative analysis of reports of

CoIs into unlawful killings found in four sources of data. The first is that, though one might hope that the four institutions, given their shared goals and visions, have identical information, or publicize the information they do have in such a way that they act as one another's auditors, they do not. The second point is that the discrepancies in this information cannot be explained solely on the grounds of the mandates of the various institutions. We have attempted to demonstrate this by looking at reporting about specific CoIs, and showing that gaps in information of various institutions do not depend on their mandates necessarily. The point is that not only is the human rights monitoring of none of the organizations comprehensive, but that even in situations in which one of the institutions, such as an NGO, limits the focus of its monitoring to a particular country or issue, its monitoring is not comprehensive. The third point is that these information deficits have real impacts for all of the institutions. In the case of NGOs, it means suggesting potentially inefficient solutions to problems. In the case of the SR, it means perhaps endorsing solutions that have little possibility of success.

The preceding analysis dealt primarily with the problem of information being dispersed across the various data sources. But there are also additional dimensions concerning the quality of the reporting. The first of these concerns a lack of follow up, and especially situations in which an actor calls for the setting up of a CoI into a killing but then fails to monitor or report on its effectiveness. The second concerns situations in which the effectiveness of a CoI simply cannot be determined based on the information about the CoI made available by the institutions.

The first issue is not an uncommon one. For example, in 2001 Algeria set up a CoI to look into the deaths of demonstrators in the Kabilya region. HRW sent an open letter to the President commending him for his action and urging, in particular, that the commission work with the special prosecutor to bring to justice those responsible for unlawful killings. Both AI and SD reported, at the conclusion of the CoI within the year, that no prosecutions had in fact taken place, although indemnities had been paid to the families of those killed. For its part, however, HRW does not seem to have followed up specifically on this CoI. In 2003, in the context of a new Algerian CoI inquiring into disappearances during the civil war, it urged the CoI not to relinquish the goal of pursuing prosecutions.

A comparable case study concerns an AI letter to the Governor of Rivers State in Nigeria in 2004 urging him to set up a CoI similar to one undertaken in a neighbouring state. However, AI did not follow up either in relation to this call for a new CoI or in relation to the existing

CoI to which its statement had referred, despite the stated objective of seeking to combat impunity.

Failure of institutions to follow up is problematic in two principal respects. First, it plays into the hands of those governments which have set up CoIs precisely in order to placate those calling for action, although the government concerned has no intention of ensuring a proper accounting. Secondly, it undermines the effectiveness of the strategy of naming and shaming by failing to ensure that the remedy that has been identified as appropriate is actually embraced in an authentic and meaningful manner.[7]

The second issue in this context concerns the extent to which the data provided by the reporting institutions in relation to CoIs are often very incomplete. In some cases this might be understandable even if not optimal. For example, where the reference is essentially a historical recounting of what has or has not been done, one might not expect to see a very detailed account. But even in these situations there might be much to be said in favor of a more extended analysis. In other situations, providing details would seem to be important both to enable an assessment to be made of the adequacy of the arrangements and to facilitate effective follow up by those with a stake or an interest in the inquiry. But many of the references to CoIs identified by our survey are in fact very brief. Thus, for example, the SD reports mention the creation of a CoI into deaths during a protest outside a mosque in Thailand, and give a concluding indication of the outcome before moving on to a separate and unrelated issue. An HRW report on the 2006 war in Lebanon with Hezbollah refers in a footnote to a CoI established in Israel. AI, after noting the existence of a CoI in Burundi and observing that it is unclear to what extent the inquiry was able to fulfill its mandate, makes no further mention of the CoI. These examples could be multiplied. We are not suggesting that the judgment call made by the reporting institution was necessarily problematic, but ideally there would be more information easily accessible somewhere in relation to the details of these inquiries.

Information Politics

The results that emerge from an empirical review of the reporting of each of these entities in relation to such CoIs may be succinctly stated as follows. None of the entities, on its own, provides anything like a comprehensive survey of the inquiries that have been set up to examine significant incidents of extrajudicial execution. While there is some overlap in reporting, it is far less than might be expected, given the attention that is usually generated at the national level as a result of the creation of a CoI. Reporting by one source is often not picked up in the reports or analyses of the others. Indeed, in many cases, information on major incidents involving extrajudicial executions seems to be the preserve of just one of the relevant monitoring groups. In other words, the picture that emerges is one of "dispersed information." The available information remains in the hands of a wide range of actors who are not in effective communication with one another. This raises the question as to how feasible it is either for the dispersed actors to pool their resources or for external actors to take steps to bring together at least some of the disparate sources in order to create a more comprehensive and integrated knowledge base. That question, in turn, is premised upon the assumption that this dispersal effect is in some respects problematic. In other words, there are costs that flow from the inability of the actors themselves, or of other interested parties, to obtain the broader, more detailed, and nuanced picture that would result from having access to the overall picture.

Formulating the issue in this way enables us to see that there are two quite separate analytical levels at which we need to operate. The first, the micro level, concerns the aspirations, claims, policies and methodologies of the individual entities. Are they happy with, or at least resigned to accepting, the situation that emerges from the survey? In other words, would they defend the rather selective and partial nature of the information that each of them accumulates and publicizes? Would they be content to proffer the simple defense that such selectivity and partialness are an inevitable and proper result of factors such as resource constraints, staffing limitations, the need to pick and choose by way of prioritizing certain situations and issues over others at any given time, and the limits imposed upon them by their mandates or missions?

While we would question the desirability of the *status quo* from the perspective of each of the individual entities, those are policy issues for the relevant actors to consider and not for us to resolve. Instead, our concern is with the macro level implications so that the question becomes whether the international human rights "community" or "movement," for want of better terms, is best served by contenting itself with an outcome that results in the relevant information remaining widely dispersed? In other words, are there alternatives to the existing system in which the key monitors do not seek to pool the information they collect, despite the fact that their respective staffs are in regular contact with one another? Are there reasons relating not to logistics or technical problems but rather to the politics of information that explain why the extremely valuable information that they generate remains dispersed and not effectively integrated into a larger, more coherent, and perhaps ultimately even more compelling pool of data? Can the problems of fragmentation and limited accessibility which seem to characterize the existing situation be overcome, at least in some measure?

Before proceeding, it needs to be acknowledged that each of the major reporting institutions surveyed in this article has strong and even compelling justifications for not taking on more than they have chosen to do with the inevitably limited resources available to them. But this is also where the politics of information management within the human rights regime comes into play. In other words, we need to focus on the broader questions of who collects what information, by what means, and from which sources, how is it shared and disseminated, and how these decisions are made. Detailed responses to such questions go well beyond the scope of the present analysis, but we have sought above to make the case for the need to have the debate, and in what follows we will explore one option among many others that seems worth pursuing. But, first, we need to clarify the addressees of our proposal.

The SD, for all its aspirations to be objective and impartial and whatever else, clearly has limitations on what it can and will do in terms of monitoring and reporting, if only because it is a government agency. There seems to be relatively little to be gained in the present context from examining where its interests lie in terms of the global politics of information, although that is certainly a topic worth pursuing elsewhere. The SR, for his part, simply does not have the resources to expand the coverage provided, nor necessarily the agreement of governments and the UN to such a move. But the information his mandate generates is all, sometimes with some delay, in the public domain and can thus be readily incorporated into any larger database.

The focus for present purposes is thus on the leading international NGOs. While the data analysis above has been limited to an examination of the approach adopted by AI and HRW, there is no reason to confine the observations that follow to these two groups. The reality is that there is strong competition among the principal international human rights NGOs in a variety of ways that influence, among other things, the approaches they adopt, the coalitions and partnerships that they build, and the policies they adopt towards information sharing. There is nothing wrong with this competition; it is in many ways crucial and healthy. Nor does competition mean that there is not extensive and sometimes intensive consultation and even collaboration at the staff level. But it is important to acknowledge that competitive concerns influence, and perhaps even dictate, the information policies with which we are concerned here. While their size, focus, constituencies, supporters, and funders vary dramatically across the spectrum, the reality is that they compete at a range of different levels.

Most importantly, perhaps, they compete for brand name recognition, and thus have a strong interest in being able to claim "credit" for their reporting. This is linked in turn to concerns about quality and reliability, thus imposing significant limits on collaborative undertakings. Reports come in various formats and serve a variety of functions, although there is a significant premium on what might be termed the HRW model, a style that originated with HRW but has been emulated or adapted by a range of other groups. The report should be not much longer than, say, 50 pages. It should contain a section describing the methodology used, but the information provided there will be mainly defensive and designed to counter possible criticisms, rather than being especially informative as to the particular challenges faced. The report should be thoroughly, even exhaustively, edited and honed to eliminate not just rough edges but idiosyncrasies and major diversions from a reasonably standardized approach. Innovation is to be avoided, and tailoring the style to fit the situation in hand is both cautious and limited. The report is, in most instances, written for an intelligent lay audience with no deep familiarity with the country or the issues. It will employ a limited range of rhetorical strategies and techniques and avoid undue technicality and detail. There will be deliberately few references to reports by other groups, and the tone will seek to combine an element of objectivity and authoritativeness with materials designed to put a human face on the violations. And, finally, there will be an executive summary and a premium placed on "actionable" recommendations directed to a range of specific entities ranging from the amorphous international community, through specific international agencies and donors, to the government concerned and perhaps also specific agencies or officials. While HRW did not "invent" this model, it has honed it more thoroughly than any other NGO and it has, by dint of its professionalism and the sheer number of reports it has produced, set a benchmark against which other groups seem to feel they have little alternative but to seek to emulate as far as possible.

While our description of some of these characteristics would doubtless be contested by some of the organizations concerned, the point for present purposes is that this model does not lend itself to "sharing" or being made a part of a broader enterprise. Indeed a huge amount is invested in distinguishing the "final product" from other information sources. This is in the very nature of the branding process that seems to lie at the core of the politics of information in this field.

In addition, and closely linked to the branding dimension, groups compete for influence and perceived authoritativeness. Again this militates against sharing or collaborative approaches. And, finally, they compete for funding. AI is almost alone in relying essentially on membership contributions rather than foundations, large individual donors, or governments. These funding sources will generally need to be convinced that they are getting something identifiable and distinctive for their money; funding a more amorphous undertaking with multiple partners, and a "final" product whose shape and orientation cannot readily be predicted, let alone assured, is more problematic and less attractive. Nevertheless, in the overall scheme of this analysis of the politics of human rights information, it is the funders who will need to be convinced that other models deserve to be explored. They will need both to have the vision to support alternative approaches and the strength to encourage or induce the mainstream groups they presently support to develop means by which to cooperate in more innovative and collaborative ways with a community of monitors and fact finders. . . .

Notes

1. Cassese, "A Plea for a Global Community Grounded in a Core of Human Rights," in A. Cassese (ed.), *Realizing Utopia: The Future of International Law* (2012), at 136, 143.

2. See Inter-American Court of Human Rights, *Velasquez Rodriguez Case*, Judgment of 29 July 1988, Inter-Am.Ct.H.R. (Ser. C) No. 4 (1988).

3. See Summary or Arbitrary Executions, Report by the Special Rapporteur, UN doc. E/CN.4/1983/16 (31 Jan. 1983), at www.extrajudicialexecutions.org /reports/E_CN_4_1983_16.pdf.

4. Poe, Carey, and Vazquez, "How Are These Pictures Different: A Quantitative Comparison of the US State Department Reports and Amnesty International Human Rights Reports, 1976–1995," 23 *Human Rights Quarterly* (2001) 650, at 654.

5. For an early critique see de Neufville, "Human Rights Reporting as a Policy Tool: An Examination of the State Department Country Reports," 8 *Human Rights Quarterly* (1986) 681.

6. For example, Hathaway, "Do Human Rights Treaties Make a Difference?" 111 *Yale LJ* (2002) 1935; and K. Sikkink, *The Justice Cascade* (2011).

7. Roth, "Defending Economic, Social and Cultural Rights: Practical Issues Faced by an International Human Rights Organization," 26 *Human Rights Quarterly* (2004) 63.

19

Trafficking of Women:
Norms, Realities, and Challenges

Rashida Manjoo

It ought to concern every person, because it's a debasement of our common humanity. It ought to concern every community, because it tears at the social fabric. It ought to concern every business, because it distorts markets. It ought to concern every nation, because it endangers public health and fuels violence and organized crime. I'm talking about the injustice, the outrage, of human trafficking, which must be called by its true name—modern slavery.

—US President Barack Obama, September 25, 2012

Human trafficking for sexual and labor exploitation is a transnational, global phenomenon having an impact on all countries—whether as source, origin, or destination countries. It is a prevalent human rights abuse perpetrated mostly against women and children. The abolition of the slave trade has not ended the exploitation and tragedy of human trafficking and sexual slavery. It is prevalent in many countries and manifests in different ways. Despite advancements in technology, data collection, and legislative developments, human trafficking for exploitative purposes is currently on the rise in different parts of the world. Women and children are trafficked and exploited for numerous reasons including poverty, lack of education, civil wars, conflict and disaster related displacements, peer pressure, inducements, vulnerability, and lack of access to adequate information. In the 2006 report of the United Nations (U.N.) Secretary-General, it is "asserted unequivocally that violence against women [including trafficking and sex slavery] constitutes a form of gender-based discrimination and that discrimination is a major cause of such violence."[1]

The issue of trafficking of women for sex and labor exploitation is of such gravity that a number of special procedures mechanisms of the

Reprinted from *Albany Government Law Review*, vol. 7: 5–33. © 2014 by Albany Law School. Reprinted by permission of the publisher. Edited for length.

United Nations Human Rights Council . . . have paid particular attention to specific aspects of this topic. The Mandate on Violence Against Women was created in 1993 and has consistently raised the issue, particularly in country mission reports.[2] In 2004, a specific mandate devoted to "Trafficking in Persons, especially women and children," was also established.[3] This paper highlights the focus and analysis of the work carried out by both mandates, including legal frameworks for the protection for women trafficked for sexual exploitation. The focus will be on the transnational trafficking of women. This paper also discusses challenges militating against effective remedies for victims of trafficking.

Trafficking in persons must be viewed within the context of international and national movements and migrations that are increasingly occurring due to economic realities, globalization, the feminization of migration, armed conflict, the breakdown or reconfiguration of the State, and the transformation of political boundaries. . . .

In its 2012 Global Report on Trafficking in Persons ("Global Report"), the United Nations acknowledges the gravity and global nature of human trafficking.[4] Nevertheless, it notes that estimating the severity of the problem remains a challenge as trafficking largely remains a hidden crime, which is scarcely reported to state agencies. . . . The Global Report states that women and girls account for seventy-five percent of all trafficked victims worldwide. It is acknowledged that trafficking in women and girls is one component of a larger phenomenon of trafficking in persons, including both male and female adults and children.

Human trafficking for sexual exploitation and sex slavery involves the exercise of powers attaching to the right of ownership of another, and involves the commodification and sale of human beings for purposes of exploitation. Both concepts limit the options available to the victim and infringe on individual autonomy to decide whether to engage in intimate relationships, and with whom. . . .

Forced labor is closely linked to human trafficking, but these manifestations are not the same. A distinction must be made between victims subjected to some form of compulsion to accept egregious labor conditions because they simply lack alternatives, and those where a third party forces them to work against their will. In this context, in many countries bonded or forced labor falls within the category of trafficking.[5] . . . [The] International Labour Office (ILO) . . . estimated the minimum number of persons in forced labor as a result of human trafficking to be around 2.4 million at any given time.[6] . . . As illustrated in Table 19.1, it is evident that there are huge geographic disparities between regions and that more than half (about 1.36 million) of the total figure of trafficked persons in forced labor are from Asia and the Pacific. . . .

Table 19.1 Regional Distribution of Trafficked Forced Labourers

Asia and the Pacific	1,360,000
Industrial Countries	270,000
Latin America and the Caribbean	250,000
Middle East and North Africa	230,000
Transition Countries	200,000
Sub-Saharan Africa	130,000
World	2,450,000

Source: Patrick Belser, *Forced Labour and Human Trafficking: Estimating the Profits* 17 (International Labour Office, Geneva, Working Paper No. 42, 2005), p. 14.

Causes and Consequences of Human Trafficking

. . . Two major causes of human trafficking and sexual slavery are poverty and globalization. Poverty and unemployment have made many families susceptible to traffickers who prey on their ignorance, lack of education, and lack of economic means. The root causes of trafficking and migration under coercive circumstances share common and overlapping features. Often, violations of women's human rights are the primary causative factor. The failure of the State to respect, protect, and fulfill women's rights can lead to sexual and economic exploitation of women in both public and private spaces. . . .

In a number of countries with porous borders and weak institutions, and where the rule of law is not enforced, trafficking is pervasive. [In] Somalia, for example, . . .

> [t]rafficking occurs through the country's border areas with Ethiopia where a significant number of [Somali and Ethiopian] women and children . . . often find themselves in involuntary domestic servitude or other types of forced labour. Often these women do not speak the language and find themselves with no other options.[7]

Some women are also

> attracted by the opportunity to cross the Red Sea and often find themselves trafficked by pirates who operate along the coast and who are actively involved in commercial sexual exploitation. Often young women are offered jewels and other presents by local Somali women recruiters. They are offered marriage proposals or promised employment to pay their passage across the sea.

. . . The consequences of trafficking include exposure to physical, sexual, and psychological violence. Trafficking impacts victims in virtually all areas of their lives, carrying a prolonged and continued trauma, which can continue well after their experience. Throughout the period in which victims are being trafficked, acts of physical, sexual, and psychological abuse, violence, ill-treatment, deprivation, the forced use of drugs, exploitation, and poor living conditions can be part of the experience. Victims are usually at high risk of sexually transmitted disease, including HIV infection. . . . Also, the stigma attached to them can be a source of rejection in their family and in the community. . . . There is no guarantee that a victim will recover from the long-term consequences of their experience, and many women and girls experience re-victimization in similar ways.

Once trapped or bought by those who desire their services, victims of human trafficking and sexual slavery "are at the mercy of those to whom they must repay a debt or to those who have seized their documentation or are threatening to harm their families back home." According to Louise Shelley,

> The costs of human trafficking are experienced on the individual, community, national, regional, and global level. They affect not only source countries but also transit and host countries. . . . Trafficking challenges states' control over their borders and their ability to determine who will reside on their territory. It undermines states because trafficking can survive only with the corruption and complicity of government officials.[8]

International Normative Framework

International law relating to the exploitation of human beings has an extensive history that dates back to 1904, when the first binding international instrument, the International Agreement for the Suppression of the White Slave Trade, was adopted under the auspices of the League of Nations. This was adopted by thirteen European countries that wanted to put an end to the sale of women into prostitution as a result of the economic stagnation experienced during that period. However, the agreement did not contribute much to the suppression of human trafficking for sexual exploitation, as there was no enforcement mechanism to ensure its success. This resulted in the adoption of the International Convention for the Suppression of White Slave Traffic in 1910. . . .

The campaign to end human trafficking and sexual exploitation led to the adoption of numerous other international instruments. . . .

The first explicit mention of trafficking appears in the 1949 Convention for the Suppression of the Traffic in Persons and of the Exploitation of the Prostitution of Others. . . . The 1979 Convention on the Elimination of All Forms of Discrimination Against Women (CEDAW), in Article 6, provides that States Parties shall take all appropriate measures, including legislation, to suppress all forms of traffic in women and exploitation of prostitution of women. Furthermore, CEDAW General Recommendation No. 19 added the issue of violence against women to the terms of the Convention and into the international legal norm of non-discrimination, on the basis of sex. According to General Recommendation No. 19, poverty and unemployment broaden opportunities for trafficking in women and girls, tending to drive them into prostitution and exposing them to gender-based violence, which emanates from social stereotyping and stigmatization of prostitution. . . . More importantly, the CEDAW Committee has broadened the scope of gender-based violence to include "acts that inflict physical, mental or sexual harm or suffering, threats of such acts, coercion and other deprivations of liberty."

In 2000, the Protocol to Prevent, Suppress and Punish Trafficking in Persons, Especially Women and Children, commonly referred to as the Palermo Protocol, was adopted by the United Nations General Assembly and was the first international legal instrument on trafficking in persons which contained a legally binding definition of trafficking. This instrument forms part of the United Nations Convention against Transnational Organized Crime, and contains important standards for the protection and assistance of victims, including a mandated state responsibility to cooperate to prevent and combat trafficking. The Protocol defines human trafficking as:

> [T]he recruitment, transportation, transfer, harbouring or receipt of persons, by means of the threat or use of force or other forms of coercion, of abduction, of fraud, of deception, of the abuse of power or of a position of vulnerability or of the giving or receiving of payments or benefits to achieve the consent of a person having control over another person, for the purpose of exploitation. Exploitation shall include, at a minimum, the exploitation of the prostitution of others or other forms of sexual exploitation, forced labour or services, slavery or practices similar to slavery, servitude or the removal of organs.[9]

To qualify as human trafficking, the process or conduct in question should involve three elements: [1] an action of recruitment, transportation, transfer, harboring or receipt of persons; 2) an unlawful threat or use of force or other forms of coercion, of abduction, of fraud, or deception; 3) it must be done to achieve a particular criminal goal, namely, the exploitation of the trafficked person.] . . . These dimensions of exploitation and the other elements of trafficking briefly discussed above suggest that human trafficking is not a single crime, but rather a process designed to achieve broad and specific criminal ends. Generally, the approach taken in the Protocol on Trafficking in Persons recognizes that the majority of perpetrators of human trafficking and sex slavery function in large and complicated networks of organized crime. . . .

The definition of trafficking is a welcome development, as it provides a minimum standard for the protection of victims of human trafficking. However, some scholars have argued that a weakness of the definition is "its excessive focus on criminalizing traffickers to the detriment of making protection of trafficked person[s] the priority."[10] . . .

Nevertheless, the Protocol has become the key international instrument that has accelerated legislative and policy actions to respond to and prevent trafficking. . . . Many countries have introduced the specific offence of trafficking in persons in their national laws after the Palermo Protocol entered into force. Prior to that, many countries had no specific anti-trafficking legislation, but this figure was reduced to twenty percent by November 2008. The Palermo Protocol does not include an international review mechanism to strengthen the ability to monitor its implementation at the national level.

The United Nations Office of The High Commissioner for Human Rights has adopted a "soft law," namely, the Recommended Principles and Guidelines on Human Rights and Human Trafficking ("Guidelines"). The Guidelines encourage States to "adopt appropriate legislative and other measures necessary to establish, as criminal offences, trafficking, its component acts and related conduct." The latest development in the field of non–legally binding standard setting initiatives is the adoption of the Global Plan of Action to Combat Trafficking in Persons in 2010 by the General Assembly. This plan urges governments to take coordinated and consistent measures to fight trafficking, and calls for the integration of the fight against trafficking within the U.N.'s broader programs, and for the establishment of a voluntary trust fund for victims of trafficking.

[According to] the Slavery Convention, slavery is "the status or condition of a person over whom any or all of the powers attaching to the right of ownership are exercised." In practical terms, slavery exists when one person owns another and is entitled to the services of the latter person without any obligation to give remuneration for such services. From this definition it can be deduced that sex slavery exists when one person is coerced to provide one's sexual services (or offer their bodies for the sexual gratification of another person) without receiving any of the proceeds that emanate from one's services. However, not all sex labor amounts to human trafficking and sex slavery. Instances of voluntary prostitution, where sex workers sell their services for an agreed upon price, do not constitute sex slavery. Arguably, this can be so even where the persons may have been initially transported to a particular country or place by force or deception, and later regained their freedom, whether by accident or by design. The critical factor appears to be the relative freedom of the exploited individual to continue selling or to terminate his or her "employment" and return to his or her home.

Nonetheless, there are other compelling legal reasons why the idea of slavery in general, and sex slavery in particular, should be construed or applied in ways that extend their reach to situations that are generally associated with trafficking, including debt bondage, forced labor, and obligatory prostitution. Expanding the definition of sex slavery to include all forms of sexual exploitation would protect many victims who are often trafficked and used as objects for the benefit of persons who are holding them in circumstances of physical control by force, threat of serious harm, or through deception. The prohibition on slavery constitutes a rule of customary international law which applies universally, and the state's non-ratification of relevant treaties would not be a bar to holding a State accountable for non-action on any form of sex slavery taking place within its territories. The prohibition on slavery has generally been categorized as forming part of *jus cogens* or peremptory norms of international law. . . . A *jus cogens* is . . . a norm accepted and recognized by the international community . . . from which no derogation is permitted. . . . Regardless of these possible interpretations, there is no consensus on whether human trafficking amounts to slavery and whether sex slavery should include other forms of sexual exploitation. . . .

Implementation of International Norms

[The] Special Rapporteur on Trafficking has emphasized a number of components of anti-trafficking responses, namely the "5 Ps" (protection, prosecution, punishment, promoting international cooperation, and partnership), the "3 Rs" (redress, recovery, and reintegration), and the "3 Cs" (capacity, cooperation, and coordination).[11] . . . They are designed to bring clarity to the concept of the right to an effective remedy and to elaborate on specific factors to be taken into account when this right is applied to trafficked persons. . . .

[Many governments, however, have] adopted a "law and order" approach with accompanying strong anti-immigration policies, which are often at odds with the protection of human rights. The definition and criminalization of trafficking at the national level is often not consistent with the Palermo Protocol. In some States, for instance, the crime of trafficking in persons does not cover labor exploitation, such as slavery and forced labor, or the law focuses only on trafficking for sexual exploitation. Furthermore, despite the increase in anti-trafficking legislation around the world, evidence seems to indicate that the total number of prosecutions and convictions of traffickers is still low, owing to a variety of factors, including the limited understanding of the crime of trafficking in persons on the part of law enforcement authorities.

With respect to protection, recovery, and reintegration of trafficked persons, there has been some positive progress with legislation requiring trafficked persons to be provided with appropriate facilities and services, such as housing, legal assistance, medical, psychological, and material assistance, employment, and educational and training opportunities. . . . However, effective implementation remains a challenge. For example, many States still do not have appropriate shelters for trafficked persons, particularly for specific groups of trafficked persons, such as domestic victims of trafficking.

A number of States provide for a legal right of trafficked persons to a recovery and reflection period in accordance with Article 7 of the Palermo Protocol. Some States make this period conditional upon the trafficked person's willingness to cooperate with law enforcement authorities in investigating and prosecuting traffickers, or they simply fail to grant it in practice, due to the lack of knowledge on the part of the authorities.

As for prevention of trafficking, challenges remain in implementing the State Parties' obligations to establish comprehensive policies, programs, and other measures. A number of States have implemented initiatives mainly in the form of information and mass media campaigns on risks of trafficking in persons, but insufficient attention is paid to addressing the root causes of trafficking, such as demand for cheap labor, sex tourism, widespread poverty, gender discrimination, conflicts, corruption, and restrictive immigration policies of favored countries for migrants. Prevention initiatives are not necessarily based on the recognition that trafficking in persons is caused by the lack of comprehensive protection of human rights, such as the freedom from discrimination, the right to work, the right to an adequate standard of living, and freedom of movement, amongst others.

The right to an effective remedy should include "restitution, compensation, rehabilitation, satisfaction and guarantees of non-repetition."[12] Rights of access to remedies, such as access to information, counseling and legal aid, and regularization of residence status, are critical pre-conditions to provide effective remedies, including compensation. The ability of trafficked persons to claim remedies hinges upon regularization of residence status in countries where remedies are sought, as it would be difficult for them to obtain remedies if they were at risk of expulsion or had already been expelled from the countries. Thus, unless trafficked persons are guaranteed certain procedural rights, the right to seek remedies would be relegated to a mere theoretical possibility for many trafficked persons.

The pervasiveness of patriarchal attitudes in law enforcement and justice systems, coupled with a lack of resources and insufficient knowledge on existing applicable legislation, leads to inadequate responses to cases involving violations of women's rights and the persisting social acceptance of such acts. . . .

[Procedures] and rules of evidence in the criminal justice system are often infiltrated by strong gender stereotypes, which can result in gender-biased behavior by court officials and discrimination against women by the criminal justice system, in general. . . . [Common] gender-biased rules of evidence and procedure [include]: 1) having to prove physical violence to show that there was no consent; 2) viewing women as likely to lie, therefore only accepting evidence if corroborated; 3) assuming that women are constantly sexually available; 4) inferring that women consent to sex even if forced, threatened, coerced, or if they remain silent; 5) taking into consideration previous sexual experience as a predisposition for women to be sexually available, or to automatically consent to sex; 6) perceiving women as bearing the responsibility for sexual attacks when they have been out late, in isolated places, or dressed in a particular manner; 7) thinking that it is impossible to rape a sex worker; and 8) viewing raped women as dishonored, shamed, and guilty, rather than as victims. . . .

State Responsibility to Act with Due Diligence

"Under international human rights law, states are compelled to prevent and respond to all acts of violence against women."[13] The 1993 Declaration on the Elimination of Violence Against Women urges States to

> Develop penal, civil, labor and administrative sanctions in domestic legislation to punish and redress the wrongs caused to women who are subjected to violence; women who are subjected to violence should be provided with access to the mechanisms of justice and . . . to just and effective remedies for the harm that they have suffered; States should also inform women of their rights in seeking redress through such mechanisms[.][14]

The enactment of adequate legislation on violence against women is the first preventative step. Shortcomings in legislation have particularly negative effects in contexts where women's subordinate status within intimate relationships, their economic dependence on male partners, and their fear of being abandoned or assaulted make them more vulnerable to trafficking.

The due diligence standard has increasingly become the parameter which measures the level of State compliance with its obligations to prevent, and respond to acts of violence against women. . . . The investigation, prosecution, protection, and redress measures offered to women victims of violence will have a direct effect on the prevalence rates of such violence. Therefore, it is crucial to promote offender-focused prosecutions, which take into consideration the histories of alleged perpetrators, and to offer victim-centered responses to trafficking of women, addressing the immediate, medium, and [long-term] needs of victims. Such responses must be sensitive to the safety needs and cultural considerations with respect to victims' positions within their families and their wider communities. The ultimate objective of States' efforts when investigating and punishing acts of violence against women, and when protecting and offering redress to victims, should be the prevention of re-victimization and future acts of violence, by addressing structural discrimination and ensuring the empowerment of women. Comprehensive remedial schemes for women victims of trafficking should consider measures of restitution and compensation, rehabilitation and reintegration, substantive recognition of the harms suffered, as well as guarantees of non-repetition.

Many States have exercised due diligence in their measures to prevent and combat trafficking as a form of violence against women. . . . [They have adopted appropriate legislative measures, including anti-trafficking, labor and immigration legislation.] The importance of integrated training that promotes a rights-based approach and provides technical skills for criminal justice agencies and institutions, who have the responsibility to investigate, prosecute, and adjudicate trafficking crimes with due diligence, has also been emphasized.

. . . While many States have made progress in developing a criminal justice response, the human rights of trafficked persons are often not the primary consideration in the pursuit of effective prosecution and punishment. Criminalization *per se* is not an end in itself. It must be accompanied by the effective enforcement of the law, and the imposition of appropriate punishments for trafficking, and related offences. In this regard, low prosecution and conviction rates around the world confirm that even those States with advanced criminal justice systems and sophisticated anti-trafficking strategies need to improve their interventions.

Correct identification of trafficked persons remains complex, and in practice, trafficked persons are often arrested, detained, and charged as smuggled or undocumented workers. Timely and accurate identification of victims is crucial for effective criminal justice responses to trafficking, as it affects the ability of law enforcement officials to prosecute traffickers and allows for the provision of necessary support services to trafficked persons. . . . In order to facilitate quick and accurate identification of trafficked persons, numerous States have conducted "specialized training sessions to enhance the capacity of front-line officers, especially the police, immigration, border guards and labour inspectors."[15] . . .

Ideally, the provision of protection and support to victims of trafficking would play a critical role in promoting the effective investigation and prosecution of traffickers. Unfortunately, too many States still link the provision of assistance and protection to cooperation with national criminal justice agencies. Practices include victims of trafficking being mandatorily detained in shelters, which, in some circumstances, violates the right to freedom of movement, and the prohibitions on . . . arbitrary detention.

Creating opportunities for safe migration as a way of preventing trafficking in persons has often been overtaken by concerns for the protection of national sovereignty, and border security. Article 11 of the Palermo Protocol clearly stipulates that States shall strengthen border controls to prevent trafficking in persons "without prejudice to international commitments in relation to the free movement of people."[16] Trafficked persons are subject to arrest and detention in some States on the basis that they are "illegal migrants" in violation of immigration laws, or in violation of anti-prostitution laws, in the case of trafficking for the purpose of commercial sexual exploitation. The promotion of cooperation and partnership—which are cross-cutting elements in all aspects of the efforts to combat trafficking in persons—is also crucial. Without international cooperation and collaboration, effective investigation and prosecution of the crime of human trafficking may be almost impossible. In this regard, it is critical to develop cooperation mechanisms between States, to share and exchange information and to conduct joint investigations by law enforcement authorities.

Restitution, [if implemented to mean simply returning trafficked women to the pre-existing situation, may place her at the risk of further human rights violations.][17] Where trafficked persons are repatriated, restitution may thus imply that States have an obligation to undertake broader measures to address root causes of trafficking, and to provide the necessary support for the reintegration of trafficked persons.

Recovery is a crucial form of remedy for trafficked persons not only in itself, but also as a means to seek other forms of remedy, such as compensation. Yet there are often obstacles in ensuring the non-discriminatory and unconditional provision of services to assist the full recovery of trafficked persons. Recovery services may only be available to certain categories of trafficked persons to the exclusion of others, or upon cooperation with law enforcement authorities.

Compensation, while being the most widely recognized form of remedy, is often not readily accessible to trafficked persons, whether in criminal, civil, or labor proceedings. In these proceedings, the possibility of obtaining compensation hinges upon identification, arrest, trial, and conviction of traffickers, which remains difficult. Civil proceedings tend to be time-consuming, expensive, and complicated, which may effectively preclude trafficked persons from seeking this course of action. The possibility for trafficked persons to obtain compensation through labor proceedings may be restricted by a number of eligibility criteria, such as the type of their work and their immigration status. Legal assistance is also essential in order to claim compensation, as judicial and administrative proceedings are often complex in many jurisdictions and trafficked persons may not be familiar with the legal system of the country concerned.

Asset recovery plays an important role in effective criminal justice responses to trafficking, not only because it undermines the financial gain of traffickers, but also linking asset seizure to victim support is in line with a rights-based approach to human trafficking. Laws which explicitly provide that restitution and compensation be made to victims of trafficking out of the proceeds of assets seizure do exist in some countries. In some instances, such proceeds have reportedly failed to be distributed to victims.

The role of other influential stakeholders, such as businesses, consumers, and the media, in the fight against human trafficking in supply chains should also be stressed when discussing anti-trafficking strategies. Businesses are a significant part of the human trafficking chain, as they could be directly linked to it through the recruitment, transport, or receipt of workers for purposes of exploitation. Businesses may be linked to human trafficking at various stages of production of their goods or delivery of their services through the conduct of their suppliers, subcontractors, or business partners, given the complexity of supply chains in today's global economy. Ethical consumerism and other consumer-targeted initiatives, such as product certification and labeling, are powerful ways to influence corporate behavior.

Conclusion

Throughout the world, violence against women is pervasive, widespread, and unacceptable. Rooted in multiple and intersecting forms of discrimination and inequalities, and strongly linked to the social and economic situation of women, violence against women constitutes a continuum of exploitation and abuse. It occurs both in the public and the private spheres, including in the family, the community, in State institutions, and at the transnational level. . . .

Violence occurs at the intersections of various elements, which characterize women's realities. Trafficking of women is yet another illustration of how discriminatory practices, prior experiences of violence and exploitation, economic and social conditions, ethnicity, and other elements interplay and contribute to fuelling trafficking. As such, States' responses must reflect a holistic framework and have regard to due diligence in preventing trafficking, punishing and prosecuting perpetrators, and assisting and providing remedies to victims.

[Accurate] identification of trafficked persons is a pre-requisite for trafficked persons to be able to exercise the right to an effective remedy, as it is almost impossible to do so if they are misidentified as irregular migrants or criminal offenders. They must also be provided with a reflection and recovery period as well as support and assistance necessary for their recovery on a non-conditional basis, so that they can make an informed decision as to what course of action they would like to pursue. If trafficked persons wish to seek compensation for the harms suffered, it is necessary that they are equipped with information about their rights and avenues available to exercise their rights, legal assistance, interpretation, and other necessary services, including regular residence status. . . .

[Instances] of violence against women generally feed into pre-existing patterns of crosscutting structural subordination and systemic marginalization, and as such measures of redress for victims need to link individual remedies with structural transformation. This means that remedies provided to victims of violence should aspire, to the extent possible, to subvert, instead of reinforce, pre-existing patterns of structural subordination, gender hierarchies, systemic marginalization, and structural inequalities that may be the root cause of the violence that women experience. Eliminating discriminatory practices in all spheres of women's lives, addressing the root causes of trafficking of women, addressing women's empowerment, and most importantly transforming societies so that equality, non-discrimination, dignity, and accountability are the rule rather than the exception, has to be part of a more intensive response. This is a global challenge that needs urgent attention.

Notes

1. U.N. Secretary-General, *In-Depth Study on All Forms of Violence Against Women: Rep. of the Secretary General*, 31, U.N. Doc. A/61/122/Add.1 (July 6, 2006).

2. Declaration on the Elimination of Violence Against Women, G.A. Res. 48/104, U.N. Doc. A/RES/48/104 (Feb. 23, 1994). Special Rapporteur on Violence Against Women, Its Causes and Consequences, *Report of the Special Rapporteur on Violence Against Women, Its Causes and Consequences*, Human Rights Council, U.N. Doc. A/HRC/23/49/Add.2 (Mar. 18, 2013).

3. G.A. Res. 2004/110 (Apr. 19, 2004).

4. U.N. Office on Drugs & Crime, *Global Report on Trafficking in Persons 2012*, 68 (Dec. 2012).

5. Special Rapporteur on Contemporary Forms of Slavery, Including Its Causes & Consequences, *Promotion and Protection of All Human Rights, Civil, Political, Economic, Social and Cultural Rights, Including the Right to Development*, Human Rights Council, ¶ 60, U.N. Doc. A/HRC/12/21 (July 10, 2009).

6. International Labour Office [ILO], *A Global Alliance Against Forced Labour*, Rep. of the Director-General, Rep. I (B) (2005).

7. Special Rapporteur on Violence Against Women, Its Causes and Consequences, *Report of the Special Rapporteur on Violence Against Women, Its Causes and Consequences*, Human Rights Council, ¶ 30, U.N. Doc. A/HRC/20/16/Add.3 (May 14, 2012).

8. Louise Shelley, Human Trafficking (Cambridge Univ. Press 2010).

9. Palermo Protocol, G.A. Res. 55/25, Annex II, art. 3(a), U.N. Doc. A/RES/55/25 (Jan. 8, 2001).

10. Elzbieta M. Gozdziak & Elizabeth A. Collett, *Research on Human Trafficking in North America: A Review of Literature*, 43 INT'L MIGRATION 99, 104 (2005).

11. Special Rapporteur on Trafficking in Persons, Especially Women and Children, *Report of the Special Rapporteur on Trafficking in Persons, Especially Women and Children*, Human Rights Council, Annex I, U.N. Doc. A/HRC/17/35 (Apr. 13, 2011) (by Joy Ngozi Ezeilo).

12. G.A. Res. 60/147, ¶18, U.N. Doc. A/RES/60/147 (Mar. 21, 2005).

13. Special Rapporteur on Violence Against Women, Its Causes and Consequences, *Statement by Ms. Rashida Manjoo*, 2, 66th Session of the General Assembly (Oct. 10, 2011) (by Rashida Manjoo); Declaration on the Elimination of Violence Against Women, *supra* note 8, at art. 4.

14. Declaration on the Elimination of Violence Against Women, *supra* note 8, at art. 4(d).

15. Special Rapporteur on Trafficking in Persons, Especially Women and Children, *Report of the Special Rapporteur on Trafficking in Persons, Especially Women and Children*, Human Rights Council, ¶ 72, U.N. DOC. A/HRC/20/18 (June 6, 2012) (by Joy Ngozi Ezeilo), *supra* note 146, at ¶ 25.

16. Palermo Protocol, G.A. Res. 55/25, Annex II, art. 3(a), U.N. Doc. A/RES/55/25 (Jan. 8, 2001), *supra* note 72, at art. II(1).

17. Special Rapporteur on Trafficking in Persons, Especially Women and Children, *Report of the Special Rapporteur on Trafficking in Persons, Especially Women and Children*, Human Rights Council, Annex I, U.N. Doc. A/HRC/17/35 (Apr. 13, 2011) (by Joy Ngozi Ezeilo), *supra* note 103, at ¶¶ 20–21.

Part 6

International Organizations and the Future

20

Reforming the United Nations:
Lessons from a History of Progress

Edward C. Luck

The never-ending quest for reform, for improving the functioning of the United Nations, has been an integral part of the life of the world body since its earliest days. Indeed, one of the more controversial issues at the UN founding conference in San Francisco during spring 1945 was how the process of amending its Charter should be structured and when a general review conference of its provisions should be called.[1] Those delegations unhappy with some of the compromises reached in San Francisco, especially concerning the inequities of the veto power granted the "big five" permanent members (P-5) of the Security Council, wanted to schedule a general review relatively soon and to make the hurdles to amendment relatively low. The Soviet Union and, to a lesser extent, the other "big five" powers, on the other hand, naturally preferred to keep the barriers to Charter change relatively high.

On a more operational level, the UN had barely passed its second birthday before members of the U.S. Congress started to call for sweeping reforms of UN finance and administration. In October 1947 the Senate Expenditures Committee launched a study that found serious problems of overlap, duplication of effort, weak coordination, proliferating mandates and programs, and overly generous compensation of staff within the infant but rapidly growing UN system.[2] Similar complaints have been voiced countless times since.

Through the years, scores of independent commissions, governmental studies, and scholars have put forward literally hundreds of proposals aimed at making the world body work better, decide more fairly, modify

Reprinted from Jean Krasno, ed., *The United Nations*, pp. 359–397. © 2004 by Lynne Rienner Publishers. Reprinted by permission of the publisher. Edited for length.

its mandate, or operate more efficiently. Not to be left behind by the reform bandwagon, successive Secretaries-General and units of the Secretariat have engaged in frequent, if episodic, bouts of self-examination and self-criticism, offering their own reform agendas.

What explains this apparently irresistible impulse for reforming the United Nations? Six factors suggest themselves:

1. Public institutions depend on recurring processes of criticism, reassessment, change, and renewal to retain their relevance and vitality. Reform is a sign of institutional health and dynamism, not a penalty for bad behavior.
2. Highly complex, decentralized, and multifaceted institutions, like the UN system, offer more targets for criticism and more opportunities for change. The temptation to tinker with the United Nations is only magnified by its high visibility, symbolic aura, and broad agenda.
3. The diversity of UN membership and the ambitious nature of its mandates make it highly likely that some constituencies will be seriously disappointed with its power-sharing arrangements and/or its accomplishments at any point in time. Persistent disappointment or feelings of disenfranchisement have often led to calls for reform.
4. As the world changes, so do the politics of the UN and the priorities of its Member States. In looking to the UN to fulfill new mandates that exceed its capacities, influential nongovernmental organizations (NGOs) often look to structural innovations or to the creation of new bodies to close the gap between expectations and capabilities. In both cases, proposals for reform usually follow.
5. Critics keep calling for reform in part because the United Nations has been so slow in delivering it. As the major powers hoped in San Francisco, formal institutional and structural reforms have proven hard to achieve in the UN system. The concerns about UN management and finance voiced by Congress in the late 1940s, moreover, were echoed a half-century later in the late 1990s.
6. The universality of the UN has fueled a dual pattern on the intergovernmental level: frequent calls for change by one Member State or group, followed by blocking moves by others with divergent interests or perspectives. At times, it seems as if every Member State is in favor of some sort of reform, but their individual notions of what this should entail differ so markedly as to make consensus on the direction reform should take hard to achieve.

These dynamics ensure almost continuous attention to the reform agenda, but much slower progress on the intergovernmental than Secretariat plane. If gauged by the sheer quantity of deliberations, debates, studies, and resolutions devoted to it, reform has become one of the enduring pastimes and primary products of the UN system. For example, from 1995 to 1997, the General Assembly was consumed with no less than five working groups on different aspects of reform, its president was engrossed in developing his own reform package, the Security Council reviewed its working methods, the Economic and Social Council (ECOSOC) adopted new procedures for relating to NGOs, and the new Secretary-General offered a comprehensive, if generally modest, plan for Secretariat reform. Before the dust had settled from these battles, the U.S.-led drive to have the Member State assessment scales revised took center stage in the Assembly from 1998 to 2000. And in September 2002, a reform study led by the Deputy Secretary-General called for aligning activities with the priorities voiced in the Millennium Declaration, trimming reporting, improving coordination, streamlining the budgeting process, and improving human resource management.

The hardest reforms to achieve, of course, are those entailing amendments to the UN Charter. As noted above, after a good deal of divisive debate, the big five managed at San Francisco to set the political bar quite high for any modifications of the Charter. Contending that their unity was key to making the new body more successful at securing the peace than its predecessor, the League of Nations, the five insisted on their having individual vetoes over amendments to the Charter. As a result, Article 108 stipulates:

> Amendments to the present Charter shall come into force for all Members of the United Nations when they have been adopted by a vote of two thirds of the members of the General Assembly and ratified in accordance with their respective constitutional processes by two thirds of the Members of the United Nations, including the permanent members of the Security Council.

Some of the other delegations not only objected to the inequity of these provisions but also fretted that those Member States in the minority opposing a particular amendment were given no recourse. Unlike the League Covenant, the Charter offers no mechanism for a dissatisfied member to withdraw from the UN—a practice that had disabled the League in the years preceding World War II. As a gesture toward these concerns, Article 109 offers the possibility of convening a general conference to review the Charter. While a number of delegations at San

Francisco expected this to take place within the Organization's first decade, the polarization of the membership during the Cold War years made this look like an unpromising course.[3]

As discussed in the next section, the Charter has been amended only three times in over half a century. The Security Council has been enlarged once and the Economic and Social Council twice. The last of these moves took place almost three decades ago. So, while much of the public debate on reform continues to focus on possible Charter amendments, such as further expanding and diversifying the composition of the Security Council, in practice this has proved to be difficult to accomplish. Much of the action, instead, has occurred below this level and often with little publicity. The rules of procedure for the Security Council, the General Assembly, and ECOSOC have repeatedly been modified, as have their rosters of subsidiary bodies.[4] The latter, naturally, have been more prone to expansion to meet new priorities than to contraction as old mandates fade. The relationships among UN bodies have provided material for successive waves of reform aimed at greater coordination, coherence, or even unity of purpose among the UN's many and disparate pieces. The activities of one principal organ, the Trusteeship Council, were suspended when the task of eliminating it from the Charter appeared too ambitious.[5] Financial, administrative, and personnel matters have been the target of so many reform and retrenchment campaigns through the years that some wags in the Secretariat have suggested that the most useful reform would be to declare a moratorium on introspection and reform so that the UN's workers could get back to their assigned tasks. More serious, the dizzying diversity of initiatives and proposals labeled "reform" has led to some reflective inquiries about the proper meaning of the term.[6]

In theory, it would be analytically cleaner to adopt a relatively narrow and rigorous definition, such as the following: reform is the purposeful act of modifying the structure, composition, decisionmaking procedures, working methods, funding, or staffing of an institution in order to enhance its efficiency and/or effectiveness in advancing its core goals and principles. In terms of the UN, this would encompass those steps intended to make the Organization more efficient, more effective, and/or more capable of fulfilling the purposes laid out in Article 1 of its Charter, consistent with the principles expressed in Article 2.

In practice, however, many other endeavors have also been called "reform" by one party or another in the world body; in this field, as in others, the seemingly irresistible impulse at the UN to expand the definition and scope of basic terms until they begin to lose their meaning, as well as their analytical value, is much in evidence. Reform has taken on so many guises through the years as to be almost unrecognizable. When there appears to be political momentum behind a reform exercise, various delegations are quick to repackage some of their favorite perennial hobbyhorses as innovative reform measures. Few Member States, for example, are reticent about claiming that measures to reduce their assessments or to increase their voice in the Organization qualify as essential reforms that would make the United Nations both more effective and more equitable. Seen in that context, of course, what looks like reform to one national delegation may appear regressive to others. At other points, when the term "reform" has taken on negative connotations, there has been a reticence to label reform measures by their real name. It was telling, for example, that during the intergovernmental deliberations of the late 1990s none of the five reform working groups established in the General Assembly had the term included in their elongated and carefully negotiated titles.[7] Clearly the notion of reform is more popular with larger and richer delegations than with others these days.

Another unsettled question—whether reform should encompass changes in what the UN does, for example, in its mandates and priorities, or only modifications in its administration, budgeting, financing, structure, and decisionmaking methods—also directly affects the scope of the concept. Judging from the titles and mandates of the five reform working groups in the General Assembly referred to above, it would seem that some believe that adjustments in programmatic substance should be included, as well as steps related to structure and procedures. In addition to the more traditional areas of Security Council, financial, and management reform, there were also working groups on an agenda for peace and an agenda for development that ranged over most of the UN's extensive substantive interests.

Reform was not treated as an abstract phenomenon, but rather as one of the potential tools for strengthening the Organization's capacities for dealing with specific issue areas.[8] Given this context, it is understandable why the United Nations has not sought to develop a single definition of reform that would be acceptable to all or most of the Member States. Such an undertaking might well prove as frustrating, controversial, and time-consuming as the decades-long attempts to negotiate universal definitions for terms such as "aggression" or "terrorism."

The first step toward understanding the twisting course of UN reform efforts through the years and the confusing maze of reform proposals that have been put forward is to bear in mind the fundamentally political nature of the United Nations. Within the UN context, even seemingly routine matters of administration, personnel, and finance have a way of assuming a political character, should one group of Member States or another come to perceive potential slights to their interests, stature, or priorities. To put it crudely, much of the reform debate, at its basest level, is a struggle over political turf, over who is perceived to gain or lose influence within the Organization if the proposed changes are enacted or implemented. One of the most frequently voiced questions in UN corridors during the late 1990s reform exercise was: "Reform for what purpose?" To gain support, the answers needed to be on two levels: substantive and political. Even if the goal of a particular proposal was to enhance efficiency, to some it mattered a good deal in which priority areas these efficiencies were to be carried out, who headed those programs, and whether the balance of attention and resources vis-à-vis other priorities would be affected. In short, much of the reform debate has been about three things: who makes decisions, who implements them, and who pays. If these political questions are settled, then international cooperation on moving the reform agenda will most assuredly flourish.

Who Decides? Reforming the UN's Intergovernmental Organs

For the UN's first three decades, reform of its intergovernmental bodies was largely a question of numbers. How large should ECOSOC and the Security Council be to represent properly the UN's rapidly growing membership?[9] What should the balance be between different geographical or ideological groups of states? In other words, who decides? For the past two-plus decades, however, the emphasis has shifted. While debates about numbers and names have continued without agreement, the action in terms of reform progress has moved to matters of working methods and of relations with other organs and with civil society.

The key "Who decides?" questions have become: "How are decisions reached, including whether there should be limitations on the use of the veto in the Security Council?" and "Who is consulted along the way, even if the formal composition of these bodies has not changed?"

During the 1950s and 1960s, one of the UN's cardinal achievements was to serve as midwife to the decolonization process. With the resulting influx of newly independent Member States, the ranks of UN members swelled from 51 in 1945 to 114 in 1963 (compared to 191 in 2003). Though only three African and three Asian countries were among the founders at San Francisco, by the early 1960s more than half of the Member States came from those two regions.[10] In 1956, after 20 new Member States were admitted to the UN over the two previous years, the calls for enlarging the two Councils came into the open. The original "gentlemen's agreement" on the geographical distribution of nonpermanent seats in the Security Council could no longer hold, since Latin America and Europe increasingly appeared to be "overrepresented" and the new majority "underrepresented." Unresolved squabbles over the six nonpermanent seats led to the constitutionally questionable practice of dividing a two-year term between countries from different regions. At one point, the Soviet Union favored redistributing the existing six nonpermanent seats, a step that would not have required Charter amendment. But this would have entailed a major sacrifice on the part of the West-leaning nations of Latin America and Europe, something Washington opposed.

The expansion of ECOSOC, in contrast, appeared to be a simpler and less consequential step. One-third of its eighteen members were elected each year for three-year terms, with each member having a single vote and equal rights. Not only were there no permanent members or vetoes in ECOSOC, but its mandate avoided core security issues, its primary task was coordination not policy, and its decisions were only recommendations, with none of the binding character of Security Council decisions under Chapter VII.[11] So as early as 1956, U.S. representatives acknowledged that both Councils should eventually be enlarged and suggested that the initial focus be on ECOSOC expansion.[12]

The developing countries, on the other hand, were especially keen on having a louder voice in the Security Council, which had become increasingly active in dispute resolution and peacekeeping efforts in the developing world. Some complained that their second-class status in the world body seemed to mirror the colonial status that they had recently struggled to overcome. For example, the heads of state of the members of the new Organization of African Unity (OAU), at their founding meeting in 1963, made this the topic of their very first joint summit resolution. In this context, and given their competition for influence in what was then known as the "Third World," neither Washington nor Moscow wanted to be the first to oppose openly the growing campaign for enlargement, whatever their actual misgivings.[13]

The expansion debate came to a head at the eighteenth General Assembly session in fall 1963.[14] Despite the building momentum, there was no consensus during the Assembly debate on either the need for an immediate expansion or the dimensions and voting rules of the enlarged bodies. On the final day of the session, none of the P-5—all of whose ratifications would be needed for formal amendment—voted in favor of the resolution to expand ECOSOC, and only China, of the five, voted for the resolution to expand the Security Council. During the debates preceding the votes, all P-5 members had called, in one form or another, for more time and further consultation before action was taken.

Nevertheless, on December 17, 1963, the General Assembly passed resolutions 1990 (XVIII) and 1991 (XVIII), the latter for the first time calling for amendments to the UN Charter. The first resolution, which passed 111 votes to none, enlarged the General Assembly's gate-keeping General Committee to permit fuller representation of the new African and Asian members. The second resolution was divided into two parts, each subject to its own roll call vote. Part A, to expand the Security Council from eleven to fifteen members, to increase the majority required from seven to nine, and to specify the geographical distribution of the ten non-permanent members, was adopted by a vote of 97 to 11, with 4 abstentions. Those opposed included France and the Soviet bloc, while the United States and the UK were among those abstaining. Part B, which passed 96 to 11, with 4 abstentions, enlarged ECOSOC from eighteen to twenty-seven members and indicated the geographical breakdown of the nine new members. The only difference in the voting pattern was that the Republic of China shifted from an affirmative vote in Part A to an abstention on Part B, dealing with ECOSOC, a body on which it had been denied a seat in recent years. Adding a note of urgency, both parts called on the Member States to ratify the amendments by September 1, 1965, less than two years away.

Following the Assembly vote, the expansion bandwagon inexorably gathered momentum. Of the P-5, the Soviet Union was the first to reverse course and to ratify the amendments (followed, of course, by the rest of the Soviet bloc). By the time the U.S. Senate Foreign Relations Committee held hearings on this question in late April 1965, the United Kingdom had also announced its intention to ratify the alterations in the Charter, and 65 of the required 76 Member State ratifications had already been completed. When the Senate gave its consent to ratification in June, France had added its intention to ratify, and 71 of the 76 required ratifications were in hand. Though none of the permanent members had voted for both amendments in the General Assembly, within nineteen months all had overcome their reservations and ratified them.

The reasons for this remarkable about-face could be instructive for future efforts to amend the Charter. In theory, because of the need to attain ratification by all P-5 members, the amendment process is ultimately subject to a veto by any of them, including a pocket veto in which one or more of them simply fail to act. In practice, however, this step can be invoked only after at least a two-thirds majority of the Member States have expressed support for the amendment through their votes in the Assembly and possibly through their national ratification processes. So, in terms of the politics of the UN, the costs of vetoing a proposed Charter amendment can be quite high, and this has never been done once an amendment has cleared the Assembly. The political costs are disproportionately high, of course, if one permanent member has to cast a lonely veto, so there is a premium on cooperation among the five.

Cold War politics and the lack of coordination among the five were not the only explanations for this historic reversal. The UN's precarious financial position also contributed. In the early 1960s, the United Nations was in the midst of a severe financial and constitutional crisis, brought on by the refusals of the Soviet Union, France, and some developing countries to pay their assessments for the UN's first two large-scale peacekeeping operations, in the Congo and the Middle East, despite the decision of the International Court of Justice that they were required to do so. Washington and most Western capitals were very concerned with rallying the support of developing countries on these questions. The Article 19 crisis reached its boiling point in 1964, when the Soviet Union threatened to quit the UN, the United States pushed to have Moscow denied its vote in the General Assembly under Article 19 of the Charter for its accumulated arrears, and as a result, voting was suspended in the Assembly session that fall.[15] For those capitals concerned about preserving the fiscal and political integrity of the UN—and in those days Washington was in the front ranks—this was no time to veto reforms sought so fervently by the developing-country majority.

Then, as now, the dominant argument for expansion of both Councils was equity, not performance in fulfilling their august missions. In their statements before the Senate Foreign Relations Committee on this matter, none of the Johnson administration witnesses raised cautions about whether the expanded Councils would be better equipped to carry out their missions effectively, or whether due regard would be paid to the first Charter qualification for Security Council membership: the Member State's contribution to the maintenance of international peace and security.[16] Nor, in turn, did any of the committee members ask such pointed questions about the effects of the amendments during the public hearings, which ranged over a wide spectrum of UN and foreign policy matters. On the floor of the House, several representatives spoke in favor of the amendments and none raised these issues.[17] Prior to giving its consent to rati-

fication virtually without dissent, by a 71–0 vote, the Senate held a per-
functory debate on the floor.[18] Only Strom Thurmond, the conservative
Republican from South Carolina, spoke against the measure.[19] So, with
ringing words of endorsement from the Johnson administration and a
unanimous vote by the Senate, the United States acceded to the proposition that bigger is better in terms of UN fora.

A scant six years later, with this precedent firmly in place, the
United States put forward a package of ECOSOC reform measures that
included a substantial enlargement.[20] Many developing countries
wanted to go further and faster, proposing a doubling of the size of
ECOSOC, from twenty-seven to fifty-four members. In opposing this
step, the French representative complained that the General Assembly
had not "devoted as much time to this problem as it did 10 years ago,
the last time the membership of the Economic and Social Council was
enlarged."[21] Arguing that the Council's "authority is not necessarily a
function of the size of its membership and the distribution of seats
among regions" he suggested that already "the number of seats is too
large."[22] Along similar lines, the Soviet delegate stressed that "the belief
that the work of the Council can be improved solely through enlargement and through corresponding changes in the United Nations Charter is
unfounded."[23] The United States, however, had accepted the principle of
proportional growth in ECOSOC to parallel the proliferation of UN members, which reached 135—well beyond State Department predictions—by
the end of 1973, the year the second expansion of ECOSOC came into
force.[24] When the question of doubling the membership of ECOSOC
came to a head in 1971, first in ECOSOC and then in the General Assembly, on both occasions the United States was the only P-5 member to vote
in favor.[25] In terms of ratification, however, the United States was the last
of the P-5 (including China) to complete the process, with the others
deciding once again not to resist the international political tide. With the
deposit of the U.S. ratification on September 24, 1973, this second expansion of ECOSOC, the last Charter amendment to be accomplished, came
into force.

Calls for ECOSOC reform, of course, hardly subsided with this second increment to its membership. Indeed, many Member States went
along with the two expansion steps on the assumption that they would
be followed by measures to enhance ECOSOC's working methods, to
bolster its capacity to coordinate systemwide programs, and to rationalize its structure.[26] By the early 1970s, it had become increasingly
apparent that the UN system was failing to fulfill the expectations of
Member States—from the North as well as the South—in the realm of

economic and social development, despite the fact that some four-fifths of its outlays then went to such programs.[27] A group of high-level experts, appointed by the Secretary-General under a mandate from the General Assembly, concluded in 1975 that the revitalization of ECOSOC would be one of the keys to more effective global policy-making.[28] Their report urged ECOSOC to adopt a biennial calendar, with a series of short subject-oriented sessions, a one-week ministerial session, and annual reviews of program budgets, medium-term plans, and operational activities. It stressed the utility of the Council establishing small negotiating groups to facilitate the search for common ground on key economic issues, as well as initiating consultations at an early stage with the most affected states on each issue. In addition, the report identified steps to raise the level of participation in ECOSOC sessions and called on the Council to assume the responsibilities of many of its subsidiary bodies.

A number of UN-sponsored and independent studies have proposed even more sweeping reorganizations of ECOSOC.[29] Some would enlarge it further, while others would eliminate it altogether or divide it in two. Several have advocated the creation of a smaller executive body to set priorities and negotiate key issues, and most urge that the specialized agencies be made more subservient to the Council. Some of the more modest reform proposals have been realized—the institution of a high-level segment, shorter sessions, a somewhat more theme-oriented agenda, and greater use of panels of independent experts on selected issues—but there has been no agreement among the Member States on a more fundamental restructuring. One area where ECOSOC has been somewhat more innovative, however, is in recasting and clarifying the rules for the engagement of NGOs in the work of the UN.[30] In this respect, ECOSOC reform progress compares favorably to that of the General Assembly, which has resisted the adoption of new rules for NGO access.

In retrospect, however, the effects of ECOSOC expansion appear to have been mixed at best. As some developing countries have gained a stronger sense of ownership of the Council, developed countries on the whole have been more prone to question its relevance and effectiveness.[31] In part because of its unwieldy size—too big for serious negotiation and too small to represent the membership as a whole—ECOSOC has been the target of repeated reform campaigns during the 1970s, 1980s, and 1990s. It is not evident, moreover, that ECOSOC has found it any easier to coordinate the disparate and decentralized pieces of the UN system as it has itself grown larger and more diverse. After all, ECOSOC's powers have not expanded appreciably, its decisions remain only recommendations, it is still subservient to the Assembly on political questions, and the specialized agencies and the Bretton Woods institutions (the World Bank and the International Monetary Fund [IMF]), as always, have their own political and financial constituencies, charters, and governing bodies. For these and similar constitutional reasons, the enlargement of ECOSOC has been irrelevant to addressing that body's core weaknesses.

Though they were linked in the package of Charter amendments that came into force in 1965, the efforts to reform ECOSOC and the Security Council have followed quite distinct paths since then. The Security Council, for instance, has not undergone a second tranche of expansion. Yet the pressures for enlarging the Security Council, at least judging by the public expressions of Member State policies, have been far greater than has been the case for ECOSOC. But then, of course, so too has been the resistance to tinkering with a body charged with such awesome security responsibilities. The mixed results of ECOSOC expansion are often cited as reasons not to enlarge the Council. The end of the Cold War, moreover, has had a far more profound effect on the debate over changes in the Security Council than in ECOSOC. On the one hand, the Council was rejuvenated as East-West divisions began to fade and the scope of its possible actions grew dramatically. Its new-found activism led some to declare that there had been nothing wrong with its structure and working methods, only a lack of political will, and that if there was nothing amiss in its performance, then there was no need to fix it. On the other hand, once the Council was freed of its Cold War shackles, it appeared to become, more than ever, the most dynamic and consequential piece of the system. The attractiveness of becoming a member rose, as did the stigma of being excluded from this inequitable and, some said, anachronistic club. In the consensus-driven atmosphere of this new era, moreover, the casting of vetoes came to appear decidedly out of step with the tenor of the times.

In 1993 the General Assembly convened the "Open-Ended Working Group on the Question of Equitable Representation and Increase in the Membership of the Security Council and Other Matters Related to the Security Council," a body whose very title embodied the complexities, uncertainties, and general awkwardness of its mandate. It divided its task into two clusters: one on membership, including expansion, the veto, and voting; the second on enhancing transparency through improved working methods and decisionmaking processes. While the first cluster has attracted far more public attention and Member State rhetoric, the second has spurred the greater progress.[32] By 2003 the 191 members of the General Assembly had not been able to come close to agreement on any Council reform package. But their high-profile debate has encouraged the Security Council to take a number of parallel steps on the second cluster, working methods.

As the pace and profile of Security Council activities rose during the 1990s, a series of modifications in its working methods were adopted.[33] Among these were the following:

- Under the Arria formula, a member of the Council invites the others to meet with one or more independent experts for a candid exchange of views on a pressing issue before the Council. This innovative practice, which permits more direct input from civil society and encourages Council members to reflect on the complexities of the choices facing them, has proven quite popular, as have more formal meetings with agency heads and others with knowledge of developments in the field.
- The Council has also participated in a number of retreats, away from headquarters, with the Secretary-General, other UN officials, and sometimes leading independent experts.
- Council members have undertaken a number of missions to visit areas where developments are of particular interest or concern to the Council. This has allowed much more extensive contact with government officials, NGOs, and UN personnel on the ground in regions of crisis.
- The Council has met a number of times over the past decade at either the foreign minister or summit level.
- To assist transparency and accountability, it has become common practice for the president of the Council to brief nonmembers, and often the press, on the results of informal (private) consultations.
- Tentative forecasts and the provisional agendas for the Council's upcoming work are now provided regularly to nonmembers, as are provisional draft resolutions.
- Consultations among Security Council members and troop contributors, along with key Secretariat officials, are now held on a more regular basis.

While acknowledging the progress that has been made on the second cluster, most Member States contend that it has not gone nearly far enough. The ten nonpermanent members of the Security Council called for the institutionalization of the steps that had been taken, for taking several of them further, and for more public meetings and fewer informal consultations.[34] It is questionable, however, whether all of the transparency and reporting measures called for would result in a more efficient or effective Security Council. The bulk of the negotiations among the members are bound to be carried out in private, and the public sessions of the Council have become opportunities largely for restating official positions and for public rationalizations. Even nonmembers of the Council frequently complain of the number and repetitiveness of the speeches given in the formal, public sessions. While it would aid accountability to require states to explain why they cast each veto, and the Council could be more forthcoming in its reports to the General Assembly, excessively detailed or frequent reporting could make it that much harder for an already overburdened Council to devote sufficient time and attention to its wide-ranging substantive work.

The first cluster has proven more problematic. Most distinct, the volume of complaints about the veto privilege of the P-5, a point of contention since the founding conference in San Francisco, seemed to rise precipitously during the 1990s.[35] Most of the other 186 Member States, as well as numerous scholars and blue ribbon commissions, have criticized the veto provision for being inequitable, undemocratic, and debilitating to the capacity of the Council to fulfill its core responsibility for the maintenance of international peace and security. Others, however, have stressed that the principle of unanimity among the major powers was central to the conception of the UN, and that principle has permitted it not only to survive the tensions of the Cold War, but also to play a role in helping to resolve them.

The veto controversy has complicated progress on the array of first-cluster issues in several ways:

- Since Article 108 gives the permanent members a veto over Charter amendments, they can trump any efforts to weaken formally their veto power.
- Those seeking to expand the number and geographical spread of the permanent members face a dilemma: Should additional permanent members, in the name of equity, be given the very veto power that critics claim is so debilitating to the work of the Council? Wouldn't a Council with eight or ten permanent members be even more restricted in terms of where it could act, and wouldn't the common denominator for Council action be even lower in most cases?[36]
- Alternative formulas for coping with the veto dilemma raise additional concerns. A number of delegations criticized the proposal by Ismail Razali, when he was president of the General Assembly in

1997, to add five permanent members without veto power because they said it would add a third layer to the Council hierarchy.[37] Asking the current permanent members to exercise greater restraint in their use of the veto, for example, by restricting it to matters under Chapter VII of the Charter, offers no guarantees and sets a precedent of calling on selected Member States to relinquish rights given them under the Charter.[38]

- Divisive questions about which states should have the veto have exacerbated splits within each region about which local states should be on the Council, especially since most security threats come from within one's own region, not from afar. Moreover, there is no provision in the Charter suggesting that one Member State may or should represent the interests and positions of others, neighbors or not.

So, while the General Assembly working group has made progress on narrowing differences over the size of a reformed Council, there has been little agreement either about names or about vetoes.

In sum, though it has now been almost thirty years since the Assembly last voted to amend the Charter, in retrospect, the three Charter amendments did make participation in the Security Council and ECOSOC accessible to more Member States, more of the time. They made some accommodation, if not full places, at the decisionmaking table for the scores of new members. They demonstrated a degree of flexibility, for example, some willingness to adapt to changing circumstances. But clearly they did not address the root shortcomings of either body, nor quench the public's thirst for stronger tools and machinery for dealing with the world's persistent security, economic, and social problems. Indeed, the fact that the only Charter revisions that have proven capable of sparking wide support among the members have been those to increase the size of limited membership bodies has also served to fuel skepticism about whether Charter reform is the best route to a stronger and more effective United Nations.

Who Implements? Coordination and Management

Though lacking the high drama of the debates over who decides, the question of implementation—how the mandates agreed upon by the intergovernmental bodies are to be carried out—has generated sustained attention since the UN's infancy. At its opening session in London, Arthur H. Vandenberg, the influential Republican senator who led the administrative and financial committee in both San Francisco and London, warned his colleagues against mistaking "pomp for power" and letting their aspirations for the United Nations "outrun its resources."[39] The next year, in November 1946, he wrote to Secretary of State James Byrnes that the specialized agencies "are being created entirely too rapidly and too ambitiously."[40] The following year, as noted above, the U.S. Senate initiated its first critical review of UN management and administration. The problems identified—overlap, duplication, coordination, proliferation of papers and mandates, and staff competence and compensation—have formed the core of the reform agenda ever since, in part because such challenges are common in, perhaps endemic to, complex multilateral organizations.

International bodies may properly be assessed first and foremost by what they stand for and seek to accomplish, the things determined by their constitutions and principal intergovernmental decisionmaking bodies. Yet over time, the most stinging rebukes are often about their failure to perform, about the gaps between their high purposes and meager capacities to carry them out. It has been to this second set of challenges, to narrowing the implementation gap, that most of the UN's internal reform efforts have been devoted.

From early on, two characteristics of the UN system underlined the value of developing effective practices and/or mechanisms for coordination: one was the interdisciplinary and multisectoral nature of many of the key issues on the international agenda, and the other was the complex and horizontally segmented mix of agencies, funds, and programs that composed the "system." The whole, it seemed, often acted as less than the sum of its parts. The Charter, in Articles 57 and 63, called on ECOSOC to "enter into agreements" with the various specialized agencies, several of which predated the world body, so as to bring them "into relationship with the United Nations." ECOSOC was asked to coordinate their activities "through consultations and recommendations," while Article 64 gave ECOSOC permission to seek reports from the agencies. Nowhere in the Charter, however, is there any suggestion that ECOSOC would have any binding power over them.

In practice, of course, a number of the agencies had their own boards, bylaws, mandates, and funding sources, giving them every reason to maintain a substantial degree of independence from the General Assembly, which lacked budgetary authority over them (Article 17[3] of the Charter). Since the major donor countries were members of most of these agencies, they could, if they worked together, enforce substantial discipline and coherence on the pieces of the system. But this would have required a degree of coordination among national ministries and within capitals that was only occasionally achieved. According to the 1948 Senate review, "a considerable portion of the problem of coordination seems to be due to the failure of national governments to achieve coordination in their own policy formulation. As a result, various departments of government often tend toward an autonomous handling of relationships with specific international organizations.[41] Within the UN system, weaknesses in program coordination were compounded by an inability to set and maintain clear priorities. . . .

Of course, the Member States, with their disparate interests and priorities, have been as much or more to blame as the Secretariat for the proliferation of mandates and the mismatch between ambitions and resources, problems that continue to plague the world body. To be fair, however, at times the various agencies and programs have managed to pull together to respond to emergencies and special opportunities with a sense of common purpose. When the goal is clearly articulated by the Secretary-General and the Member States pull together, so do the programs and agencies. On the whole, though, the highly decentralized nature of the system and its resistance to integrative reforms have tended to fuel perceptions of institutional disarray and fragmentation.

No one has more pungently described the malady or more painstakingly detailed possible remedies than Sir Robert Jackson, a former high-ranking international civil servant from Australia who had been tapped in 1968 by the United Nations Development Programme (UNDP) to carry out a "study of the capacity of the United Nations system to carry out an expanded development program."[42] Unlike the more pessimistic premises of recent reforms, which have been identified with cost and post retrenchments, this assessment was undertaken at a time of rapid growth in development funding through multilateral channels. The challenge was not whether the world body could do more with less, but whether the UN could handle another doubling of its development programs in the course of a few years time.

Sir Robert and his small team of researchers produced a report of almost 600 pages, laying out a detailed plan for restructuring the way the UN goes about assisting the development process. Yet it was a few unvarnished comments in the report's foreword about the shortcomings of the existing arrangements that gained the study almost instantaneous notoriety around the world. Sir Robert noted that he had been left with two strong impressions: one positive, one negative. On the plus side, he was "convinced that technical co-operation and pre-investment are one of the most effective ways of assisting the developing countries in achieving economic and social progress. I believe the United Nations, despite its present limitations, has demonstrated conclusively that it is the ideal instrument for the job."[43] There was, according to Sir Robert, "an unprecedented opportunity to revitalize the United Nations development system. Yet he doubted that the governments of the world could grasp this chance given "the great inertia of this elaborate administrative structure which no one, it seems, can change. Yet change is now imperative."

The UN development "machine," in Sir Robert's view, had evolved into "probably the most complex organization in the world." He pointed out that "about thirty separate governing bodies" tried to exercise control over different pieces of the administrative machine, yet "at the headquarters level, there is no real 'Headpiece,' no central coordinating organization which could exercise effective control." He luridly described the "administrative tentacle" that ran down to a vast complex of regional, subregional, and field offices in over ninety developing countries. Governments could not control the process, and "the machine is incapable of intelligently controlling itself." As a result, "unmanageable in the strictest sense of the word," the machine "is becoming slower and more unwieldy, like some prehistoric monster." While praising the largely good work of UNDP, he concluded that management lapses and structural shortcomings had permitted about 20 percent of the programs to qualify as "deadwood," or "nonessential projects."

He had surmised, moreover, that his preferred solution was not politically feasible: "In theory, complete control of the machine would require the consolidation of all of the component parts—the United Nations and the Specialized Agencies—into a single organization, which is not within the realms of possibility." Movement in this direction, even restructuring UNDP into "a strong central coordinating organization," would be resisted, he feared, by UN officials, by agencies that had "become the equivalent of principalities," and by those national ministries that tend to take positions in UN agencies that conflict with their "government's policies toward the UN system as a whole."

An alternative way to reform the machine without amending the Charter, in his view, "would be to centralize the budgets of all of the Specialized Agencies and bring them under effective coordinated control in ECOSOC. Then you really would see opposition to change! That battle was fought out when I was at Lake Success in the early days and the supporters of the sectoral approach won the day." Moreover, the UN system had become "a disproportionately old and bureaucratic organization," plagued with a pervasive sense of "negativism." Based on his consultations, Sir Robert had concluded that the "UN system has more than its fair share of 'experts' in the art of describing how things cannot be done."

For all of his doubts, Sir Robert saw some rays of light ahead. He urged his readers to reflect on how much the developing countries had already achieved, on the advances of science and technology, on the growing interdependence of nations, on the principles the General Assembly had articulated for relations between the UN and the Third World, and on the complementary roles that had been carved out for UNDP and the specialized agencies. With greater funds and top-flight managerial talent, he argued, a great deal could be accomplished given these favorable conditions. "The sheer force of political circumstances," he concluded, "will compel governments to act sooner or later."

The study emphasized the importance of clarifying and defining the respective roles of the various pieces of the system. "The World Bank Group should be the chief arm of the UN system in the field of capital investment, while UNDP should perform the same function for basic technical co-operation and pre-investment." UNDP should serve "as the hub of the UN development system," coordinating the efforts of the specialized agencies and other UN operational programs at the country level through UNDP resident representatives; at headquarters through a new program policy staff, four regional bureaus, and a technical advisory panel; and at the highest interagency level through the replacement of the Inter-Agency Consultative Board (IACB) with a more powerful Policy Coordination Committee. The specialized agencies would serve both as executing agents for projects contracted with UNDP and as technical advisers in their respective fields of expertise, but "UNDP would assume full responsibility for all development activities carried out under its aegis, and with its funds, irrespective of which agency or other institution expedited a particular programme or project on its behalf."[44] Therefore, the agencies would have to be accountable to the administrator of the UNDP for these projects, just as he would be accountable to governments and to the UNDP Governing Council.

Following the suggested reorganization of UNDP, the study urged consideration of the merger of the governing bodies of the World Food Programme (WFP), the UN Children's Fund (UNICEF), and UNDP. Calling for a decentralization of line authority within UNDP, the report recommended a strengthening of the role of the resident representatives, an enhancement of the authority of the administrator, and a focus on policymaking by the Governing Council. To facilitate a more decentralized apparatus, the report also stressed the need to upgrade the quality of the Secretariat, especially the resident representatives, and to improve communications throughout the system.[45]

While much of Sir Robert's plan depended on establishing this more integrated organizational structure, in many ways the operational heart of his vision centered on the institution of country-based programming and a "UN Development Cooperation Cycle."[46] The latter would consist of five phases: country program and annual review; formulation and appraisal of projects; implementation; evaluation; and follow-up. The country program would be prepared by the recipient government and the UNDP resident representative, hopefully with the participation of the agencies and in association with the World Bank, and then submitted to the UNDP Governing Council for approval. This process would provide each developing country with "a comprehensive view of the total cooperation it might expect from the UN development system during the whole period of its national development plan." For developed countries, it would provide an overview of the use of resources, facilitate forward planning, and permit bilateral and multilateral programs to be harmonized country by country.

Much of the thrust of Jackson's vision has been implemented, some at that point and some over time. But the core dilemmas that he identified have not disappeared. In particular, though his proposed combination of central authority and country-based programming has its attractions, it does not eliminate the possibility of disputes between the priorities of field-level and headquarters-level decisionmaking. This tension between centralization and decentralization has plagued UN reform efforts from the organization's early days.[47]

Because the Secretary-General lacks the power either of the purse or of appointment in dealing with the specialized agencies and the Bretton Woods institutions, he must rely on persuasion, personality, and indirect appeals to publics and Member States to give a sense of direction and coherence to the system as a whole.[48] Some Secretaries-General, and Kofi Annan has set an especially good example, are better at pulling the disparate pieces of the system together than others have been. More fundamentally, the capacity of the Member States to set and hold priorities has been markedly episodic. Divisions or indifference among the Member States, in turn, provide ample opportunities for agency heads to engage in splitting tactics or to pursue independent agendas. As a 1987 blue ribbon commission convened by the United Nations Association of the United States of America (UNA-USA) put it, the system's potential for interdisciplinary analysis and integrated implementation efforts has been hampered by the fact that "there is no center at the center of the U.N. system."[49]

The next wave of social and economic restructuring, undertaken between 1974 and 1977, unfolded in a much less propitious political context than had Jackson's capacity study a few years before.[50] The early 1970s saw growing strains between developed and developing countries on a host of economic, energy, trade, and financial questions of a bilateral, regional, and global nature. While solutions to problems of the magnitude of the oil crisis far transcended the bounds of the UN system, the world body, with its broad-based membership, became the favorite forum for the countries of the South to raise their concerns about the equity of the existing economic and political system. Through their numbers in the one-nation, one-vote General Assembly, the developing countries sought to codify a series of principles, targets, and procedures that would define a new set of global economic relationships. In this larger political context, the question of UN reform took on a more intense and divisive meaning in terms of the control, direction, and priorities of UN bodies. Amid calls by the developing countries for a new international economic order (NIEO), in 1974 the General Assembly (resolution 3343 [XXIX]) asked the Secretary-General to appoint a group of experts to prepare "a study containing proposals on structural changes within the UN system so as to make it fully capable of dealing with problems of international economic co-operation in a comprehensive manner." With Professor Richard N. Gardner of Columbia University as its rapporteur, the group of experts reached a consensus on a broad-ranging report in only four months of deliberations during the first half of 1975.

The experts' report acknowledged that "no amount of restructuring can replace the political will of Member States to discharge their obligations under Article 56 of the Charter."[51] It stressed that the group viewed efficiencies and financial economies at best as secondary factors in its deliberations, though they expected that some of their recommendations could lead to staff reductions and budgetary savings. Of higher priority to the group was the need to bring much greater coherence to the planning, programming, and budgetary processes of the UN system. According to the report, at that point, of the almost $1.5 billion expended annually by the system, less than one-quarter was covered by the regular budget, one-quarter by fifteen largely autonomous specialized agencies, one-quarter by UNDP, and one-quarter by voluntary contributions. Recognizing that this arrangement made policy direction and priority-setting that much more problematic, the experts called for a series of steps to make the budgetary and programmatic reporting of the various pieces of the system at least sufficiently compatible to permit the possibility of cross-sectoral planning and monitoring.

The proposed innovation that attracted the most attention was for the creation of the post of director-general for development and international economic cooperation, to be placed above agency heads and undersecretaries-general, as the second highest official in the world body. The director-general would be supported by two deputy directors-general, one for research and policy and the other to head a new United Nations development authority. While the director-general could not exercise authority over the relatively autonomous specialized agencies, he or she would be in charge of interagency coordination and operational activities and would chair a new interagency advisory committee on economic cooperation and development. It was suggested that the post be occupied by "a national of a developing country at least during those years when the post of Secretary-General is occupied by a developed country."[52]

The report also advocated the consolidation of all of the funds for technical assistance and preinvestment activities—except for those of UNICEF—into a new UN development authority. In a politically charged recommendation on a matter of high priority to the capitals of both developed and developing countries, the group urged that the weighted voting systems in the IMF and World Bank be revised "to reflect the new balance of economic power and the legitimate interest of developing countries in a greater voice in the operation" of those institutions.[53] The report did not specify how this should be done, and in any case the General Assembly has no authority over the Bretton Woods institutions and the specialized agencies. Though the experts from around the world had managed to reach a consensus on a shared vision in short order, the same could not be said either of the Member States or of the heads of the various parts of the UN system. Though welcoming some aspects of the report, the West cautioned against any changes that might worsen the unstable North-South political dynamic of the time or weaken its control of the Bretton Woods institutions. The East opposed steps that would entail Charter amendment or additional costs. The Group of 77 (G-77) lacked a coherent view, other than placing a higher priority on the achievement of the NIEO and on expanding the authority of the General Assembly than on restructuring the system. Wary of the implications of greater institutional integration, the G-77 preferred to stress the need for a third expansion of ECOSOC.[54]

Finally, on December 20, 1977, more than three years after the economic and social restructuring exercise was launched with the mandating of the group of experts, the General Assembly, without vote, endorsed a substantially weakened version of the group's proposals (resolution 32/197). The parallels also included measures to rationalize the work of the Second and Third Committees, to biennialize the agenda of ECOSOC, to institute shorter and more frequent subject-oriented sessions of ECOSOC over the course of the year, to hold periodic sessions of the Council at the ministerial level, and to have the Council "assume to the maximum extent possible direct responsibility for performing the functions of its subsidiary bodies." Lost, however, was the experts' core notion of small negotiating groups in both bodies on key economic issues. Instead, the Assembly predictably called for the consideration of ways to enable all Member States to participate in the work of the Council and to make "the Council fully representative." The idea of facilitating agreement through the convening of smaller groups of states on an ad hoc basis, for all of its appeal to logic, simply cut across the grain of the current political dynamics at a time of continuing North-South struggles over an array of macroeconomic issues.

Though the post of director-general survived the negotiating process, it was stripped of the authority and support structures that would have allowed it to be a powerful new locus for policy coordination and advocacy within the system. The two new deputy director-general posts were not established, none of the existing undersecretary-general posts were eliminated, the funds were not consolidated into a UN development authority, and their governing boards were not merged. The resolution called for greater uniformity in financial and administrative procedures and extolled UNDP's country-based programming process, but essentially the director-general was superimposed on the existing highly decentralized structure, without the authority to reshape or redirect it. Kenneth Dadzie, the Ghanian chairman of the Ad Hoc Committee, was appointed to be the first director-general. Though widely liked, he had little real power and was never fully accepted by the Secretary-General.

Over the years, the post came to be seen at best as marginally useful at moving these issues within the Secretariat, and at worst as a high-level appendage with little influence. Fourteen years later, in a sweeping gesture of unilaterally imposed reform, incoming Secretary-General Boutros Boutros-Ghali unceremoniously included the position of director-general as one of a list of eighteen high-level posts he was abolishing "to redress the fragmentation which existed in the Secretariat" and "to consolidate and streamline the Organization's activities into well-defined functional categories."[55]

Nevertheless, below the intergovernmental level, the efforts to bolster the system's capacity for coherent implementation of mandates have continued. The Joint Inspection Unit (JIU) has undertaken a number of assessments of how these efforts have been faring or might be enhanced. For example, a 1999 JIU report reviewed the history of steps to strengthen the Administrative Committee on Coordination (ACC), and called for further modifications, including of its name.[56] Established by ECOSOC in 1946 (resolution 13 [III]), the ACC was the only forum that convened the executive heads of all of the Organizations of the UN system, under the chairmanship of the Secretary-General, to focus on questions of coordination and crosscutting policy issues. While its effectiveness had varied with the personalities involved, its agenda had become increasingly substantive in recent years. In 2000 the name of the ACC was changed to the Chief Executives Board (CEB) and the responsibilities for coordination were divided into a High-Level Committee on Management (HLCM) and a High-Level Committee on Programmes (HLCP).

Achieving greater unity of purpose was a central theme of Secretary-General Kofi Annan's 1997 reform plan. Earlier that year, he organized four sectoral executive committees to bring together all relevant departments, funds, and programs under the headings of peace and security, the UN Development Group, humanitarian affairs, and economic and social issues.[57] He established a senior management group to act as a sort of cabinet on management issues, and a strategic planning unit to identify and assess crosscutting issues and trends. He also asked the General Assembly to establish the post of Deputy Secretary-General to address, among other things, questions that "cross functional sectors and Secretariat units."[58] While seeking to improve communication and the sense of common purpose at headquarters level, the Secretary-General also recognized the value in delegating authority and initiatives to the country level for operational development and humanitarian programs. In this regard, he called for "decentralization of decision-making at the country level and consolidation of the UN's presence under 'one flag.'"[59] Consolidations were undertaken to create a single Department of Economic and Social Affairs and a unified office to combat crime, drugs, and terrorism in Vienna.

While these steps have modified in significant ways the internal workings of the United Nations, they have had relatively little impact either on the way intergovernmental decisions are made or on the way others perceive the world body. As Kofi Annan has often pointed out, reform is a process, not an event. In closing his reform report, he captured these points nicely:

> In an organization as large and complex as the United Nations, reform necessarily consists not of one or two simple actions but a multitude of tasks that amount to a major agenda that must be pursued over time. But the world will not measure the reform process by the number of items on the agenda, by how many more or fewer activities are undertaken, or how many committees are formed or disbanded. The Organization will be judged, rightly, by the impact all these efforts have on the poor, the hungry, the sick and the threatened—the peoples of the world whom the United Nations exists to serve.[60]

Who Pays? Assessments, Finance, and Budgeting

. . . The UN Charter is quite explicit about who decides on other matters; however, when it comes to revenues and outlays, the Charter has relatively little to say, leaving these core matters to be determined by the Member States over time. According to Article 17:

1. The General Assembly should consider and approve the budget of the Organization.
2. The expenses of the Organization shall be borne by the Members as apportioned by the General Assembly.

Article 18(2) lists "budgeting questions" as among those "important questions" requiring "a two-thirds majority of the members present and voting." The skeletal nature of these provisions did not reflect a downplaying of the potential importance of these issues at the San Francisco founding conference or the preparatory meetings that led up to it. Rather, it was widely believed that open debates on finance and burden sharing would become so contentious and divisive as to threaten the sense of unity and common purpose the founding members were seeking to achieve.[61] Recognizing how acutely political questions of outlays and assessments would be, moreover, the founders of the world body felt it best to let the answers be adjusted periodically according to the ebb and flow of political power and economic means among the Member States over time. Thus, in seeking to postpone or finesse the issue, they ensured that finance would be a hardy perennial on the reform agenda for years to come.

No doubt, the most highly charged issue has been the assessment scale, which determines the relative burden borne by each member for financing the UN's regular budget and, since the late 1950s, its peacekeeping operations.[62] Other than assigning the task of apportionment to the Assembly, the Charter provides neither a mechanism nor a set of principles by which this determination should be made. These tasks were assigned in 1945 to an expert committee on contributions, which encountered politically turbulent seas when it sought to lay down both a set of criteria and its initial recommendations for the percentage assessments for each Member State.[63]

The capacity to pay has been the underlying principle for assessing states. Yet as more and more developing nations with very low capacities to pay joined the UN, placing more demands on the Organization, the United States began to complain. As Jeane Kirkpatrick testified before the Senate Committee on Governmental Affairs in May 1985, soon after she stepped down from the post of UN Permanent Representative: "The countries who pay the bills do not have the votes, and the countries who have the votes do not pay the bill. . . . The countries which contribute more than 85 percent of the U.N. budget regularly vote against that budget, but are unable to prevent its increases because the countries who pay less than 10 percent of the U.N. budget have the votes."[64] . . .

Fair or not, these arguments found a ready audience in Congress. Finding that the UN and its specialized agencies "have not paid sufficient attention in the development of their budgets to the views of the member governments who are major financial contributors," in August 1985 Congress passed the Kassebaum-Solomon Amendment as part of the Foreign Relations Authorization Act for fiscal years 1986 and 1987.[65] It precluded for fiscal year 1987 and beyond payment of assessed contributions of over 20 percent to the UN or any of its specialized agencies—which meant the withholding of 20 percent of the U.S. contribution—until they adopted weighted voting on budgetary matters "proportionate to the contribution of each such member state." In seeking to assert greater control by the major contributors over spending, Republican senator Nancy Kassebaum insisted that her aim was to strengthen, not weaken, the world body.[66] Putting their intent more bluntly, her cosponsor, the veteran Republican representative Gerald Solomon of New York, later remarked that "the way to get the attention of a mule is to hit him in the head with a 2x4. The way to get the attention of the United Nations was to pass the Kassebaum-Solomon amendment."[67]

The worsening financial crisis and the growing U.S. withholdings gave the UN's fortieth General Assembly session a markedly somber cast. After weeks of sharp debate, much of it directed toward U.S. withholding tactics, the Assembly agreed to establish a group of eighteen experts, though with a limited mandate, as most developing countries preferred. The group's purpose was to conduct a thorough review of the administrative and financial matters of the United Nations, with a view to identifying measures for further improving the efficiency of its administrative and financial functioning, which would

- contribute to strengthening its effectiveness in dealing with political, economic, and social issues; and
- submit to the General Assembly, before the opening of its forty-first session, a report containing the observations and recommendations of the Group.[68]

The experts were to stick to questions of efficiency and to avoid political matters, such as the relative priority of security and economic/social questions in the work of the UN.[69]

Meanwhile, Secretary-General Perez de Cuellar and his top managers had been undertaking a review of possible personnel and spending cuts in parallel to the deliberations of the Group of 18. In January and March of 1986, the Secretary-General announced two series of economy measures, such as reductions in travel, consultants, overtime, recruitment, promotions, benefits, and maintenance. While not eliminating any mandated posts or activities, these initial steps produced an estimated $30 million in savings.[70] Department heads were asked to identify how an additional 10 percent reduction in outlays could be achieved, if required. Deeper cuts and more far-reaching reforms, however, would require action by the Member States, since they are responsible for setting program mandates and priorities. So the Secretary-General asked the General Assembly to resume its fortieth session in late April 1986 to consider further economies to ease the worsening financial crisis. In the end, the Assembly, despite the considerable reluctance of many developing countries, adopted the Secretary-General's interim package of austerity measures with the caveat that "no project or programme for which there was a legislative mandate would be eliminated if adequate financial resources were available."[71]

The Group of 18 had only six months to try to forge a consensus on matters on which the Member States were deeply divided. It soon became painfully obvious that there was little chance of the group reaching agreement on a proposal for a new scale of assessments, something the Secretary-General had urged them to examine.[72] Reportedly, the U.S. expert in the group rebuffed suggestions by some of the other members that the possibility of lowering the U.S. assessment rate, as had been proposed by Olaf Palme and others, be considered in their deliberations.[73] Likewise, questions relating to the elimination of marginal intergovernmental bodies, to a restructuring of the UN's programs, or to recasting priorities among activities and budget line items also proved too divisive to be tackled. The group's report acknowledged problems of duplication and insufficient coordination of agendas and programs, but stated that the group did not have time to undertake an in-depth review, which "should be entrusted to an intergovernmental body."[74] The group likewise called for a streamlining of the machinery for interagency coordination, but failed to specify how this should be done (recommendations 9–13). It urged reductions in the number and duration of conferences, and in documentation, travel costs, and conference facilities (recommendations 1–7, 38). To improve the monitoring, evaluation, and inspection of UN activities, the group recommended an upgrading of the Joint Inspection Unit, a broadening of its mandate, amid closer coordination and a clearer division of labor between the JIU and external auditors (recommendations 63–67).

As seems perennially to be the case with intergovernmental bodies, the one target the Member States can readily agree to criticize is the Secretariat.[75] In this respect, the group's report was both specific and far-reaching. Noting that the number of posts funded through the UN regular budget had grown more than sevenfold in forty years, from 1,546 in 1946 to 11,423 in 1986, the report devoted two full chapters to Secretariat-related questions. Of greater concern to coherent management than these aggregate numbers was that the structure was "both too top-heavy and too complex," with twenty-eight posts at the Under-Secretary-General level and twenty-nine posts at the Assistant Secretary-General level under the regular budget, plus an additional seven and twenty-three, respectively, financed through extrabudgetary sources.[76] The experts thus called for a 15 percent reduction in the overall number of regular budget posts and a deeper 25 percent cut in Under-Secretary-General and Assistant Secretary-General regular budget posts, both to be achieved within a three-year period (recommendation 15). They also proposed a consolidation of the political departments, a review of those devoted to economic and social affairs, a streamlining of administration, and a review of public information activities, though these recommendations were mostly expressed in general terms (recommendations 16–40).

While the Group of 18 report, which included a consensus-based decisionmaking process, was generally well-received, many delegations were wary of institutionalizing a U.S. financial veto over the UN's budget and programs, which would be the result of the consensus requirement. Delegations did not want to appear to buckle in the face of U.S. financial and political pressure. The developing countries, in particular, seemed far less concerned about Secretariat retrenchment than about how their own voice and influence in the United Nations might be affected by modification in the procedures for intergovernmental decisionmaking. The one-nation, one-vote rule mattered to them in terms of both principle and national interest. This sensitivity was especially apparent in the question of budgeting, the one area in which the Charter permits the Assembly to make binding decisions on its own accord.

Yet on December 19, 1986, a weary Assembly approved by consensus resolution 41/213, calling for implementation of the agreed upon proposals of the Group of 18 and of a new consensus-based planning, programming, and budgeting process. Three factors helped to turn the tide. First, throughout the fall, the financial straits of the UN had grown more desperate. According to UN officials, the Organization, which opened 1986 with a $240 million deficit, had since depleted its contingency funds and exhausted ways of shifting funds among different accounts, leaving it increasingly vulnerable to financial pressures imposed by Member State withholdings.[77] At the end of October, the Secretary-General terminated ten top officials, while maintaining the cuts and freezes announced earlier in the year. There was growing talk of "payless paydays" if the United States—and other countries—did not make substantial additional payments before year's end.[78] Second, top U.S. officials and legislators began to make a positive linkage between UN reform and congressional restraint, contending that together they could produce a more effective and sounder world body.[79] The U.S. administration lobbied key capitals in the developing world on the value of consensus-based decisionmaking, including sending an envoy with this message from Washington to selected capitals in Africa in early December—seen as the key to moving the process in New York.[80] Third, in New York, the president of the General Assembly, Humayun Rasheed Choudhury of Bangladesh, helped shape a diplomatically worded description of the new budget process that would be relatively inoffensive to all parties.

Despite Choudhury's reassuring language, many delegations wanted an opinion from the UN Legal Counsel that these provisions would not undermine Article 18 of the Charter, which stipulates that "each member of the General Assembly shall have one vote" and that "important questions," including budgetary ones, require a two-thirds majority. The Counsel's opinion, included as Annex II of the resolution, found that "these draft proposals read separately or together do not in any way prejudice the provisions of Article 18 of the Charter of the United Nations or of the relevant rules of procedure of the General Assembly giving effect to that Article."[81]

With all of the horse-trading, however, opinions were divided about whether the multilateral negotiations had produced a mouse or something of historic proportions. Maurice Bertrand, a member of the group and a former JIU inspector, was skeptical. In his view, the resolution "defined the process of decision-making regarding the size and content of the programme budget so obscurely that everyone could declare himself satisfied but nothing was really settled."[82] As U.S. Permanent Representative Vernon Walters acknowledged, "we got most of what we wanted and so did nearly everyone else."[83] But he also claimed that "what has been done here is something really historic. We have gotten the things that the United States intended."[84] Based on these results, he said that he would urge Congress to repeal the Kassebaum-Solomon Amendment and to appropriate the full U.S-assessed contribution to the world body. Yet critics could argue that very little had changed, given the option to resort to voting if consensus fails. On the other hand, while the new process fell well short of weighted voting, the emphasis had shifted toward the presumption that consensus was the preferred way to determine the size and shape of the budget. The new system, however, offered no guarantees. Small contributors, as well as large ones, could conceivably prevent the attainment of a consensus in the Committee for Programme and Coordination (CPC). While traditionally the P-5 had regularly been elected to the CPC, there was no formal rule requiring that the United States or any of the others be seated.[85] Even if the CPC reached a consensus, the Assembly retained its prerogative to accept, modify, or reject those recommendations. As President Choudhury asserted, the new mechanism would depend on a tacit agreement between the big contributors and the developing countries, as well as on Congress's willingness to provide sustained financial support.[86] In the State Department's view, the new system would change relationships and assumptions among the Member States:

> This process has the effect of reducing the ability of the numerical majority to dictate decisions about the size and use of UN resources. If the resort to majority power cannot simply be assumed, real compromise becomes essential. Trade-offs must be achieved between minority and majority viewpoints, involving the exchange and modification of tangible interests. That is why the reform program budget decision-making process is so significant.[87]

More bluntly, Assistant Secretary of State Alan Keyes cautioned that the United States would consider further funding cuts down the road if the CPC failed to maintain a consensus. The hesitant steps toward implementing the 1986 reforms were monitored closely by Congress and the Reagan administration. The week after the General Assembly in 1987 decided to expand the CPC membership from twenty-one to thirty-four, Congress enacted legislation placing new conditions on U.S. payments to the UN, this time geared to the implementation of the provisions of resolution 41/213.[88] Though a range of assessments could be heard in Washington about the degree of progress being made in carrying out these provisions, over the course of 1988 the Reagan administration seemed to gain greater confidence that UN reform, on balance, was moving forward. The Secretary-General had not yet reached the 15 percent personnel cut targeted for the end of 1989, but he appeared to be closing in on that goal.[89] The 1988–1989 budget estimates were revised modestly upward, but with the United States joining the consensus because the additional outlays related to UN peacekeeping operations in Afghanistan and the Western Sahara, which the United States strongly supported. These add-ons were termed by the U.S. delegation as ones that were "critically important" or would "strengthen the Organization," unlike ones in earlier years that "were marginally useful, and, in some cases, politically divisive." Though the 41/213 procedures had not yet been fully operationalized, the United States was pleased with the way the 1990–1991 budget outline had been developed and, again, joined in the consensus approval of it.

More fundamentally, the larger political context within which relations with the UN had been viewed was changing in important ways. The Soviet Union had agreed to withdraw its forces from Afghanistan, and Mikhail Gorbachev was bringing "new thinking" to Soviet domestic and foreign policy. The prospects and utility of UN peacekeeping operations were rising in Washington's strategic calculations. In the U.S. presidential election campaign, both candidates pledged to repay U.S. arrears to the world body. On the eve of the president's final speech to the General Assembly, the White House announced its decision to authorize the release of outstanding 1988 dues and to develop a multiyear plan to pay back the accumulated arrears.[90]

These years of crisis in U.S.-UN relations produced a number of intriguing ironies and lessons for the process of UN reform and renewal. Most striking was the metamorphosis in Reagan administration attitudes toward, and perceptions of, the UN. The question of reform played a major role in this transformation, at first seeming to confirm the widely held assumption that the Organization would never change and later, after resolution 41/213, fueling a sense that the world body had been somehow transformed into a far more effective and promising vehicle. Positive developments in the larger political atmosphere mattered a great deal in the end, boosting both reform and U.S.-UN relations. By the latter stages of the second Reagan term, U.S. officials seemed inclined to see the reform glass as half full, when earlier it appeared at best as half empty. The ultimate irony was that the Reagan team had left office and the United States was committed to full funding and to repaying the arrears before the supposedly pivotal consensus-based budgeting mechanism was fully realized in December 1989.[91] Ultimately, it required carrots, as well as sticks, to accomplish durable fiscal reform.

The progress of the 1980s hardly satiated the financial reform agenda and the debate was rekindled in the 1990s. Indeed, it took the terrorist attacks on the United States of September 11, 2001, and mounting pressure from the Bush administration for the House finally to vote to pay the arrears to the UN body (and for the Senate to confirm John Negroponte as the U.S. Permanent Representative to the UN, after some nine months of waiting). To those hoping for a promising new chapter in U.S. relations with the United Nations or an end to the squabbles over dues and assessments, these developments could not offer much encouragement.

Conclusion

As this historical review makes abundantly clear, the process of institutional change at the UN works in subtle, complex, and uneven ways. The dual phenomena of reform and adaptation have not been widely studied and are not well understood.[92] Some of the following lessons, drawn from this review, are consistent with prevalent assumptions, but others seem counterintuitive.

1. Reform does not come easily to the UN system. The Secretary-General has little leverage, the system is diffuse, and the Member States are rarely united behind specific reform goals. Any number of reform initiatives have fizzled because the sponsors lacked the time, patience, political capital, or commitment to see the process through to the end.
2. On the other hand, the process of reform is a constant. Big waves of high-visibility initiatives may only come every five to seven years, but less publicized and less contentious tinkering closer to the surface never seems to cease. In the UN, as the premier multilateral political entity, a premium is put on consultative processes. At times, process seems more important than results, while at other times process *is* the desired result.
3. Those unaware of the history of reform may indeed be condemned to repeat it. Since conditions change, it may make sense to test the waters again from time to time with proposals that have been tried before. But a lot of time and aggravation can be saved by learning the history first, especially because the UN is such a precedent-dependent institution. Delegations that are uncertain or reluctant to press forward on a particular initiative can be counted on to recite their version of the history of past efforts and steps on that subject.

4. The key to UN reform, in that sense, may lie less in trying to be innovative than in understanding why past initiatives have failed and how the strategies and tactics for achieving them could be improved. Scholars and commissions thus might utilize their time more productively in thinking through how to advance existing proposals than in developing new ones that have little chance of implementation.

5. More study is needed of how scholars and commissions have helped to shape the UN reform process.[93] In a few of the cases addressed here, such as the Jackson capacity study, the Group of 18, the Razali plan, and Kofi Annan's July 1997 package, there have been direct, creative, and productive interactions between idea producers from civil society and the official reform processes. In each case, of course, the independent voice is sought by those actors who believe that this expert input will help to bolster their case for or against a particular step. In turn, the perspectives, values, and positions of official actors may well have been shaped to some extent by what scholars and blue ribbon commissions had been saying and/or writing. At the same time, however, it is striking how often the reform debates have proceeded with only modest or marginal input from civil society, which is readily excluded from these processes and which tends to gravitate to less technical and tedious topics. Though they took place at the height of the clamor for greater NGO access to UN proceedings, the five General Assembly working groups established during the mid-1990s largely operated behind closed doors and interacted regularly with only a handful of enterprising NGO representatives.

6. When it comes to moving an agenda for reform in the UN, it is not always clear where power dwells (or who, if anyone, is in charge). In the 1960s, none of the P-5 voted for the expansion of both ECOSOC and the Security Council, yet all eventually found it easier to go along with the tide for expansion. In the 1990s, by contrast, their mere ambivalence helped to foster doubts and divisions among the rest of the membership regarding enlarging the Security Council. Through dues withholding, the United States has been able to achieve some of its financial goals, but has less to show in terms of structural, institutional, or programmatic change. And to the extent that financial leverage matters, the United States has worked hard to ensure that it has less and less of this dwindling asset at the UN. Some Secretaries-General, moreover, have been far more adept than others at playing their modest reform cards.

7. Change happens even if reform doesn't. The UN is highly adaptable to changing world conditions. Sometimes formal reform follows (it never leads). When reform fails to keep pace with changing needs or conditions, entrepreneurial UN officials, Member States, and civil society representatives are all adept at circumventing the rules and procedures to get things done. Given the often glacial pace of institutional reform, it is not surprising that through the years more and more funding and programmatic initiatives have avoided the regular budget and scrutiny by the Assembly, finding voluntary and ad hoc routes instead.

8. The course of reform tends to be decidedly unpredictable. Rarely does a reform wave end up where its initiators expected. Sometimes the detour takes place at the negotiating stage, sometimes during implementation. Given the number and diversity of players in the UN community, as well as the episodic nature of the engagement of national leaders in these matters, it is very difficult to map the political course reform initiatives are likely to take. They invite free-riding, empty gestures, and a playing to domestic audiences along the way.

9. As this review has demonstrated, the temptation to mistake modest and short-term adjustments for epochal change has proven irresistible time and again. Unfortunately, such repeated overselling of reform accomplishments has tended to undermine support for reform in two ways: it has led to overly high expectations and resulting disillusionment with the whole enterprise; and it has too often made the best the enemy of the good, encouraging flashy proposals that squeeze out sound but incremental ones.

Where do these lessons leave us in terms of future prospects? . . . In terms of historical lessons, perhaps the most important is also the most obvious: UN reform has an unusually full and rich history. The impulse to improve the workings of the world body has been present since San Francisco. It ebbs and flows, of course, but it keeps coming back. The tensions, divisions, and distasteful compromises of the last reform drive have left delegations, officials, specialists, and even private foundations with a mighty antireform hangover. In UN circles, congressional withholdings have given reform a bad name. But a lot of parties have also been left with a sense of incomplete agendas and unfulfilled ambitions. Very few delegations, in particular, got what they wanted. . . .

As this chapter documents, the pace of UN reform has become markedly skewed. There have been repeated incremental refinements to the UN's response to the question, "Who implements?" Likewise, the struggle over "Who pays?" never ends. The most disgruntled party, the United States, has been forcing its will on the rest and getting results. Others are deeply resentful of its tactics, but can live with the results. There has been no new answer, however, to the core question of "Who decides?" for the past three decades. The ongoing debate about Security Council reform, in particular, increasingly revolves around complaints about the inequity of the current system. . . .

The question of "Who decides?" raises a related dilemma: Should the goal of UN reform be to make its decisionmaking processes more reflective of the membership as a whole or more in line with the prevailing balance of power and capacity outside of its halls? Clearly, most Member States, in calling for democratization, equity, and transparency, have the former in mind. The founders, as noted earlier, recognized this dilemma and sought, in the creation of an Assembly and a Council, to have it both ways. Today, however, the question is more pointed because of the growing imbalance of power in the real world outside. The United States has not only built an unrivaled power position, including importantly in the projection of military force, but has also shown a growing willingness to go it alone on a number of issues of great concern to the rest of the membership. The latter, in turn, have begun to see multilateral organization as a way of discouraging or even countering the unilateral instincts of the United States. It is frequently said, as well, that the UN is an organization for smaller countries and should be restructured to reflect this. . . . The question of U.S. power and influence within the world body, it seems, will become the subtext for much of the debate about what kind of a UN the world will need in the future: one that constrains or multiplies U.S. power?

. . . In terms of the "Who implements?" issues, the only ones over which the Secretary-General can exercise decisive influence, the possibility of slippage is always present. So too are pressures to create new posts and increase spending, especially after so many years of relative austerity. The next Secretary-General will have some big shoes to fill, since it is never easy to succeed a popular leader. The political dilemmas noted above, moreover, suggest that the dual task of political management and institutional management will be merged in a most challenging way. But after all, in the United Nations, reform has always been about politics. This is what history teaches us.

Notes

1. Ruth B. Russell, *A History of the United Nations Charter: The Role of the United States 1940–45* (Washington, D.C.: Brookings Institution, 1958), pp. 742–749.

2. Senate Committee on Expenditures in the Executive Departments, *United States Relations with International Organizations*, 80th Congress, 2nd sess., 1948, Senate Report 1757, pp. 11–19.

3. For ideas for a 1995 review conference, see Francis O. Wilcox and Carl M. Marcy, *Proposals for Changes in the United Nations* (Washington, D.C.: Brookings Institution, 1955).

4. Sidney D. Bailey and Sam Daws, *The Procedure of the UN Security Council*, 3rd ed. (Oxford: Oxford University Press, 1998).

5. See A/49/1, para. 46, and A/50/1, para. 69. For a proposal to revive and reorient the Trusteeship Council, see Kofi Annan, Report of the Secretary-General, *Renewing the United Nations: A Programme for Reform*, A/51/950, July 7, 1997, paras. 84–85, 282; Note by the Secretary-General, *United Nations Reform: Measures and Proposals: A New Concept of Trusteeship*, A/52/849, March 31, 1998; and Report of the Secretary-General, *United Nations Reform: Measures and Proposals, Environment and Human Settlements*, A/53/463, October 6, 1998, para. 61 and recommendation 24(b).

6. For example, see W. Andy Knight, *A Changing United Nations: Multilateral Evolution and the Quest for Global Governance* (New York: Palgrave, 2000), pp. 41–50.

7. The five groups included the Open-Ended Working Group on the Question of Equitable Representation and Increase in Membership of the Security Council and Other Matters Related to the Security Council; the Ad Hoc Open-Ended Working Group of the General Assembly on an Agenda for Development; and the High-Level Open-Ended Working Group on the Strengthening of the United Nations System.

8. See, for example, the so-called Brahimi Report, on UN peace operations. A/55/305, August 21, 2000.

9. Of the UN's four principal intergovernmental organs, this review focuses on the two that have been the targets of the most reform attention: the Economic and Social Council and the Security Council. For the results of the latest drive to improve the General Assembly's performance, achieved by the Strengthening Working Group in 1997, see *Report of the Open-Ended High-Level Working Group on the Strengthening of the United Nations System*, A/51/24, July 18, 1997.

10. This count of founding members deletes Australia, New Zealand, and several countries of the Middle East.

11. One of the few studies of ECOSOC was by Walter R. Sharp, *The United Nations Economic and Social Council* (New York: Columbia University Press, 1969).

12. Report by the President to the Congress for the Year 1963, *U.S. Participation in the U.N.*, Department of State (Washington, D.C.: U.S. Government Printing Office, 1964), pp. 143–161.

13. Nikolai Fedorenko, the Soviet Permanent Representative to the United Nations, to the Special Political Committee on December 10, 1963, A/SPC/96, pp. 1–9.

14. See A/PV.1285, December 17, 1963, pp. 6–17; A/5487, September 4, 1963, pp. 1–4; and A/5502, July 16, 1962–July 15, 1963, pp. 95–96.

15. Edward C. Luck, *Mixed Messages: American Politics and International Organization, 1919–1999* (Washington, D.C.: Brookings Institution Press, 1999), pp. 233–238.

16. But see U.S. Senate Committee on Foreign Relations, *Hearings on United Nations Charter Amendments*, 89th Congress, 1st sess., 1965 (Washington, D.C.: U.S. Government Printing Office, 1965), no. 89-51678-1, p. 22.

17. U.S. House of Representatives, *Congressional Record*, 89th Congress, 1st sess., 1965, vol. III, pt. 7 (Washington, D.C.: U.S. Government Printing Office, 1965), pp. 8713–8716.

18. U.S. Senate, *Congressional Record*, 89th Congress, 1st sess., 1965, vol. III, pt. 9 (Washington, D.C.: U.S. Government Printing Office, 1965), pp. 12547–12559.

19. Ibid., pp. 12548–12549.

20. Report by the President to the Congress for the Year 1971, *U.S. Participation in the U.N.* (Washington, D.C.: U.S. Government Printing Office, 1972), pp. 134–136.

21. A/PV.2026, p. 1.

22. Ibid., pp. 1–2.

23. Ibid., p. 3.

24. Statement of Martin F. Herz, acting assistant secretary of state, Bureau of International Organization Affairs, to the Senate Foreign Relations Committee, July 24, 1973, reproduced as an appendix in the committee's report, *Amendment to Article 61 of the Charter of the United Nations*, July 26, 1973, 93rd Congress, 1st sess., Executive Report no. 93-9, pp. 2–4.

25. See *Report of the Economic and Social Council on the Work of Its Fiftieth and Fifty-first Sessions, General Assembly, Official Records: Twenty-sixth Session, Supplement no. 3* (A/8403), pp. 9–13. See also A/PV.2026, p. 2. China was not a member of ECOSOC and was absent for the Assembly vote.

26. Ronald I. Meltzer, "Restructuring the United Nations System: Institutional Reform Efforts in the Context of North-South Relations," *International Organization* 32, no. 4 (Autumn 1978): 993–1018.

27. Report of the Group of Experts on the Structure of the United Nations System, *A New United Nations Structure for Global Economic Co-operation*, E/AC.62.9 (New York: United Nations, 1975), p. 1.

28. Ibid., pp. 13–19.

29. Sir Robert G. A. Jackson, *A Study of the Capacity of the United Nations Development System*, vols. 1–2, DP/5 (Geneva: United Nations, 1969); Peter J. Fromuth, ed., *A Successor Vision: The United Nations of Tomorrow* (New York: United Nations Association of the United States of America, 1988); Independent Working Group on the Future of the United Nations, *The United Nations in Its Second Half-Century: The Report of the Independent Working Group on the Future of the United Nations* (New York: Yale University/Ford Foundation, 1995); Commission on Global Governance, *Our Global Neighborhood* (New York: Oxford University Press, 1995); South Centre, *For a Strong and Democratic United Nations: A South Perspective of UN Reform* (Geneva: South Centre, 1996); and South Centre, *The Economic Role of the United Nations* (Dar-es-Salaam and Geneva: South Centre, 1992).

30. ECOSOC, resolution 1996/31, July 25, 1996. Also see the NGLS Roundup of November 1996, available at www.globalpolicy.org/ngos/docs96/review.htm.

31. Maurice Bertrand, *Some Reflections on Reform of the United Nations*, Joint Inspection Unit, JIU/REP/85/9 (Geneva: United Nations, 1985), p. 59.

32. See GA/9945, November 1, 2001; GA/9692 and GA/9693, December 20, 1999; and A/149-55]/47 (1994 to 2000).

33. See Note by the President of the Security Council, S/2002/603 and A/AC/247/1996/CRP.4.

34. Memorandum by the Elected Members on Transparency in the Security Council, December 22, 1997, www.globalpolicy.org/security/docs/memo1297.htm.

35. Russell, *History of the United Nations Charter*, pp. 713–749.

36. As the Commission on Global Governance phrased it, "to add more permanent members and give them a veto would be regression, not reform." *Our Global Neighborhood* (New York: Oxford University Press, 1995), p. 239.

37. The Razali plan can be found at www.globalpolicy.org/security /reform/raz497.htm.

38. Razali called for such restraint, as did the Independent Working Group on the Future of the United Nations in *The United Nations in Its Second Half-Century*, p. 16.

39. Arthur H. Vandenberg Jr., ed., *The Private Papers of Senator Vandenberg* (Boston: Houghton Mifflin, 1952), pp. 238–239.

40. U.S. Department of State, *Foreign Relations of the United States, 1946*, vol. 1, *General: The United Nations* (Washington, D.C.: U.S. Government Printing Office, 1972), p. 494.

41. Senate Committee on Expenditures, *United States Relations*, pp. 16–18.

42. UNDP, *Progress Report by the Administrator to the Governing Council*, May 9, 1968, DP/L.79, p. 2.

43. Jackson, *Capacity Study*, vol. 1, pp. ii–x, 10, 21, 34–36, 49.

44. Ibid., vol. 2, pp. 302, 329, 335–337.

45. Ibid.; see vol. 2, chaps. 8 (pp. 339–372) and 6 (pp. 215–278) respectively.

46. Ibid., vol. 1, pp. 25–29.

47. Johan Kaufmann, "The Capacity of the United Nations Development Program: The Jackson Report," *International Organization* 25, no.1 (Winter 1971): 946.

48. This was lamented in the 1948 Senate report. Senate Committee on Expenditures, *United States Relations*, p. 18.

49. Fromuth, *Successor Vision*, p. xx.

50. Rosemary Righter, *Utopia Lost: The United Nations and World Order* (New York: Twentieth Century Fund, 1995), pp. 155–184.

51. Report of the Group of Experts on the Structure of the United Nations System, *New United Nations Structure*, p. 1.

52. Ibid., p. 23.

53. Ibid., pp. 56–57.

54. *Contributions by the Executive Heads of the Organization of the United Nations System*, A/AC.179/16, October 20, 1977, and *Note by the Secretary-General*, A/AC.179/6, April 15, 1976.

55. A/46/882, February 21, 1992, and A/C.5/47/2, June 2, 1993. Ironically, by that point the last few incumbents of the post of director-general had been French nationals, so the goal of making this a high-level post for developing-country nationals was not being served in any case.

56. E/1999/L.61, December 15, 1999.

57. For a listing of these units, see Annan, *Renewing the United Nations*, p. 31.

58. Ibid., p. 17, para. 38.

59. Ibid., p. 6, plus p. 20, paras. 49–51. For the rationale and workings of the new UN Development Group and other aspects of development cooperation, see pp. 49–56, paras. 46–169 and actions 9–11.

60. Ibid., p. 90, para. 283.

61. J. David Singer, *Financing International Organization: The United Nations Budget Process* (The Hague: M. Nijhoff, 1961), pp. 122–123; and Russell, *History of the United Nations Charter*, pp. 62–63.

62. While voluntary payments for particular agencies, programs, or trust funds have grown very substantially over time, they have not proven nearly so controversial as assessments either in UN fora or in capitals.

63. For a more detailed account of these early debates, see Singer, *Financing International Organization*, pp. 122–146.

64. *U.S. Financial and Political Involvement in the United Nations*, 99th Congress, 1st sess., 1985 (Washington, D.C.: U.S. Government Printing Office, 1985), p. 6.

65. Section 143 of Public Law 99-93 (H.R. 2068), August 16, 1985.

66. See U.S. Congress, *Congressional Record*, 99th Congress, 1st sess., 1985, vol. 131, pt. 11 (Washington, D.C.: U.S. Government Printing Office, 1985), pp. 14937–14940. Also see U.S. House of Representatives, *Congressional Record*, May 8, 1985, 99th Congress, 1st sess., vol. 131, pt. 8 (Washington, D.C.: U.S. Government Printing Office, 1985), pp. 11096–11098.

67. House Subcommittee on Human Rights and International Organizations and Subcommittee on International Operations, Committee on Foreign Affairs, *Recent Developments in the United Nations System*, 100th Congress, 2nd sess., 1988 (Washington, D.C.: U.S. Government Printing Office, 1988), no. 88-H381-61, p. 66.

68. Subparagraphs 2(a)–2(b) of resolution 40/237, December 18, 1985.

69. See A/40/PV.121, pp. 7–8, 16, 27, 41.

70. See Tapio Kanninen, *Leadership and Reform: The Secretary-General and the UN Financial Crisis of the Late 1980s* (The Hague: Kluwer Law International, 1995), pp. 44–45; and A/40/1102, pp. 5–8, paras. 15–31.

71. Subparagraph (c) of resolution 40/572, and A/40/1102 and its addenda.

72. Kanninen, *Leadership and Reform*, p. 51. The Secretary-General called for a reduction in the U.S. assessment to 15 or 20 percent and for the five permanent members to pay "more or less the same amount." Elaine Sciolino, "U.N. Chief Suggests U.S. Contribution Be Cut," *New York Times*, April 29, 1986.

73. Kanninen, *Leadership*, p. 73.

74. *Report of the High-Level Intergovernmental Experts to Review the Efficiency of the Administrative and Financial Functioning of the United Nations*, A/41/49, p. 4, para. 19. Also see p. 7, para. 22, and recommendation 8, pp. 7–8.

75. Maurice Bertrand, *The Third Generation World Organization* (Dordrecht, Netherlands: M. Nijhoff, 1989), p. 111.

76. A/41/49, pp. 1, 10.

77. Michael J. Berlin, "U.N. Adopts Agreement to Trim Costs; Weighted Voting, Staff Cuts Approved," *Washington Post*, December 20, 1986.

78. Don Shannon, "State Department to Lobby Congress for U.N. Budget," *Los Angeles Times*, September 15, 1986; and James F. Clarity, Milt Freudenheim, and Katherine Roberts, "U.N.'s Bloated Bottom Line," *New York Times*, August 24, 1986.

79. See Alan L. Keyes, "Why Imperil U.N. Reform?" *New York Times*, September 25, 1986; José S. Sorzano, "The Congress Is Not 'Bashing' the UN," *Christian Science Monitor*, August 19, 1986; and Dante B. Fascell, "Enough U.N.-Bashing," *New York Times*, September 19, 1986.

80. The United States circulated a UNA-USA report that proposed a similar consensus-based budgeting mechanism and that was signed by four African leaders, a Latin American foreign minister, and Senator Kassebaum, among others. See United Nations Management and Decision-Making Project, *U.N. Leadership: The Roles of the Secretary-General and the Member States* (New York: UNA-USA, December 1986).

81. A/41/PV.102, pp. 7–8.

82. Bertrand, *Third Generation*, p. 115.

83. Quoted in Elaine Sciolino, "U.N. Assembly Favors Plan to Alter the Budget Process," *New York Times*, December 20, 1986.

84. "Walters Says U.S. Should Restore U.N. Dues," *New York Times*, December 21, 1986.

85. The CPC was established by ECOSOC as a subsidiary body by resolution 920 (XXXIV) of 1962. Also see ECOSOC resolutions 1171 (XLI) of 1966, and 2008 (LX) of 1976. It serves as the principal subsidiary body of both ECOSOC and the General Assembly for planning, programming, and coordination. Its members are nominated by the Council and elected by the Assembly for three-year terms, according to a formula for equitable geographical distribution.

86. Berlin, "U.N. Adopts Agreement."

87. *United States Participation in the UN* (Washington, D.C.: U.S. Government Printing Office, 1986), p. 306.

88. Public Law 100-204, sec. 143, December 22, 1987, Foreign Relations Authorization Act, fiscal years 1988 and 1989. In essence, Congress—a full year after the passage of 41/213—decided to ease one condition but to add two new ones before the United Nations could receive full funding.

89. Report by the President to the Congress for the Year 1988, *United States Participation in the UN* (Washington, D.C.: U.S. Government Printing Office, 1989, pp. 305–306, 309, 310.

90. Elaine Sciolino, "Reagan, in Switch, Says U.S. Will Pay Old U.N. Dues," *New York Times*, September 14, 1988; and Lou Cannon, "U.S. to Pay Dues, Debt to U.N.; White House Offers Olive Branch, Praise for Fiscal Reforms," *Washington Post*, September 14, 1988.

91. See U.S. statement, A/44/PV.84, pp. 17–21.

92. But see Knight, *Changing United Nations,* and Kanninen, *Leadership and Reform.*

93. Edward C. Luck, "Blue Ribbon Power: Independent Commissions and UN Reform," *International Studies Perspectives*, no. 1 (2000): 89–104.

Index

About the Book

Covering decisionmaking processes, peace and security affairs, and economic, social, and humanitarian issues, *The Politics of Global Governance* helps students of international organizations to understand the major themes, theories, and approaches central to the subject. The fifteen new selections in this fully revised edition reflect an increased emphasis on transnational governance and emerging global norms. The editors' section introductions underscore the importance of the essays, which have been selected not only for their relevance, but also their accessibility.

Brian Frederking is professor of political science at McKendree University. His publications include *The United States and the Security Council: Collective Security Since the Cold War.* **Paul F. Diehl** is associate provost and Ashbel Smith Professor at the University of Texas–Dallas. His recent publications include *Evaluating Peace Operations* (with Daniel Druckman) and *The Scourge of War: New Extensions of an Old Problem.*